Problems in MODERN LATIN AMERICAN HISTORY *A Reader*

Edited by JOHN CHARLES CHASTEEN
and JOSEPH S. TULCHIN

SR BOOKS

A Scholarly Resources Inc. Imprint
Wilmington, Delaware

The paper used in this publication meets the minimum requirements of the American National Standard for permanence of paper for printed library materials, Z39.48, 1984.

Scholarly Resources Inc.
104 Greenhill Avenue
Wilmington, DE 19805-1897

Library of Congress Cataloging-in-Publication Data

Problems in modern Latin American history : a reader / edited by
    John Charles Chasteen and Joseph S. Tulchin.
        p.   cm. — (Latin American silhouettes)
    Includes bibliographical references.
    ISBN 0-8420-2327-5 (cloth : alk. paper). — ISBN 0-8420-2328-3
(pbk. : alk. paper)
    1. Latin America—History—1830–   I. Chasteen, John Charles,
1955–   . II. Tulchin, Joseph S., 1939–   . III. Series.
F1413.P76   1994
980.03—dc20   93-17715
                                                                            CIP

Contents

About the Contributors

LESLIE BARY earned her Ph.D. in comparative literature at the University of California, Berkeley. She teaches Latin American and comparative literature at Louisiana State University, Baton Rouge, focusing particularly on literature and society in modern Latin America. Her research centers on questions of subjectivity and identity, both individual and collective, in modern Latin American literature and culture. She has published articles on twentieth-century Spanish American and Brazilian poets in journals such as *Hispania*, *Chasqui*, *Latin American Literary Review*, and *Revista de crítica literaria latinoamericana*. Her *Postcolonial Subjectivities: César Vallejo in the Latin American Avant-Garde* will be published in 1993 by the University of Minnesota Press.

MARY BUTLER has taught Latin American history at Rider College, at Colgate University, and the University of North Carolina at Chapel Hill. Her research interests focus on comparative slavery and emancipation in the Americas and the Caribbean. She has published several articles in the *Journal of Caribbean History*, including "Mortality and Labour on the Codrington Estates, Barbados" (1984) and "A Fair and Equitable Compensation" (1988).

HUGO F. CASTILLO has taught at the University of North Carolina at Greensboro, the Universidad de Concepción (Chile), and the University of North Carolina at Chapel Hill. His research interests focus on revolutionary movements and on agrarian structures and credit systems in Chile and Argentina. He is working on a monograph, "The Settlement of the Chilean Frontier, 1850–1930."

JOHN CHASTEEN is assistant professor of history at the University of North Carolina at Chapel Hill. His research on the southern borderland between Brazil and Spanish America appears in a number of edited books and scholarly journals, including the *Hispanic American Historical Review* and the *Latin American Research Review*, as well as in a biography, *Heroes on Horseback: The Saravia Brothers of Brazil and Uruguay*, now in preparation.

MICHAEL L. CONNIFF, Ph.D. Stanford, 1976, teaches history at Auburn University, where he also directs the Institute for Latin American Studies. He has written and edited books on populism, Brazil, Panama, and African-American history.

LYMAN L. JOHNSON is professor of history at the University of North Carolina, Charlotte. His research interests include colonial social and economic history and crime and the police in modern Argentina. Among his recent publications are *Colonial Latin America* (with Mark A. Burkholder, 1989), *The Problem of Order in Changing Societies* (1990), and *Essays on the Price History of Eighteenth-century Latin America* (with Enrique Tandeter, 1990).

PETER F. KLAREN is professor of Latin American history and international affairs and director of the Latin American Studies Program at the Elliott School of International Affairs at the George Washington University. A specialist in the sociopolitical history of twentieth-century Latin America, he is the author of *Modernization, Dislocation and Aprismo* (1973). He is a contributor to *Land and Labour in Latin America: Essays in the Development of Agrarian Capitalism* (1977) and the *Cambridge History of Latin America* (1986). He also coedited (with Thomas J. Bossert) *Promise of Development: Theories of Change in Latin America* (1986), which he is currently revising for a second edition (1991). Dr. Klaren is writing a new *History of Peru* for the Latin American country history series of Oxford University Press.

JOSEPH S. TULCHIN is the director of the Latin American Program of the Woodrow Wilson International Center for Scholars in Washington, DC. Previously, he was professor of history at the University of North Carolina at Chapel Hill. He served as associate editor and as editor of the *Latin American Research Review*. He has traveled throughout Latin America. His research interests are Argentine history and inter-American relations. *Argentina and the United States: The History of a Conflicted Relationship* (1990) is his most recent book.

GERTRUDE YEAGER is associate professor of history at Tulane University. Her published works include *Barros Arana's Historia jeneral de Chile: Politics, History, and National Identity* (1981) and *Bolivia* (1988).

Preface

This reader, like its predecessor, *Problems in Latin American History: The Modern Period* (1973), is intended as a support to both teachers and students in survey courses on the history of the region since its independence. We make no pretense of having defined a canon of primary problems in modern Latin American history. Instead, our choice of topics has been essentially pragmatic, shaped by our experience in teaching the survey course, limited by the restrictions of a one-semester format, and motivated by our desire to help students understand the complexities and contradictions of the Latin American past. We only hope professors and students will find the issues selected for this volume to be provocative and challenging. Both of us have spent a lot of time in Latin America and hold a deep affection for the region. We would like to help a new generation of students share our affection.

Surviving the final stages of the publication process was made possible by the invaluable help of Allison Garland, who demonstrated patience, tact, a keen eye for detail, and a clear sense of organization in pulling the chapters together and serving as an intermediary among the unit authors, the editors, the publisher, and the seemingly endless number of those whose permission was required to reprint copyrighted material. We also are especially indebted to the staff at Scholarly Resources for their patience, efficiency, and hard work throughout the many editorial and production stages of this book.

John C. Chasteen
Joseph S. Tulchin

Introduction

The survey course in Latin American history since independence presents a number of unique problems to both student and teacher. Few commonly taught history courses surpass the organizational difficulties inherent in covering almost two centuries of life in complex, multiracial societies divided into more than a score of separate states. Moreover, university students in the United States typically have little background useful to them in making sense of Latin American history. Most of them crave structure and information; thus, not surprisingly, textbooks are organized chronologically and by country or groups of countries. A thematic approach is another way of helping them find coherence in the flood of new information. To focus their attention and, perhaps, to deepen their understanding of Latin America, we offer this volume of documents and essays organized into "problems."

Problems require students to develop critical skills in analyzing potentially conflicting evidence. They also present complex puzzles of social, cultural, and political interpretation that lend themselves to class discussion and short writing assignments. In selecting nine *Problems in Modern Latin American History*, we have favored issues that complement most survey texts and endeavored to create a geographic and chronological spread that would maximize the book's usefulness in the classroom. Our objective has been to create a flexible collection that can be used in many different ways.

Since one of us published an earlier reader in 1973, the emphasis in the field has changed, and the changes are reflected in our selection of chapter topics. The result is a new book, not merely an updated second edition. For example, since political history no longer dominates our approach to teaching the Latin American past, we have condensed political themes to make room for chapters on social and cultural themes. Other chapters on standard topics—especially those analyzing discourse—reveal how much interpretations have changed with a generation of scholarship.

Aside from the fact that each has an introduction, a selection of documents, and a bibliography (or suggestions for further reading), the chapters do not follow a rigid model. Some include only primary sources, some use only secondary materials, and some mix the two. Nor is the political outlook or scholarly style uniform. All of the chapters, however, aim at conceptualization. They strive to explain broad patterns and trends, not merely to describe specific moments in the past.

The chapters on traditional political topics span the nineteenth and twentieth centuries. On the process of independence, Lyman Johnson presents an analytical collection drawn mostly from scholarly studies. His chapter explores the powerful impact of the long and bloody wars that transformed the political landscape of Spanish America while leaving perfectly intact many enduring social and economic patterns. Next, John Chasteen describes the turbulent political life of the early national period, trying to show the coherence within the apparent chaos of frequent civil wars and powerful personalistic leaders. He illustrates his points by excerpting nine political narratives written by nineteenth-century Latin Americans, most appearing for the first time in English. Using a mix of secondary accounts and primary materials, Michael Conniff shows how oligarchical politics was ended forever in most Latin American countries by urban populists who invited the masses into the electoral arena in the midtwentieth century. Through his collection of primary materials on Central America in the 1980s, Hugo Castillo invites students to encounter the revolutionary impulse central to the political history of Latin America since 1959.

Topics such as slavery, economic development, and U.S. policy in the region provoke lively student interest now, just as they did twenty years ago. In her chapter on African slavery in Brazil, Mary Butler uses contemporaneous descriptions to confront students with the horrifying spectacle of human bondage that remains overwhelmingly the single most important theme in the history of Latin America's largest country. Peter Klaren walks the reader through the complex and changing interpretations of the perennial dilemmas of development from "the age of self-incrimination" in the nineteenth century through the age of import substitution in the midtwentieth, down to the present day. This chapter includes interpretive and theoretical writings by leading Latin American and U.S. social scientists. Joseph Tulchin provides background on U.S. policy in Latin America, a matter seldom more important than now, as hemispheric relations emerge from their Cold War configurations. He attempts to highlight features of U.S.- Latin American relations that remain constant across long periods of time.

Issues of gender and culture have been somewhat tardy arrivals among the intellectual concerns of Latin American historians. Few history courses emphasized them in the 1970s, but many more do so now. Gertrude Yeager employs a variety of primary and secondary materials, which ranges from independence to the political struggles of the late twentieth century, to show students the importance of restoring women to Latin American history. Also taking a broad conceptual approach, Leslie Bary explores the processes of transculturation as diverse peoples encountered one another all across the region. She has selected an array of influential texts that constitute key evidence for tracing the slow formation of new collective identities in the nineteenth and twentieth centuries.

Together these chapters present a wide variety of perspectives and a multiplicity of voices—the majority of them Latin American. Here students will encounter the voices of guerrillas, poets, presidents, economists, peasants, philosophers, and industrial workers, as well as the voices of scholars. There is ample room here for disagreement, and the chapter editors themselves have taken markedly contrasting attitudes toward some issues. This creative confusion expresses our conviction that, while certain consensual facts constitute a necessary part of any introductory course on the Latin American past, the true excitement of historical scholarship arises from conflicting interpretations such as may be found in the following pages.

I

Spanish American Independence and Its Consequences

This intro is boring.
All about curriculum.

Lyman L. Johnson

At most colleges and universities, introductory courses on the history of Latin America use the independence period as a convenient point to separate the semesters. Although the significance of independence is now disputed by some historians, this well-established academic custom owes its durability to more than mere chronological convenience. The struggle for political independence in Spanish America along with the conquest and the great twentieth-century social revolutions have been widely accepted as important regional watersheds by both professional historians and the political leaders of Spanish American nations. The calendars of these nations mark the major events of this struggle with days of celebration, and public parks and buildings are commonly decorated with the images of the liberators.

A strong case can be made for both this traditional periodization and its underlying historical interpretation. There is little doubt that the men and women of the time thought that they were living in a heroic era. Among the politicized minorities that led these struggles (mostly drawn from elite and urban professional classes), there was a clear desire to break with the past and eliminate vestiges of the colonial order. This would lead in some places to an enthusiasm for a romanticized Indian past and in others to an evocation of an idealized republican future. Neither of these abstracted ideals would prove to be much help in the difficult business of organizing new nations.

Nor was the cost of independence small. With some exceptions the transition to independence was gained by the expenditure of great amounts of blood and treasure. Although Argentina and Paraguay gained effective independence with little difficulty, many nations, including Venezuela, Colombia, and Mexico, paid dearly for their freedom. For an entire generation this long struggle was the crucible that forged a new national consciousness.

In recent years, historians have raised questions about the significance of independence for Spanish America. Some have proposed a new historical periodization that would replace the traditional independence era (1808–1825) with a long transitional period of nearly one hundred years. They argue that the breakdown of the mature colonial order began in the mideighteenth century with an effort by the Spanish monarchy to reform administrative and economic structures. In this interpretation the long transition was punctuated by armed conflicts and political instability including late colonial rebellions, the wars for independence, and the civil wars of the early national period. An essentially new order finally appeared in the second half of the nineteenth century with the creation of stable central governments and the maturation of new trade linkages with Great Britain and the United States.

Economic and social historians have been particularly dissatisfied with the earlier periodization that emphasized the importance of political independence. They note that independence failed to change in fundamental ways the structures of production, exchange, and social organization found in the late colonial era. According to this revisionist reading of the historical record, the nations of Spanish America after independence merely traded formal economic and political dependence on Spain for a less formal, but more comprehensive, dependence on Great Britain and, in the twentieth century, on the United States. Evidence arrayed on behalf of this argument includes unfavorable loan terms, the development of economies based on the exchange of raw material exports for industrial imports, and, perhaps most important, the willingness of Britain and the United States to use both economic and military means to protect and preserve these imbalances.

The social historical literature of the last two decades provides convincing evidence of the persistence of colonial hierarchies of race, ethnicity, and class long after the achievement of political independence. In fact, these hierarchies often were strengthened by the increased levels of economic specialization that characterized the postindependence era. Were the lives of Caribbean cane cutters, Andean miners, Argentine ranch hands, or village agriculturalists in Mexico or Central America altered essentially by independence? Is there, then, any reason to treat independence as an important watershed in the history of Spanish America?

Despite this recent inclination to deflate the importance of independence, I remain convinced that these long struggles had a lasting impact on the nations of Spanish America. The political landscape, indeed the political culture, of this region was altered in fundamental ways by independence. Colonial government within the Spanish empire permitted, even encouraged, the appeal of administrative and judicial decisions to higher levels, culminating in Europe with king and council. The creation of new nation-states foreshortened the political distance between local economic interests and networks of class and ethnicity and the governments that sought to regulate and control them.

Colonial practice tended to put off the implementation of controversial policies, especially those that broke with well-established local custom. In the colonial system, threatened individuals and groups were offered plentiful opportunities to stall or reverse decisions that affected their interests by lodging appeals to viceregal and metropolitan levels. That is, the Spanish imperial system tended to diffuse political anger and reward political patience. The historical record of the colonial period, therefore, provides innumerable protests, an unbelievable level of litigation, even riots and assaults on hated officials, but few significant rebellions before the era of the Bourbon Reforms. Because these reforms made lower levels of government more effective, narrowing the temporal gap between decision making and policy implementation, they seem to have promoted an increase in both urban and rural unrest. The tide of conflict that flowed from these changes rose after independence with the elimination of potential appeals to distant authority.

The newly created national governments of Spanish America clearly were more representative of local interests and therefore more likely to avoid challenging established practices and customs. Nevertheless, conflicts occurred with surprising frequency. Because the creation and implementation of laws and the adjudication of disputes were now determined by local leaders and domestic institutions, the contest for political ascendancy took on greater importance. Government initiatives in the areas of religious freedom and public education as well as obviously contentious issues such as taxes and tariffs often provoked armed resistance. Although delays and appeals were retained as political tactics, their utility was much diminished by the loss of the geographically vast imperial context.

Across the region, independence led to a crisis in legitimacy that made more difficult the often confused and conflictive efforts to create new political institutions. With the elimination of kings, viceroys, and royal judges the question of who would rule and in what circumstances proved difficult to resolve. The cachet of Enlightenment-era enthusiasm for constitutions and democratic institutions and the practical example of the newly minted constitutional experiment in the United States led to the widespread adoption of republican principles and democratic institutions in Latin America. Support for these political novelties was found across the region, but this support would prove to be shallow. Within a decade a range of authoritarian alternatives to democracy had appeared, from traditional monarchies in Mexico and in the former Portuguese colony of Brazil to forms of dictatorship in Argentina, Gran Colombia, and Bolivia.

Just as independence had been resisted by many American-born loyalists in the Spanish empire, early democratic experiments produced a potent native resistance as well. In many cases the military leaders of revolutionary forces withheld support from civilian politicians or ignored the decisions of new institutions. Accustomed to a culture of hierarchy and command, they quickly grew impatient with the rough-and-tumble discourse of partisan politics. The failure of early governments to resolve successfully the inherent tension between legislative and administrative branches now combined with deep fiscal difficulties to focus the political anger of disaffected elements within the elite and their military allies. The result was a cycle of popular risings and military rebellions. As public order deteriorated and many national governments faced secessionist threats, a reinvigorated conservative tendency took hold in Spanish America.

A number of distinctive authoritarian types flourished during and after independence. José de San Martín maintained monarchist sentiments while leading revolutionary forces against the royalists of Chile and Peru. Simón Bolívar, the single most important figure of the era, demonstrated deep ambivalence about Latin America's democratic potential. Even his strongest articulations of republican and constitutional principles generally coincided with his role as a personalist leader whose real power rested on charisma and military muscle. Among the most theatrical of these new authoritarians was Agustín de Iturbide, a native-born general in the service of Spain, who led a military revolt that brought independence to Mexico in 1821. After a discrete hesitation, Iturbide accepted a crown and briefly ruled a jerry-rigged Mexican empire as Agustín I.

Regardless of the specific form that these authoritarian tendencies took, Spanish American liberalism was challenged by a resurgent indigenous conservatism within decades of independence. Even where liberalism succeeded in eventually gaining and holding power, constitutions and representative institutions operated in the shadow of larger-than-life political leaders such as Benito Juárez of Mexico. The weakness and vulnerability of these new political institutions and forms in responding to conservative challenges were consequences of the deep crisis of legitimacy that marked the region's break with its European monarchical past.

Unable to rely on tradition or habit, new national elites needed to organize and sustain popular support in order to gain and hold power. They were compelled, therefore, to organize supporters by self-consciously inventing or modifying ideologies to fit local circumstances. As a result, in the decades following independence, political parties found a place in Spanish American political culture alongside older forms of political organization based on family, patron-client relationships, and regional loyalties. The most successful politicians of the early national period were adept innovators who used symbols, rituals, and spectacles to draw followings. Yet even where adroit political leaders succeeded in achieving some stability, the political culture of the early national period was, in comparison to the imperial era, miniaturized in scale, often violent in character, and polemical in style.

This changed environment called forth a new type of political leader. The highest levels of political authority were closer to the average citizen. What resident of Buenos Aires, Santiago, or Caracas had not often seen or been addressed by the president, junta leader, or victorious general who momentarily commanded the political heights of his nation? Political proximity produced a more familiar political style. Commonly the personality, or more accurately the manufactured image, of a leader was injected into churches, taverns, and workplaces. National symbols, flags, and party colors proved to be powerful tools for the mobilization of illiterate populations. But at its roots this new political culture relied on loyalty and personal relationships to provide the bonds that tied individual citizens to their political leaders. No group was better prepared by events to thrive in this environment than the military leaders of the revolutionary armies, whose skills had permitted them to create and sustain armies despite limited fiscal resources and shaky governmental authority. The readings that follow provide an excellent introduction to the role of the military in organizing national political culture in the newly independent nations of Spanish America.

Historians seeking to revise the traditional interpretation of independence have emphasized the continued economic dependence of Spanish America after the defeat of Spain. This argument relies heavily on an analysis of foreign trade. Here the former Spanish colonies concentrated on low value-added production of raw materials while simultaneously becoming dependent on high value-added imported manufactures. That is, the nations of Spanish America retained, even perfected, the characteristics of underdevelopment after independence.

This formulation, I believe, ignores the complexity of the colonial economy and therefore underestimates the significance of the postindependence changes. Although the economy of the Spanish empire was increasingly uncompetitive relative to the most advanced nations of Europe, it sustained and protected a vast and diverse range of agricultural and factory production. Exports intended for the European market, such as tobacco, cacao, sugar, dyes, and silver, were centrally important to imperial commerce and to imperial finances, yet they represented only a small part of the total colonial economy. High levels of profitability in these products provided much of the region's investment capital and helped develop complex urban networks.

Exports were crucial components in a dense and intricate network of regional production and exchange. Wine producers in Arequipa, Peru; weavers in Quito, Ecuador; and ranchers in Córdoba, Argentina, were all dependent on the economic vitality of the silver mines in Potosí, Bolivia. Mexico's silver mines supported an even larger and more diverse system of colonial production and exchange. Similar, if less important, networks formed around indigo production in Central America and cacao production in Venezuela. Spanish commercial policies worked to protect the hand-loom weavers of Quito, the mining tool manufacturers of Mexico City, and other colonial producers from the competition of more efficient European factories. Independence brought an end to this protected form of regional and international trade.

The colonial state was an important, if not the most important, participant in the economy before independence. The colonies enjoyed a uniform and stable monetary union and well-established credit conventions. Administrative devices such as the repartimiento, or forced sales of goods to Indian communities, created vast markets for colonial production. Quito's textiles and Córdoba's mules relied on the colonial government's ability to force Indian communities to consume nontraditional goods. The size and scale of the colonial state and its ability to appropriate wealth in the form of taxes gave it an enormous weight in the economy. Prodigious public-sector expenditures for construction, salaries, and supplies helped to compensate for structural weaknesses in consumer demand caused by the endemic poverty of most of the colonial population. The urban economies of colonial Lima, Mexico City, Buenos Aires, and other major cities were largely dependent on public-sector spending.

With the end of the empire the economies of Spanish America lost these traditional protections and traditional markets. The loss of the colonial state's economic resources and its ability to sustain complex networks of structurally weak producers often meant the destruction of whole industries. Many new governments in Spanish America attempted to protect marginal economic sectors. However, ambitious plans for public-sector participation in the economy and the reality of reduced fiscal resources led more often to inflationary monetary policies than to the protection of local producers. Regardless of the specific character of the changes in individual countries, all of the economies of Spanish America were more specialized and more vulnerable after independence.The economic significance of independence will become clearer, I believe, as the colonial economy is understood in greater detail.

The utility of these competing interpretations remains in doubt. Students should feel free to explore critically the meaning of independence. The readings that follow offer a beginning to this process.

1. National Consciousness and
Alternative Myth ◆ Simon Collier

*While the generals and politicians of the patriot cause met the practical
challenges of defeating Spanish armies and creating new political institutions,
intellectuals struggled to invent new nations. That is, they sought to convince
their kinsmen and neighbors that they shared a common history and common
destiny separate from that of Spain. As long as Spanish authorities and
native-born loyalists resisted independence, this invented nationality had to
meet the practical test of convincing men and women to risk their lives and
their property on behalf of an abstraction—national sovereignty.*

*Simon Collier has provided a very useful introduction to the Chilean
experience. The poems, plays, and essays of patriot intellectuals were
infused with the dramatic, emotionally charged language of Romanticism.
The era's orators and writers gave the nation a feminine character, not only
beautiful and bountiful but also dependent and vulnerable. Unable to protect itself, this feminized nation required the heroic self-sacrifice of its male
citizens to protect it from "oppressors" and "tyrants" just as a mother
depended on the courage of her sons to protect her honor. In addition to
manipulating this maternal metaphor, patriot intellectuals imitated Oedipus's
crime by rejecting this colonial society's historical origins in the violent
actions of Spanish conquistadores. In this new version of the past, Creoles
invented a fictive descent from native Araucanian Indians. Instead of being
the disaffected cultural heirs and material beneficiaries of Spanish
conquistadores, Creoles now claimed a heroic legacy based on the
Araucanians' long resistance to Spain.*

*Although Professor Collier points to a number of symbolic initiatives in
the era of independence, this appropriation of Araucanian history was not
accompanied by any sustained effort to address the real needs of Chile's
indigenous peoples. Following independence, growing population and
increased integration in world markets led to new pressures on traditional
Araucanian lands. A series of military campaigns in the 1860s and 1870s
broke Araucanian resistance and subjected the survivors to an impoverished
dependence on the state.*

The revolutionary rejection of Spain and the Empire was, it is fair to say,
closely linked to what may be regarded as the single most important
aspect of the new ideology: the sense of national identity which was growing up. The revolution undoubtedly extended and enlarged that feeling of

From Simon Collier, *Ideas and Politics of Chilean Independence, 1808–1833*
(New York, 1967), 207–17, footnotes omitted. © 1967 by Cambridge University
Press. Reprinted by permission of Cambridge University Press and the author.

regional and provincial pride which can be observed at the end of the colonial period. The events of 1808 and 1810 compelled the creole leaders to act in a distinctively "national" manner. As [the revolutionary journalist] Henríquez put it in 1811, "In the present circumstances [Chile] should be considered as a nation. Everything has combined to isolate her. Everything impels her to seek her security and happiness on her own." The need to *form* a new nation, and to give it specific national characteristics, was implicit in Juan Egaña's treatise on education, presented to Congress in 1811. Egaña's aim in the treatise was to persuade Congress "not so much to reform abuses and to correct a People inveterate in its habits, as to create, give existence, politics and opinions to a Nation which has never had them before." Chile, thought Egaña, was in a good position to undergo this treatment; she was "free from the influence and violences of corrupt Europe" and "placed at the extremity of the earth." Egaña, then, appreciated the inner significance of the events of 1810–11. Later on, after independence many others shared this appreciation that a new nation was being built. *La Clave* was able to exhort its readers in 1827: "Let us not lose sight of the epoch in which we live, and the fact that we are the founders of a nation."

It can be argued, I think, that many attitudes . . . point to a new and more concrete sense of nationality. . . . The rejection of Spanishness and the total condemnation of the colonial period reflect the torments of emergence from the chrysalis, . . . but more direct evidence of national feeling should be noted. The word "patriot" itself is significant. The word *patria* (homeland, fatherland), frequently used at the start of the revolution to denote the whole Spanish Empire, soon began to acquire a much more exclusively local character. An unknown patriot writer of early 1811 considered it essential, for instance, to uphold the "integrity and good name of the homeland" by opposing the pretension of the Peruvian Viceroy. During the wars of the *Patria Vieja*, the cry of "¡*Viva la Patria*!" became common, and it was the permanency of the Chilean homeland rather than the imperial community that was being encouraged.

[Bernardo] O'Higgins, in a draft proclamation to Chilean soldiers fighting on the royalist side, included an openly nationalistic note in his propaganda: "How could you forget that you are Chileans, our brethren, from the same homeland and with the same religion, and that you must be free despite the tyrants who are deceiving you?" The fact that Chileans of the lower class could fight on the royalist side (as they did in large numbers) as well as on the patriot side shows that patriotic sentiment had not penetrated very far below a certain level of society. But amongst the creole intelligentsia and the aristocracy it was already a major theme. The concept of *patria* as it developed through the revolution was not a narrow racial one, though it was certainly geographical. European Spaniards and foreigners were welcomed into the community of the homeland provided they supported the cause. Thus, Carlos Spano, a peninsular, died in battle against the royalists and was suitably honored by the government, which publicly recalled that his last words had been: "I die for my Homeland, for the land which adopted me as one of its children!"

When Chile was liberated in 1817 by the Army of the Andes, the same themes of patriotism recurred. Those creoles who returned from a harsh and bitter exile on Juan Fernández could take renewed delight in the land they had lost, as did Juan Egaña: "Oh, adorable fatherland! How delightful is your beautiful aspect to one who has suffered! He who had lost you blesses your soil on seeing you once more!" "Our dear homeland, beautiful Chile," triumphantly proclaimed Bernardo O'Higgins as his army descended the Cordillera, "once again occupies the rank of nation!" Up and down the country, Chileans celebrated their return to freedom with tributes of a lyrical kind to their native earth. At Ligua a patriot styling himself "El Americano del Sud" produced a typical effusion, part of which may be quoted here.

> There is no single being whose soul is not cheered merely by pronouncing . . . *beloved, adorable homeland*. . . . Did the enemies of American freedom perhaps imagine that the sweet word *homeland* would once again be proclaimed in Chile, as has been done today? . . . Those monsters succeeded in silencing it for more than two years, not even permitting the word to be framed on the lips of men. (Oh, enchanting homeland!) But now, freed from her oppressors, she calls on her sons publicly to name her as Mother. . . . Thus the despotic name of *King* will never more be revived in our territory, and the enchanting name of Mother Country alone will resound even in the forests.

Chileans had a very clear notion of what constituted their homeland. Definite geographical limits were always borne in mind. Differences of opinion between the provinces of the country did not mean that these provinces had ceased to form part of the homeland. "There," wrote Carrera in 1812, referring to [distant] Concepción, "are our brothers, the sons of the same mother." Chile was no exception to the general Latin American pattern in this. Most of the former viceroyalties or captaincies-general had accepted what Giménez Fernández has called the "provincialist thesis" as far as their boundaries were concerned, though it might just as well be referred to as the "commonsense" thesis. Bernardo de Vera y Pintado observed as early as 1813 that Spanish America would, on the whole, choose to divide itself along the lines of "those limits which the provinces have comprehended up to now." Within these limits, however, Chileans were agreed that a basic political uniformity should prevail. This was shown very clearly in the case of the island of Chiloe. In the 1823 Congress, it was maintained that "Chiloe, as an integral part of the state, must yield to the majority, and since the majority has freely expressed its will to become constituted, Chiloe must submit."

There can be small doubt that many men experienced a genuine and profound affection for their fatherland during the revolutionary period. Juan Egaña, born a Peruvian but emotionally a Chilean, could write of his "love for this country, which I regard as my only fatherland." Nicolás Matorras . . . could proclaim that "there is no fate, no glory equal to that of being a Citizen of our great Chile." Supreme Director Freire was able to denounce "innovations contrary to the *national spirit.*" The Cabildo of Santiago could urge greater efforts in the military struggle against the Spaniards, for "we shall, in the end, possess a land of our own."

This national sentiment invested the revolution with its fundamental significance. It was not merely a question of political rights rediscovered; it was the birth of a nation. "Chile is raised to the rank of Nation," ran a line from a poem recited in the theater on February 12, 1820. The Proclamation of Independence of February 1818 made this fact known, finally and unequivocally, to "the great confederation of the human race," of which Chile now became a member. . . . The colonial epoch, then, was not simply an earlier epoch, but different in kind. It was, in Egaña's words, a time "before there was a fatherland." In short, the theme of national genesis was a strong one in the revolution, and it may fairly be regarded as the one emotion which carried all the others in its wake. . . .

National feeling, having fiercely rejected the legacy of Spain, was compelled to turn elsewhere for an alternative myth. The conquistadores had to be condemned as monsters; they could no longer be regarded as the legitimate heroes of the nation. But the Chileans did not have to travel far to find a suitable and acceptable object for their historical reverence. The new national myth was waiting for them on the doorstep, in the form of the Araucanian Indians, "the proud republicans of Araucania," as Simón Bolívar called them in his Jamaica Letter. Here, the Chileans quickly discovered, was a pantheon of timeless heroes who could hold their own in any company.

> What are the Demi-Gods of antiquity alongside our Araucanians? Is not the Greeks' Hercules, in every point of comparison, notably inferior to the Caupolicán or the Tucapel of the Chileans?

. . . Alonso de Ercilla's epic poem *La Araucana*, with its stirring description of the Araucanian resistance to the Spanish conquest, had played its part in the stimulation of Chilean self-consciousness at the close of the colonial period. The example of Araucanian valor now began to inspire the patriots in their first military campaigns against the royalists. At a celebration in honor of one patriot success, Henríquez toasted "Araucanian valor, superior to European tactics," and not long afterwards the names of the ancient heroes were invoked to spur on the armies to greater victories.

> Oh, patriots . . . recover your rights, imitating in unity and constancy your Araucanian ancestors, whose ashes repose in the urn of the sacred cause of liberty. . . . May Colo Colo, Caupolicán, and the immortal Lautaro (the American Scipio) be reborn amongst us, so that their patriotism and valor can serve . . . to frighten the tyrants.

The creoles regarded themselves as the true heirs of the Araucanians. Freire could speak of "our fathers, the Araucanians," Francisco Calderón could toast the Chileans as "the sons of Caupolicán, Colocolo and Lautaro," and Henríquez could proclaim, somewhat condescendingly, that "ancient and meritorious Araucania . . . looks with pleasure on the youthful and glorious exploits of Colombia, Peru and Buenos Aires." The adjective "Araucanian" became a poetic way of saying "Chilean." Thus, Carrera referred to Chile's struggle as "the war of Araucanian independence." Many of the newspaper titles of the period also indicated the identification very clearly.

The realities of Araucanian life, past and present, did not influence the Chilean vision of the ancient Indian as the true precursor of the modern patriot. Juan Egaña saw Araucania as "the happy region ignorant of the usages of Europe and the vices of the outside world." The distinctly aggressive and bloodthirsty nature of the Indians at the time of the Conquest was either ignored or presented as "valor," "constancy," and so on. . . .

The Chileans found many parallels, however idealized and artificial, between the Araucanian situation in the sixteenth century and their own in the early nineteenth. The Indians had, after all, put up a commendably tough resistance to oppression.

> The territories of Concepcíon and Valdivia will always be classic lands of liberty. Oh! The Whole of America had bent the knee, and was kissing the hand of the oppressor, and only the standard of Araucania opposed the banners of the House of Austria!

Araucanian government, too, was superior to the government which had attacked it: "The Araucanians governed themselves according to democratic standards which were infinitely more perfect than those of the Republics in Europe at that time.". . .

Given these historical precedents, it became important to establish a sense of solidarity with the remaining Araucanians of the South. Purely political considerations doubtless helped in this process. O'Higgins, for instance, tried to attract Indian support against the royalists by proclaiming to them: "We know no enemy but the Spaniard; . . . we are all descended from the same fathers, we inhabit the same clime." But a rejection of the Spanish Empire and a cultivation of the Indians did not mean that the creoles, descendants of the conquerors, had to vacate the lands formerly occupied by the Indians. If the Spaniards, in their efforts to maintain control of America, claimed the "right of conquest," then the creoles could retort, with Henríquez, "If conquest gives rights, then we alone are the owners of these lands. For we can all indisputably claim descent from the conquistadores." The Conquest might be condemned. But it was, after all, an accomplished fact, and after three hundred years the creoles surely had rights of tenure. As Henríquez asked, "Who can find a region which has always been inhabited [only] by natives?"

This practical consideration did not, and could not, absolve the creole Chileans from trying to form a common community with the Araucanian brethren they now idealized. A most interesting reflection of this optimistic aspiration is to be found in a short dramatic sketch written by Bernardo de Vera y Pintado during the O'Higgins government. The scene is set at the mouth of the River Bío-Bío. The last descendant of the old Araucanian heroes stands meditating alone. A Chilean frigate approaches from the sea. Significantly enough, it bears the name Lautaro—the "name of the chief whose eternal fame inspires pride and draws forth tears of tender gratitude to the native." The captain then prophesies utopia in a stirring invocation to the trees of Araucania:

> Oh, sturdy *maitenes*, whose trunks were once watered by unmixed blood—the indomitable Araucanian's blood with which he sealed his eternal independence. Today behold beneath thy shade the patriots who are renewing liberty in all the land. A day will come when, associated with the natives of this beautiful forest, we shall form a single family together. Her brilliant ferocity softened, Araucania will then taste the fruits of trade, the arts and the sciences. Agrarian laws will regulate her fields. Industry, and those connections which bring pleasure and wealth, will replace rusticity and indigence.

Having delivered this oration, the captain of the frigate informs the Indian of the liberation of Chile and of O'Higgins's martial prowess. The Indian fetches his wife to join in the celebrations. She is somewhat diffident at first, but the captain reassures her: "We are not enemies; we are your compatriots." The two Araucanians finally go aboard the frigate, where everybody sings an appropriate paean of praise to O'Higgins. Much of the mystique of the revolution is present in these lines of Vera's: the utopian optimism, the identification of the modern patriot cause with the ancient Araucania, and the belief that all Chileans, whether white or Indian, could live together in a reformed and ideal state.

When it came to practical approaches to the Araucanians, ironically enough, relatively little was achieved by successive Santiago governments. In fact, the revolutionaries experienced one set of troubles after another in their dealing with the Indians, who remained stubbornly unappreciative of the advantages of the new liberal order. The patriots' failure to propagandize effectively along the Southern "Frontier" was exacerbated by the vigorous activity of the royalists. The Peruvian task forces of 1813–14 were able to mobilize the Indians on their side, and the Church was active in promoting the royalist cause. After the liberation in 1817, Indians were more often than not involved in proroyalist guerrilla activities under Benavides and later the Pincheirias. Their recalcitrant attitude proved a recurrent problem for the army in the South. . . .

In view of the rosy attitude of the revolutionaries towards the glorious Araucanian past, it was unfortunate that the Indians did not take a more positive stance in relation to the revolution. Nevertheless, this did not prevent a few moves in the direction of greater justice for the Indian, even though the question remained largely academic as long as the vast majority of Indians lived beyond the influence of the central government. The first Congress provided for the admission of Indians on equal terms into the Colegio Carolino and other schools, hoping that this would end "the shocking discrimination that maintains them in their depressed condition." In 1813 the Junta decreed certain economic aid measures which, it believed, would destroy "the caste difference" in what by rights should be a nation of brothers. In O'Higgins's time the principle of equal rights was used to establish that the Indians were eligible for military service, perhaps a somewhat unhappy way of indicating their equality. Amongst the instructions which O'Higgins's Senate tried to force on San Martín before he set off to liberate Peru (where the Indian issue had a far greater practical importance than in Chile) was an article insisting that the Indians there should be granted the same civil rights as everybody else. Later governments were more interested in crushing the last remnants of royalist resistance in the South and the endemic lawlessness which followed, an aim finally achieved by Prieto. Despite this, there were some signs that earlier attitudes were being maintained. In the 1828 Congress, some deputies urged that the Araucanians should be regarded as an integral part of the nation, even if in the past they had been treated separately. In 1829, Nicolás Pradel recommended the appointment of a Consul for Araucania, a measure designed to bring creoles and Indians closer together. A scheme of wider and more utopian proportions, embracing the whole Amerindian race, was sponsored by O'Higgins in exile. It illustrated with some force the philanthropic motives so prominent in the revolutionary attitude towards the "noble savage."

2. Islands in the Storm: Quiet Cities and Violent Countrysides in the Mexican Independence Era ◆ Eric Van Young

Throughout Spanish America, the leaders of revolutionary movements attempted to mobilize mass support for independence. This was a difficult enterprise. Patriot leaders had to overcome widespread loyalty to the king as well as political inertia while legitimizing rebellion and manufacturing a new sense of nationality. Despite their efforts, political organizations and political agendas were increasingly local in character as the old colonial order crumbled. Ethnic and racial animosities, regionalism, and the appearance of local personalist leaders hindered the achievement of independence and undermined the creation of stable national institutions.

Important differences in social and economic structure separated the countryside and city. Late colonial cities were more prosperous than the villages and isolated settlements of the countryside. The benefits as well as the institutional and cultural symbols of empire were more visible in the cities and larger towns. It is not surprising, then, that when the struggle for independence began, cities and rural areas often responded quite differently.

Eric Van Young offers an interesting preliminary analysis of the Mexican experience. He argues that rural populations provided the revolution's most enduring support while urban populations generally remained on the sidelines, despite efforts by leaders such as Hidalgo and Morelos to attract an urban following.

In Mexico conspiracies have almost always been brewed in the cities and serious rebellions in the countryside. One is hard put to think of exceptions to this rule, which might be extended more generally to Latin America as a whole. Surely for this reason incidents of major upheaval in cities, such as the riots of 1624 and 1692 in Mexico City, the "Tragic Week" of 1919 in Buenos Aires, and the "Bogotazo" of 1948 in Colombia, infrequent as they have been and enjoying different social etiologies, jump to the observer's attention as anomalous urban blips in a continual sea of rural riot and rebellion. The passivity of cities is especially remarkable in periods of generalized and protracted rural insurrection, such as the one which gripped Mexico in the years 1810 to 1816 and which eventuated in the country's

From Eric Van Young, "Islands in the Storm: Quiet Cities and Violent Countrysides in the Mexican Independence Era," *Past and Present: A Journal of Historical Studies* 118 (February 1988): 130–55, footnotes omitted. Reprinted by permission of The Past and Present Society (Oxford, England) and the author.

political independence from Spain in 1821. Indeed, the rurality of the rebellion which broke out in 1810—that is, that armed violence was almost exclusively carried out by rural people from small villages, hamlets, and towns all over New Spain (as the colony was then called)—is one of its most notable characteristics. The absence of large-scale urban uprising is still more striking if one recalls its ubiquity in contemporary European social upheavals. The French Revolution, for example, though it encompassed a significant rural component, both revolutionary and counterrevolutionary, was of course initiated in Paris and developed there, supported largely by the urban lower classes. Popular direct action in the form of riots of varying degrees of seriousness gave the English in the eighteenth and nineteenth centuries, and particularly Londoners, a reputation for riotousness throughout Europe. Why, then, as insurrection engulfed most of rural Mexico, did the cities of the realm remain so quiet and loyal? Outlining an answer to this question can provide insights into two larger issues. The study of why a major segment of the Mexican population did not rebel can provide some useful indications as to why yet others did so. Furthermore, a close look at the reasons for this late colonial urban passivity can tell us much about the nature of cities and their development in colonial Mexico and, more generally, about the evolution of colonial society as a whole.

The major hypotheses that have guided my present research on this question are as follows. First, it appears that the mass of inhabitants of the Mexican cities did not take up arms against Spanish authority because there was no issue to mobilize them in 1810 or thereafter. There is very little, if any, evidence to indicate that the programmatic elements espoused by the creole directorate of the independence movement and its allies, in the early phase of the insurrection up to 1815 or so, had any attraction for the urban masses, and they certainly appear to have had little for the overwhelming Indian rural masses of the colony. These issues included the contradictions brought forth by the Bourbon reforms of the late colonial decades, longings for some sort of local political autonomy on the part of New Spain's white elite, and the breakdown of imperial legitimacy connected with events in Napoleonic Europe. One would think that if such ideological elements had the power to mobilize the popular classes at all, it would have been in the cities of the realm, sharing, as they did at least to some degree, many of the characteristics of late preindustrial cities in Europe: greater population densities, higher literacy rates, extensive poverty, easier communications, and so forth; but such was not the case. Second, even if the mass of the urban population had been inclined to rebel in the name of such issues, it would have been incapable of doing so because the social and economic conditions of most late colonial Mexican cities militated against concerted forms of popular political action. Finally, conditions prevailed in Mexican cities which tended to eliminate mass armed uprising as a possible course of action, and which were both conjunctural (that is, recent and circumstantial) and structural (long-term and developmental) in nature.

Before concentrating our attention on late colonial cities as social environments, it will be helpful to discuss the chronology and some of the characteristics of rural rebellion in New Spain. The colony found itself in a continual political crisis from 1808 onwards as a result of Napoleon's seizure of the Spanish throne, which sent shock waves across the Atlantic. In September 1810, Father Miguel Hidalgo, the parish priest of the town of Dolores in central Mexico, raised the standard of revolt and quickly gathered an enormous army which sacked a number of major cities, came near to capturing the viceregal capital, and occupied the important provincial city of Guadalajara for about two months. Hidalgo's improvised army melted away after a climactic battle against numerically inferior but regular royalist troops in early 1811, and the priest was betrayed, captured, tried, and executed. The mantle of Hidalgo's authority then passed to another priest and former student of his, José María Morelos, but was disputed by rival factions within the rebel camp, despite Morelos's charismatic leadership and military successes. Morelos in his turn was finally captured and executed by the royalists at the end of 1815. During these first five years of the independence struggle there occurred—sometimes separate and sometimes overlapping the mass mobilizations, more or less formal campaigns and pitched battles fought between rebels and royal armies—a steady incidence of local uprisings in towns and villages widely dispersed over New Spain, as well as activities by lesser chieftains, small guerrilla forces, and groups of bandits. The exuberance in the form and energy of rebellion all but died out with Morelos's passing in 1815, and royal arms had largely pacified the country by the following year. Pockets of resistance continued to flare in isolated areas of New Spain throughout the next few years, accompanied by occasional pitched battles and the digging in of the remaining rebels in a handful of fortified positions. Then in 1821 a military rebellion led by the conservative creole military officer Agustín de Iturbide, a response to the proclamation of a liberal constitution in Spain, joined forces with a rump insurrectionary force and declared the effective independence of the Mexican colony, an ironic turn not lost upon subsequent writers.

Certainly, violent collective action by rural people against constituted authority was not new or unusual in colonial Mexico, nor was it to disappear during the century between 1810 and the outbreak of the revolution of 1910. Unusual, however, were the scale of the early nineteenth-century uprisings and their preternatural violence. In terms of the numbers of people involved, the geographical extent of that involvement, and the duration of the popular participation, there had been nothing like the independence period in previous Mexican history and there would be nothing on a similar scale for a century after it. Consisting largely of peasants and other rural people, Hidalgo's army came to number as many as 100,000 men by January 1811, and even after the mass mobilization phase of the movement had crested with the defeat and dispersion of that force, armed contingents of several thousand men fighting over periods of many months were quite common right up until 1812. The size of these armies clearly dwarfed anything which might be called a peasant rebellion during the preceding colonial period. Furthermore, the sustained character of the movement was unusual. While it is true that insurgent armies and guerrilla bands shared a certain evanescent quality, and while it is also true that the royalist government succeeded in pacifying virtually all of New Spain by 1816, one may still speak of a certain degree of continuity in the rebellion as a peasant movement. This generalization certainly extends to regions which endured as focuses of sustained rebellion, and even to individuals who fought over the course of several years, sometimes obtaining one royal pardon after another.

Finally, the violence perpetrated in individual incidents of village riots and paramilitary rebel activity was markedly different in tone from that which generally characterized interpersonal and village violence before 1810. An illustrative incident was a riot by Indian peasants in the small town of Atlacomulco, near Toluca just to the west of Mexico City, which broke out on All Saints' Day (November 1) 1810. A mob of several hundred Indian villagers launched a furious assault on the house and shop of a European-born Spanish merchant of the town, sacked the house thoroughly, and killed the owner with stones, knives, and clubs. The man was so mutilated as to be virtually unrecognizable, testified his wife, and was left by his assassins "a misery, covered with stones." One of the alleged Indian assailants remarked ingenuously that the victim "had a very hard head, that he had hit him with a club and with stones and he still hadn't died." Nor was this incident particularly unusual for the period. While it is true that large numbers of European Spaniards were killed by the rebels in the cities they captured in late 1810 and early 1811, even at their worst these mass executions look like brutal but clinical excisions of scapegoats or social enemies rather than ritualistic, sacrificial killings in which not just the death but the annihilation of the victim was the goal, and in which the acting-out of the aggressive affect itself was as important as the elimination of its object.

On the other hand, several characteristics of rural rebellion in 1810 and after which are of a piece with smaller-scale, localized revolts before that time include the jacquerie-like nature of many local movements ostensibly linked to national leadership, the feudalization of the movement for independence as a whole, the prepolitical quality of popular ideology, and hints of antiurban sentiment which show up in rebel attacks on cities. Most often, rather than form the basis for a definitive mobilization for rebellion on a long-term footing, such uprisings quickly faded. The feudalization of the movement in general—that is, its tendency to breed factional struggle within the rebel leadership, to be organized on extremely localized lines and dominated by local clans or strongmen, its effective failure even under Hidalgo and Morelos to coalesce militarily, and so forth—is acknowledged by most investigators. The prepolitical quality of popular ideology—that is to say, peasant, but not exclusively Indian, rebel ideology—is evident in its almost total lack of formal programmatic elements, its tendency to be cast in terms of some sort of distorted legitimism and the intriguing messianic and millenarian beliefs that show up in it from time to time. Among these was the belief that the ferociously reactionary deposed King Ferdinand VII of Spain was actually present in Mexico in 1810 and 1811, disguised as a masked man and cooperating with the rebels themselves.

Finally, there are hints in revolts and conspiracies in the pre-1810 period, and rather clearer through still largely inferential signs in 1810 and after, of a sentiment of antiurbanism on the part of rural rebels. For example, in 1797 a not-altogether-unfounded rumor was circulating in the provincial city of Celaya that a local Indian resident named Agustín de la Rosa, alias "Tachuela," had hatched a conspiracy to raise the Indian population of the city itself and the surrounding pueblos in a rebellion "against the city" with the object of having himself crowned king of an unspecified political entity. The lurid descriptions left by eyewitnesses to the capture and sack of Guanajuato in 1810, and the famous slaughter of some three hundred Spaniards in the city's fortified granary, are echoed in accounts of the rebel capture of the major provincial city of Valladolid in the same year, in which the rebels were given, according to one accused, "one hour of pillage and one hour of fornication."

While it is difficult to tease out elements of antiurban feeling from those of the natural frenzy of riot or Indian-white racial tensions, they are almost certainly there. Nor were small towns exempt from such treatment. Describing the rebel capture and its aftermath in the modest town of Jocotitlán in March 1812, a local priest likened the town to "Babylonia, crying at the edge of the river for its past sins, with its houses still smoking and its plazas and streets nothing but sepulchres, bloodied even the walls of the church . . . since soldiers both enemy and friend seem to have agreed to reduce it to ashes and both to make of it their victim."

While periodic mass mobilizations, revolts, riots, and lynchings racked the countryside of New Spain, the major cities of the realm remained relatively quiet and, except for Guanajuato and one or two others, experienced no uprisings from within. It would be most illuminating to analyze the case of Guanajuato and the other rebellious towns of the Bajío region of which it formed the center, but this would take me beyond the scope of the present article. Some of the elements at play there were an unusually complex regional economy, an ethnically heterogeneous population, a well-developed urban hierarchy, and certain marked signs of economic downturn at the end of the colonial period following upon several decades of robust expansion. This is not to say that large cities elsewhere remained unscathed by ten years of intermittent violence or that they experienced no signs of internal unrest, but only that such disturbances as occurred tended to take forms other than mass collective action. . . .

Despite occasional fears of plebeian insurrection, rumors, and paranoia on the part of the central authorities, the royalists would not have been surprised by the failure of urban uprisings to materialize. In fact, it is abundantly clear that the royalist government expected the greatest danger to the regime to come in the form of rural-based insurrection, rather than from within the cities. Timothy Anna has put this succinctly in his book on Mexico City during the revolutionary era: "From 1810 until 1815, the royal regime in New Spain was threatened chiefly by armed insurrection in the countryside." Perhaps the clearest and most famous example of the failure of the rebellion to draw forth a sympathetic response from a major urban population in the central part of the country is that of Hidalgo's advance on Mexico City at the end of October and beginning of November 1810. The passivity of the capital city's lower classes was echoed by that of the surrounding villages in the Valley of Mexico, which generally refused to aid the insurgents or to contribute men to their cause. Explanations for Hidalgo's failure to attack the city as it lay vulnerable before him have varied, but the fact is that no urban uprising was forthcoming, and this painful reality probably weighed heavily in Hidalgo's decision to retreat. . . .

To conclude, my brief consideration of the reasons for urban passivity within the context of widespread rural insurrection in early nineteenth-century Mexico leads to an important observation, though hardly an unanticipated one: that the grievances which fueled popular rebellion were essentially agrarian in nature, and did not engage the sympathies of urban people. Surprisingly, direct attacks by rebels on the institutions of landlord rule and commercial agriculture in the countryside were not as common as one might be led to predict from this conclusion, and the reasons for the deflection and the nature of the intervening variables would make for a fascinating study in and of themselves. But the other term of the equation, embracing the social characteristics of late colonial Mexican cities, is just as important. The cities' rapid growth through migration from the countryside and the peculiarly fluid nature of their class and ethnic structure made for a situation in which the propensity to collective violence at the lowest level, and programmatic protest at the highest, was minimal. Thus, the dynamic of mass rebellion was not from the city out, nor a parallelism of action or sympathy between city and country, but from the countryside in. From this point of view, the mass of city-dwellers may have had their complaints, but these were not the same as those of peasants. Despite the presence of poverty and powerlessness, then, late colonial Mexican cities were hardly roiling cauldrons of discontent, nor would they, for the most part, subsequently become so.

3. War to the Death ◆ Simón Bolívar

Throughout Spanish America, independence was achieved by violent means. Levels of violence, however, varied from colony to colony and within colonies from place to place. Buenos Aires and its immediate hinterland gained effective self-government with little bloodshed, while Uruguay witnessed nearly two decades of violence. Armed conflict was persistent and pervasive in Venezuela and Colombia, where colonial authorities recruited a potent loyalist force by effectively exploiting class and race divisions that separated the masses from the patriot elite that favored independence.

By 1813 the struggle had attained a brutal character with expropriation of property and execution of prisoners common to both sides. It was in this context that Simón Bolívar, the Liberator of Venezuela, issued his proclamation of "War to the Death" from his headquarters at Trujillo on June 15. Like many of the era's constitutions and laws, this official document had only limited impact on the actual conduct of patriot forces. Few Spaniards were executed and many native-born enemies were cruelly punished.

However, because this proclamation usefully demarcates the altered nature of political discourse in the postcolonial period, it remains important. Notice here the hyperventilating prose where political enemies become "the monsters who infest Colombian soil, who have drenched it in blood." Encoded in this self-serving reconstruction of events is a celebration of military virtue, without a clear acknowledgment of legal restraints, and Venezuelans are urged to "fear not the sword that comes to avenge you." In this construction of a new, less institutionalized, political reality, we can locate the origins of modern personalism and militarism.

From *Simon Bolivar, Selected Writings, 1810–1830*, comp. Vicente Lecuna, ed. Harold A. Bierck, Jr., trans. Lewis Bertrand (New York: Colonial Press, 1951), 31–32. Reprinted by permission of the Banco de Venezuela, Caracas.

Venezuelans: An army of your brothers, sent by the Sovereign Congress of New Granada, has come to liberate you. Having expelled the oppressors from the provinces of Mérida and Trujillo, it is now among you.

We are sent to destroy the Spaniards, to protect the Americans, and to reestablish the republican governments that once formed the Confederation of Venezuela. The states defended by our arms are again governed by their former constitutions and tribunals, in full enjoyment of their liberty and independence, for our mission is designed only to break the chains of servitude which still shackle some of our towns, and not to impose laws or exercise acts of dominion to which the rules of war might entitle us.

Moved by your misfortunes, we have been unable to observe with indifference the afflictions you were forced to experience by the barbarous Spaniards, who have ravished you, plundered you, and brought you death and destruction. They have violated the sacred rights of nations. They have broken the most solemn agreements and treaties. In fact, they have committed every manner of crime, reducing the Republic of Venezuela to the most frightful desolation. Justice therefore demands vengeance, and necessity compels us to exact it. Let the monsters who infest Colombian soil, who have drenched it in blood, be cast out forever; may their punishment be equal to the enormity of their perfidy, so that we may eradicate the stain of our ignominy and demonstrate to the nations of the world that the sons of America cannot be offended with impunity.

Despite our just resentment toward the iniquitous Spaniards, our magnanimous heart still commands us to open to them for the last time a path to reconciliation and friendship; they are invited to live peacefully among us, if they will abjure their crimes, honestly change their ways, and cooperate with us in destroying the intruding Spanish government and in the reestablishment of the Republic of Venezuela.

Any Spaniard who does not, by every active and effective means, work against tyranny in behalf of this just cause, will be considered an enemy and punished; as a traitor to the nation, he will inevitably be shot by a firing squad. On the other hand, a general and absolute amnesty is granted to those who come over to our army with or without their arms, as well as to those who render aid to the good citizens who are endeavoring to throw off the yoke of tyranny. Army officers and civil magistrates who proclaim the government of Venezuela and join with us shall retain their posts and positions; in a word, those Spaniards who render outstanding service to the State shall be regarded and treated as Americans.

And you Americans who, by error or treachery, have been lured from the paths of justice, are informed that your brothers, deeply regretting the error of your ways, have pardoned you, as we are profoundly convinced that you cannot be truly to blame, for only the blindness and ignorance in which you have been kept up to now by those responsible for your crimes could have induced you to commit them. Fear not the sword that comes to avenge you and to sever the ignoble ties with which your executioners have bound you to their own fate. You are hereby assured, with absolute impunity, of your honor, lives, and property. The single title, "Americans," shall be your safeguard and guarantee. Our arms have come to protect you, and they shall never be raised against a single one of you, our brothers.

This amnesty is extended even to the very traitors who most recently have committed felonious acts, and it shall be so religiously applied that no reason, cause, or pretext will be sufficient to oblige us to violate our offer, however extraordinary and extreme the occasion you may give to provoke our wrath.

Spaniards and Canary Islanders, you will die, though you be neutral, unless you actively espouse the cause of America's liberation. Americans, you will live, even if you have trespassed.

---

4. The Royalist Army of New Spain ◆ Christon I. Archer

As a result of the wars of the independence era the military grew in political importance everywhere in Latin America. The self-confident and ambitious officer corps of the revolutionary armies resented the asserted preeminence of civilian politicians, few of whom had risked their lives in battle. The difficult fiscal circumstances that confronted these new nations exacerbated this rivalry between politicians and soldiers. When civilian leaders failed to pay military salaries or provide needed supplies, the army had the means to impose new priorities. In such an environment nearly every political movement courted military support or created its own military force.

In most Latin American nations the difficult process of creating new political institutions and developing effective political parties was disrupted over and over again by military challenges to constitutional order. Election results were overturned, presidents forced from office, and constitutions brushed aside. The nearly stereotypical Hollywood image of the region's political culture—the bemedaled general greeting his followers from a balcony after overthrowing the government—has its origin in historical events.

Historians have questioned the origins of the Latin American military's political vocation. Was it the result of the experiences of the wars of

From Christon I. Archer, "The Royalist Army of New Spain, 1810–1821: Militarism, Praetorianism, or Protection of Interests?" *Armed Forces and Society* 17, no. 1 (Fall 1990): 99–116, footnotes omitted. © 1990 by Transaction Publishers. Reprinted by permission of Transaction Publishers.

independence, or did it originate in the late colonial reforms that gave the military greater power and prestige? Christon Archer, in an article on the period from 1810 to 1821, abridged here, argues that the wars were a transforming experience for the Mexican military. The officers that supported Iturbide's rebellion in 1821 were far less constrained by political custom or law than were their colonial antecedents. Once these inhibitions were discarded, Mexico's military leadership became a kind of electoral college profoundly influencing the nation's political life. From the determination of election results to the interpretation of constitutional law, officers claimed and exercised unprecedented power. One important consequence of a politicized military was the reduced authority of the presidency. In the fifty-five years following independence the office of president changed hands seventy-five times.

Reflecting upon the turbulent recent history of Mexico from the vantage points of the 1830s and 1840s, liberal observers such as José María Luis Mora attacked the national army for its negative influences upon the new republic. Mora employed terms such as "depraved," "corrupt," "destructive," to describe the military. He identified a chronic spirit of rebellion, an unbridled lust for power, an aggressive hunger for recognition and promotions and a get-rich-quick mentality in officers, who intervened in political affairs to further the interests of their corporation. Mora condemned the *espíritu del cuerpo* [esprit de corps] of the army and other privileged jurisdictions such as the church, which in his view weakened or even destroyed the *espíritu nacional* essential for the construction of a modern nation. How could the new Mexican army have developed such strong traditions of predatory praetorianism and militarism? Was Mora correct in his damning assessments of the military corporation and its dangers to the future development of the new nation?

Until 1810 the Mexican military lacked a unified corporate identity. Headed by very few regular infantry and dragoon regiments, most of the army consisted of provincial militia regiments and battalions raised and centered in the major cities and towns of the country. While some young men sought professional army careers in the regular officer corps, few volunteered to serve in the ranks. More often than not, vagabonds, delinquents, petty criminals, and even some murderers received sentences to lengthy enlistments in regular units. Garrisoned in the unhealthy coastal fortifications, [they were prone to] yellow fever, malaria, and other tropical diseases [that] provided an effective solution to criminal recidivism.

The Spanish crown was willing to concede the *fuero militar* [special legal privileges] and some other benefits to members of the Mexican elites who would accept royal militia commissions and to accord similar rights to men of the lower classes when they served on active duty. However, these privileges were granted as an incentive to recruitment rather than as part of a plan to enhance the corporate identity of the military. . . .

Compared to the army of metropolitan Spain, the Mexican army possessed much less corporate identity or political power. While a few domineering commanders in isolated provinces were able to exercise temporary ascendancy over civil administrators, they lacked controls over military appointments, patronage, and finances. These officers had to share power with provincial intendants, district subdelegates, city and town councils, and a variety of different bureaucrats, who watched over their own prerogatives and acted to prevent any growth of the martial jurisdiction. This state of affairs was extremely frustrating to aggressive army commanders such as Brig. Félix Calleja, who was anxious to strengthen the army and to enhance its authority. . . .

Effects of the Hidalgo Rebellion

Fate granted Calleja what the royal administration had refused. In September 1810 the outbreak and early successes of the rebellion of Father Miguel Hidalgo—beginning the decade of Mexican independence wars—served to underscore Calleja's arguments favoring greater military autonomy and discipline. Trained to resist foreign invasions, the Mexican army was ponderously slow in its response to mass popular uprising. Fearing that the populace would rise up behind them, many commanders delayed offensive actions beyond the precincts of their own urban garrisons.

Even at San Luis Potosí, where he commanded the 10th Militia Brigade, Calleja felt surrounded by defeatist attitudes and abandoned by petrified European Spaniards who fled to safer locations. Despite his reservations, Calleja accepted the commission of Viceroy Francisco Javier de Venegas to raise a force called the Army of the Center. From the beginning, Calleja expanded his powers unilaterally so that he exercised full personal control over those who served under his command. Calleja's successes lay in his ability to attract and retain the personal allegiance of his officers and soldiers, overcoming their provincialism to build a strong fighting force. In turn, Calleja and his senior commanders defended the Army of the Center against all critics and insisted that the regime grant recognition through awards, medals, service ribbons, and promotions for those who fought in the battles and campaigns.

Often surrounded by a Mexican population that he believed desired independence and by "egotistical and greedy" European Spaniards who appeared cowardly or indifferent to victory, Calleja developed a loyal force with an esprit de corps that had not been seen in Mexico since the time of

Hernando Cortés. As the general of an army of beleaguered *buenos criollos* [royalist Creoles], Calleja became much more than a military commander. He defended Mexican creole interests, pointed out their grievances against the imperial regime, and exercised control over promotions. In the process, he detached the army from the narrow base of its earlier mission and launched it into the political theater.

The corporate spirit absent in the colonial army prior to 1810 emerged quickly in the Army of the Center and in other royalist forces. In part, this development originated from the deep suspicions of commanders who felt real or imagined pressures from a variety of known and unknown opponents. Calleja described the Mexican populace as "immoral, without character, and lacking in customs." Insurgent soldiers amnestied after supporting the rebels often rejoined the uprising as soon as they were free from the risk of punishment. Towns were loyal only when actually garrisoned by royalist soldiers. Even troops of the operational armies evaded their duties or sometimes deserted on the slightest provocation to return to their home provinces. Calleja informed Venegas, "Enemies surround us on all sides.". . .

To prevent loss of morale and desertions, officers sought to separate their soldiers as much as possible from the civilian populace. If the insurgents offered recruits the lure of booty, royalist commanders permitted their troops freedom to sack and pillage rebel properties. Commanders worked to develop a special military identity or spirit of solidarity and encouraged soldiers to denounce enemy agents who sometimes infiltrated royalist units. On one occasion in 1812, Col. Ciriaco de Llano offered cash rewards to his men if they apprehended enemy agents responsible for desertions from his column. Two grenadiers received 30 pesos each for reporting seven followers of rebel chief José María Morelos, who had been active in "seducing and entrapping" royalist soldiers into going over to the insurgents. . . .

Military Corporatism

The emergence of the term Callejista to identify the followers of one general underscored the movement of the army away from an apolitical existence dependent upon the civil regime to a more active situation in which soldiers defended the military corporation and their commanders. Officers closed ranks against critics of the army, whom they dismissed as being ignorant of martial affairs. By as early as 1812, Calleja's men engaged in aggressive political lobbying on behalf of their leader and adopted firm positions on other political matters. So strong was their personal loyalty to Calleja that some men denounced their own brothers who tried to seduce them into joining the party of insurrection. Calleja's officers feared that such personal links with their general might prevent the soldiers from accepting the orders of any other commander. If their loyalties terminated, such men would desert the army to rejoin their families.

Besides strengthening already strong personal ties between officers and soldiers of the operational forces, the years of insurgency altered the basic system of governance within Mexico. The Bourbon colonial administration and political structures suffered permanent damage. During the Independence wars, the royalist army produced regional military-political bosses who manipulated the levers of power. Justo Sierra described the creation of "some real satrapies" ruled by a new breed of army officers who became accustomed to controlling the social, economic, and political lives of their provinces. Army commanders dominated enormous territories, often cut off from any central control from Mexico City. Many of these officers were controversial figures whose careers were marked by disputes and scandals involving such matters as the misappropriation of funds, corruption, and power struggles.

The central viceregal administration, provincial intendants, district subdelegates, and urban governments lost powers to the army. In some provinces such as Puebla and Veracruz, military officers had been appointed to the post of governor-intendant ever since the implementation of the reformed Bourbon administrative system in the 1780s. After 1810, however, many of the senior administrative offices changed to reflect the decentralization required by the fragmented insurgency and the rising pre-eminence of army commanders in what had been predominantly civil administrations. During wartime, regional army leaders paid little heed to intendants, subdelegates, urban *ayuntamientos*, or other officials who stood in their way. . . .

In provinces with separate army commanders and provincial intendants, conflicts often produced acrimonious debates and clashes of jurisdiction. Although the military usually won, some intendants caused hardships and desertions by withholding army pay and provisions. At San Luis Potosí, Intendant Manuel de Acevedo fought for years unsuccessfully against the provincial brigade commander, Col. Manuel María de Torres. Acevedo complained about erosion of his authority by army officers who were encroaching upon his economic, political, and military powers. While he was the chief administrator of all treasury accounts, Acevedo lacked any specific knowledge about the large-scale recovery and disposition of confiscated insurgent property. He heard rumors that army officers were distributing booty among their own troops and keeping a large share for themselves. The intendant became particularly incensed about the low level of moral guidance provided by Torres, who in 1815 converted an army barracks to stage nightly theatrical comedies for the troops and the urban populace. Torres took it upon himself to parade captured rebel chiefs through the city, and he gave every indication that he, rather than the intendant, was the senior official in San Luis Potosí. In addition, the army commander bypassed the city government and removed traditional patronage powers by taking over officer appointments. Torres infuriated the regional elite by awarding commissions to men considered to be of low social status and lax morality. According to Acevedo, many of Torres's garrison officers were chronic gamblers, drinkers, and womanizers. In addition, the intendant complained about conscription abuses in which Torres drafted too many young men from agriculture, stockraising, and industry. While Acevedo appealed every quarrel, Viceroy Juan Ruíz de Apodaca sided consistently with the military jurisdiction. . . .

The length of the Mexican insurgency became increasingly significant in changing the attitudes of officers and soldiers. The inability of the metropolitan army to send fresh replacements after 1816 accentuated growing problems with morale. Officers and soldiers who believed that they had little chance of returning to Spain, or simply because they had spent so long in Mexico, ceased to think of themselves as Spaniards and became Mexicanized. Time blurred family ties and connections with the metropolis and allowed for new links with Mexico. Some officers, left out for so long from the competition for promotions in the metropolitan army, felt little desire to reenter the struggle to develop patronage links with military benefactors. Of equal importance, the Spanish expeditionary units were Mexicanized through local recruitment and through the potentially dangerous practice of accepting large numbers of amnestied insurgents directly into the regular regiments. Gradually, some units came to be composed in large part of men who had fought with the insurgents. In 1817, for example, of 902 rebels from the town of Tehuacán and its region, 118 men were sent to serve in the expeditionary Infantry Regiment of Zamora and many more went to the royalist militias of Zacapala that were manned almost totally by former rebels.

Officers such as Juan Rafols, who in 1820 commanded the district of Temascaltepec in the heart of guerrilla country southwest of Toluca, expressed doubt that the royalist army could ever subdue the insurgents. Rafols's mission to pacify Sultepec, Texupilco, and other communities situated in rugged mountainous terrain convinced him that the rebels remained strong. Moreover, some officers believed that even apparently loyal subjects were insurgents at heart, who would bide their time until the royalists weakened. With no end in sight to the insurgency and with exhaustion taking a greater toll upon the royalist army, soldiers had excellent reasons to accept Agustín de Iturbide's Plan de Iguala as the only certain way to achieve peace.

There were other forces at work that influenced the thinking of soldiers in Mexico's royalist army. The long and difficult conflict had produced a top-heavy officer corps; there were far too many senior ranks for an army of the size in question. Examining the state of the Mexican army in 1818, the Marqués de Reunión [former Viceroy Venegas] described "repeated and precipitous advances" for almost all officers who had satisfactory combat records. He accused Viceroys Calleja and Apodaca of excessive generosity with promotions in order to inspire soldiers to greater activity against the insurgents. Younger officers of limited seniority advanced so rapidly that they caught up in rank with older officers who had earned their promotions through time and careful consideration of seniority. Soldiers who had achieved recognition for leadership, heroism, and military excellence faced demotions in rank owing to their lack of seniority should they return to service in the metropolitan Spanish army. Others retired from active duty in Mexico, but they retained the full privileges of the *fuero militar* and continued to support the military corporation. In addition, the expansion of military privileges granted during the war to numerous urban and rural militias and the fact that demobilized soldiers retained their *fueros* in retirement meant that they would continue to back the army during the political crises following independence.

Given these attitudes, it is not difficult to see why royalist officers in Mexico opposed or at least feared the 1820 liberal revolution in Spain and the restoration of the 1812 constitution. It was well known that the liberals of 1820 would remove or at least severely diminish army privileges. The metropolitan army appeared to have adopted political directions that simply could not be supported by most officers of the Mexican army. Moreover, it became clear that the politicization of the Spanish army ended any chance of replacements or reinforcements being sent to Mexico. The level of turbulence increased at an alarming rate in Mexico as news of the restored constitution spread throughout the country. From all over Mexico, there were reports of clubs, juntas, and conversations favoring independence. In many garrisons, soldiers became insubordinate, and there were incidents of violence between Spanish and Mexican troops. Officers felt that they might soon lose control of the situation entirely and find themselves confronting mass insurrection similar to that of 1810.

Besides politicizing elements of the Mexican population, the Spanish constitution struck directly at the military system that permitted officers to develop and maintain their regional and district bases of power. In a Royal Order dated February 11, 1820, King Fernando VII prohibited army commanders from imposing and collecting taxes for the subsistence of militia units in their jurisdictions. This legislation and the constitutional requirement for a national militia system granted Mexican city and town governments an escape from damaging militia-support taxation. Throughout the country, the urban population resisted entrenched military governors, rescinded taxes, and disbanded units that had been used by army officers to maintain their regional military authority. Almost overnight, the counterinsurgency system that had worked for so long in many provinces simply ceased to exist. No longer could the army guard major roads, patrol towns, and watch over rural districts. Regional commanders discovered that their powers and incomes had diminished.

---

5. The Black Legions ◆ G. Reid Andrews

As the military and political crises of the independence struggles deepened after 1810, both royalist and patriot leaders broadened their recruitment efforts to include the nonwhite masses. Indian villagers, mestizo cowboys, and black freemen and slaves were coaxed or compelled into military service. G. Reid Andrews has provided one of the most detailed analyses of the experience of black troops during this era. In this abridged essay, he discusses recruitment, the experience of the campaigns, and the motivations of these black troops.

Efforts to draft and motivate slaves commonly included the promise of freedom, and it is clear that the accumulated weight of these promises and the military achievements of black soldiers played a crucial role in bringing about the end of slavery in Spanish America. Military service also allowed some blacks and other nonwhites to improve their social status and income. Among veterans, a small minority rose to high levels in the military or gained high political office, but this was certainly exceptional. More commonly, victorious commanders of the revolutionary and civil war eras rewarded the loyalty and courage of black soldiers with minor commands and petty bureaucratic offices. Nevertheless, this expanded access to power and wealth when combined with the end of slavery represented a significant alteration in the social structure that evolved during the colonial period.

The phenomenon of armed black men has always been a troublesome one for the multiracial societies of the Americas. The spectacle of present or former bondsmen, or their descendants, organized into disciplined fighting units inevitably suggests the possibility that those units may acquire

From G. Reid Andrews, *The Afro-Argentines of Buenos Aires, 1800–1900* (Madison, 1980), 113–27, footnotes omitted. © 1980 by The University of Wisconsin Press. Reprinted by permission of The University of Wisconsin Press.

institutional autonomy and strike against the very government and society that created them. Armed forces always present this threat, but especially so when the members of those forces belong to a class or social group consistently exploited and confined to a subordinate position. Even if the black soldiers never use their power to redress their legitimate grievances, the fear that they will do so is a constant in the mind of the greater society.

Another drawback of black participation in the armed forces is that the services rendered the state by its black soldiers entitle those men, and the rest of the black population as well, to recognition and repayment of the collective debts owed them by their nation. Black assistance in defending the country against invasion can form the basis for demands that official and unofficial discrimination against black people be ended. This assistance, plus the potential of mutiny or rebellion if the demands are not met, can provide black people with the bargaining power to force societal change.

Thus, while black military units have proved useful and even irreplaceable as defenders of various North, South, and Central American states, their very existence has implied a force potentially hostile to the social bases on which those states rest. The problem of black men serving in the armed forces has therefore proved to be an extremely complex and delicate issue, not only for military policy makers but for historians as well. To acknowledge black participation in a nation's military history is to acknowledge the contributions which entitle black citizens to equality with whites. Such acknowledgment is obviously undesirable in societies dedicated to maintaining racial inequality. . . .

Battalions and Regiments

Afro-Argentines served in a succession of units in colonial and nineteenth-century Buenos Aires. As early as the 1660s black men formed segregated militia units in the province; by 1801 black troops formed 10 percent of the city's 1,600-man militia. These troops were easily overcome by a British expeditionary force which occupied the city in 1806, but when the British were driven out six weeks later, free and slave Afro-Argentines fought side by side with white militiamen. A second British invasion a year later was defeated by a defending force of some 5,000 men, of whom 876 belonged to the Corps of Indians, Pardos, and Morenos.

Officers and enlisted men from these black militia units went on to fight in the independence wars. Free black troops from Buenos Aires constituted two all-black units in the revolutionary army—the Sixth Infantry Regiment of Pardos and Morenos, and the Battalion of Pardos and Morenos of Upper Peru. Both units distinguished themselves against the Spanish in Uruguay, Bolivia, and northwestern Argentina before being mauled at the Battle of

Sipe-Sipe in November 1815. In the worst defeat suffered by Argentine arms during the revolution, over 1,000 men were killed, wounded, and captured, while the Spanish suffered 20 dead and 300 wounded. The surviving Afro-Argentines were sent back to Buenos Aires to recuperate; they saw no further action against the Spanish.

Another black unit, the Seventh Infantry Battalion, also fought at Sipe-Sipe, but the Seventh was of a very different type from the free black units, being composed entirely of slaves bought by the state or donated by their owners. . . . [I]n 1813 the government initiated the first of a series of *rescates* (possible translations of this word include ransom, redemption, and exchange), decrees by which owners were required to sell their able-bodied slaves to the state in varying proportions, depending on the economic use to which the slaves were being put. Owners of domestic slaves were to contribute one third of their holdings, owners of bakeries and *fábricas* one fifth, and owners of slaves engaged in agriculture one eighth. In Buenos Aires province, this draft produced 1,016 slave soldiers, who were organized into two battalions, the Seventh and the Eighth Infantry. Subsequent rescates in 1815, 1816, and 1818 yielded 1,059 more *libertos*, who were aggregated to the Eighth Infantry and the Second Battalion of Cazadores (literally Hunters).

When Englishman Emeric Vidal wrote an account of his trip to Buenos Aires, as part of his discussion on the humaneness of porteño slavery he mentioned a particularly benevolent government program by which slaves could be sold to the state as soldiers, whereupon they would be free men. In one respect Vidal was quite right: slaves were free as soon as they entered the armed forces, acquiring liberto status which they would retain for the duration of their military service, afterwards becoming completely free men. This program therefore had obvious attractions for Buenos Aires male slaves, though there is no record of their responding to it as enthusiastically as the slaves of Santiago, Chile, three hundred of whom hired a lawyer in 1813 to sue the government for their right to enter the army and win their freedom. Instances of slave resistance to the rescate program in Buenos Aires were rare, much rarer than those of owner resistance. After an initial flurry of enthusiasm in which a number of porteño families donated slaves to the state as a patriotic gesture, slave owners began to flood government offices with petitions for exemptions for their slaves, usually based on their economic dependence on the slave's labor. Many owners resorted to the crime of spiriting their slaves out of the city and hiding them in the countryside, where law enforcement was looser. By 1816 the government had decreed the uncompensated expropriation of slaves belonging to any master caught illegally withholding eligible slave males, and an especially long term of service for any slave who failed to turn himself in when called for service. Slaves who informed on such recalcitrant owners would be released from service after a mere three-year term of duty, considerably less than the hitches served by the other libertos.

Vidal's description of the rescate system as a benevolent one is a bit wide of the mark. The libertos' freedom came neither easily nor frequently. Those drafted earliest signed up for the comparatively short term of five years; later decrees required liberto troops to serve until two years after the cessation of hostilities before acquiring complete freedom. To what extent these original terms were honored is unclear. Many libertos died during the campaigns and thus never lived to claim their freedom. The numerous libertos discharged for medical reasons before completing their term of service did not always win their freedom, but rather were frequently returned to their owners—whether as slaves or libertos is not clear.

Many other libertos deserted to escape the miserable conditions of campaign life. Those who succeeded in this enterprise may have won a precarious freedom which conceivably could have proved permanent, but those who were recaptured were usually sentenced to lengthy terms of extra service as punishment. In any case, deserting libertos forfeited hopes of legally winning their freedom through the originally established mechanism of service. There is even serious doubt that the remnants of the revolutionary regiments that made it back to Buenos Aires after years of campaigning were allowed to enjoy the freedom they so richly deserved. An official history of the liberto Eighth Infantry Regiment reports that when its few survivors returned to Buenos Aires in 1824 after eight years of campaigning in Chile, Peru, and Ecuador, they were promptly incorporated into regiments preparing for the approaching War with Brazil, an incorporation which must have been forced on them since it is impossible to imagine that those broken survivors would have gone off voluntarily to fight in yet another war.

Despite the shortcomings of the rescate program from the Afro-Argentines' point of view, it was undeniably successful in furnishing the revolutionary armies with much-needed manpower. Following the destruction of the free black battalions at Sipe-Sipe, the Afro-Argentine representation in the armed forces consisted almost entirely of libertos. When General José de San Martín led his army across the Andes into Chile in 1816 to liberate that country from Spanish rule, half of his invading force consisted of ex-slaves recruited from Buenos Aires and the provinces of western Argentina and organized into the all-black Seventh and Eighth Infantry Battalions and the integrated Eleventh Infantry. San Martín's conquest of Chile and Peru is the stuff of which military legend is made. Leading his small army with a rare combination of skill and luck, he succeeded in throwing off Spanish rule in two centers of royalist resistance and sympathy. Even more remarkable was the career of the black battalions that accompanied him. Between 1816 and 1823 they fought and won battles in Chile, Peru, and Ecuador in an odyssey of campaigning that took them as far north as Quito, thousands of miles from their homes in Argentina. By the time they were finally repatriated, fewer than one hundred fifty men remained out of the approximately two thousand black soldiers who had crossed the Andes with San Martín.

A focus on the all-black regiments, however, obscures the importance of Afro-Argentines in integrated units. Though segregation of the military was more strictly observed during the colonial period than after independence, there is considerable evidence that even prior to 1810 black and white soldiers served side by side in the local militias. It was not unusual, for instance, for well-to-do merchants or professionals to send their slaves to substitute for them at militia drills and in actual combat, so that a de facto integration resulted through slaves' serving in supposedly all-white units. Sometimes integration was officially condoned. During the English invasions a company of free mulattoes was attached to the First Squadron of Hussars, a prestigious white cavalry unit. At least two petitions survive from black officers in this company appealing to the viceroy to allow them to continue to serve in "this distinguished unit" rather than be transferred back to the Battalion of Castes. So badly did these two men want to stay in the white unit that they both offered to serve without pay, supplying their armament and horses at their own expense. Despite their pleas, both men were reassigned to the Castes.

Given the liberal rhetoric of the revolution, integration of regular army units was almost inevitable. At first the revolutionary junta sought to keep Afro-Argentine companies in separate battalions, allowing only the Indians to serve with the whites, but eventually they relented, and in 1811 several companies of free Afro-Argentines were aggregated to the Second Infantry Regiment. These companies were later separated from the regiment to form the basis of the Tenth Infantry, another integrated unit. The Eleventh Infantry, which accompanied the black Seventh and Eighth Battalions on their eight-year campaign through the Andean countries, was also integrated. . . .

Death, Desertion, and Disease

A potentially explosive question concerned with segregation and the existence of all-black units is the possibility that commanders used them as assault troops in preference to white units, consciously killing off Argentina's black population while achieving military objectives. No Argentine historian has suggested in print that such a genocidal policy existed, but several mentioned it in conversation as one explanation for the demographic decline of the Afro-Argentines. Simón Bolívar, the liberator of northern South America, once argued frankly in favor of such a policy:

> Is it right that only free men die to free the slaves? Would it not be just for the slaves to win their rights on the battlefield and diminish their dangerous number by this powerful and legitimate means? In Venezuela we have seen the free population die and the slaves remain; I do not know if this is politic, but I do know that if in [Colombia] we do not make use of the slaves [as soldiers] the same thing will happen.

Let it stand to Argentina's credit that there is no evidence of such thought or practice in the country's military history. Although black males were drafted in numbers disproportionate to their representation in the population, it does not appear that they were singled out for consistently hazardous duty. It is true that the Seventh and Eighth Infantry Battalions eventually melted away to nothing during their years of campaigning, but the white units that accompanied them did no better. The First Cazadores was almost completely destroyed at the Battle of Maipu, and very few of the Mounted Grenadiers ever returned from Peru to Buenos Aires. No casualty counts are available for the disaster at Sipe-Sipe, but a list of officers killed and captured suggests that the mainly white Ninth Infantry suffered more heavily than the two black regiments combined. The Ninth Infantry lost fifteen officers, while the Sixth and Seventh Infantry between them lost six. Or consider the Fourth Cazadores, which quietly sat out the War with Brazil in Buenos Aires while the integrated regiments battled Brazilians and the cold in Uruguay. . . .

The devotion with which thousands of Afro-Argentines fought for their country is a puzzling phenomenon, when one considers the meager rewards they received in return. Perhaps they actually believed the appeals to defend God and country with which their officers fired them before battle, but it is more likely that their bravery and even ferocity in battle sprang from two sources. The first source included the resentments and frustrations they suffered due to their position in Buenos Aires society. The discontent and rage that they had to repress in the city could be released on the battlefield without fear of punishment, and the occasional testimonials to the "blood-thirstiness" and "savagery" of the Afro-Argentine soldiers suggest that they did not hesitate to take advantage of this opportunity. The fury they displayed on the battlefield was truly above and beyond the call of duty and hints at some deeper motive than mere love of country. The second source was the hope for promotion: upward mobility in the army and perhaps even in the greater society.

Suggestions for Further Reading

Anna, Timothy E. *The Fall of the Royal Government in Mexico City*. Lincoln: University of Nebraska Press, 1979.

———. *The Fall of the Royal Government in Peru*. Lincoln: University of Nebraska Press, 1979.

———. *Spain and the Loss of Empire*. Lincoln: University of Nebraska Press, 1983.

Bushnell, David, ed. *The Liberator, Simon Bolivar: Man and Image*. New York: Knopf, 1970.

Collier, Simon. *Ideas and Politics of Chilean Independence, 1808–1833*. Cambridge, England: Cambridge University Press, 1967.

Dominguez, Jorge I. *Insurrection or Loyalty: The Breakdown of the Spanish American Empire*. Cambridge, MA: Harvard University Press, 1980.

Halperin-Donghi, Tulio. *The Aftermath of Revolution in Latin America*. New York: Harper and Row, 1973.

———. *Politics, Economics, and Society in Argentina in the Revolutionary Period*. Cambridge, England: Cambridge University Press, 1975.

Hamill, Hugh M., Jr. *The Hidalgo Revolt: Prelude to Mexican Independence*. Gainesville: University of Florida Press, 1966.

Hamnett, Brian R. *Roots of Insurgency: Mexican Regions, 1750–1824*. Cambridge, England: Cambridge University Press, 1986.

Lynch, John. *The Spanish-American Revolutions, 1808–1826*. 2d ed. New York: Norton, 1986.

Lynch, John, ed. *Origins of the Latin American Revolutions, 1808–1826*. New York: Knopf, 1965.

Masur, Gerhard. *Simon Bolivar*. 2d ed. Albuquerque: University of New Mexico Press, 1969.

Rodriguez O., Jaime E. *The Emergence of Spanish America: Vicente Rocafuerte and Spanish Americanism, 1808–1832*. Berkeley: University of California Press, 1975.

Russell-Wood, A. J. R., ed. *From Colony to Nation: Essays on the Independence of Brazil*. Baltimore: Johns Hopkins University Press, 1975.

Sloan, Stephen K. *Pablo Morillo and Venezuela, 1815–1820*. Columbus: Ohio State University Press, 1974.

Timmons, W. H. *Morelos of Mexico: Priest, Soldier, Statesman*. El Paso: Texas Western Press, 1963.

II

Making Sense of Caudillos and "Revolutions" in Nineteenth-century Latin America

John Charles Chasteen

The political history of nineteenth-century Latin America confronts us with a maze of shifting alliances and a succession of leaders who rise or fall by force more often than by elections. The ubiquity of these generals on horseback, called *caudillos*, and the proliferation of their sometimes theatrical "revolutions" pose one of the oldest riddles to confront historians of Latin America. Nineteenth-century historians either sang the praises of caudillos or vilified them, depending on each author's political allegiance. In the early twentieth century, most historians saw caudillismo as a disorder, a sickness in the body politic, and their diagnoses often involved imputations of racial and cultural inferiority or references to the "political inexperience" of a newly independent people. More recent (and better) interpretations have emphasized the place of caudillismo within larger political, social, and economic patterns—the disappearance of effective state power, centrifugal regionalism, and the disorganization of trade—which emerged in the wake of independence.

By definition, a caudillo was a man with a personal following largely independent of any institutional leadership role. The great majority were military men. Few caudillos attracted their followers by proposing specific changes in government policy. Instead, they tended to mobilize support through family and friends, and through the networks of patronage and clientele that linked them to people below them in the social hierarchy. Large landowners were the best gatherers of voters or fighters because so many poor country people had no land and depended on them for a livelihood, and most caudillos were landowners. Once in power, caudillos acted as guarantors of the social order, almost never questioning the existing social hierarchy. Nevertheless, they often attracted intense devotion from their popular following.

Caudillos also differed from one another in many ways. Argentina's Gen. Juan Manuel de Rosas began as a powerful landowner and entrepreneur before his political rise, whereas Mexico's Gen. Antonio López de Santa Anna and many others acquired fortunes after their political triumphs. In Central America, the Liberal caudillo Gen. Francisco Morazán was a white Creole, while Conservative caudillo Gen. Rafael Carrera was a mestizo. Gen. José Antonio Páez shared the portion of African ancestry so common among his followers on the Orinoco Plains of Venezuela. Although caudillos were usually military men, some university-educated "doctors" (usually lawyers by training) functioned as caudillos, more frequently in the later nineteenth century. Benito Juárez—Zapotec Indian, jurist, president of Mexico, and friend of Abraham Lincoln—is among the most famous.

The native-born elites of nineteenth-century Latin America were intensely involved in building networks of personal alliances and vying with each other for political dominance. (The qualifier "native-born" is important, since immigrants often wielded great economic power but seldom took an active role in politics.) The best alliance builders were men with a talent for gaining other people's confidence and loyalty. Santa Anna has not won the admiration of later generations of Mexicans, but in his own time he seldom failed to impress people who met him, whether humble countrymen or foreign dignitaries. A successful caudillo became known as a good friend but also as a fierce enemy. In Argentina, Rosas dispensed vast expanses of public lands to his supporters and harassed his political adversaries with implacable brutality. Political dominance often included an element of violent force.

The selections that follow this introduction were written by nineteenth-century Latin Americans, many of whom took part in the political conflicts they describe. They reveal the frequency of rebellions and the importance of face-to-face transactions among the small groups of upper-class males who played the leading roles in politics. We begin with the autobiographical account of José Antonio Páez, the hero of Venezuelan independence, who describes an encounter of mounted lancers in the 1830s (Doc. 1), then turn to the memoir of Peruvian caudillo José Rufino Echenique, who describes a series of barracks revolts in the 1840s (Doc. 2). Next, we will look at Mexico in the 1850s, where Benito Juárez championed the Liberal cause in a major civil war (Doc. 3), and at Chile, where turbulence in the 1820s gave way by the 1840s to a long period of stable, oligarchical rule (Doc. 4).

A schematic idea of caudillo politics will help students to interpret these readings. Much nineteenth-century political life was shaped by competing networks of friends and followers, often called patronage structures. Such networks were social pyramids composed of several tiers of "vertical" patron-client relationships. At the top stood a national caudillo who counted the powerful heads of the country's great families among his friends and supporters. In the next tier down, these powerful supporters had followers of their own in the regions dominated by their families: lawyers, merchants, landowners, and military men. Such men competed for local judgeships and administrative offices. Below them were clerks, artisans, and landless rural men who depended economically on the lawyers and landowners and were expected to back them politically. People without property could rarely vote or hope to hold office, nor could women do so. Although women became involved in political struggles through brothers, fathers, and husbands, leadership remained a male prerogative.

As often as not, politics was a matter of fighting. In fact, bearing arms in a revolution was one of the main forms of political participation for nonelite Latin Americans in the aftermath of independence. Most nineteenth-century rebellions were not intended to rearrange the social order. Instead, the word "revolution" often implied simply the overthrow of a tyrant—any ruler believed to abuse power. Such revolutions were typically brief trials of strength between one elite faction, which controlled the government, and another, which aspired to do so. A challenger to the current government, encouraged by his friends and followers, issued a pronouncement declaring the current government immoral, specifying his own lack of political ambition, and announcing his willingness to sacrifice personal interests to deliver the country from the scourge of tyranny. People watched the prospective leader parade through town and countryside, gathering supporters. En route, the caudillo displayed loyalty to his friends, gallantry with women, and generosity with his social inferiors. In battle, he had to demonstrate (or conceal his lack of) physical courage and a commanding presence. The leadership quality that Latin Americans call "political prestige"—the special attraction associated with caudillos—commonly derived from their behavior in a revolution. One or two battles usually revealed the preponderance of power, and the weaker side saw little to be gained by persisting in a hopeless cause. If the revolution were defeated the rebellious caudillo would go into exile, but if fortune smiled he would make a triumphal entry into the capital city and assume the presidency. There, he would distribute the spoils of office to his loyal friends and they, in turn, would reward their own followers, down to the level of the servants and laborers who had composed the bulk of the insurgent army. Members of powerful families received cabinet ministries or lucrative business concessions and local supporters could expect preferment in government employment, while the humblest followers enjoyed at least a few days of festive largesse on the part of the *patrón*. In this way, patronage flowed down through the tiers of clientele like sap through a branch, thus making the control of the government its own reward for the victorious faction.

So frequent did insurgency become after independence in Latin America that "revolution," or the permanent threat of it, constituted an integral part of the political process. A full enumeration of all the military coups, guerrilla wars, regional revolts, and local uprisings that occurred during the middle decades of the nineteenth century would number in the hundreds. Brazil constitutes an important exception to this generalization, however. Given the country's size and diversity, the number of revolutions in nineteenth-century Brazil pales by comparison with Spanish American patterns. Fortunately for the poor, who did most of the fighting in both Brazilian and Spanish American civil wars, limited aims and a general shortage of firearms kept routine political warfare from producing huge death tolls. Indeed, it may well be that more combatants died on the battlefields of the U.S. Civil War than in all the political warfare of Latin America's tumultuous midnineteenth century. The indirect social and economic costs of these wars, on the other hand, were incalculably great.

Like most people, the authors of the following selections usually rationalize their self-serving politics as a matter of principle. Joaquim Assis Brasil, taking inspiration in a past rebellion, justifies the attempted secession of a southern Brazilian province in 1836 as a result of abusive taxation and governmental neglect reminiscent of the complaints of the English colonists of North America (Doc. 5). Many people of the midnineteenth century used the tenets of Anglo-French liberalism to attack Hispano-Catholic traditionalism, but the influence of formal ideologies was frequently subordinate to other influences and fails to explain fully the behavior of leaders and followers. For example, it was fairly common for people to switch parties to avoid opposing friends or supporting enemies. The logic of personal alliance and enmity frequently overrode all else, at least during a "revolution."

Moreover, the formal political ideologies then available were all incompatible with the defense of upper-class privilege in highly stratified societies, a fact which significantly reduced their appeal among those active in politics. Venancio Ortiz provides a cautionary tale of some young upper-class males in Colombia who took up the cause of social equality in order to gain a following among urban artisans. According to Ortiz, the young hotheads were playing with fire in order to advance their own ambitions, and the fire quickly burned out of control (Doc. 6). Lower-class participation in the political process appears to these upper-class authors as a sign of dangerous disorder, with good reason: When the people at the bottom of the social hierarchy felt their own collective power, they sometimes used it against their "betters."

The authors of these narratives have sometimes revealed something of how they saw their political world in the way they have "constructed" their descriptions of it. Domingos Antonio Raiol describes a race riot as an inversion of the social order, a blasphemous version of the traditional Brazilian carnival, when servants sometimes dressed up like masters. As the author recognizes explicitly, the fury of the rioting blacks and Indians flowed from centuries of mistreatment, yet he concentrates on the perversion of ritual and order rather than on matters of cause and effect. By framing events in this manner, readers and writers made sense of the violence without any unpleasant scrutiny of the tensions in their hierarchical society (Doc. 7).

Nineteenth-century Latin American politics often turned on symbolic issues of identity and values. The most famous political narrator of Argentina, Domingo Faustino Sarmiento, denounced the symbol-mongering of his hated foe, Rosas, in his description of the red ribbons that everyone in Buenos Aires was supposed to wear as a badge of loyalty to Rosas (Doc. 8). In addition, caudillos seemed to have been viewed as protagonists with whom followers could identify, and their "revolutions," as occasions in which to dramatize their scorn for danger and characterize themselves as bold leaders. Somewhat surprisingly for modern readers, emotional sensitivity and disposition to self-sacrifice were central motifs in the autobiographies of many caudillos, who sought to appear as moral exemplars rather than problem solvers. The autobiography of Mexico's Santa Anna offers a notable example (Doc. 9).

The following selections represent seven Latin American countries at the height of their postindependence turmoil. They illustrate the frequent use of armed force in political life; the terms of conflict among elite factions; the face-to-face style of patronage politics, with its emphasis on the character of leaders rather than on their programs; and the discourse of gesture and image in which political conflict was partly transacted. In entering the political world of our nineteenth-century narrators, readers should try to get a feel for the period rather than strive to understand the details of particular events. Students should simply ignore the profusion of names unaccompanied by adequate identifying information. Because they wrote for the small political class of their own countries, these authors assume a familiarity with the people and places they describe. By looking past the intricacies of the individual cases, we can better see the general patterns that explain caudillos and revolutions in nineteenth-century Latin America.

1. The Lions of Payara ◆ José Antonio Páez

The Venezuelan caudillo José Antonio Páez was a rural man of middling social origins who became a leader during the wars of independence and, afterward, the first president of Venezuela. Such social mobility was uncommon, and it usually stemmed from fighting ability. Páez's original supporters were the mounted herdsmen of the Orinoco plains, famous for their military prowess. Charging lancers, roll calls of heroes, and paternalistic bonds between Páez and his followers give his account of 1836–37 an archaic tone reminiscent of a medieval epic. In this passage from his autobiography (written in an elevated style he would have required assistance in composing), the caudillo describes events that occurred between his two presidencies of the 1830s. Although out of office, he remained the real power behind the government at the time.

After the triumph of Independence, the cattle of the Province of Apure had been distributed among the valiant warriors of the army whose lances doomed Spanish despotism there. By distributing the herds, our country repaid their services and gave them a stake in the prosperity of the territory which they had conquered with heroism and defended with unfailing courage. Cornelio Muñoz, intrepid captain of my former guard, had property there; so did Rafael Ortega, my constant companion in hardship and glory, whose recent death still grieved me at the time of these events; then there were Francisco Guerrero (second in command of the army in Apure), Remigio Lara, Juan Angel Bravo, Facundo and Juan Antonio Mirabal, Doroteo Hurtado, León Ferrer, Andrés Palacio, Marcelo Gómez, and others whose names I have recorded already when describing my campaigns in the Llanos. Also among them were Juan Pablo and Francisco Farfán, who had aided me on more than one occasion to succeed in my desperate struggle. These two were true bedouins of the Llanos: gigantic in stature, with athletic musculature and valor bordering on the ferocious, obedient only to naked force. They had served at first in the ranks of the royalist Yánez. But when I had offered to give the rank of captain to any Llanero who brought me forty fighters, they enlisted with their followers and rode with me in Apure from that time on. If I had been strict with my troops, I would have had to punish these brothers severely, because they often deserted for a time with their men to go on plundering raids. Then they would appear again,

From José Antonio Páez, *Autobiografía* (New York, 1869; reprint ed., H. R. Elliot and Company, 1946), 2:297–301. Translated by John Chasteen.

claiming some excuse for their absence. But in those days my only prudent course was tolerance of their behavior, for I needed brave fighters.

Just before the Battle of Mucuritas the Farfán brothers disappeared on one of these escapades, and I finally threatened to lance them through if they did not get out of my sight with all their people. That is why they did not share in the glory of Mucuritas. Later I allowed them to return, and I have told elsewhere how valuable the Farfán brothers proved in the capture of Puerto Cabello in 1823. They eventually returned to their herds in Apure, and there they lived peacefully until the year 1836.

In that year they raised the flag of rebellion—according to some, in connivance with other rebels on the coast; according to others, in response to a personal affront—without even a pretext of principles to justify their uprising against the government. The government directed the governor of Apure, Gen. Cornelio Muñoz, to organize a column to march against them, providing him with men, horses, arms, money, and a few troops from other provinces. The president also authorized General Muñoz to extend any sort of clemency compatible with the dignity of the government. He well knew that an insurrection based in Apure could put the whole Republic in danger. For my part, I sent several letters to the rebel leaders, reminding them of their patriotic duty. In reply, they tried to convince me that what they demanded was no more than I had promised to the Apureños during the war: that in a free Venezuela they would have to pay no taxes. "Your demands are unjust, quite unjust," I wrote back to them. "In no American republic are taxes lower than in Venezuela. The customs house supplies our treasury. The only internal taxes are those essential for the maintenance of public works in the provinces, which must have schools to educate the young and roads for the betterment of trade. The provinces should supply these needs with their own funds. Refusal to pay taxes for ends so important would mean an eternity of backwardness and misery."

The rebels finally accepted the clemency offered by Muñoz in his decree of July 9, and Francisco Farfán wrote me that "ignorance of the situation, the influence of others, and the lack of any adviser who could discern right from wrong had plunged him into an error that grieved him in his heart. He had fallen into it despite his good intentions and persisted in it thoughtlessly." He wrote: "I am aware of all the good Your Excellency has done for me, more than I can repay. But if gratitude would serve as repayment, I could bestow a wealth of it upon you, my friend and comrade, to whom I look up as a son to his father."

What happened next will show whether Farfán's repentance was sincere. Early in 1837 he rebelled again, this time in the Province of Guayana, proclaiming reunification with Colombia, the reform of the Constitution, the reestablishing of special judicial privileges for military officers and clergy, the institution of trial by jury, the abolition of all taxes on rural property, a decree of amnesty for various conspirators fleeing justice, and finally the proclamation of General Mariño (the instigator of all of this) as Supreme Chief.

Cornelio Muñoz mobilized against Farfán, but his subordinates failed in their operations. Major Navarrete was defeated on the banks of the Orinoco and Colonel Mirabal was beaten on the plains of the Merecure. The rebels took Achaguas and obliged Muñoz to entrench himself in San Fernando. The president then decreed the formation of an army under my orders, naming Col. Agustín Codazzi chief of staff for the Division of Apure. . . .

Codazzi marched to the aid of Muñoz, besieged by Farfán in San Fernando, and managed to force his way into that beleaguered town. I moved my troops to San Fernando as well and, on arrival, sent Captain Mirabal's infantry and Major Calderín's cavalry to reconnoiter. The enemy had crossed the river and withdrawn about a mile from the city just before my arrival. My men's horses were exhausted, so at nightfall I had the advance parties return so that the entire force would be able to resume the pursuit together. When the moon rose, I had the men take their horses across the river, and we set out at eight the next morning. Reaching the place called Rabanal, I learned that the rebels had passed hours earlier. I saw that it would be impossible to catch them with our whole army, so I took the best-mounted men on ahead, leaving the rest to come along afterward. With sixty fighters, I trotted in pursuit of a rebel force that numbered three times that. At the place called Yuca, about fifteen miles from San Fernando, I heard that they were only slightly ahead of us and, increasing the pace, I caught up with their rear guard a couple of miles from the town of Payara.

We entered the fight with that rear guard (composed of eighty men armed with carbines) and defeated them. As we chased these routed rebels through the town, my small force was divided into two groups. The enemy was waiting in a field to the west of the town: three columns of cavalry with a reserve force of infantry. The group to my right charged ahead impetuously but was repulsed, and the whole enemy army bore down upon them. Seeing this, I rushed to join them with my own group in order to face the onslaught with a compact mass of sixty lancers. In the extraordinary battle which followed, each man defended the ground within the radius he could reach with his lance, leaving an adversary sprawled there or dying there himself. Juan Pablo Farfán came personally to put me out of action, but the robust lance of my servant Rafael Salinas knocked him dead out of the saddle.

The rebels finally gave up the field, and the soldiers of the government were not less ardent in the pursuit than they had been in the heat of combat. We lost a mere two men dead and seven wounded; the rebels lost one hundred and fifty dead, among them a brother and an uncle of the ringleader, Francisco Farfán. Farfán sought his own salvation in the swiftness of his horse, and his followers fled in such disarray that one could not see ten of them together in their flight.

This deed of arms took place on April 26, 1837. I received a thousand congratulations for the victory, but they would have been more pleasant if the glory had not been won at the cost of Venezuelan blood. Such bravery, had it been displayed in the face of a foreign foe, would have moved the grateful nation to erect a battlefield monument to THE LIONS OF PAYARA.

---

2. "I Met Vidal on His Way to the Palace" ◆ José Rufino Echenique

The most famous caudillos were those who became president of their countries, as did José Rufino Echenique of Peru (1851–1854). This extract from his memoir describes what occurred in the 1840s, before he became president. Echenique shows how personal alliances and barracks revolts structured political life after highland-based rural caudillos wrested leadership from the aristocracy of Lima in the 1830s and 1840s. When the scene opens, a friend of Echenique's has just tried a revolution and failed.

I had left my hacienda and come to Lima to buy some mules that I had heard were on sale near the port. Passing the street which runs in front of the Palace of Government, I met my friend Colonel Ros, who told me of Hercelles's defeat. He also said that Hercelles himself had been captured and was presently being brought as a prisoner to Lima, but that an order had been issued to execute him before arriving. Ros added that I could probably save Hercelles if I tried, because of the great influence that I had with [Acting President] Vidal. It was true that I did have influence with Vidal, and since I was Hercelles's friend I went straight to the Palace. Vidal was not there, but they told me that I might speak with La Fuente, a government minister with particular sway over Vidal, so I went to speak with him about the matter. I found him surrounded by many important figures, among them the minister Lazo, all talking about Hercelles. With his characteristic emphasis, La Fuente spoke of the order which had been given, saying that Hercelles should be shot the moment it was received, and declared that the government would do the same five hundred times to stop revolutions.

From José Rufino Echenique, *Memorias para la historia del Perú (1808–1878)*, Part 2 (Lima: Editorial Huascar, 1952), 1:119–22. Translated by John Chasteen.

Several of his interlocutors voiced their agreement. You may be sure that this resolution wounded my patriotism because I considered it tyranny. Overcome by my feelings, I said nothing, but withdrew, determined to reach Vidal. They had told me he was at his house, and I headed that way.

As it happened, I met Vidal on his way to the Palace, and we returned there together. As soon as we were alone, I told him why I was looking for him, and I was astonished to hear him simply repeat the same words I had heard from La Fuente. Sensitive by nature, I also have an unfortunately violent temper, and I took offense that he should speak to me in that way. His arbitrary threats constituted a horrible tyranny for the nation, and furthermore, the man he intended to destroy was my good friend. I made up my mind first to save my friend, and then to help overthrow a government of methods so antithetical to laws and rights. This decision, unhappily, became the cause of all that befell me later: the loss of my privileged situation and of the bright future which corresponded to it.

As soon as I got home, steadfast in my purpose, I sent for a well-known war captain named Contreras who was extremely loyal to me. I told him to gather twenty-five men of absolute trustworthiness, to arm them, to lead them out the road to Chancay, to ambush the party that was bringing Hercelles prisoner, and to rescue him. He agreed but, as he gathered the men and arms, the news arrived that Hercelles had been executed immediately upon receipt of the order to that effect. Not only that, his head had been cut off and sent to the place where he began the revolution, to be displayed as an example and a warning. Lazo, the Minister of Government, gave that order, and it was the last straw for me. I determined to move against the government at the first opportunity.

Shortly thereafter we learned of a revolution in favor of General Vivanco, which had taken place in Arequipa. The well-known patriotism, ability, honesty, and honorable sentiments of General Vivanco gave everyone high hopes for the future progress and stability of the country. By this time the government had fallen into complete disrepute. Besides not doing anything to benefit the nation, the government had lost even institutional legitimacy because, at the death of Gamarra, the presidency should have gone to Menéndez, who was chairman of the Executive Council, or to Vice President Figuerola, and not to Vidal, who had been merely assistant to the Vice President. Consequently, the revolution spread quickly to Cuzco, and then to Ayacucho, where General Pezet joined with his division. In Lima, there were four corps which I decided to bring into the revolution without having communicated with Vivanco. I began by establishing contact with some of the officers, and I found them favorably disposed. When Figuerola assumed the presidency and made Castilla Minister of War, these corps were now under his command. But I could not turn back because I had already made commitments to some supporters of Vivanco. In addition, I had the highest opinion of Vivanco and felt it my patriotic duty to help put him in power. Foolishly, I thought that my responsibilities would end with the triumph of the revolution and that I would then be able to return to the peace and quiet of my hacienda. Most important, two high officers had solemnly committed themselves to move the moment that I gave the command.

I do not know whether or not Castilla found out about the revolutionary plans, but for some reason he sent the four corps under his command to spend the night in the main plaza of Lima. I received word of this maneuver, which was taken for a sign that the revolution had been discovered, and without hesitation I went to talk with the officers loyal to me, judging that the time was ripe. We encountered little resistance from the officers in command of the other two corps. They, too, put themselves at my orders when I proclaimed Vivanco to be Supreme Chief of the Republic. The next day, most of the leading citizens of the city met to proclaim the same thing. They also named me mayor and military commander of Lima. I could find no way to decline these honors and so accepted them, trusting that it would be only until the arrival of Vivanco, at which time I could get rid of these responsibilities and go back to my private occupations. In the meantime, I persecuted no one and allowed Castilla himself to remain free in his own house.

A few days later I heard that Castilla was conspiring with another officer to bring down the revolution on a certain night. That night I went to the barracks where the reaction was supposed to begin, and I stayed there until dawn. Nothing happened, and people's apprehension began to dissipate. Then I learned that Colonel Alvarado Ortiz was on his way to Lima from Jauja with two battalions. Some said that he supported Vivanco; and others, that he meant to restore the constitutional government. When he arrived, I had him bivouac his troops in Lurín as a precaution, but without letting him know that I did not trust him. Next, General Pezet arrived with the force which had announced for Vivanco in Ayacucho. Because of his rank I put my soldiers at his disposition, but I continued in the office of mayor.

Everyone knows how well I executed my duties as mayor. It is enough to say that I neglected nothing and enjoyed wide popularity. Pezet and I got along excellently. He continued the policy of not bothering anyone for political reasons. Still, we could not rest easy because we had no news of Vivanco, not a word, and all the time we heard rumors of thriving conspiracies to bring back the constitutional government.

Finally, we learned that Vivanco had arrived in Jauja and was continuing to Lima, so we prepared him a splendid reception with the enthusiastic participation of the people, who seemed well pleased with the new order of things. Immediately after reporting on everything concerning the current situation of Lima, I asked Vivanco to appoint a new mayor, explaining my determination to return to my personal affairs, which were suffering from my neglect. But he asked me—one could even say he begged me—not to desert him at a time when my services were urgently needed for the regeneration of our country. I have always been too soft to deny a favor to a friend, and. believing that it would be unpatriotic to abandon Vivanco at this moment, I agreed to continue.

---

3. "Juárez Was Indeed a Man" ◆ Justo Sierra

This account of Mexico's Three Years' War (1858–1860) was published at the turn of the century by Mexican historian and political thinker Justo Sierra, a leading Liberal. Sierra praises the Liberal president Benito Juárez, whose moral virtues contrast sharply with the selfish ambition of his opponents. Bold use of force was admired, but nineteenth-century Latin Americans stressed matters of character in their descriptions of caudillos. The career of Juárez also shows that, although frequently disobeyed, constitutional authority remained an important political asset for those who could claim it. The Three Years' War ended a generation of Conservative hegemony closely associated with the Mexican caudillo Antonio López de Santa Anna (see Doc. 9).

Santa Anna's dictatorship, with unflagging zeal, had set about restoring the vigor and refurbishing the splendor of the army. And a group of young, ambitious officers, trained in the Military College or in the practical school of civil strife, had begun, in the dictator's flamboyant new regiments, to push aside such veterans of his revolts and of the war with the United States as Félix M. Zuloaga, Manuel Robles Pezuela, Miguel Echegaray, and Adrián Woll. Between these and the youngest of the new generals, Luis G. Osollo and Miguel Miramón, leaders of the forces which overthrew Comonfort, the transition was represented by a number of terribly fanatical warriors whose archetypes were Leonardo Márquez, Tomás Mejía, and the two Cobos, José María and Marcelino R. Nearly all of these men, forming a narrow circle in the capital of the Republic, were devout believers in military privilege, contemptuous of those governments that tried to lean on the national guard, and, from professional pride, lovers of war for war's

From Justo Sierra, *The Political Evolution of the Mexican People*, notes and intro. Edmundo O'Gorman, pro. Alfonso Reyes, trans. Charles Ramsdell (Austin, 1969), 281–85. © 1969 by the University of Texas Press. Reprinted by permission of the University of Texas Press.

sake. They could count on the applause of high society, of the rich, whose hatred of reformist ideas had become a religion; they could count on the coffers of the clergy, and, confident of their military prowess, they resolved to conquer the Republic at sword's point and then see who could stay on top. This was to be, for them, an exciting adventure, which they undertook without compunction and with boundless valor.

First, they had to have a president. So they called together, in the capital, the most prominent politicians, lawyers, clergymen, journalists, generals, and landowners of the reactionary party, who then picked General Zuloaga, author of the Plan of Tacubaya, as being the candidate least apt to collide with the highly explosive ambitions of the rest. Then the army was set in march for the interior, the heartland. With what objective?

In the center of the Bajío, between Querétaro, Guanajuato, and Jalisco, a nucleus of resistance to the anticonstitutionalist coup had been organized. This became a vital nucleus when Juárez arrived, seeking the protection of the tristate coalition, which forthwith proclaimed him legitimate head of the nation. In the face of such catastrophes as Comonfort's flight and the apparent triumph of the reaction, he raised the banner of legality. He himself, in truth, was all that remained of legality, for no other officer or organ of the constitutional government was in a position to function: he exercised every power—the executive, the legislative, and the judicial—all at the same time and represented the whole people. Nothing of the sort was provided for by the Constitution, but, in the circumstances, nothing else could be done. The rights of individuals had to be suspended, and the grim specters of execution for political offenses, of confiscation, of banishment, sat on the closed book of a Constitution that survived only in the person of one man.

Juárez was indeed a man. As an intellectual, he was far inferior to his two collaborators, Ocampo and Lerdo de Tejada. Ocampo, his thought pervaded by a passion for liberty and a love of nature, was a true pagan, like the authors of the French Encyclopedia, and the strength of his basic optimism inspired him to prophetic heights. Although less of a philosopher, Lerdo de Tejada had an acute understanding of the economic problems intrinsic in the social and political structure; a Mexican Turgot, he devoted his entire life to the diagnosis of the malady, and his entire energy to its cure. Juárez possessed the great virtue of the indigenous race, to which, without a single drop of admixture, he belonged, and this virtue is perseverance. His fellow believers in Reform had faith in its inevitable triumph. So did he, but success, to him, was a secondary matter. What came first was the performance of his duty, even if the consequence was to be disaster and death. What he sought, far beyond the Constitution and the Reform, was the redemption of the indigenous people. In his pursuit of this ideal he never faltered: to free his people from clerical domination, from serfdom, from ignorance, from mute withdrawal—this was his secret, religious longing, the reason why he was a liberal and a reformist, the reason why he was great. It is not true that he was stolid. Deeply emotional, he suffered much, but nothing could move him from his path. He towers, morally, above any other figure of our civil wars. Beside him, the reactionary leaders, with all their words and deeds, seem as shadows, fading into the past, while he stands, immutable, for the future, for the conscience of a nation.

When the crusaders of the reaction, heaped with blessings by Archbishop Garza as God's instruments to remedy the Church's ills, marched out to win laurels and Te Deums, the coalition had an army waiting for them, under the command of the honorable and experienced General Anastasio Parrodi. Meanwhile, Juárez and his ministers made their headquarters in Guadalajara. But not for long. By the middle of March the coalition had been completely shattered by Osollo, and Manuel Doblado, governor of Guanajuato, capitulated without a fight. In a mutiny of soldiers at Guadalajara the president was captured and about to be executed when the eloquence of Guillermo Prieto persuaded the firing squad to raise their rifles first and then to release him. The history of our country came near taking an utterly different turn.

The young generals of the reaction swept everything before them. The president fled to the United States by way of the Isthmus of Panama, thence to Veracruz, where, with the cooperation of Governor Manuel Gutiérrez Zamora, he established a formal government. The simple fact that a constitutional government whose authority was based not on proclamations but on law was functioning in the principal port of the Republic made the outcome of the struggle merely a question of time, no matter how many victories the reactionaries might score. And they scored a great many.

---

4. The Powerful Minister Portales ◆ Diego Barros Arana

In Chile as throughout Latin America, struggles over government patronage became a frequent type of political conflict. This passage by the late-nineteenth-century historian Diego Barros Arana illustrates how elite males competed for a commodity in limited supply: office and rank appropriate to their social station. It also shows how the period's historians searched for legitimating images of political consensus. Barros Arana describes the creation of a stable oligarchical state under Diego Portales, a dictatorial

From Diego Barros Arana, *Historia jeneral de Chile*, 16 vols. (Santiago: Imprenta Cervantes, 1884–1902), 16:78–80, 347–48. Translated by John Chasteen.

leader of the 1830s. Because Portales put an early end to Chile's postindependence instability, Barros Arana portrays him as a patriotic hero. When the narrative opens in 1830, Portales is extending his influence in the absence of Bernardo O'Higgins, the caudillo of Chilean independence, who has left the country.

Although the stability of the new order of things seemed firmer every day, one could also detect certain seeds of discontent which were no doubt worrisome to the government. Men whose cooperation had been rather important in the triumph of the [recent] revolution now showed their displeasure with the way things were going, either because of their own political ill fortune, or because of the sometimes immoderate and offensive manner in which government minister Diego Portales increased his control of the ruling party. Two of the senators recently elected to the new Congress—men whose experience and intelligence could have contributed much—resigned their seats in the Senate. The senator-elect for Valdivia, don Diego José Benavente, who had quarreled with Portales over an extremely vexatious personal incident, resigned his Senate seat, declaring that his health and the administration of his family's property would keep him away from the capital. In a similar fashion, Dr. José Antonio Rodríguez resigned his seat representing the Province of Concepción, alleging that his health and his family business necessitated a total withdrawal from public life. Rodríguez's principal motive for participation in the revolution of 1829 had been a desire to restore Gen. Bernardo O'Higgins to his titles, honors, and political influence; but Portales, wary of the sway which O'Higgins might exercise over the new president, had opposed the general's return to Chile. The Senate could not prevail on either of these two senators to withdraw his resignation. Adamant in their decisions, both refused to attend sessions of the legislature and isolated themselves from political life. Benavente's attitude was such that he became regarded as an enemy of the administration.

The alienation of these two figures clearly lessened the prestige of the government, without yet causing alarm to those interested in maintaining the country's political stability. On the other hand, the continuing dissatisfaction of the ousted party and of the many officers who lost their commissions because of the revolution could not but inspire the most serious misgivings. The pecuniary hardship which these men now suffered through the loss of their titles and salaries (a loss which they sincerely believed to have been flagrantly unjust), and the idea that, as in previous years, the troops could be led easily to mutiny and revolt, effectively turned these men into habitual conspirators. So, beginning in 1831, Chile suffered a more or less unconnected series of subversive plots. Neither the vigilance through which these plots were detected nor the severity with which they were repressed could quench the rebellious spirit that inspired them. . . .

Then, in June 1837, came the terrible mutiny of Quillota, which cost Portales his life and was instigated by a military leader enjoying the favor and confidence of the famous minister. That revolt was put down and severely punished owing to the reigning spirit of order in the country (represented in this case by the National Guard, an institution developed from its inception by Portales). Quillota constitutes one of the most painful pages of our history. Whatever errors might have been committed by Diego Portales, the elevation of his character, his absolute honesty, the purity of his patriotism, and his clear understanding of the need to give our country a solid and stable political organization have made him deserving of the gratitude of posterity and of the aureola of glory which surrounds his name.

That bloody mutiny was, we repeat, punished with implacable severity; but in the following months the government's actions grew less harsh. This deplorable crisis seems to have demonstrated to the powerful minister's successors in the government of Chile that Portales's style of rule, with its permanent courts-martial and irrevocable death sentences, was not the most conducive to stability of the state. A more moderate and conciliatory policy, initiated shortly after the repression of the mutiny, reduced the frequency of conspiracies; it contributed more effectively to the public tranquility than had the persecutions and trials. A glorious foreign war, conducted with rare good fortune, laid firm foundations for Chile's international power and credit. In a matter of months we had destroyed the Peruvian-Bolivian Confederation which sought to achieve an overbearing hegemony on our continent. The victories won in that struggle, by exalting our national pride and turning our spirits away from civil strife, were largely responsible for the peace and well-being subsequently enjoyed by the Republic.

The new policy gained momentum under the presidency inaugurated in 1841. Elevated to the office of chief executive after his recent triumphs in Peru, Gen. Manuel Bulnes was determined to put an end to the political enmities produced by earlier civil wars. Domestic peace fostered all the manifestations of progress in our country. Though its well-being has not been uninterrupted, and though its moral and material development has encountered unfortunate obstacles from time to time, still, the Republic of Chile, no more than a poor and obscure Spanish colony in 1810, can be proud of the degree of progress achieved since independence.

5. The Brief Rio Grandense
Republic ◆ Joaquim Assis Brasil

In large countries such as Brazil, regional conflict was common throughout the middle years of the nineteenth century. During the attempted secession of the Brazilian province of Rio Grande do Sul from 1836 to 1845, rebellious elites mobilized support against the central government partly through appeals to regionalist sentiment, identifying their class interests with those of the Rio Grandense people as a whole. In the 1880s, Joaquim Assis Brasil, a law student and future political leader, described the origins of the Rio Grandense Republic to invoke historical antecedents for the federal republic that he and other young Republicans still dreamed of creating. Brazil finally became a republic in 1889.

People who are not prosperous naturally assign much of the responsibility for their problems to the government. That is what occurred in the province of Rio Grande, except that the complaints of people there were absolutely justified, even more justified than they supposed. The central government declared wars which required the services of the courageous sons of the province; the central government siphoned off the wealth of the province, leaving it prostrate; but the central government never tried to give the province the kind of protection which every young settlement needs at the beginning. To the contrary, the central government seemed always to be trying to frustrate the creation of wealth in the poor province of Rio Grande.

It levied taxes which were exorbitant in scale and absurd in conception, weighing heaviest on precisely those activities which the laws should have stimulated most. An extremely high tax of six hundred *réis* was exacted on each exported *arroba* [a measure of about thirty pounds] of jerked beef. As a result, Rio Grande's all-important cattle industry declined rapidly when it should have thrived. Meanwhile, the cattle industry of the Río de la Plata (which paid very light taxes) supplied increasing amounts of competing products to the Brazilian market. Cowhides shipped out of the province of Rio Grande paid an onerous tax of *one fifth* their value when destined for the domestic market and even more when destined for foreign ports. And what made this absurd tax still more absurd was the fact that it had to be paid in kind rather than in money. For example, if a man had traveled through the

From Joaquim Assis Brasil, *História da República Riograndense* (1882; reprint ed., Porto Alegre: ERUS, n.d.), 42–47, 161–64. Translated by John Chasteen.

interior and endured enormous hardships to buy hides and had managed to collect a thousand of them, he would then have to deliver two hundred of these hides to revenue agents, losing a major part of his profit-making potential. . . .

The evils of centralization, which deprive people of liberty, had never been so evident. The central government did not know the needs of the province or, at any rate, those needs did not affect the Empire directly, so nothing was done. The exploited and exhausted province itself had no way to meet its own pressing needs; local initiative could not exist in a system where everything depended on the center. The province had many large rivers and wide, open plains which offered easy communications in any direction, and yet this potential could not be developed without vessels to ply the rivers or bridges to cross them when the waters were high. The bridge at Rio Pardo was the only one in the province.

Education was supported exclusively by private funds. As late as 1820 the government did not maintain even one primary school, and a Latin school existed only in Porto Alegre. When the government finally decided to create public schools in a few localities, it budgeted a laughable one hundred *réis* a year for the teachers' salaries. As could have been foreseen, none of these schools was ever opened since they could never get teachers at less than nine *réis* a month. Only the Rio Grandense's natural inclination for education, still evident today, explains why there were many tolerably educated men in the province in those years. Those who educated themselves out of their own pockets could not but be enemies of that unnatural government which took so much without giving anything in return.

The disappointments and resentments smoldered and became hatred. In the spirit of each Rio Grandense emerged the conviction that the province desperately needed liberty: the sovereign power over what pertains to oneself alone. With that idea, the road to federation had been opened, and the people would soon gather the momentum needed to burst the ties which kept them from traveling down it. . . .

[A revolt against the central government began in 1835 and enjoyed a number of victories during its first year. But the Brazilian Empire had resources far greater than those of its rebellious province.]

Continual reinforcements of men and materiel arrived from the Imperial capital of Rio de Janeiro, where the government justified its actions (more from partisan hatred than love of country) by painting the Rio Grandense revolutionaries as bloodthirsty beasts. Almost everyone in the province patriotically supported the revolution; those who fought against it were mostly natives of other provinces or of other countries, especially Portugal. The patriot leaders were repelled by the idea of surrendering their arms, sterilizing the revolution, putting themselves at the mercy of foreigners, and subjecting themselves to an unavoidable reaction (only disguised by an amnesty). Reconciliation remained impossible, since both sides hoped for victory, but an indefinite continuation of the war would be unbearable for the Rio Grandenses. An attempt to overthrow the central government was certain to be defeated in the end.

Considering these alternatives, the revolutionaries soon came to the unanimous conclusion that there existed only one road out of their difficulties: the separation of the province from the Brazilian union, with whose government all chance of harmony had been lost. And that is how the crisis was resolved.

On September 12, 1836, General Netto camped on the left bank of the Rio Jaguarão, the extreme southern edge of Brazilian territory. That afternoon, he rode before his comrades in arms and addressed them. It had been a year already, he said, since the province had risen in revolution. The aim of the revolution was to free Rio Grande from a despised faction of political retrogrades, most of whom were outsiders. But the government persecuted the revolutionary leaders and frustrated their efforts to expel the retrogrades. In the present circumstances, he went on, only two courses of action lay open: submission, with loss of liberty; or secession of the province, with enormous sacrifice but a triumph of principles. The latter course alone was honorable and patriotic. For his part, he was disposed to any sacrifice. Seceding from Brazil, the Rio Grandenses would form a free and independent republic but would continue to love their Brazilian brothers and would be ever ready to accept an equitable confederation with the other provinces. The general proclaimed that the great majority of Rio Grandenses would support independence since they were for the revolution and only foreigners opposed it. The cause of independence attracted all the peoples of the earth, especially those of the neighboring republics, which would surely lend a hand. For all these reasons, he called for his brothers in arms to raise the cry of Rio Grandense independence and liberty, and he shouted: "Long Live the Rio Grandense Republic, Long Live Its Defenders, Long Live Our Religion, and Long Live Bento Gonçalves!" The column of troops responded with an enthusiastic roar. And that is how the Rio Grandense Republic was proclaimed, on September 12, 1836, on the left bank of the Rio Jaguarão.

6. The Subversive "Democratic Society" in New Granada ◆ Venancio Ortiz

Liberal assaults against conservative traditionalism constituted a major axis of conflict in nineteenth-century Latin America. Like other conservative spokesmen, Colombian historian Venancio Ortiz developed intellectual critiques of political experimentation and attempted to justify upper-class privilege in a hierarchical society. The ideological innovators, for their part, opened some new opportunities for social mobility, but their friends and followers were the principal beneficiaries of the innovations. Liberalism (and even early socialist ideas) held little appeal for the common people, and elite factions avoided social radicalism for reasons obvious in this cautionary tale written in the 1850s, shortly after the events it describes.

After New Granada was set up as an independent republic, its citizens began to display various political leanings. Some wanted a strong government to be the guarantor of the social order, and they wanted our religion to serve as the foundation of the republic. This party, which was more or less intolerant of opposing ideas, received the appellation of "retrograde." Others viewed religion as a barrier to intellectual progress and as a bastion of despotism, and they wanted a government that could in no way circumscribe individual liberty. These men composed the party called "progressive."

Both parties represented extremes, though one must recognize that sincere men within each party believed the triumph of their ideas would redound to the good of the country; and both parties tried to manipulate the ignorant multitudes, attracting them into their ranks with flattering promises. Now, the multitudes did not understand much about political matters, but they did have respect and affection for the Catholic religion, which the "retrogrades" vowed to protect, and so the majority soon supported the retrogrades. . . .

This ruling party counted among its members almost all of the country's principal businessmen and many fine minds, men belonging to families which, because of lineage or wealth, boasted long and distinguished participation in the affairs of the Republic. Since public life already abounded in capable and powerful men, it was hard for new men to enter influential circles. One had to be extremely rich, well connected, or intelligent; and

From Venancio Ortiz, *Historia de la Revolución del 17 de Abril de 1854* (1855; reprint ed., Bogotá: Biblioteca Banco Popular, 1972), 17, 22–23, 28, 36–38. Translated by John Chasteen.

most ambitious young men were treated with a degree of disparagement. Young men who wanted to make a name for themselves generally failed unless they had outstanding qualities. Therefore, a good part of that element of society which Pericles compared to the springtime of the year, the youth, became convinced that the Republic lay in the hands of an oligarchy, and they swore to fight it with any means at their disposal.

So a number of these young men established contact with leading artisans and formed a "Progressive Artisans' and Laborers' Society," later given the nickname of "Democratic Society." Here they preached to the common people a doctrine essentially abolitionist in nature and argued that the ruling party, supported by the church and the wealthy, had created a tyranny. The fact that one man named Mosquera was archbishop and another Mosquera was president, and that former president Herrán had married Mosquera's daughter—with other facts of similar insignificance—were used cleverly to persuade people that a certain circle wanted to perpetuate its own power. The speakers referred to that group as "nobles" with a bitter, ironic smile, making the members of the Society twist in their seats as if touched with a hot iron. . . .

Most of the rich people were conservative, and since they got richer all the time and wanted to have less to do with the poor people, the educated leaders of the Democratic Society presented the rich as oppressors and exploiters. And when they preached humanitarian ideas, they founded them on communist principles, calling all property a form of robbery. All good faith then disappeared, and they organized bands of brigands to terrorize the capital. In daily dealings, everyone tried to deceive everyone else, and trade was crippled due to the lack of trust. The fairer sex, in whose heart is rooted the tree which nourishes society, became contaminated by these anarchic principles; women began to scoff at religious practices and to sell their favors. If this sort of thing happened among educated people, you can imagine how the lower classes behaved. The social edifice had been undermined and threatened to come crashing down. . . .

[The Democratic Society centered its attention on a tariff matter under consideration in the legislature.]

From very early in the morning, the crowd began to occupy the hall of the legislature, the large gallery at the entrance of the building, and part of the plaza in front. They had been convinced that their interests would be favored by a measure prohibiting the importation of articles against which the artisans of Bogotá could not compete. They were no less attracted by the idea of punishing those whom they believed to be their enemies. At ten o'clock, the House of Representatives began its session with consideration of a committee resolution whereby the proposal of the Democratic Society would be sent to the Senate so that it might be taken into account later during the debate on tariffs. The discussion had hardly opened when insults and threats against members of the legislature rang out from the gallery, and next, cries of "Down with" this and that. But then answering cries were heard from decent young men from both parties who had mingled with the crowd of Democrats and were determined to sacrifice their lives, if necessary, to defend our country's representative institutions. The Democrats saw that they could not bully and kill with impunity, but that they would have to fight and defeat noble adversaries whom they could not but fear. This sudden realization made them change their plan. Though they were already numerous, they tried to gain a crushing advantage by calling upon the crowd outside. The cry was raised in the plaza: "Inside!" And the multitude surged into the building where the representatives were meeting. While several citizens worked prodigiously to restrain the mob, the secretaries of government and finance, Sr. Patrocinio Cuéllar and Sr. José María Plata, urged the chairman to call in the armed forces. . . . In spite of everything, the discussion continued and, disregarding the danger which surrounded them, the representatives fulfilled their duty with a steadiness worthy of their high station. Suddenly, the shouting increased, and the crowd again pushed its way into the hall, this time almost reaching the first row of seats. . . . Some young men jumped down from the upper gallery, thinking that a fight with the mob was inevitable, and others from the lower gallery leapt onto the floor of the chamber to join them. The rioters contained themselves, and the representatives voted on, and approved, the resolution. So the Democrats left the hall, determined to find a more open battleground on which to attack the representatives, who, for their part, continued calmly at their business and adjourned the session at the accustomed hour. They left the building escorted by citizens determined to defend them against their assailants. Thwarted by such courage, the hecklers kept their distance and threw rocks.

---

7. Uproar in Pará: Blasphemous Carnival or Race Riot? ◆ Domingos Antonio Raiol

Nineteenth-century writers such as the Brazilian Domingos Antonio Raiol often put symbolic constructions on political events which modern analysts would view strictly in terms of cause and effect. Looking back from later in

From Domingos Antonio Raiol, *Motins políticos ou história dos principáis acontecimentos políticos da província do Pará desde o ano de 1821 até 1835* (1865–1890; reprint ed., Belém: Universidade Federal do Pará, 1970), 3:921–25. Translated by John Chasteen.

the century, Raiol describes how the rebel capture of the provincial capital of Pará, or Belém, in 1835 became a race riot. Raiol explains that the blacks and Indians harbored "a long-repressed desire for revenge" against their white masters, but he pictures the events not as the natural result of oppression but as a grotesque, totally aberrant inversion of the social order. Episodes of this kind were rare, but their power over the upper-class imagination will be evident here.

After the government forces were withdrawn to Tatuoca Island, the capital of Pará lay in rebel hands! In the early dawn of August 23, 1835, Eduardo Angelim was out inspecting and reinforcing the city's riverside defenses! Some say he knew nothing about the Marshal's withdrawal during the night, because he had not opposed the slightest resistance, as if knowing nothing about it. Indeed, he may not have known, or he may have feared for the well-being of the families who embarked in the same warships. Angelim himself told me that he had desired no further bloodshed. However that may be, the only people who remained in Belém unwillingly were those who had not heard in time that the ships were leaving.

Angelim's first responsibility was to control the unthinking violence of his men, and in justice it must be said that he used all the means at his disposal to do this. Still, the frenzy of the rebellious population was such that his efforts often failed. Groups scattered through the main streets of the city, breaking down doors, entering houses, plundering commercial establishments, abusing and raping decent women, and murdering any man in their paths, without respecting even the sanctuary of the churches in which many of their victims had taken refuge!

The night before, a government detachment had occupied the Church of the Virgin of Carmo and, through an oversight, these men had not been notified when the Marshal's forces were withdrawn. On the morning of August 23, this group was caught by the rebels, who spared no one in the church. A few managed to escape over the wall behind the convent, but others thought they would be safer hiding behind the altar or among the various shrines. The villains found them there, however, and dragged them in brutal triumph out to the street, where the victims were rent by machete blows and shotgun blasts amid hellish howling!

That horrid butchery claimed sixteen victims, among them, retired Cols. José Narciso da Costa Rocha and Manuel Pinto Gomes, Maj. João Inácio Cavallero, Antônio Rodrigues Neves, and other prominent citizens. In their anguish, neither pleas for mercy nor the presence of sacred images could save them. Upon hearing their cries and lamentations, the bishop sent Geraldo Gavião to intercede on behalf of the few whom the rioters had not yet sacrificed, and Gavião escorted these fortunate few to the bishop's house nearby.

But no power could long restrain the incredible cruelty of the rioters, and the capital descended into total anarchy. When the rebels learned that the Marshal had left during the night, they opened the churches and set the bells ringing in jubilation, and they chanted strings of prayers in the cathedral. They shouted "Long Live Liberty" and "Death to the Government and to the Cowardly Fugitives"; they exploded fireworks, and they decorated the streets with banners. They greeted the people and congratulated their leaders, and finally they dispersed in unruly bands through the city, threatening the safety of person and property!

Foremost among those guilty of atrocities were certain slaves and freedmen who left their masters' houses and went to tell on them. These men committed the greatest outrages against the sanctity of the home: making foul, threatening advances to white women and, upon being rejected with natural repugnance, beating them as punishment! And let us not forget to say that during three days and three nights there were meetings, speech-making, singing of hymns and serenades, and parades and celebrations of every kind. Houses were required to put lights in their windows. All this in tribute to the solemn triumph of the morality and justice of so holy a cause, according to the proclamations of the apparent victors, delivered in scenes of indescribable uproar and disorder. While so diverting itself, a mob will forget its suffering, and such entertainments are the best means of distracting it from more serious matters.

The anarchy increased with the immoderate use of alcoholic drinks. The excesses of the seditious crowds knew no limits. They entered brazenly into the houses which they found open and broke into those which were closed against them, searching for suspected Masons and *caramurus* [members of the most reactionary party], which they generally considered all white men to be. And they thought the same of the Portuguese, whom they called "sailors" or "long beaks." Fortunately, almost all the Portuguese had left. The few who had hidden themselves in the city, though they might be unarmed, sick or decrepit, and completely harmless, were murdered without compassion. . . .

The rioters perpetrated countless outrages during their rampage through the province. Like the grim struggle between Roman plebeians and patricians, the revolt of the *cabanos* [as these Brazilian rebels were called] became a fight to the death against the upper classes, only more cruel and savage because unmotivated by any higher principle or general interest. Since it did not offer solutions to any social problems, the rebellion degenerated naturally into a chaotic bloodbath fueled by racial hatred. It was a hatred arising from the insults and abuses which the Indians, the blacks, and the people of mixed blood believed they had suffered—a hatred they had carried inside from colonial times and held back for many years and which burst forth in those dark days against their real or imagined oppressors. Nothing else explains the tremendous savagery of the rebels, whose every act demonstrated a long-repressed desire for revenge.

8. Rosas's Ribbons and Rituals ◆ Domingo Faustino Sarmiento

One can often interpret political actions as symbolism. The Argentine caudillo Juan Manuel de Rosas used lapel ribbons and church rituals to signify public conformity under his rule. His enemy Domingo Faustino Sarmiento (who later became president himself) ridiculed Rosas's symbol-mongering in this passage taken from Facundo, or Civilization and Barbarism, *the single most influential interpretation of nineteenth-century Argentina, but the book's own case is heavily symbolic, too. Facundo Quiroga, the apparent subject of the biography, was a lesser caudillo whom Sarmiento uses merely to personify the barbarity of Argentina under Rosas. Here, Facundo himself does not appear at all.*

Finally, Rosas has the government in his hands. Facundo has died a month earlier; the city has placed itself at his discretion; the people have candidly confirmed their surrender of all rights and institutions. The State is a blank slate on which he will write something new and original. He is a poet, a Plato who will now bring into being the ideal republic which he has conceived; he has meditated upon this labor for twenty years, and now he can finally bring it forth unimpeded by stale traditions, current events, imitations of Europe, individual rights, or existing institutions. He is a genius, in short, who has been lamenting the ills of his century and preparing himself to destroy them with one blow. All will be new, a work of his creative faculty. Let us observe this prodigy.

Leaving the House of Representatives, where he went to receive his staff of office, he withdraws in a coach painted red expressly for the ceremony. Yoked to the coach by cords of red silk are the men who, with criminal impunity, have kept the city in a state of continual alarm since 1833; they style themselves the People's Society, and they wear *knives* at the waist, *red* vests, and *red* ribbons with the slogan: "Death to the Unitarians." At the door of his house, these same men form an honor guard. Next he gives audience to citizens, and then to generals; everyone must show his limitless personal loyalty to the Restorer.

From Domingo F. Sarmiento, *Facundo o civilización y barbarie* (1844; reprint ed., Caracas: Biblioteca Ayacucho, 1977), 206–8, 123–24. Translated by John Chasteen.

The next day, a proclamation appears with a list of proscriptions. (One of the proscribed is a relative by marriage, Doctor Alsina.) This proclamation, one of Rosas's few writings, is a wonderful document that I am sorry not to have on hand. It was his program of government, undisguised and unambiguous: WHOEVER IS NOT WITH ME IS MY ENEMY. That is the axiom of policy enshrined in the document, which announces that blood will flow, and promises only that property will be respected. Woe to those who provoke his fury!

Four days later, the parish of San Francisco announces its intention to celebrate a Mass and Te Deum to give thanks to the Almighty, etc., inviting the people of the neighborhood to solemnize the event with their presence. The surrounding streets are dressed with banners, bunting, and carpets. The place becomes an Oriental bazaar displaying tapestries of damask, purple, gold, and jewels in whimsical array. People throng the streets: young people who are attracted by the novelty, ladies who have chosen the parish for their afternoon stroll. The Te Deum is postponed for a day, and the city's excitement—the agitated coming and going, the interruption of all work—lasts for four or five days in a row. The *Gazette* supplies the most insignificant details of the splendid event. And eight days later, another parish announces its Te Deum. The people of that neighborhood are determined to surpass the enthusiasm of the first parish, to outdo the first celebration. What excess of decoration! What ostentation of wealth and adornment! The portrait of the Restorer is placed on a dais in the street, swathed in *red* velvet, with golden cords and braid. The hubbub returns, for as many more days. In the privileged parish, people seem to live in the street. And, a few days later, there is another celebration, in another parish in another neighborhood. But how long can this go on? Do these people never tire of spectacles? What sort of enthusiasm is this, which does not subside in a month? Why do not all the parishes have their celebrations at the same time? No, it is a systematic, organized enthusiasm, administered a little at a time. A year later the parishes still have not concluded their celebrations. The official giddiness has passed from the city to the countryside; it appears endless. The *Gazette* of the period is occupied for a year and a half with descriptions of Federalist celebrations. The famous portrait appears unfailingly, pulled along by generals, by ladies, by the *purest* of Federalists, in a carriage made especially for the purpose. "Et le peuple, enchanté d'un tel spectacle, enthousiasmé du Te Deum, chanté moult bien à Notre-Dame, le peuple oublie qu'il payait fort cher tout, et se retirait fort joyeux."*

*Sarmiento displays his erudition by quoting a French history of the Middle Ages, *Chronique du moyen âge*: "And, enchanted by such a spectacle, thrilled by the Te Deum sung very well in Notre Dame, the people forget that they have paid dearly for everything, and they went away quite happy."

After a year and a half of celebrations, the color *red* emerges as the insignia of loyalty to "the cause." The portrait of Rosas first graces church altars and then becomes part of the personal effects of each and every man, who must wear it on his chest as a sign of "intense personal attachment" to the Restorer. Last, out of these celebrations comes the terrible Mazorca, the corps of amateur Federalist police, whose designated function is, first, to administer enemas of pepper and turpentine to dissenters, and then, should this phlogistic treatment prove insufficient, to slit the throat of whomever they are told.

All America has scoffed at these famous celebrations of Buenos Aires and looked at them as the maximum degradation of a people; but I see in them nothing but a political strategy, and an extremely effective one. How does one teach the idea of personalist government to a republic which has never had a king? The red ribbon is a token of the terror which goes with you everywhere, in the street, in the bosom of the family; you must think of it when dressing and undressing. We remember things always by association; the sight of a tree in a field reminds us of what we were talking about as we walked under it ten years ago. Imagine what ideas the red ribbon brings with it by association, the indelible impressions it must have joined to the image of Rosas. . . .

The story of the red ribbon is, indeed, curious. At first, it was an emblem adopted by enthusiasts; then they ordered everyone to wear it in order "to prove the unanimity" of public opinion. People meant to obey, but frequently forgot when they changed clothes. The police helped jog people's memories. The Mazorca patrolled the streets; they stood with whips at the church door when ladies were leaving Mass and applied the lash without pity. But there was still much which needed fixing. Did someone wear his ribbon carelessly tied?—The lash! A Unitarian!—Was someone's ribbon too short?—The lash! A Unitarian!—Someone did not wear one at all?—Cut his throat! The reprobate!

The government's solicitude for public education did not stop there. It was not sufficient to be a Federalist, nor to wear the ribbon; it was obligatory also to wear a picture of the illustrious Restorer over one's heart, with the slogan "Death to the Savage, Filthy Unitarians." Enough, you think, to conclude the job of debasing a civilized people, robbing them of all personal dignity? Ah! They were not yet well enough disciplined. One morning, on a street corner in Buenos Aires, there appeared a figure drawn on paper, with a ribbon half a yard long floating in the breeze. As soon as someone saw it, that person backed away in fright and spread the alarm. People ducked into the nearest store and came out with ribbons half a yard long floating in the breeze. Ten minutes later, the entire population was out in the street wearing ribbons half a yard long. Another day the figure reappeared with a slight alteration in the ribbon. The maneuver repeated itself. If some young lady forgot to wear a red bow in her hair, the police supplied one free—and attached it with melted tar! That is how they have created uniformity of public opinion! Search the Argentine Republic for someone who does not firmly believe and maintain that he is a Federalist!

It has happened a thousand times: a citizen steps out his door and finds that the other side of the street has been swept. A moment later, he has had his own side swept. The man next door copies him, and in half an hour the whole street has been swept, everyone thinking it was an order from the police. A shopkeeper puts out a flag to attract people's attention; his neighbor sees him and, fearing he will be accused of tardiness by the governor, he puts out his own. The people across the street put out a flag; everyone else on the street puts one out; other streets follow suit; and suddenly all Buenos Aires is bedecked with flags. The police become alarmed and inquire what happy news has been received by everyone but them. And these people of Buenos Aires are the same ones who trounced eleven thousand Englishmen in the streets and then sent five armies across the American continent to hunt Spaniards!

Terror, you see, is a disease of the spirit which can become an epidemic like cholera, measles, or scarlet fever. No one is safe, in the end, from the contagion. Though you may work ten years at inoculating, not even those already vaccinated can resist in the end. Do not laugh, nations of Spanish America, when you witness such degradation! Look well, for you, too, are Spanish, and so the Inquisition taught Spain to be! This sickness we carry in our blood.

---

9. The Caudillo as Protagonist ◆ Antonio López de Santa Anna

The autobiography of Antonio López de Santa Anna constitutes the histrionic self-dramatization of one of the most powerful men in nineteenth-century Mexico. The caudillo presents himself not as a decision maker or a power broker but as a vulnerable, introspective protagonist, the leading figure on a national stage. The modern reader may recoil from the unmitigated vanity of this "leading man," but Santa Anna's self-absorption seems not to have disqualified him in the eyes of his audience. When the excerpt begins in the early 1840s, Santa Anna is about to become president of Mexico for the fourth time.

From Antonio López de Santa Anna, *The Eagle: The Autobiography of Santa Anna*, ed. and trans. Ann Fears Crawford (Austin: Pemberton Press, 1967), 65–69.

Sixty-two days after my foot had been amputated, Gen. Guadalupe Victoria called on me at the instigation of the government. He informed me that a revolution was threatening, and that the government desired me to take Bustamante's place as temporary president in this time of trials. How well the people knew me! They knew I would never desert my principles and would always be on hand when my country needed me!

I was carried to the capital on a litter. Although my trip was made with extreme care, the hardships of the journey and the change of climate weakened me. However, despite my poor health, I assumed the office of president immediately. The tasks involved completely overwhelmed me, but without ill results. The government forces triumphed throughout the country. Gen. Gabriel Valencia captured and executed the hope of the revolution, José A. Mejía, in the vicinity of the town of Acajeta. The dreaded threat of revolution died, and peace was restored.

Bustamante once again took up the reins of government, and I retired to [my estate] to complete my recovery. However, Bustamante's loss of prestige with the people caused his government to fail. In the town of Guadalajara, in the early months of 1841, arrangements were made for Bustamante to abdicate and for the reform of the Constitution of 1824. In Tacubaya, a council of generals agreed upon a set of provisional bases to help bring about these reforms, and once again I assumed the office of provisional president. . . .

In order to conform to public opinion, I called together a junta of prominent citizens from all states in the nation to instigate needed reforms. This group drew up *Las Bases de Organización Política* on June 12, 1844. This constitution was circulated by the government, and each of the states accepted and ratified it without dissension.

In September 1844, my beloved wife died. Greater sorrow I had never known! General of Division Valentín Canalizo substituted for me while I devoted myself to family matters.

During the first session under our new Constitution, I was duly elected president and called to the capital to administer the customary oath. The election saddened me. My deep melancholy drove me to abhor the glamorous life of the capital and to prefer a life of solitude. I resigned the noble office to which I had been called, but the public intruded upon my privacy, pleading that I return. My friends, with the greatest of good faith, also begged me to resume my office. Their pleas led me to sacrifice myself to the public good. I withdrew my resignation.

Near the end of October, General Paredes rebelled against the government in Guadalajara. When the news was communicated to me by the government, they ordered me to take the troops quartered in Jalapa and march to the capital. I instantly followed the full instructions of the orders.

Paredes had been relieved of his command of the Capital District due to excesses of intoxication while he was commanding his troops. He bore a grudge and was determined to take revenge. In our country one spark was sufficient to set aflame a revolution.

I was marching toward Guadalajara under orders, when I received the news of an upheaval in the capital and the imprisonment of Canalizo, the president ad interim. The situation seemed serious, and I stopped my march at Villa de Silao.

The details of the revolt in the capital arrived soon after my halt. The infamous words the messenger read me are repeated here:

> The majority of Congress openly favor the Paredes revolution. The government, in self-defense or wishing to avoid revolution, has issued a decree by which the sessions of Congress were suspended and the Constitutional President invested with extraordinary powers. This decree has served as a pretext for General José T. Herrera to rise against the current government, a service for which he was rewarded with the appointment of *ad interim* President. The rioters imprisoned President Canalizo and extended their aversion to the President, Santa Anna. They tore down a bronze bust erected in his honor in the Plaza del Mercado. They stripped his name from the Santa Anna Theater, substituting for it the National Theater. Furthermore, they have taken his amputated foot from the cemetery of Santa Paula and proceeded to drag it through the streets to the sounds of savage laughter and regaling . . . .

I interrupted the narrator, exclaiming savagely, "Stop! I don't wish to hear any more! Almighty God! A member of my body, lost in the service of my country, dragged from the funeral urn, broken into bits to be made sport of in such a barbaric manner!" In that moment of grief and frenzy, I decided to leave my native country, object of my dreams and of my illusions, for all time.

At the head of eleven thousand well-trained and well-armed men and with partisans in the capital, I could have taken it easily. However, I was drained of all vengeance and was determined merely to leave my country forever. I countermarched toward Puebla, avoiding everyone.

Suggestions for Further Reading

Students will find authoritative political narratives for most countries in *Spanish America after Independence, c. 1820 – c. 1870*, edited by Leslie Bethell (Cambridge, England: Cambridge University Press, 1987). A more concise comprehensive account can be found in David Bushnell and Neill MacCauley, *The Emergence of Latin America in the Nineteenth Century* (New York: Oxford University Press, 1988).

To explore changing interpretations of nineteenth-century caudillismo, students should read an early twentieth-century version such Charles E. Chapman, "The Age of the Caudillos: A Chapter in Hispanic American History," *Hispanic American Historical Review* 12 (1932): 281–300, along with Eric R. Wolf and Edward Hansen, "Caudillo Politics: A Structural Analysis," *Comparative Studies in Society and History* 9 (1967): 168–79. Hugh M. Hamill provides a useful selection of readings in *Caudillos: Dictators in Spanish America* (Norman: University of Oklahoma Press, 1992), and John Lynch offers a comprehensive interpretation in *Caudillos in Spanish America, 1800–1850* (Oxford: Clarendon Press, 1992).

For more general treatments of political instability, one should begin with an analytical overview: Frank Safford, "Politics, Ideology, and Society," in Bethell, *Spanish America after Independence*. For the long-term perspective see Claudio Véliz, *The Centralist Tradition of Latin America* (Princeton: Princeton University Press, 1980), and Richard M. Morse, "The Claims of Political Tradition," in his *New World Soundings: Culture and Ideology in the Americas* (Baltimore: Johns Hopkins University Press, 1989), 95–130, both of whom emphasize the Hispanic roots of Latin American political culture. These should be compared to Stanley J. and Barbara H. Stein, *The Colonial Heritage of Latin America: Essays on Economic Dependence in Perspective* (New York: Oxford University Press, 1970), who stress the economic legacy of colonialism, and Fernando Henrique Cardoso and Enzo Faletto, *Dependency and Development in Latin America* (Berkeley: University of California Press, 1979), who follow the same logic through the nineteenth and into the twentieth century. At a different level of analysis, students can examine the behavior of powerful clans over several generations in Diana Balmori, Stuart F. Voss, and Miles Wortman, *Notable Family Networks in Latin America* (Chicago: Chicago University Press, 1984).

On Brazilian patterns in the period, students should consult a concise overview in Emilia Viotti da Costa, "Liberalism: Theory and Practice," in

The Brazilian Empire: Myths and Histories (Chicago: University of Chicago Press, 1985); a detailed narrative of national politics in Roderick Barman, *Brazil: The Forging of a Nation* (Stanford: Stanford University Press, 1988); and a general interpretation of political culture in Richard Graham, *Patronage and Politics in Nineteenth-century Brazil* (Stanford: Stanford University Press, 1990).

III

African Slavery in Brazil

Mary Butler

The history of African slavery in Brazil is one of cruelty, exploitation, courage, and resistance. It is the history of the millions of black men, women, and children who provided the blood and muscle for the economic development of the nation and of their continual resistance to a dehumanizing situation. It is also the history of the slave owners, of their determination to maintain the system despite domestic and international condemnation, and of the eventual triumph of the slaves and their abolitionist sympathizers over a system that existed in Brazil for nearly four hundred years.

When the conditions of conquest and enslavement drastically reduced the indigenous populations of Brazil during the early sixteenth century, the Portuguese quickly turned to Africa to satisfy their insatiable demand for servile labor. Already familiar with black slavery in the Iberian Peninsula, the Portuguese merely extended their existing slave trade to the New World. Historians such as Philip Curtin have estimated that at least nine million Africans arrived in the Americas between the beginning of the Atlantic slave trade in 1502 and the final suppression of the trade in 1870.[1] Many captives died on their way from the African interior to the coast, and approximately 20 percent died at sea during the so-called middle passage to the Americas (Doc. 1). Thus, one can only speculate on the total number originally taken into captivity.

Of the nine million Africans who survived the journey, over one third were destined for Brazil. Approximately 1,552,00 were sent to the Spanish American colonies. By comparison the combined British, French, Dutch, and Danish sugar islands of the Caribbean imported about 3,800,000 Africans, and British North America an estimated 399,000. The following table gives

[1]Philip D. Curtin, *The Atlantic Slave Trade: A Consensus* (Madison: University of Wisconsin Press, 1969), 86.

a clear indication of the relative importance of slavery in Brazil and in the various regions of Spanish America.

Estimated Slave Imports into Latin America, 1502–1870

Spanish America	
Cuba	702,000
Puerto Rico	77,000
Mexico	200,000
Venezuela	121,000
Peru	95,000
La Plata, Bolivia	100,000
Chile	6,000
Santo Domingo	30,000
Colombia, Panama, Ecuador	200,000
Central America	21,000
	1,552,000
Brazil	3,646,800
Total	5,198,800

Source: Adapted from Curtin, *Atlantic Slave Trade*, 268, Table 77.

Note: More recent estimates range as high as twelve million. Robert Conrad puts the number of slaves arriving in Brazil alone at five million. See Robert Conrad, *World of Sorrow: The African Slave Trade to Brazil* (Baton Rouge: Louisiana State University Press, 1986), 34.

African slaves worked in all sectors of the Brazilian economy: on the sugar estates of the northeast; in the gold and diamond mines of the interior; on the coffee plantations of the south; and as sailors (Doc. 3), prostitutes, carpenters, masons, cowboys, vendors, wet nurses, and personal servants in virtually every region of the country. By far the greatest proportion, however, worked on the rural plantations; as late as 1887, 85 percent of all Brazilian slaves were agricultural workers. As in other similar societies, slavery in Brazil was a status, not an occupation. It encompassed the cities and the countryside and included both skilled and unskilled labor.

Despite the enormous numbers imported during the 350 years of the slave trade, only about 1.5 million slaves remained in Brazil when slavery was abolished in 1888. As with virtually every other slave society, except the United States, it proved impossible to maintain the size of the labor force through natural increase. Brazilian slave owners accepted the high death rates and low birth rates common to slave populations. Most owners firmly believed that it was cheaper to work their slaves to death within six or seven years and then replace them than to carry the financial burden of nonproductive children. Not only cruelty and overwork destroyed the slaves, but also malnutrition, lack of medical care, poor housing, primitive sanitation, and insufficient numbers of female slaves of childbearing age were all important factors.

The notion of Brazilian slavery as milder and more humane than slavery in the West Indies and the United States grew out of nineteenth-century proslavery propaganda.[2] In the face of increasing calls for abolition, apologists for the system painted Brazil as a veritable haven for blacks, far better than anything they could have hoped for in their African homelands. Their rhetoric influenced students of slavery well into the twentieth century. As late as the 1940s scholars such as the Brazilian sociologist Gilberto Freyre and the North American historian Frank Tannenbaum held to this belief.[3] They based their argument on the existence of legislation intended to protect the lives, families, and property of the slaves and to allow for ease of manumission. Moreover, they argued, the mildness of the system meant that Brazil experienced fewer problems with race relations in the twentieth century than did the United States. Modern historians clearly refute these ideas, and even a cursory glance at contemporary documents reveals the falseness of the earlier picture.

Brazilian slave owners controlled their slaves through the use, or threat, of ferocious discipline. Authorities rarely questioned the right of a master to sell, punish, maim, or even kill his slaves. Even more rarely did they punish even the excessively cruel. Brazilian slaves could purchase their freedom under certain circumstances, but the master and his social peers set the price demanded for freedom.

Recently, historians have become more sensitive to the slaves' reactions to their condition and to the part they played in bringing about their own emancipation. Slaves never resigned themselves to the brutality and injustice of their situation. They rebelled and resisted individually and collectively at every opportunity: attacking overseers, burning crops, destroying tools, working as slowly and poorly as possible, or running away. The fear of slaves organizing in open rebellion left their owners in constant dread of a widespread revolt.[4] Consequently, any act of rebellion brought fearsome

[2]Robert Conrad, ed. and trans., *Children of God's Fire: A Documentary History of Black Slavery in Brazil* (Princeton: Princeton University Press, 1983), xx.

[3]Gilberto Freyre, *The Masters and the Slaves* (New York: Alfred A. Knopf, 1946); Frank Tannenbaum, *Slave and Citizen: The Negro in the Americas* (New York: Vintage Books, 1946).

[4]Owners particularly feared a repetition of the successful slave rebellion which occurred in Haiti between 1791 and 1804.

retribution, ranging from flogging to castration or breaking on the wheel.[5] To those suffering under the worst punishments, death must have seemed a merciful relief from the tortures which masters devised to discourage revolution.

Thousands of slaves escaped into the backcountry to set up runaway communities known as *quilombos*. Most were stable settlements based on agriculture and organized along the lines of African villages. Separate political and military leaders ruled the carefully hidden settlements and demanded complete obedience from the inhabitants. Hidden ditches lined with sharpened stakes surrounded many *quilombos*, and a system of armed lookouts gave advance warning of approaching slave hunters. Occasionally the people negotiated treaties with the white authorities. The runaways promised to return future escapees in exchange for their own freedom and the right to continue as an independent entity, but the whites rarely honored the resulting treaties.

Runaway communities could be found throughout the Americas from the earliest days of slavery. Palmares, the most famous and certainly the most enduring, was established in the early 1600s in northeastern Brazil and survived repeated attacks from Portuguese forces before being destroyed in 1694 (Doc. 4). Sizable runaway communities existed in seventeenth-century Mexico and Colombia, and others were reported as late as the nineteenth century in Brazil.[6]

Until the late 1690s the majority of the country's slaves worked on the sugar estates of Bahia and Pernambuco. With the discovery of gold in Minas Gerais in the 1690s and of diamonds in Mato Grosso in the 1720s, planters in the declining sugar regions of the northeast diverted thousands of able-bodied slaves to the mines of the interior provinces. By the 1820s the growing international demand for coffee created a new export economy in southern Brazil. Planters established extensive estates in Rio de Janeiro, Minas Gerais, and São Paulo. Like their counterparts in the northeast, the coffee growers demanded a servile labor force for their new enterprise (Doc. 2). A booming interprovincial trade sent thousands of the youngest

[5]Slaves broken on the wheel were tied to a wooden frame while the executioner broke their bones beginning with the smallest in the fingers and toes, and progressing to the arms, legs, and ribs before delivering final, massive blows to the genitals and head.

[6]Gerald Cardoso, *Negro Slavery in the Sugar Plantations of Veracruz and Pernambuco, 1550–1680* (Washington: University Press of America, 1983), 54; Anthony McFarlane, "Cimarrones and Palenques: Runaways and Resistance in Colonial Colombia," in *Out of the House of Bondage: Resistance and Marronage in Africa and the New World*, Gad Heuman, ed. (London: Frank Cass and Company, 1986), 134–35.

and healthiest slaves from the stagnant sugar plantations and worn-out mines to the expanding coffee estates of the south.

Brazil soon outstripped Cuba and Puerto Rico as the world's leading coffee exporter. Increased production meant a growing demand for labor which could not be satisfied simply through the internal transfer of slaves. Consequently, coffee planters became even more reluctant to end, or even reduce, their participation in the Atlantic slave trade.

After Britain abolished its slave trade in 1807 it had immediately begun coercing its sugar-producing rivals to follow suit. Its efforts met with varying degrees of success. By 1815 every American nation except Cuba, Puerto Rico, and Brazil had abolished its trade. Spain ended the trade to Cuba and Puerto Rico in 1815, but Brazil remained free to continue importing Africans quite legally. In 1826, under intense pressure from Britain, Brazil finally agreed to abolish its trade. Its congress passed legislation which freed any African brought into the country after November 7, 1831. Nevertheless, the demand for slave labor proved so great, and the trade so lucrative, that an estimated fifty thousand Africans per year were smuggled into Brazil between 1831 and 1852 (Doc. 5). Nor was it the only country to ignore the ban. As their sugar economy expanded, Cuban planters smuggled five hundred thousand Africans into the island between 1827 and 1865. By 1869 only Cuba, Puerto Rico, and Brazil still considered slavery vital to their economic survival. Most of the former Spanish colonies had emancipated their slaves during the 1850s. Spain abolished the system in Cuba and Puerto Rico in 1886, due more to conditions within the islands than to diplomatic pressure. Only the Brazilian plantocracy refused to relinquish its hold.

Until the 1870s the majority of free Brazilians saw no logical reason for ending such a well-entrenched labor system. People of all classes owned at least a few slaves, and life without them seemed virtually impossible. In urban areas, slaves did everything from lighting streetlamps, clearing the garbage, and nursing the indigent sick to tailoring clothes, selling food, and working as servants in private homes. Who would do all this if slavery ended? Most important, who would work on the coffee and sugar estates that kept the rich and influential in their comfortable situation?

Most Brazilian statesmen had close family ties with the powerful slave-owning classes. Middle-class professionals and merchants depended on the patronage of the great slave owners for their livelihood. Given the intertwining of family and business ties, who would seriously foster abolitionist ideas? Until Brazil became the last outpost of slavery in the western world, few people saw any real need to change their long-accepted way of life.

With the end of slavery in the United States, however, Brazilians began to question the moral and economic implications of forced labor. The

Rio Branco Law of 1871 marked the first move toward gradual abolition. The law automatically freed all children born to slave women after September 28, 1871. Such children, called *ingenuos*, were to remain in the slave yards and work for their mothers' masters until they reached the age of twenty-one.

By the early 1880s it was clear that the 1871 law had merely created a subculture of semifree people and that de facto slavery could continue well into the twentieth century. Abolitionists renewed their efforts (Doc. 6), especially in the cities where individual owners had fewer slaves. New antislavery societies were formed and new legislation introduced, but each additional move met with increased resistance from the more reactionary owners. In 1885 the Cotegipe ministry freed all slaves over the age of sixty but, since the law did not require owners to reveal the ages of their slaves, it did nothing to identify the thousands of Africans smuggled into Brazil after 1831. In retaliation, influential slave owners forced the ministry to approve a more stringent Fugitive Slave Law. The new legislation imposed stiffer penalties for harboring runaways and authorized the use of the military in recapturing escapees.

The Fugitive Slave Law produced an immediate backlash. Both dedicated abolitionists and ordinary citizens resented the high-handed methods of slave catchers who invaded public buildings and private homes in search of runaways. Formerly moderate sympathizers became increasingly radical and joined the ranks of the abolitionists. Sympathetic judges began to rule against irate owners as ordinary citizens complained about slaves being returned to the plantations in chains.

By 1886 tens of thousands of slaves, encouraged by the abolitionists, began deserting the plantations and risking their lives to reach freedom. Antislavery groups established an underground railway with a system of safe houses to assure runaways of sanctuary once they reached areas such as Rio Grande do Sul or Santos where the local populations had already emancipated their slaves. In São Paulo many owners, hoping to gain some credit, freed those slaves who remained. In 1887 the Military Club petitioned the Crown to relieve the army of the distasteful, undignified, and dangerous duty of recapturing runaway slaves. The abolitionists and the slaves themselves won their final victory in 1888 when the Princess Regent approved the unconditional and uncompensated abolition of slavery. The passage of this Golden Law dismantled the shattered remnants of Brazilian slavery but left future generations to deal with its legacies.

Despite the claims of Tannenbaum, Freyre, and others, race relations in Brazil have proved as difficult as in other slave-based societies. The country never resorted to institutionalized segregation such as bedeviled the United States. It has had no need of formal laws. After nearly four hundred years of oppression the descendants of its slave population understand only too well the subtler forms of racism. For the most part, Brazilian blacks remain at the bottom of both the social and economic ladders.

The legacies of slavery, however, extend beyond the sphere of economics. The black population has made many positive contributions to the cultural life of the nation. Its influence is clearly apparent in music, where, for example, African rhythms dominate the samba; in the color and sensuality of Carnival in Bahia and Rio de Janeiro; in art, in literature, and in the widespread practice of Candomblé, which synthesizes elements of Christianity and older African religions. None of these legacies can justly be ignored when considering the problem of African slavery in Brazil.

---

1. This Accursed Trade ◆ Olaudah Equiano

The slaves' ordeal began with their capture and forced march to the "factories," or holding forts, which the European traders maintained along the African coast. The journey could take several weeks, and those too weak to keep up were released from their shackles and left to die. At the coast the traders sorted the slaves, branded them like cattle, and loaded them aboard the waiting ships for transportation to the mines, plantations, and cities of the Americas. Aboard the slave ship, men and women crowded together below decks with scarcely enough room to lie down and rarely sufficient space to sit or stand. In good weather the ship's captain allowed the chained slaves on deck for air and exercise under the watchful eyes of an alert and anxious crew. In foul weather the slaves remained battened down in the hold to endure hunger, thirst, disease, and death.

Olaudah Equiano's account, written in the eighteenth century, is one of the few firsthand descriptions of the "middle passage." Captured as a child in Benin, in West Africa, Equiano survived captivity in his homeland, the United States, and the West Indies before gaining his freedom. His account vividly illustrates the terror and horrors which the newly enslaved Africans endured on their journey to the New World.

When I was tossed on board I was immediately handled, and tossed up, to see if I were sound, by some of the crew; and I was now persuaded that I had got into a world of bad spirits, and that they were going to kill me. . . . When I looked round the ship too, and saw a large furnace or copper boiling, and a multitude of black people of every description chained together, every one of their countenances expressing dejection and sorrow, I

From Olaudah Equiano, *The Interesting Narrative of the Life of Olaudah Equiano, or Gustavus Vassa, the African* (London: n.p., 1789), 1:42–57, passim.

no longer doubted my fate; and quite overpowered with horror and anguish, I fell motionless to the deck and fainted. When I recovered a little, I found some black people about me, who I believed were some of those who brought me on board, and had been receiving their pay; they talked to me in order to cheer me, but all in vain. I asked them if we were not to be eaten by those white men with horrible looks, red faces, and long hair. They told me I was not; and one of the crew brought me a small portion of spiritous liquid in a wine glass; but being afraid of him, I would not take it out of his hand. One of the blacks therefore took it from him, and gave it to me, and I took a little down my palate, which, instead of reviving me, as they thought it would, threw me into the greatest consternation at the strange feeling it produced, having never tasted any such liquor before. Soon after this, the blacks who brought me on board went off, and left me abandoned to despair. I now saw myself deprived of all chance of returning to my native country, or even the least glimpse of hope of gaining the shore, which I now considered as friendly; and I even wished for my former slavery, in preference to my present situation, which was filled with horrors of every kind, still heightened by my ignorance of what I was to undergo.

I was not long suffered to indulge my grief; I was soon put down under the decks, and there I received such a salutation in my nostrils as I had never experienced in my life; so that, with the loathsomeness of the stench, and the crowding together, I became so sick and low that I was not able to eat, nor had I the least desire to taste anything. I now wished for the last friend, death, to relieve me; but soon, to my grief, two of the white men offered me eatables; and, on my refusing to eat, one of them held me fast by the hands, and laid me across, I think, the windlass, and tied my feet while the other flogged me severely. I had never experienced anything of this kind before; and, although not being used to the water, I naturally feared that element the first time I saw it; yet, nevertheless, could I have got over the netting, I would have jumped over the side; but I could not; and, besides, the crew used to watch us very closely who were not chained down to the decks, lest we should leap into the water: and I have seen some of these poor African prisoners most severely cut for attempting to do so, and hourly whipped for not eating. This indeed was often the case with myself. In a little time after, amongst the poor chained men, I found some of my own nation, which in a small degree gave ease to my mind. I inquired of them, what was to be done with us? They gave me to understand we were to be carried to these white people's country to work for them. I then was a little revived, and thought, if it were no worse than working, my situation was not so desperate; but still I feared I should be put to death, the white people looked and acted, as I thought, in so savage a manner; for I had never seen amongst any people such instances of brutal cruelty; and this not only shown towards us blacks, but also to some of the whites themselves. One white man in particular I saw, when we were permitted on deck, flogged so unmercifully with a large rope near the foremast, that he died in consequence of it; and they tossed him over the side as they would have done a brute. This made me fear these people the more. . . .

The stench of the hold while we were on the coast was so intolerably loathsome, that it was dangerous to remain there for any time, and some of us had been permitted to stay on deck for the fresh air; but now that the whole ship's cargo were confined together, it became absolutely pestilential. The closeness of the place, and the heat of the climate, added to the number in the ship, which was so crowded that each had scarcely room to turn himself, almost suffocated us. This produced copious perspirations, so that the air soon became unfit for respiration, from a variety of loathsome smells, and brought on a sickness amongst the slaves, of which many died, thus falling victims to the improvident avarice, as I may call it, of their purchasers. This wretched situation was again aggravated by the galling of the chains, which now became insupportable, and by the filth of the necessary tubs, into which the children often fell and were almost suffocated. The shrieks of the women, and the groans of the dying, rendered the whole scene of horror almost inconceivable. Happily perhaps for myself I was soon reduced so low here that it was thought necessary to keep me almost always on deck; and from my extreme youth I was not put in fetters. In this situation I expected every hour to share the fate of my companions, some of whom were almost daily brought upon deck at the point of death, which I began to hope would soon put an end to my miseries. Often did I think many of the inhabitants of the deep much more happy than myself; I envied them the freedom they enjoyed, and as often wished I could change my condition for theirs. Every circumstance I met with served only to render my state more painful and heighten my apprehensions and my opinion of the cruelty of the whites. One day they had taken a number of fishes; and when they had killed and satisfied themselves with as many as they thought fit, to our astonishment who were on deck, rather than give any of them to us to eat, as we expected, they tossed the remaining fish into the sea again, although we begged and prayed for some as well as we could, but in vain; and some of my countrymen, being pressed with hunger, took an opportunity, when they thought no one saw them, of trying to get a little privately; but they were discovered, and the attempt procured them some very severe floggings.

One day, when we had a smooth sea, and moderate wind, two of my wearied countrymen, who were chained together (I was near them at the time), preferring death to such a life of misery, somehow made through the nettings, and jumped into the sea; immediately another quite dejected fellow, who, on account of his illness, was suffered to be out of irons, also followed their example; and I believe many more would very soon have done the same, if they had not been prevented by the ship's crew, who were instantly alarmed. Those of us that were the most active were in a moment put down under the deck; and there was such a noise and confusion amongst the people of the ship as I never heard before, to stop her and get out the boats and go after the slaves. However, two of the wretches were drowned, but they got the other, and afterwards flogged him unmercifully, for thus attempting to prefer death to slavery. In this manner we continued to undergo more hardships than I can now relate, hardships which are inseparable from this accursed trade.

2. A Day on a Coffee Estate ◆ Stanley Stein

Stanley Stein describes life on a Brazilian coffee estate during the second half of the nineteenth century. He depicts the hierarchy within the labor force and the ever-present fear of discipline represented by the slave driver's whip. The lives of the slaves were monotonous but not without a touch of humor, as can be seen in Stein's account of a typical day on a coffee estate in the valley of Vassouras.

The first signs of dawn brightened the sky as slaves separated to their work. A few went into the main house; most merely placed the long hoe handles on their shoulders and, old and young, men and women, moved off to the almost year-round job of weeding with drivers following to check stragglers. Mothers bore nursing youngsters in small woven baskets (*jacás*) on their backs or carried them astraddle one hip. Those from four to seven trudged with their mothers, those from nine to fifteen close by. If coffee hills to be worked were far from the main buildings, food for the two meals furnished in the fields went along—either in a two-team ox-cart which the slaves called a *maxambomba*, or in iron kettles swinging on long sticks, or in wicker baskets or two-eared wooden pans (*gamelas*) on long boards carried on male slaves' shoulders. A few slaves carried their own supplementary articles of food in small cloth bags.

Scattered throughout the field were shelters of four posts and a grass roof. Here, at the foot of the hills where coffee trees marched up steep slopes, the field slaves split into smaller gangs. Old men and women formed

From Stanley J. Stein, *Vassouras: A Brazilian Coffee County, 1850–1900* (Cambridge, 1957), 162–54. © 1957 by Harvard University Press. All rights reserved. Reprinted by permission of Harvard University Press.

a gang working close to the rancho; women formed another; the men or young bucks (*rapaziada nova*), a third. Leaving the moleques [little boys] and little girls to play near the cook and assistants in the rancho, they began the day's work. As the sun grew stronger, men removed their shirts; hoes rose and fell slowly as slaves inched up the steep slopes. Under the gang-labor system of *corte beirada* used in weeding, the best hands were spread out on the flanks. . . . [The] four lead-row men were faster working pacesetters, serving as examples for slower workers sandwiched between them. When a coffee row (*carreira*) ended abruptly due to a fold in the slope, the slave now without a row shouted to his overseer: "Throw another row for the middle," or "We need another row"; a feitor [overseer] passed the information to the flanking lead-row man who moved into the next row, giving the slave who had first shouted a new row to hoe. Thus, lead-row men always boxed in the weeding gang.

Slave gangs often worked within singing distance of each other, and to give rhythm to their hoe strokes and pass comment on the circumscribed world in which they lived and worked—their own foibles, and those of their master, overseers, and slave drivers—the master-singer (*mestre cantor*) of one gang would break into the first "verse" of a song in riddle form, a *jongo*. His gang would chorus the second line of the verse, then weed rhythmically while the master-singer of the nearby gang tried to decipher (*desafrar*) the riddle presented. An ex-slave, still known for his skill at making jongos, informed that "Mestre tapped the ground with his hoe, others listened while he sang. Then they replied." He added that if the singing was not good, the day's work went badly. Jongos sung in African tongues were called *quimzumba*; those in Portuguese, more common as older Africans diminished in the labor force, *visaria*. Stopping here and there to "give a lick" (*lambada*) of the lash to slow slaves, two slave drivers usually supervised the gangs by crisscrossing the vertical coffee rows on the slope and shouting, "Come on, come on"; but if surveillance slackened, gang laborers seized the chance to slow down while men and women slaves lighted pipes or leaned on their hoes momentarily to wipe sweat away. To rationalize their desire to resist the slave drivers' whips and shouts, a story developed that an older, slower slave should never be passed in his coffee row. For the aged slave could throw his belt ahead into the younger man's row and the youngster would be bitten by a snake when he reached for the belt. The overseer or master himself, in white clothes and riding boots, might ride through the groves for a quick look. Alert slaves, feigning to peer at the hot sun, "spiced their words" to comment in a loud voice, "Look at that red-hot sun," or intermixed African words common to slave vocabulary with Portuguese as in "*Ngoma* is on the way" to warn their fellow slaves (*parceiros*), who quickly set to work industriously. When the driver noticed the approaching planter, he commanded the gang: "Give praise"; to which slaves stood erect, eager for a brief respite, removed their hats or touched hands to forehead, and responded, "Vas Christo." Closing the ritual greeting, the senhor too removed his hat, spoke his "May He always be praised," and rode on. Immediately the industrious pace slackened.

To shouts of "lunch, lunch" or more horn blasts coming from the rancho around ten A.M., slave parceiros and drivers descended. At the shaded rancho they filed past the cook and his assistants, extending bowls, or *cuias*, of gourds split in two. On more prosperous fazendas, slaves might have tin plates. Into these, food was piled; drivers and a respected or favored slave would eat to one side while the rest sat or sprawled on the ground. Mothers used the rest to nurse their babies. A half hour later the turma [field gang] was ordered back to the sun-baked hillsides. At one P.M. came a short break for coffee, to which slaves often added the second half of the corn-meal cake served at lunch. On cold or wet days, small cups of *cachaça* distilled from the plantation's sugarcane replaced coffee. Some ex-slaves reported that fazendeiros often ordered drivers to deliver *cachaça* to the slaves in a cup while they worked, to eliminate the break. *Janta*, or supper, came at four P.M., and work was resumed until nightfall when, to the drivers' shouts of "Let's quit" (*vamos largar o serviço*), the slave gangs tramped back to the sede [plantation house]. Zaluar, the romantic Portuguese who visited Vassouras, wrote of the return from the fields: "The solemn evening hour. From afar, the fazenda's bell tolls Ave-Maria. (From hilltops fall the gray shadows of night while a few stars begin to flicker in the sky). . . . From the hill descend the taciturn driver and in front, the slaves, as they return home." Once more the slaves lined up for roll call on the terreiro [drying floor] where the field hands encountered their slave companions who worked at the sede.

---

3. Life Aboard Ship ◆ Mahommah G. Baquaqua

Mahommah G. Baquaqua served as a slave sailor aboard one of the merchant ships that traded along the coast of Brazil during the 1840s. Although his daily routine was possibly more varied than that of his planta-tion brethren, he still lived precariously. This firsthand account of his insecure life aboard ship shows the slave's complete lack of rights and the

From Mahommah G. Baquaqua, *Biography of Mahommah G. Baquaqua, A Native of Zoogao in the Interior of Africa*, Samuel Moore, ed. (Detroit: George F. Pomeroy and Company, 1854), 46–50.

degree to which his safety, and even his life, depended solely upon the whim of his master.

I was at length sold to a captain of a vessel who was what may be termed "a hard case." He invited me to go and see his Senhora. I made my best bow to her, and was soon installed into my new office, that of scouring the brass work about the ship, cleaning the knives and forks, and doing other little matters necessary to be done about the cabin. I did not at first like my situation; but as I got acquainted with the crew and the rest of the slaves, I got along pretty well. In a short time I was promoted to the office of under-steward. The steward provided for the table, and I carried the provisions to the cook and waited at table; being pretty smart, they gave me plenty to do. A short time after, the captain and steward disagreed, and he gave up his stewardship, when the keys of his office were entrusted to me. I did all in my power to please my master, the captain, and he in return placed confidence in me. The captain's lady was anything but a good woman; she had a most wretched temper. The captain had carried her off from St. Catherine's, just as she was on the point of getting married, and I believe was never married to her. She often got me into disgrace with my master, and then a whipping was sure to follow. She would at one time do all she could to get me a flogging, and at other times she would interfere to prevent it, just as she was in the humor. She was a strange compound of humanity and brutality. She always went to sea with the captain.

During this voyage I endured more corporal punishment than ever I did in my life. The mate, a perfect brute of a fellow, ordered me one day to wash down the vessel, and after I had finished, he pointed to a place where he said there was a spot, and with an oath ordered me to scrub it over again, and I did so, but not being in the best of humor he required it to be done a third time, and so on again.

When finding it was only out of caprice and there being no spot to clean, I in the end refused to scrub any more, when he took a broomstick to me, and having a scrubbing brush in my hand I lifted it to him. The master saw all that was going on, and was very angry at me for attempting to strike the mate. He ordered one of the hands to cut a piece of rope for him: he told me I was to be whipped, and I answered "very well," but kept on with my work with an eye continually turned towards him, watching his movements. When I set the breakfast ready, he came behind me before I could get out of his way, and struck me with the rope over my shoulders, and, being rather long, the end of it swung down and struck my stomach very violently, which caused me some pain and sickness; the force with which the blow was struck completely knocked me down, and afterwards he beat me whilst on the deck in a most brutal manner. My mistress interfered at this time and saved me from further violence.

4. The Negro Republic of Palmares ◆ R. K. Kent

R. K. Kent has used official seventeenth-century Portuguese and Dutch documents to provide a fascinating description of Palmares, Brazil's quint-essential quilombos. *Established in the lucrative sugar region of Pernambuco in the early seventeenth century, Palmares endured for almost one hundred years before its final destruction in 1694. The settlement threatened more than the system of slavery. As a virtual state within a state, the highly organized community challenged Portugal's tenuous hold on its New World colony.*

Nothing, however, compares in the annals of Brazilian history with the "Negro Republic" of Palmares in Pernambuco. It spanned almost the entire seventeenth century. Between 1672 and 1694, it withstood, on average, one Portuguese expedition every fifteen months. In the last *entrada* against Palmares, a force of six thousand took part in forty-two days of siege. The Portuguese Crown sustained a cumulative loss of four hundred thousand cruzados, or roughly three times the total revenue lease of eight Brazilian captaincies in 1612.

"In the captaincy of Pernambuco," reported a high official in 1612, "some 30 leagues inland, there is a site between mountains called Palmares which harbors runaway slaves . . . whose attacks and raids force whites into armed pursuits which amount to little, for they return to raid again. . . . This makes it impossible to . . . end the transgressions which gave Palmares its reputation. . . .

"[Palmares] is equally half a mile long, its street six feet wide and running along a large swamp, tall trees alongside. There are 200 *casas*, amid them a church, four smithies, and a huge [council house]; all kinds of artifacts are to be seen. . . . [The] king rules . . . with iron justice, without permitting any [sorcerers] among the inhabitants; when some Negroes attempt to flee, he sends [others] after them and, once retaken, their death is swift and of a kind to instill fear, especially among the Angolan Negroes; the king also has another *casa*, some two miles away, with its own rice fields. . . . We asked the Negroes how many of them live (here) and were told some 500, and from what we saw around us as well we presumed that there were 1,500 inhabitants all told. . . . This is the Palmares *grandes* of

From R. K. Kent, "Palmares: An African State in Brazil," in *Journal of African History* 6 (1965): 161–75. Reprinted by permission of Cambridge University Press.

which so much is heard in Brazil, with its well-kept lands, all kinds of cereals, beautifully irrigated with streamlets."

All the inhabitants of Palmares considered themselves "subjects of a king called *Ganga-Zumba*, which means Great Lord, and he is recognized as such both by those born in Palmares and by those who join them from outside; he has a palatial residence, *casas* for members of his family, and is assisted by guards and officials who have, by custom, *casas* which approach those of royalty. He is treated with all the respect due a Monarch and all the honors due a Lord. Those who are in his presence kneel on the ground and strike palm leaves with their hands as a sign of appreciation of His excellence. They address him as Majesty and obey him with reverence. He lives in the royal enclave, called *Macaco*, a name which was begotten from the death of an animal on the site. This is the capital of Palmares; it is fortified with parapets full of caltrops, a big danger even when detected. The enclave itself consists of some 1,500 *casas*. There are keepers of law [and] their office is duplicated elsewhere. And although these barbarians have all but forgotten their subjugation, they have not completely lost allegiance to the Church. There is a [chapel], to which they flock whenever time allows, and [holy images] to which they direct their worship. . . . One of the most crafty, whom they venerate as [priest], baptizes and marries them. Baptisms are, however, not identical with the form determined by the Church and marriage is singularly close to nature. The king has three [women], a *mulata* and two *crioulas* [Brazilian-born black women]. The first has given him many sons, the other two none. All the foregoing applies to the [principal settlement] of Palmares and it is the king who rules it directly; other [settlements] are in the charge of potentates and major chiefs who govern in his name. The second [settlement] in importance is called *Subupuira* and is ruled by the king's brother. . . . It has 800 *casas* and occupies a site one square league in size, right along the river *Cachingi*. It is here that Negroes are trained to fight our assaults (and weapons are forged there). . . ."

The Paulistas had to fight for two years to reduce Palmares to a single fortified site. After twenty days of siege by the Paulistas, the state of Pernambuco had to provide an additional three thousand men to keep it going for another twenty-two days. The breakthrough occurred during the night of February 5-6, 1694. Some two hundred *palmaristas* fell or hurled themselves—the point has been long debated—"from a rock so high that they were broken to pieces." Hand-to-hand combat took another two hundred *palmarista* lives, and over five hundred "of both sexes and all ages" were captured and sold outside Pernambuco. Zumbi [the ruler], taken alive and wounded, was decapitated on November 20, 1695. The head was exhibited in public "to kill the legend of his immortality."

5. The Contraband Trade ◆ Thomas Nelson

During the early 1840s, Thomas Nelson served as a surgeon aboard the British frigate HMS Crescent. *His specific duties included the inspection and treatment of contraband cargoes of slaves which the Royal Navy intercepted en route to the Brazilian slave markets. Under the Aberdeen Act of 1845, the British government claimed the right to search and arrest suspected slave ships even though they flew the Brazilian flag and, if necessary, to pursue them into Brazil's territorial waters without the per-mission of its government. To escape detection, slave ships frequently displayed the flag of the United States for, as North American officials in Rio pointed out: "It alone gives the privilege and immunity from visitation and search, when on the high seas, against all pursuers, but the commissioned naval police of our own country."*

Here, Nelson describes his encounter with the illegal cargoes of three different slavers, one of which appeared to have been built in the United States.* His account plainly demonstrates how, despite the concerted efforts of governments and humanitarians, conditions aboard slave ships had scarcely changed in over 350 years.

A few minutes after the vessel dropped her anchor, I went on board of her, and although somewhat prepared by the previous inspection of two full slavers to encounter a scene of disease and wretchedness, still my experience, aided by my imagination, fell short of the loathsome spectacle which met my eyes on stepping over the side. Huddled closely together on deck, and blocking up the gangways on either side, cowered, or rather squatted, three hundred and sixty-two negroes, with disease, want, and misery stamped upon them with such painful intensity as utterly beggars all powers of description. In one corner, apart from the rest, a group of wretched beings lay stretched, many in the last stage of exhaustion, and all covered with the pustules of smallpox. Several of these I noticed had crawled to the spot where the water had been served out, in the hope of procuring a mouthful more of the precious liquid; but unable to return to their proper places, lay prostrate around the empty tub. Here and there, amid the throng, were isolated cases of the same loathsome disease in its confluent or worst form, and cases of extreme emaciation and exhaustion, some in a state of perfect stupor, others looking piteously around, and pointing with their

From Thomas Nelson, *Remarks on the Slavery and Slave Trade of the Brazils* (London: J. Halchard and Son, 1846), 43–56.

*U.S. Department of State, Senate Exec. Doc. 47, 33d Cong., 1st sess., Message to the President no. 24, Legation of the United States, Rio de Janeiro, April 26, 1852, Robert C. Schenck to Daniel Webster, secretary of state.

fingers to their parched mouths whenever they caught an eye who they thought would relieve them. On every side, squalid and sunken visages were rendered still more hideous by the swollen eyelids and the puriform discharge of a virulent ophthalmia, with which the majority appeared to be afflicted; added to this were figures shriveled to absolute skin and bone, and doubled up in a posture which originally want of space had compelled them to adopt, and which debility and stiffness of the joints compelled them to retain.

On looking more leisurely around, after the first paroxysm of horror and disgust had subsided, I remarked on the poop another wretched group, composed entirely of females. Some were mothers with infants who were vainly endeavoring to suck a few drops of moisture from the lank, withered, and skinny breasts of their wretched mothers; others were of every intermediate age. The most of them destitute even of the decency of a rag, and all presenting as woeful a spectacle of misery as it is possible to conceive.

While employed in examining the negroes individually, and separating and classifying the sick, who constituted by far the majority, I obtained a closer insight into their actual condition. Many I found afflicted with a confluent smallpox, still more with purulent ophthalmia, and the majority of what remained, with dysentery, ulcers, emaciation, and exhaustion. In several, two or three of these were met. Not the least distressing sight on that pest-laden deck was the negroes whom the ophthalmia had struck blind, and who cowered in seeming apathy to all that was going on around. This was indeed the ultimatum of wretchedness, the last drops of the cup of bitterness. Deprived of liberty, and torn from their native country, there was nothing more of human misery but to make them the victims of a physical darkness as deep as they had already been made of a moral one.

The stench on board was nearly overwhelming. The odor of the negroes themselves, rendered still stronger by their filthy and crowded condition, the sickening smell of the suppurative stage of smallpox, and the far more disgusting effluvium of dysenteric discharge, combined with bilge water, putrid jerked beef, and numerous other matters to form a stench, it required no little exertion of fortitude to withstand. To all this, hunger and thirst lent their aid to finish the scene; and so poignant were they, that the struggles to obtain the means of satisfying them were occasionally so great as to require the interference of the prize crew. The moment it could be done, water in abundance and a meal was provided them; and none but an eyewitness could form an idea of the eagerness with which the former luxury was coveted and enjoyed. For many days, it seems, the water had not only been reduced in quantity, but so filled with impurities, and so putrid, that nothing but the most stringent necessity could have induced the use of it. . . .

Early yesterday morning (11th of September, 1843) the decks of the *Crescent* were again thronged by a miserable crowd of liberated Africans. The vessel in which they had been conveyed from the "coast" was captured a few days ago by one of the boats belonging to H.M.S. *Frolic*, a little to the northward of Rio.

Previously to the removal of the negroes, Dr. Gunn (the surgeon of the *Crescent*) and myself went on board the slaver, and stepping over the side, were astonished at the smallness of the vessel, and the number of wretched negroes who had been thrust on board of her. Below, the hold was crowded to excess; and above, the deck was so closely packed with the poor creatures, that we had to walk along the top of the low bulwarks in order to get aft. Of the appearance of the negroes, no pen can give an adequate idea. In numbers, the different protuberances and anatomical peculiarities of the bones can be distinctly traced by the eye, and appear, on every motion, ready to break through the skin, which is, in fact, all that covers them. Nor has this been confined to appearance; in many, at the bend of the elbows and knee-joints, over the hip-joints and lower part of the spine, the integuments have given way, and caused the most distressing and ill-conditioned sores. A great number of the Africans, especially the younger, cannot stand upright even when assisted, and the moment they are left to themselves, they double up their knees under their chins, and draw their legs so closely to their bodies, that they scarcely retain the form of humanity. So weak and so cramped are the most of them that they had to be carried in the arms of the seamen, one by one, up the *Crescent*'s ladder. All those not affected with contagious diseases are now on board the *Crescent*, and the most of them look like animated skeletons. From one of the Portuguese crew, who is at present under treatment for smallpox, I learn that the name of the vessel is the *Vencedora*, and that she left Benguela on the coast of Africa with four hundred and sixty slaves on board. But of this number only three hundred and thirty-eight have been counted over the side, a circumstance which will appear the less surprising when the space in which they were stowed comes to be considered. . . .

Just as the negroes who remained of the *Vencedora* had entirely recovered their wonted health and vigor, and were fit to be sent to one of our colonies, H.M.S. *Dolphin*, on the 15th of November, 1843, brought into harbor a full slaver, which she had captured a day or two before, a little to the northward of Rio. The crew of the slaver had actually run her ashore, and had begun to throw the negroes overboard into the sea, in order that they might be induced to swim for the land, when the boats of the *Dolphin* came up and obliged them to stop and effect their own escape.

This vessel is the largest I have yet seen employed in this traffic, and is better fitted and found than the common run of slavers; she is American built, and several of her fittings bear the name of American tradesmen. But, as usual, the Africans benefit nothing from the greater size of the vessel. The additional room has not been devoted to give increased accommodation, but to carry a greater number from the coast. The hold, instead of being fitted with one slave deck, has two; so that, in fact, the negroes have been as badly off, if not worse, than they would have been in a smaller vessel.

On attempting to go down into the hold, and satisfy myself with an examination before the Africans were removed, I was forced, after one or two unsuccessful attempts, to give it up;—the effluvium was perfectly overwhelming, and the heat so great, that the moment I left the square of the hatchway, the sensation approached suffocation The decks furnished a melancholy spectacle of disease and wretchedness; but the most prominent and widely spread scourge is purulent ophthalmia. Numbers of the poor creatures are squatting down in corners or groping about the deck deprived of all sight. Their immensely swollen eyelids, contrasting with their haggard and wasted features, and the discharge which keeps constantly trickling down their cheeks, and which they have not even a rag to wipe away, gives them an appearance of ghastly, murky misery which it is impossible for me to describe.

Many eyes, I am afraid, are irretrievably lost, and several poor wretches must remain forever totally blind. Dysentery, too, that fellest of all diseases in the negro race, is at work amongst them, and will undoubtedly commit fearful ravages. Five hundred and seventy-two Africans were found on board. What the number was at starting there is no means of ascertaining. One of the crew, a slave, who acted on board in the capacity of a cook, and who preferred being captured by Englishmen to escaping with his master, told me that many had died and were thrown overboard during the passage. The exact number taken on board, however, he could not tell. In all probability, it was not under seven hundred; but of course this is only mere conjecture.

---

6. A Humane and Civilized Nation:
Abolition ◆ Joaquim Nabuco

Joaquim Nabuco, perhaps the best known and most active of all Brazilian abolitionists, introduced legislation for gradual abolition while serving as a member of the Chamber of Deputies between 1878 and 1881. When the

From Joaquim Nabuco, *Abolitionism: The Brazilian Antislavery Struggle*, trans. Robert Conrad (Urbana, 1977), 83–89, 92–96, 144–47. Reprinted by permission of the University of Illinois Press and Robert Conrad. © 1977 by the University of Illinois Press.

slavocracy rejected his proposals, Nabuco sought other means to achieve his aim and, in 1880, founded the Brazilian Antislavery Society. Three years later, fearful that the abolitionist movement might falter, Nabuco wrote his famous book, O Abolicionismo, *in which he urged immediate emancipation for the 1.5 million slaves and* ingenuos *still held in captivity.*

Nabuco obviously abhorred slavery and considered it an affront to humanity, yet it is interesting to note that he couched his plea as much in terms of Brazil's economic interests and international honor as in terms of the injustice of the system. Here he states his reasons for demanding immediate abolition and answers critics who claimed that, under the existing laws, slavery would die out naturally within twenty years.

We do not want to end slavery simply because it is illegitimate in the sight of the advancement of moral concepts of cooperation and solidarity; or simply because it is illegal in the presence of the laws of the era of the slave traffic; or simply because it is a violation of the public faith as expressed in treaties like the Convention of 1826, in laws like that of November 7, 1831, in solemn commitments such as the letter of Matim Francisco, the initiative of Count d'Eu in Paraguay, and the promises of statesmen responsible for the advancement of public affairs.

Obviously we desire to end slavery for these reasons, but for the following reasons as well:

1. Because slavery, as it destroys the nation economically, blocks its material progress, corrupts its character, demoralizes its basic components, saps its energy and determination, coarsens its politics, accustoms it to servility, impedes immigration, dishonors manual labor, retards the emergence of industries, causes business failures, diverts capital from its natural course, drives out machines, arouses hatred among classes, produces a misleading appearance of order, well-being, and prosperity, while it hides the chasms of moral anarchy, misery, and destitution which north to south are carved deeply into our entire future existence.

2. Because slavery is an enormous burden which retards Brazil in its growth in comparison with other South American countries that do not know it; because this system, if continued, must bring as a consequence the dismemberment and ruin of the nation; because an accounting of its losses and diminishing profits reduces to nothing its boastful claims and adds up to an enormous and continuing national injury; because only when slavery has been entirely abolished will the normal life of the nation begin, will there exist a market for labor, will individuals rise up to their true level, will wealth become legitimate, and will regard for others cease to be a mere act of compliance; because not until slavery is ended will the elements of order be founded upon freedom, and freedom cease to be a privilege of class.

3. Because only with total emancipation can members of a community, whose elements are now struggling against one another and among themselves, undertake the work of a common motherland, strong and respected. These contending elements are the slaves, who are outside the social body; the masters, who see themselves attacked as representatives of a condemned system; the enemies of that system, who are unable to reconcile themselves to it; the inactive mass of the population, who are victims of land monopolization and execration of labor; Brazilians in general, who are condemned by slavery to form, as they are now forming, a nation of impoverished men and women.

Each of these purposes, urgent in itself, would suffice to make us reflect upon the need to end, after so many years, a social system so contrary to the interests of the entire order of a modern people. Brought together, however, and intermingled, these purposes impose this suppression upon us as a vital reform which cannot be postponed without peril. Before studying the harmful influences exercised by slavery upon each of the parts of our national organism, let us see what slavery is in Brazil today at the moment of writing, when there seems little reason to expect any real or immediate improvement.

Since the law of September 28, 1871, was passed, the Brazilian government has been trying to make the world believe that slavery has ended in Brazil. Our propaganda has tried to spread to other countries the belief that the slaves were being freed in considerable numbers and that the children of the slaves were being born *entirely* free. Slave mortality is an item which never appears in those fraudulent statistics, behind which is the philosophy that a lie spread abroad allows the government to do nothing at home and to abandon the slaves to their fate.

The record of manumission—highly creditable to Brazil—dominates the official picture and obscures slave mortality, while crimes against slaves, the number of Africans still in bondage, the hunting down of fugitive blacks, the fluctuating price of human flesh, the rearing of *ingenuos* in slavery, the utter sameness of our rural prisons, and everything unbecoming, humiliating, and bad for the government are all carefully suppressed. . . .

The Brazilian people, however, understand the entire matter. They know that after passage of the law of September 28 the life of the slaves did not change, except for those few who managed to redeem themselves by begging for their freedom. It is essential that we outline the condition of the slave today as it appears before the law, before society, before justice, before the master, and before himself, so that it will not someday be said that in 1883, when this book was being written, abolitionists no longer faced the traditional slave system but another kind of slavery, modified for the bondsman by humane, protective, and comparatively just laws. I will sketch this picture of our slavery with strokes perhaps too rapid for a topic so vast.

Whoever arrives in Brazil and opens one of our daily newspapers finds there a photographic image of modern slavery more accurate than any painting. If Brazil were destroyed by a catastrophe, one issue of any of our great newspapers would adequately preserve forever the forms and qualities of slavery as it exists in our time. The historian would need no other documents to recreate its entire structure and pursue all its effects.

In any issue of any major Brazilian paper—with the exception, I understand, of those of Bahia, where the press of the capital ceased the publication of slave advertisements—one would find, in effect, the following kinds of information which describe completely the present condition of the slaves: advertisements for purchase, sale, and rental of slaves; . . . official announcements of slave sales, . . . advertisements for runaway slaves accompanied in many papers by the well-known vignette of a barefoot black with a bundle on his shoulder, in which the slaves are often distinguished by the scars of punishment they have suffered and for whom a reward is offered . . . to anyone who can catch him and bring him to his master—an encouragement to the bush-captain's profession; rather frequent notices of manumissions; stories of crimes committed by slaves against their masters, but particularly against the agents of their masters, and of crimes committed by the latter against the slaves, barbarous and fatal punishments which nevertheless comprise only a very small part of the lordly misuse of power which occurs, since this kind of abuse rarely comes to the attention of authorities or the press, owing to the lack of witnesses and informers willing to testify to this kind of crime.

One finds, finally, repeated declarations that slavery among us is a very mild and pleasant condition for the slave, better for him, in fact, than for the master, according to these descriptions a situation so fortunate that one begins to suspect that, if slaves were asked, they would be found to prefer slavery to freedom; which merely proves that newspapers and articles are not written by slaves or by persons who for one moment have imagined themselves in their condition. . . .

The legal position of the slave can be summed up in these words: the Constitution does not apply to him. In order to contain some of its more enlightened principles, our Constitution could not sanction slavery in any way. "No citizen can be forced to do or not to do anything except in virtue of the law, . . . The home of every citizen is an inviolable asylum. . . . The law will be applied equally to every person. . . . All privileges are abolished. . . . From this time forward whipping, torture, the use of branding irons, and all other cruel punishments are abolished. . . . No penalty can be inherited, nor will the infamy of the criminal be passed on to his kinsmen regardless of its degree. . . . *The right to property is entirely guaranteed.*"

For slavery to have been provided for in this code of freedoms, the following restrictions would have had to be included as well: "Aside from the citizen, to whom these rights are guaranteed, and the foreigner, to whom they will be extended, there exist in this country slaves, a class possessing no rights whatsoever. . . ."

Thus we have a *free* nation, daughter of the Revolution and the Rights of Man, compelled to employ its judges, its police, and if need be even its army and navy to force men, women, and children to work night and day without compensation. . . .

To recapitulate, I will sketch in broad strokes what slavery is *legally* in Brazil in 1883:

1. The present bondsmen, born before September 28, 1871, and today at least eleven and a half years old, are slaves until they die, *exactly* like those of earlier generations. The number of these, as will be seen, is more than a million.

2. Whoever is subject to slavery is compelled to obey without question every order received, to do whatever he is told, without the right to demand a thing: neither pay nor clothing, improved food nor rest, medicine nor change of duties.

3. The man so enslaved has no duties—to God, to his mother and father, to his wife or children, or even to himself—which the master *must* respect and allow him to perform.

4. The law does not fix maximum hours of labor, a minimum wage, rules of hygiene, food, medical treatment, conditions of morality, protection of women. In a word, it interferes as much with the organization of the plantation as it does with the supervision of draft animals.

5. There is no law whatever which regulates the obligations and prerogatives of the master; whatever the number of slaves he may possess, he exercises an authority over them which is limited only by his own judgment.

6. The master can inflict moderate punishment upon slaves, says the *Criminal Code*, which compares his authority to the power of a father; but in fact he punishes at will, because justice does not penetrate the feudal domain. A slave's complaint against his master would be fatal, as it has been in practice, and in fact the master is all-powerful. The attitudes today are what they were in 1852. It is as dangerous now, and it is just as useless, for a slave to complain to the authorities as it was then. To accuse his master, the slave requires the same will power and determination that he needs to run away or to commit suicide, particularly if he hopes for some security in his servitude.

7. The slave lives in total uncertainty regarding his future; if he thinks he is about to be sold, mortgaged, or pawned, he has no right to question his master.

8. Any person released from the House of Correction or even confined to it, however perverse he may be, whether he be a Brazilian or foreigner, can own or buy a family of respectable slaves and expose them to his whims.

9. Masters can employ female slaves as prostitutes, receiving the profits from this business with no danger of losing their property as a result, just as a father can be the owner of his son.

10. The state does not protect the slaves in any way whatsoever. It does not inspire them with confidence in public justice but instead surrenders them *without hope* to the implacable power which weighs heavily upon them, morally imprisons or constrains them, arrests their movement, and in short destroys them.

11. The slaves are governed by exceptional laws. The use of the lash against them is allowed, despite its prohibition by the Constitution. Their crimes are punished by a barbaric law, that of June 10, 1835, the sole penalty of which is execution.

12. The belief has been spread throughout the nation that slaves often commit crimes in order to become convicts, in this way escaping from slavery, since they prefer the chain gang to the plantation, as Roman slaves preferred to fight wild beasts, in the hope of achieving freedom if they survived. For this reason a jury of the interior has absolved criminal slaves to be restored later to their masters, and lynch law has been carried out in more than one case. Here we have slavery as it really is! Death by suicide is looked upon by the bondsman as the *cessation of the evils of slavery*, imprisonment with hard labor such an *improvement in his condition* that it can be an *incentive to a crime*! Meanwhile we, a humane and civilized nation, condemn more than a million persons, as so many others were condemned before them, to a condition alongside which imprisonment or the gallows seems better!

13. Not all the powers of the master, which, as we have seen, are practically without limit, are exercised directly by him, absent as he often is from his lands and out of contact with his slaves. Instead these powers are delegated to individuals without intellectual or moral education, who know how to command men only by means of violence and the whip. . . .

The worst side of slavery is not its great abuses and passions, nor its terrible retributions, nor even the death of the slave. It is, rather, the daily pressure which slavery imposes upon the slave: his constant fear for himself and his family; his dependence upon the goodwill of the master; the spying and treachery which surround him, forcing him to live forever shut up in a prison of Dionysus, whose walls repeat every word, each secret confided to another, and, even worse, each thought which he may unintentionally reveal in the expression of his face.

It is said that among us slavery is mild and the masters are good. The truth is, however, that all slavery is the same, and the goodness of the masters depends upon the resignation of the slaves. Whoever would try to compile statistics on crimes committed either by slaves or against them, whoever would inquire into slavery and hear complaints of those who suffer it would see that in Brazil, even today, slavery is as hard, barbarous, and cruel as it was in any other country of America. By its very nature slavery is all this, and when it stops being this it is not because the masters have improved. It is because the slaves have resigned themselves totally to the destruction of their personalities. . . .

"Why, then, are you not willing to wait for those twenty years?" is the question which is always put to us.

This entire book is a response to that question. Twenty more years of slavery will bring the collapse of the nation. Indeed, this period is a brief one in our national history, just as our national history is only a brief moment in the life of humanity, and the life of humanity merely an instant in the life of the earth, and so on indefinitely. But twenty years of slavery will mean the ruin of two more generations: that generation which has just recently reached maturity and that which will be educated by it. This will mean a delay of half a century in the development of a liberated national conscience.

Twenty more years of slavery will find Brazil celebrating the fourth centenary of the discovery of America in 1892 with her flag draped in black crepe! If slavery lasts so long, the whole younger generation will be condemned to live with slavery, to serve it during the greater part of their lives. They will be forced to maintain an army and a body of magistrates responsible for its enforcement and, perhaps even worse, to see their own children, destined to take their places in twenty years, brought up in the same school of servility. . . .

Moreover, twenty more years of slavery would mean a stain upon Brazil's name during that entire time. . . . It would mean dragging Brazil's reputation through the mire in Europe and America. It would make our nation the object of derision in ancient and traditional Asia and modern Australia, three centuries younger than Brazil. How can a nation thus lashed to the world's whipping post lend manly military virtues to its army and navy, perhaps to be called upon tomorrow to suppress some slave revolt? How can it inspire them with respect for the nation they serve? How will it be able to compete in equality, at the end of that era of enfeeblement, with the smaller nations developing at its side: the Argentine republic spontaneously attracting immigrants and workers at the rate of forty thousand per year, and Chile with its homogeneous free labor force, with its entire organism healthy and strong? To maintain slavery as a national institution for that period would be equivalent to giving it twenty more years to use its influence to reinforce the belief that Brazil needs slavery in order to exist—this when the North, thought of once as the section of the national territory which could not dispense with the slave, is living without him, when slavery flourishes only in São Paulo, which with its climate and prosperity is able to attract the European immigrant and to pay the wages of the workers, national or foreign, whom it employs. . . .

To give ten, fifteen, or twenty years to the planter to prepare him for free labor, to burden him, that is, with so much foresight so far in advance, to charge him with accomplishing such a complex change, is to fail to acknowledge the national tendency to do everything tomorrow which should be done today. This scorn for the future will be overcome, not by prolonging the days of slavery, but by destroying it, thereby creating new needs, the real molder of character.

Any other action will have to be seen for what it is: the sacrifice of 1.5 million people to the private interests of their owners, interests we have recognized as murderous, morally and physically, however unconscious of this fact the exploiters of slavery may be. In other words, so that a few thousand individuals will not be ruined, they demand not only a reliable and stable labor force—which they could have by simply paying wages—but also that their human property remain negotiable, that it possess value, that is, in the bank director's office and in the market place. For these reasons, 1.5 million persons must be sacrificed to the Minotaur of slavery, and we must feed it for twenty years longer with the blood of new generations. Even worse, ten million Brazilians—who perhaps during that time will become fourteen million—will continue to endure the real losses and declining profits which slavery causes, will be victims of the same corrosive spirit which impedes the country's development and the uplifting of the various classes and which keeps free backland populations in rags and, sadder still, indifferent to their own social and moral wretchedness. What concern or compassion can the world have for ten million people who confess that they will be left to starve without the forced and unpaid labor of a few hundred thousand field slaves—old men, women, and children among them—despite living in the wealthiest, most fertile, and most beautiful territory ever possessed by any nation? Does not this same underdevelopment of the instinct of self-preservation and this absence of the energy which survival demands demonstrate the compelling need to abolish slavery without the loss of another second?

Suggestions for Further Reading

Unlike their North American counterparts, students of Brazilian slavery can rely on very few firsthand accounts written by slaves themselves. Of the two used here, only Olaudah Equiano's remains in print. Collections of contemporary documents, therefore, prove extremely helpful for filling in the details of slave treatment, resistance, manumission, proslavery attitudes, and the abolition debate. One of the best collections is Robert Conrad, *Children of God's Fire: A Documentary History of Black Slavery in Brazil* (Princeton: Princeton University Press, 1983), which contains over one hundred contemporary documents dealing with various aspects of rural and urban slavery. Many of the documents appear in English for the first time.

Out of the House of Bondage: Resistance and Marronage in Africa and the New World, Gad Heuman, ed. (London: Frank Cass and Company, 1986) and the older *Maroon Societies*, Richard Price, ed. (Baltimore: Johns Hopkins University Press, 1979) offer excellent comparative studies of slave resistance in Brazil and Spanish America.

The legal and contraband slave trade is well covered in Robert Conrad, *World of Sorrow: The African Slave Trade to Brazil* (Baton Rouge: Louisiana State University Press, 1986), which also explores the participation of British and North American nationals and the fate of slaves confiscated by British naval vessels.

Since African slavery extended over three and one half centuries of Brazilian history, it is impossible to ignore the colonial era. Katia M. de Queiros Mattoso's recently translated *To Be a Slave in Brazil, 1558–1888*, Arthur Goldhammer, trans. (New Brunswick: Rutgers University Press, 1986) gives a general overview of the entire period. Stuart B. Schwartz, *Sugar Plantations in the Formation of Brazilian Society: Bahia, 1550–1835* (Cambridge: Cambridge University Press, 1985); and A. J. R. Russell-Wood, *The Black Man in Slavery and Freedom in Colonial Brazil* (New York: St. Martin's, 1982), treat the colonial experience of the African as slave and freedman.

Two of the best regional studies for the nineteenth century are Mary C. Karasch, *Slave Life in Rio de Janeiro, 1808–1850* (Princeton: Princeton University Press, 1987), which examines the enormous diversity of slave life and culture in Rio; and Stanley J. Stein, *Vassouras: A Brazilian Coffee County, 1850–1900* (Cambridge: Harvard University Press), which covers the socioeconomic life of a rural coffee region.

The best contemporary treatment of the abolition debate available in English remains Robert Conrad's translation of Joaquim Nabuco, *O Abolicionismo* [Abolitionism: The Brazilian antislavery struggle] (Urbana: University of Illinois Press, 1977). A modern treatment of the abolition process can be found in Robert Conrad, *The Destruction of Brazilian Slavery, 1850–1888* (Berkeley: University of California Press, 1972). One of the most recent comparative works is Herbert Klein, *African Slavery in Latin America and the Caribbean* (New York: Oxford University Press, 1986), which provides excellent material on the slave trade, slave society, and abolition throughout the Americas.

IV

Urban Populism in Twentieth-century Politics

Michael L. Conniff

The populist era—roughly from World War I until the 1960s—brought profound changes to Latin America. Populist leaders such as Brazil's Getúlio Vargas and Argentina's Juan Perón turned their countries into modern nation-states; their followers grasped citizenship rights and used them; their parties live on; and their statecraft has returned under new leadership, in the 1980s and 1990s. These and dozens of other populist leaders throughout Latin America forged a new style of politics that mobilized the masses and won election after election. They threatened the old elites and often stood up to the United States. Since the populists could rarely be beaten at the polls, the military eventually stepped in and removed most of them. In short, Latin America was a different place by the 1960s, due largely to the change wrought by the populists.

Toward a Definition

Populism was an expansive style of election campaigning with which politicians drew masses of new voters into their ranks and secured their loyalty by appealing to their sense of nationalism, cultural pride, and desire for a better life. Populism occurred primarily in the big cities, where tens of millions of people gradually gained the rights of citizenship and exercised them at the ballot box. The vast majority of these new voters came from the working classes, giving some of the populists a decidedly prolabor character, but populists also attracted the middle classes, who benefited from the social and educational programs that the leaders sponsored. Put simply, the populists got more voters to the polls and held their allegiance better than traditional leaders.

The populists possessed charisma, special personal qualities and talents that, in the eyes of their followers, empowered them to defend the interests of the masses and uphold the national pride. The masses no longer trusted the Church, the patriarchal families, the traditional parties, the established press, or the business elite to select their presidents. In the absence of these usual sources of legitimacy, charisma bestowed on the new leader the right to exercise power on behalf of the people. These charismatic qualities varied among the populists, who might be visionaries, intellectuals, bene-factors, gladiators, moralists, conciliators, men of the people, builders, reformers, statesmen, or saints. They towered above the ranks of ordinary politicians.

As the populists' successes and fame spread, their followers became even more devoted, convinced that they could bring salvation in troubled times. Belief in the leaders' special faculties allowed their followers to imagine that personal links joined them, transcending the limits of space and time. It may not be excessive to speak of a mass hypnotic state binding leader and followers. Such charisma, though hard to define, was a crucial element in populism.

The populists promised to reform society and to improve the lives of the masses. Such pledges rarely corresponded to ordinary ideological schemes, however, so populists cannot be easily pigeonholed as leftists or rightists. The most common label for their programs was simply *ismo* added to their names, as with Getulismo and Peronismo. Nationalism infused all of their pronouncements, and Panama's Arnulfo Arias even called his credo Panameñismo, the ultimate patriotism. Still, the populists did draw from existing sociopolitical models, like socialism, communism, democratic capitalism, fascism, and corporatism. No single doctrine prevailed among them, however, and some altered their approaches sharply over time. Their ideas, then, were eclectic and flexible. All avoided advocating genuine revolution, or the violent overthrow of the existing government and radically restructuring society. Instead, they insisted on coming to power through elections and on changing society by the rule of law.

The populists appealed to the common men and women, to the poor and working classes, and to the humble and downtrodden, not only for votes but also for legitimacy, that is, the right to rule. To do so, they appropriated elements of folklore to show their closeness to the masses, and they were in turn embraced by popular culture. Arias and Peru's Víctor Raúl Haya de la Torre expressed pride in their Indian heritage; Perón and Vargas evoked the ethos of the Pampas; Adhemar de Barros of Brazil often posed as a *caipira*, or country boy; and Jorge Eliécer Gaitán in Colombia and Brazil's Leonel Brizola always stressed the poverty of their youth and their identification with the poor. The most vivid examples of the folk acceptance of populists were their celebration in Carnival verses and minstrel songs in Brazil.

The populists arose in the 1910s and 1920s in response to new opportunities in the cities. First, the tens of thousands of migrants who streamed into the cities in search of jobs, schools, and a better life constituted a tremendous pool of potential voters available for recruitment. The urban poor were not totally controlled by landlords, bosses, factory owners, or bureaucrats and hence could be reached by ambitious politicians. The advent of streetcars, commuter trains, and buses made urban campaigning much more effective. Second, long-distance transportation service and communications media brought politicians into contact with voters throughout the national territories. The airplane and radio, in particular, revolutionized campaigning after World War I. All over the hemisphere, populists barnstormed in small planes and broadcast their hopes and promises over the radio waves. In many towns and villages it was the first time that people had ever seen or heard a national politician. The populists forged national followings drawn from the city tenements and small towns of the interior.

The newly invented techniques of public relations found application in populist campaigns of the 1940s and 1950s. Politicians created and used symbols in order to trigger desired responses from their followers. Positive terms such as "nation," "workers," "economic development," and "sovereignty," plus negative ones such as "oligarchy," "foreign exploitation," and "the wealthy," became powerful stimuli in speeches and radio spots. Leaders also developed slogans and visual images to buttress their voters' feelings of identification with them. They handed out millions of little mementos and handbills in rallies so their followers could take away some physical object. Particularly effective were the tiny brooms that Brazilian populist Jânio Quadros gave away as symbols of his commitment to sweep the rascals out of office.

To track the effectiveness of their campaigns, politicians used opinion polling, first in Brazil and then in Argentina, Chile, and elsewhere. Increasingly exact methods allowed them to chart their popularity in general or among specific target groups, such as women, youths, businessmen, high-school graduates, and factory workers. If necessary, they could rework their publicity to win over more voters. The populists were not the only ones who employed such techniques, of course, but they used them most productively. Even if they did not have formal polls, they were more attuned to the mood of the public than others. For example, the Brazilian Institute of Public Opinion, a pioneer in Latin America, wrote in 1950 that Vargas's slogan, "Ballots Don't Fill Stomachs," was extremely effective. "We are convinced that Vargas is very well informed, perhaps even with access to his own opinion polling service." He did not actually have such a service, but he was a genius at taking the pulse of the people.

To summarize this brief discussion we can make a checklist of characteristics of populists: they were reformers, possessed charismatic images, led broad-based coalitions with strong labor components, appealed to popular culture, and continually expanded their electoral followings.

The Populists

What kind of people lurked behind the populists' newsreel images and campaign hype? The question has several answers. One is simply to array them over time, from Uruguay's José Batlle y Ordóñez in the 1910s to Brizola in the 1990s. Batlle was the first major politician to woo laborers into his party coalition. As his biographer Milton Vanger writes:

> There was one Uruguayan social class, recognized by Batlle, by Uruguayan politicians, and by themselves, to which Batlle was appealing by the end of his administration. They were the workers. . . . Workers' class consciousness, shown by the General Strike [of 1911], had risen during Batlle's administration. . . . Batlle began the "Those who would be Socialists elsewhere should be Colorados in Uruguay" campaign, designed to bring in new voters, a campaign whose success would be determined in future elections.*

Although Vanger does not call Batlle a populist, several specialists regard him as the region's first.

Across the Andes a contemporary, Guillermo Billinghurst, attempted to form a similar movement recruiting Peruvian workers but was overthrown in 1914 for his efforts. He would be followed in the 1920s by the longest-lived populist in Peru, Haya de la Torre. In nearby Argentina the Radical Civic Union of Hipólito Yrigoyen successfully mobilized middle- and working-class voters recently enfranchised by the Sáenz Peña Law of 1912. Arturo Alessandri of Chile is often considered the first populist of his country.

Populism did not prosper in the decade of the 1930s, due to the economic depression and autocratic governments that swept the region, but glimpses of it were seen in Brazil, Peru, Chile, and Mexico. The 1940 elections of Arias in Panama and Fulgencio Batista in Cuba were populist triumphs. Nevertheless, social and economic forces at work in those years

---

*Milton Vanger, *The Model Country: José Batlle y Ordóñez of Uruguay, 1907–1915* (Hanover: University Press of New England, 1980), 350.

brought millions of potential voters within reach of ambitious politicians, and the hardships they suffered left them attentive to populist blandishments and promises after the war.

Populism flourished in the postwar decades, in an environment freer and more democratic than any before or since. Some of the great populists—Perón, Vargas, Haya de la Torre, Gaitán, with José María Velasco Ibarra in Ecuador, Rómulo Betancourt in Venezuela, and Víctor Paz Estenssoro in Bolivia—appeared on the political stage or returned to it with fresh approaches. Not all of them won office, for a variety of reasons, but they enlivened and expanded participatory politics. It was a time of experimentation in policy, massive growth of the voting rolls, improved methods of taking and counting ballots, flamboyant campaigns and leaders, and sheer excitement and drama on election day. This was unquestionably the heyday of populism in Latin America.

Oddly, Brazil experienced a spate of populists in the 1950s and 1960s, while Mexico had none. Six or seven vied for national leadership in Brazil, representing several regions and styles. Rio Grande do Sul predominated, sending Vargas, Brizola, and João Goulart to Rio. In São Paulo, Barros and Quadros battled for control of the richest and most populous state, a natural launching pad to the presidency. No wonder historians refer to this period as the Populist Republic. Mexico, on the other hand, fell under the sway of the so-called Revolutionary Family, a member of which was dutifully elected president every six years by the subservient government party. The frankly populist tendencies of the Lázaro Cárdenas administration disappeared, and a concerted effort to revive them by Luis Echeverría in the 1970s failed utterly. Apparently, autocracy and populism do not coexist easily.

Several Latin American presidents of the 1980s have been dubbed populists by the press, among them Argentina's Carlos Menem, Peru's Alán García, Brazil's Fernando Cóllor de Mello, and Guatemala's Marco Benicio Cerezo. Their records of accomplishments thus far do not measure up to those of the 1950s and 1960s, however, and only time will reveal the validity of the comparisons. Whether or not these cases constitute a trend toward a new era of populism, the resurgence of the style and strategy confirms the importance of the earlier legacy. Future biographical comparisons may help determine just how similar the new populism is to the old.

Profiles in Populism

New research and studies of campaign techniques allow us to profile the populists' lives in order to print a composite portrait. Although the data are not complete, they do suggest strong patterns.

The populists were born usually in small towns or the countryside, distant from the cities they would eventually dominate. Typically, they were closer to their mothers than to their fathers, who tended to be absent or unimportant. They were highly intelligent and often were sent off to the cities to continue their education. Most steered clear of military service and early became active in politics, while still in school or in local affairs. They seemed to have a drive for power, a burning need to get into the public spotlight. They might marry and start families, but in truth they were wed to politics.

Although not urbanites by birth, the populists picked up city ways quickly and excelled in the politics of the metropolis. Many used mayoral terms as springboards into gubernatorial or presidential palaces. They were not members of the elite family and social networks and hence were free to recruit votes in working- and middle-class neighborhoods. They behaved opportunistically, earning the dislike of established politicians. They harnessed the media newly becoming available, such as radio, mass circulation dailies, and television, and used them in modern-style campaigns. Their energy and enthusiasm for power—obsessive, often flamboyant, and mysterious—led the public to believe that they had special qualities and a dedication to helping the masses. Some organized parties of their own to conduct campaigns, but these were always under the direct control of the leaders and served only to exalt their popularity. Others operated independently, allying themselves with parties temporarily and then striking out on their own. In either case the populists were loners, not team or party men, and they never allowed seconds in command to emerge from the ranks.

The daring, innovative, and reformist strategies pursued by the populists tended to alienate established groups and wielders of power, and they were often overthrown before completing their terms of office. Usually this was done by the armed forces, acting on their own (populists rarely got along with the military) or on behalf of the elites. For example, Vargas was overthrown twice and was the target of two other coups; Arias was removed three times and prevented from taking office twice; and Velasco Ibarra was deposed all five times he served as president. Driven into exile, the populists became martyrs and milked the roles for the greatest possible sympathy. Vargas was known as the *solitário de Itu* when in self-imposed exile on the family ranch; Velasco Ibarra was called *el gran ausente*; and between 1956 and 1973, Perón remained the single most important player in Argentine politics from his posh exile in Madrid. The wear and tear of conflict and exile did not seem to bother them, and in fact the populists thrived on controversy.

Their drive for power never weakened, so the populists could not withdraw and retire from public life. They constantly ran for office—in power as well as out—and enjoyed the crush of the campaign agenda. Even in the 1980s those still living betrayed a thirst for the limelight and retained their followings as well. Populism, it seemed, was an all-embracing preoccupation with leadership, one that also created a natural resonance among the masses.

The populists constituted a special group of politicians and should be distinguished from other categories of leaders. For example, they were sometimes confused with the caudillos, as in John Martz's description of Velasco Ibarra (Doc. 12). The crucial differences between them were that populists ran for election and abided by the results, respecting the popular will, and they initiated genuine efforts for reform. Some authors regarded the populists as closely related to the fascists because of their preferences for corporative institutions. This misidentification ignored the expansive electoral character of populism and the leaders' usually poor relations with the Church and military. Occasionally, revolutionaries such as Augusto Sandino and Fidel Castro were likened to the populists because of their charisma and appeal to popular sentiments. Here the problems were lack of elections and the destructive strategy of renewal, unlike the populists' reformism. Finally, military reformers such as Juan Velasco Alvarado and Omar Torrijos were sometimes called populists, a label that did not fit because those leaders came to power in coups and used the armed forces to secure their administrations. Therefore, populists should be regarded as a unique group of politicians, distinct from caudillos, fascists, revolutionaries, and military reformers.

Intellectuals continue to debate populism, and its complexity rules out a consensus definition in the near future. The readings and excerpts below give glimpses of populists and their followers from various angles. They will help readers shape their opinions and will convey a sense of the drama, the excitement, and the high stakes at risk during the age of populism.

---

1. Juan and Evita Perón:
Family Portrait ◆ Maryza Navarro

No woman played a more prominent role in populism than Evita Perón, second wife and political ally of El líder, *Juan Perón. Professor Navarro*

From Maryza Navarro, "Evita's Charismatic Leadership," in *Latin American Populism in Comparative Perspective*, ed. Michael L. Conniff (Albuquerque: University of New Mexico Press, 1982), 47–66. Reprinted by permission of the author.

explores the relationship between the two, the messages and contexts of Evita's extraordinary speeches, and her charisma as recognized by the masses of poor Argentine citizens.

Although Evita is undoubtedly Latin America's most famous female politician, for most of her life she was far more interested in her acting career than in politics. Born in 1919, of a lower-class background, illegitimate and barely educated, she was a successful radio actress when she met Colonel Perón in early 1944. He was then the most controversial political figure among the group of military officers who had ruled Argentina since June 4, 1943. Her interest in politics began to develop as a result of her relationship with him and of her participation in a propaganda program sponsored by the Secretariat of Labor. Nevertheless, her career as a soap opera and film actress continued to be her main concern until October 23, 1945, when she abandoned it to marry Perón. His election to the presidency in February 1946 altered her life to such an extent that by 1949 she had become the second most powerful and influential person in the Peronist administration. By the time she died on July 26, 1952, she was Eva Perón, Argentina's First Lady; "Evita," *la abanderada de los descamisados* (the standard bearer of the shirtless ones); Perón's liaison with labor; president of the Partido Peronista Femenino (the women's branch of the Peronist party); and head of the Eva Perón Foundation.

[Juan] Perón's involvement in politics also began in the early forties. When the June 4 coup took place, he was a forty-eight-year-old colonel who had taught military history at the National War College and was highly respected by his fellow officers. Although he had taken part in Gen. José Félix Uriburu's military coup of September 6, 1930, his interest in social and political matters was recent and had been aroused by a training tour to Italy and other fascist countries in 1939–1941. These experiences would guide him for several years. On October 27, 1943, Perón took over the Department of Labor, which until then had been a second-echelon agency whose role was primarily to suppress labor independence. Perón had it raised to secretariat by the end of the next month and soon transformed it into the symbol of a new era in Argentine labor relations by implementing old laws, enacting new ones, supporting demands for unionization, and in general developing a social policy that raised the standards of living and working conditions of rural, urban, and white-collar workers.

The origins of Perón's leadership are to be found in his actions as secretary of labor and in the relationship he established with labor from 1943 to 1945. He was helped by several factors, among others Argentina's favorable economic conditions because of World War II, the existence of a fast-growing working class with large numbers of nonunionized workers, a highly bureaucratized labor movement, and an entirely new political style. He met daily with labor leaders and the rank and file in the Secretariat of Labor, visited their headquarters and factories, and attended their rallies. When he addressed them, he spoke of social justice, emphasized workers' rights, and proclaimed the beginning of a new era in which the state would end inhumane exploitation of workers. He used a radical language, previously unheard in government officials but appreciated by the workers because it was their own.

Perón's policies found strong resistance among all political parties, which already opposed the military government because of its neutralist stand in World War II (in fact, pro-Axis) and its suspension of constitutional guarantees. The Communists and Socialists, who controlled much of organized labor until 1943, were particularly antagonistic toward Perón and denounced him as a demagogue and a Nazi. Yet his personal support among labor continued to grow, even among the Socialists, and his relationship with workers remained close. In October 1945, during a crisis that gripped Argentina for nine days, it was put to a test, only to emerge strengthened.

The crisis erupted on October 9 when Perón, then also minister of war and vice president, was forced to resign from his three posts by his military opponents in the Campo de Mayo garrison. His dismissal precipitated a cabinet crisis for the president, Gen. Edelmiro J. Farrell. Cabinet members presented their resignations and Farrell set out to form a new government. Before abandoning the secretariat, however, Perón had addressed a workers' rally where he announced several measures favorable to labor. His speech so angered his enemies that on October 13 he was detained and jailed on Martín García Island. The news of Perón's arrest triggered the reaction of labor leaders and the rank and file; helped by his collaborators in the Secretariat of Labor, they began to mobilize to obtain his release. On October 15 sugar workers in Tucumán province went on strike, and that same day the General Confederation of Workers (CGT) met to consider a motion to declare a general strike. It was voted for the 18th but on the morning of the 17th, workers abandoned their factories en masse and invaded Buenos Aires. Demanding Perón's release, they converged on the Plaza de Mayo. Neither the police nor the Campo de Mayo garrison stopped them, and they were joined by throngs of men and women throughout the day. They did not leave until late that night, after Perón finally appeared on a balcony of the Casa Rosada and spoke to them.

Perón's presence in the government house and his speech, frequently interrupted by expressions of delirious enthusiasm, marked the transformation of his relationship with the Argentine working class into a bond that would unite them for the following thirty years. It was then that he emerged explicitly as "the leader" and his followers "the *descamisados*"—indeed, the terms were used shortly after to describe Perón and the crowds that flocked to the Plaza de Mayo. The latter recognized him as their "hero," their "leader," because in a decisive and unprecedented action he had taken up their defense and in a short time had changed their lives in tangible ways. Socialist and Communist accusations notwithstanding, they knew that the Secretariat of Labor had become a different institution since he began directing it. His broad smile inspired confidence when he received labor leaders in his office, and they soon found themselves at ease, chatting amicably with him. Furthermore, he knew how to address a workers' rally as if he were a seasoned labor leader. Because of his actions in support of labor, his enemies had demanded his resignation, jailed him, and even threatened his life. In the workers' eyes, Perón's enemies were therefore their enemies. In attacking him, they had threatened the gains they had achieved since 1943. Their fears were augmented by the inaugural speech of the newly appointed secretary of labor, the reaction of employers when workers went to get their October 12 salary, and the rumors about the composition of Farrell's cabinet, which indicated that the conservative oligarchy would soon be back in power. Identifying their gains with Perón, they went on strike, forcing the CGT leadership to declare it. They made themselves his followers and, as a result of their action, their hero was freed and returned to them. Their mobilization signified their express recognition of Perón's leadership, a collective recognition, according to [Max] Weber, "decisive for the validity of charisma."

The events of October 17 had the significance of a founding act: the symbolic proclamation of Perón's leadership and the surrender of the collective will because he embodied it. In the years to come, the ceremony would be reenacted every October 17 with a massive rally held in the same plaza: Perón, standing on the same balcony, would speak to the *descamisados* as he did that night. The ritual would take place on a national holiday officially called Loyalty Day, in remembrance of the loyalty he had shown to the *descamisados*, comparable only to the loyalty they had demonstrated toward him.

By their actions, both Perón and his followers had broken the accepted rules and roles of political and social behavior and repudiated past practices. Their meeting on October 17 can thus be characterized in Weber's words as revolutionary. But the charismatic relationship that revealed itself on that day did not in fact invalidate existing institutions, did not altogether destroy the accepted rules. It might better be said to have superimposed itself on top of them. Instead of acting in accordance with the new authority vested in him, Perón, the newly anointed leader, became that very day a candidate in the forthcoming presidential elections. Indeed, the following month, Perón announced his candidacy, and the mandate he received on October 17 was formalized and confirmed in February 1946, when he was elected president . . . in a campaign that pitted him against all the political parties that existed prior to the 1943 campaign. From Communists to conservatives, they were united in an anti-Perón front, but he received 1,527,231 votes out of a total of 2,734,386. He also won all but two of the Senate seats, and a large majority in the Chamber of Deputies. Nevertheless, his position was far from secure. He lacked a solid political party, having entered the presidential race backed by two organizations created after October 17. The Unión Cívica Radical (Junta Renovadora), a small offshoot of the Unión Cívica Radical [Argentina's most important party at the time], and the Partido Laborista, organized by labor leaders, were united only by the person of Perón himself, and their disagreements flared up as soon as the campaign got under way. The Labor Party itself presented a serious danger to Perón because it was headed by seasoned labor leaders who had the respect of the rank and file and who, though committed to him, also wanted to maintain some independence. Furthermore, its leadership overlapped with that of the CGT, and, as late as October 15, 1945, the labor leaders had clearly refused to put their organizations entirely in Perón's hands.

On October 15 the CGT met to consider a motion to declare a general strike. The minutes of that meeting indicate that the delegates understood the full impact of Perón's policies on Argentine labor. Like the rank and file, the labor leaders supported him because these policies had put an end to long-standing grievances. They did not disagree with the course adopted by the workers who had abandoned their jobs in protest against Perón's arrest. In fact, they saw no other alternative but to declare a general strike. However, they resisted calling a general strike for the purpose of releasing Perón because such an action would signify the surrender of their leadership to him. The motion finally adopted, setting the strike for October 18, did not include Perón's name.

The CGT attempt to maintain its legitimacy as a labor organization was thwarted by the workers' mobilization of the 17th, which left the labor leaders in a difficult position. They tried to regain some ground by founding the Labor Party, but it was too late; and in May 1946, Perón dissolved it. His action was openly resisted by some labor leaders, while others accepted it but persisted in trying to maintain a labor movement independent from him.

Perón's position was further endangered by the rapid expansion of organized labor; the massive incorporation of industrial workers, which changed the composition of the CGT membership; and the high level of worker mobilization, which led them to strike for higher wages and better working conditions. All this occurred at a time when the secretariat of labor—newly transformed into a ministry—was unprepared to meet their demands.

If Perón was to maintain the social basis of his power, he needed to continue to satisfy these demands and tighten his control of the labor movement. He also needed to be assured that the minister of labor would not undermine his contact with the *descamisados* and find some means to continue the political style he had established as secretary of labor. His election in fact threatened his relationship with the *descamisados*, but he was able to circumvent the problems posed by his presidential duties by adopting the following steps. On the one hand, he named to the Ministry of Labor a barely known labor leader, José María Freire, who owed his preeminence to Perón and thus could not easily become his rival. On the other hand, he allowed Evita to be his substitute and thus delegated to her his personal contact with the rank and file.

Shortly after Perón was inaugurated, Evita began to undertake certain activities very unusual for an Argentine First Lady. Not only did she accompany the president wherever he went, but she also met with workers' delegations in an office made available to her in the Post Office building, visited factories and union headquarters, attended rallies, and everywhere made speeches in the name of Perón. In September 1946 her office was transferred to the Ministry of Labor, which was located where Perón's old secretariat had been. By this move he informed his followers that from then on Evita was his liaison with them, that he relied on her to keep in contact with them, and that, though he was the president of Argentina, he had not ceased to be secretary of labor—a point repeatedly implied by Evita in her speeches when she called Perón "the colonel" (although he had been promoted to general) and mentioned "the secretariat" (although it had become a ministry). Furthermore, by December 1946 her role as Perón's liaison with labor was made official by a presidential press release. . . .

[Evita] acquired a political language of her own, and her personality became more distinct. Her transformation took place during the period in which Perón asserted his control over organized labor and isolated the remnants of Laborista opposition among his followers. The process was completed in 1948: by then José Espejo was secretary general of the CGT, and that year congressional elections reinforced Perón's hold on the Chamber of Deputies. It was crowned by a constitutional reform which permitted his reelection in 1951. By the time Perón consolidated his power, Evita had become an integral part of it, and her own relationship with the *descamisados* was already clearly established. In a symbolic recognition of her new status, on October 17, 1948, she addressed for the first time crowds in the Plaza de Mayo with Perón.

Her presence on the balcony of the Casa Rosada confirmed the legitimacy of her leadership. It was the "proof" or "sign" of her charisma, but it also had an additional symbolic meaning. As co-leader of the *descamisados*, she had to be a participant in the alliance that emerged on October 17, 1945. Since she had not been part of the original "covenant," she had to be integrated into the process that began that day. Her 1948 speech therefore established her link with the earlier events and made her a participant after the fact in the founding of Peronism. . . .

Although Perón was the ultimate source of Evita's authority, the basis of her leadership came from the actual work she performed with the rank and file. Every day she met with countless delegations of workers in her ministry office. They went to see her for a variety of reasons: in some cases, they wanted help because they were organizing a union or were involved in contract negotiations. In others, they needed her support to win an internal election, to force an employer to implement a specific labor law, or to improve the working conditions in a particular factory. What she did essentially was to listen to all requests, relay them to the appropriate office, and, (acting in Perón's name) exert enough pressure to speed up paper work and obtain prompt results. She soon acquired the reputation of being efficient, and workers were quick to realize that in order to get what they wanted, it was to their advantage to channel their requests through her. . . .

Evita's meetings with labor delegations remained the center of her political activities. Even after she began spending long hours—sometimes until three and four in the morning—taking care of matters related to the Fundación Eva Perón and started organizing the women's branch of the Peronist Party, she still managed to meet with the CGT secretariat and labor delegations every day. . . . Evita's leadership did not separate the *descamisados* from Perón. On the contrary, it strengthened the bond that united them to him because she was his wife, therefore part of him and at all times acted on his behalf—a point she never failed to make in her speeches.

One of her main functions from 1946–1952 was to give speeches. Her effectiveness as a public speaker was a valuable asset to Perón, and in fact, together with the work she performed on a daily basis with the rank and file, it may have been what thrust her into political prominence. Her first public speech, part of the government campaign to lower the cost of living, was followed by many others in which she explained the goals of the Five-Year Plan, urged the adoption of women's suffrage, asked unions to remain faithful to Perón as they had done in October 1945, backed Peronist deputies in the 1948 congressional elections, advocated the need of a constitutional reform, eulogized Perón's doctrine—Justicialismo and The Third Position—warned against the threats posed by Communists and oligarchs, and, even when she was very sick, begged Peronists to reelect Perón in 1951.

Although she occasionally spoke on the radio, most of these speeches were given when she was visited by labor delegations or at meetings organized by the CGT, individual unions, and the Peronist Party. Whatever the specific occasion, however, the same themes reappeared, constantly repeated with very few changes: the terrible conditions in which workers lived before 1943; the benefits they had obtained when Perón took over the Secretariat of Labor; the accomplishments of the June 1943 Revolution—multiplied tenfold by Perón, who had transformed Argentina into a country "economically independent, socially just, and politically sovereign" where workers could now live in happiness and joy; the absolute necessity for Perón to remain in power so as to further social justice in Argentina; Perón's love for the *descamisados*; his greatness and the extraordinary significance of his doctrine; the *descamisados'* duty to fight for their rights and for Perón and to defend them from their enemies—the Communists, the oligarchy, capitalism, and imperialism.

When Evita spoke from the balcony of the Casa Rosada during the May 1 or October 17 celebrations, she did not alter her themes or her objectives, but she worded and delivered her speeches very differently. They became explosions of passion and fury, veritable harangues calculated to arouse an emotional response from the audience. They contrasted with Perón's speeches, which explained and argued in a simple and clear language and were delivered in a calm, reassuring, fatherly tone. When Evita spoke, her long hands clutched the microphone or slashed the air. Her voice would rise tense and urging, and at a rapid pace she sent blast after blast against Perón's enemies, slowing down only to pronounce caressingly his name or the word *descamisados*.

Using language that was extracted from soap operas, she transformed politics into dramas dominated by relentless invocations of love: Perón's work in the Secretariat of Labor was prompted by his love for workers; they had saved him on October 17 because they loved him; she was sacrificing her life for all because of her love for them; and the love that united Perón, Evita, and the *descamisados* was the cause of the oligarchy's hatred towards them. Her scenarios never changed and her characters were stereotyped by the same adjectives: Perón was always "glorious," the people "marvelous," the oligarchy *egoista y vendepatria* (selfish and corrupt), and she was a "humble" or "weak" woman, "burning her life for them" so that social justice could be achieved, *cueste lo que cueste y caiga quien caiga* (at whatever cost and regardless of consequences). On May 1, 1951, she ended her speech with the following words:

> And if I could choose among all the things of this world, I would choose the infinite grace to die for the cause of Perón, which is to die for you. Because I, too, like the comrade workers, am capable of dying and ending the last moment of my life with our war cry, our salvation cry: our lives for Perón. . . .

But the radicalism of Evita's discourse cannot be viewed isolated from Perón's own discourse. Whether in 1946, 1949, or 1951, her speeches had the unmistakable purpose of establishing the continuity between the past and the present, reinforcing the *descamisados'* allegiance to Perón—and therefore their control—and exalting his personality as the symbol of their will, their rights, and their welfare.

Evita's leadership was defined from the very start on the basis of Perón's superiority. He was the undisputed leader, *el líder* or *el conductor*, the ideologue who elaborated the doctrine, the strategist who defined the goals and articulated the plans to achieve them. As for Evita, she concerned herself only with repeating Perón's ideas time and again to his followers, innovating only insofar as his cause would be furthered and carrying out the tactics which he outlined. As she stated in her autobiography: "He is the leader. I am only the shadow of his superior presence." She never used the word "leader" to describe herself and neither did the *descamisados*, although a few weeks before her death, Congress granted her the title of Spiritual Leader of the Nation. As the "shadow" of Perón, however, she had numerous titles: *la abanderada de los humildes* or *la abanderada de los trabajadores* (the standard-bearer of the poor or the workers); *el escudo de Perón* (Perón's shield); *la esperanza y la eterna vigía de la revolución* (the hope and the eternal guardian of the revolution); *la plenipotenciaria de los descamisados* (the plenipotentiary of the shirtless ones); and the one she seems to have preferred, because she used it most often to describe herself, *el puente de amor entre Perón y el pueblo* (the bridge of love between Perón and the people). These titles were not mere rhetorical devices created by the Peronist propaganda machinery or herself in order to satisfy her vanity, which was great, but rather they were accurate descriptions of the role she performed between 1946 and 1952, as well as reflections of her own relationship with the *descamisados*.

Perhaps the best way to understand their significance is to examine the structure of her speeches, especially those she pronounced from the balcony of the Casa Rosada during the October 17 or May 1 celebrations. On such occasions, Evita's speeches were composed of three basic elements: Perón, the *descamisados*, and herself as the nexus between them. If she began addressing the latter, she usually spoke to them as if she were Perón but keeping a certain distance from him. She would then change the direction of speech and address herself to Perón, calling him *mi general*, as if she were part of the public but speaking in its name. Finally, she would separate herself from Perón and the *descamisados* to reaffirm that she was only a humble woman who loved both Perón and the *descamisados* and who was dedicated to work until death for their happiness.

In a speech she gave during the final session of a CGT congress, for example, she began by establishing her identification with Perón: "I, who had the great honor of sharing with the general his concerns, his dreams, and his patriotic achievements, feel proud to have followed the good path, that is to say, the path pointed out to us by General Perón." Later on, she switched sides and in her inimitable syntax she spoke to him, identifying herself with the *descamisados* but separated from them: "My general: here is the CGT with its *descamisado* vanguard, with your glorious and beloved *descamisado* vanguards, present to honor you and to support you, not in a circumstantial fashion, because that support comes from men who when they shout 'our lives for Perón' did it on October 17, 1945. . . ." Still speaking to Perón, she proceeded as if she were part of the public:

> Because, my general, we fight for economic independence; we fight for social justice; we fight for sovereignty and for the honor of our flag; we fight for the happiness of our children and for the humanization of a capitalism that has only brought us sterile struggles among brothers; we fight for the consolidation in our Fatherland of the extraordinary doctrine of our celebrated workers' leader.

Finally, she separated herself from all:

> I thank you, comrade workers, for the honor bestowed upon this humble woman who works trying to interpret the patriotic dreams of General Perón. . . . This stimulates me and spurs me to continue; it is the most honorable decoration in the breast of a woman who comes from the people, who is proud to belong to the people, and whose work is to listen to the palpitations of the working people.

Blond, pale, and beautiful, Evita was the incarnation of the Mediator, a Virgin-like figure who, despite her origins, shared the perfection of the Father because of her closeness to him. Her mission was to love infinitely, give herself to others, and "burn her life" for others, a point made painfully literal when she fell sick with cancer and refused to interrupt her activities. She was the Blessed Mother, chosen by God to be near "the leader of the new world: Perón." She was the childless mother who became the Mother of all the *descamisados*, the Mater Dolorosa who "sacrificed" her life so that the poor, the old, and the downtrodden could find some happiness.

This image of Evita was a mask that hid another woman: the shrewd and jealous politician who bullied ministers, worked at a frantic pace, and ran the Eva Perón Foundation and the Partido Peronista Femenino with an iron hand. The mediator image was nurtured by her and repeated ad nauseam by government officials, party members, and labor leaders, and it became real for many Peronists. A few days after her death in July 1952, a labor union sent a telegram to the pope requesting her canonization, and twenty years later Peronists still bought Madonna pictures of her. . . .

Following Evita's death in 1952 (at the age of thirty-three), Perón's ties with labor, the military, the Church, and industrialists began to weaken considerably. His new economic policies, his growing authoritarianism, and the political vacuum created by Evita's death eroded his support; he was finally ousted by a military coup in September 1955. Perón's own charismatic relationship with the *descamisados* underwent a period of estrangement, but during his eighteen-year exile his leadership was never seriously threatened. By the early sixties he was once again the undisputed leader of the *descamisados*. In 1973 he returned to Argentina to win a third term in office with his third wife, Isabel, vice president; however, Peronism's dual leadership died with Evita.

---

2. Getúlio Vargas: "He Is the Sun that Illumines" ◆ Orígenes Lessa

Vargas grew famous among the poor people of Brazil during his first administration (1930–1945). He traveled to every state (logging ninety thousand miles by 1941), answered every letter sent to him, and mounted an impressive publicity service to spread the word that he was the "father of the poor." Tens of thousands of individuals had some contact with Vargas, and his image as a smiling, caring, accessible person became well known. In a country lacking good communications and a national press, word of mouth was the most efficient propaganda. In the Northeast, minstrels who wrote, published, and performed a unique folk poetry called literatura de cordel *adopted Vargas as a favorite theme and did much to increase his fame. Orígenes Lessa analyzes this special literature.*

Getúlio Vargas, certainly one of the greatest personalities to impress and fascinate the poor classes of Brazil, provided the themes for a great deal of popular poetry. Only Padre Cícero [a backlands priest credited with healing powers] inspired more verses than Vargas. Neither Antônio Silvino nor Lampeão [two celebrated bandits], who were even portrayed in movies, accounted for as large a literature. At least ten times more verses were dedicated to Getúlio Vargas. . . . In his lifetime and for many years after his death, Vargas provided the most frequent and popular themes among the humble customers of the minstrel singers. . . .

From Orígenes Lessa, *Getúlio Vargas na literatura de cordel* (Rio: Editora Documentário, 1973), 59. Translated by Michael Conniff.

A "good disaster" or "nefarious crime" will always inspire the songwriters more than politicians and their feats. Yet in the Northeast politicians have always made use of the minstrels in their election campaigns, knowing the broad acceptance they have among the poorest classes. . . .

The classic smile of the president—the euphoria of victory, a powerful weapon for conquering popular sentiments, an expression of his own temperament—distinguished Vargas from the other dictators of the period. [The minstrel] Athayde saw the difference in this 1938 verse:

> The most important thing/ In the president's life
> Is that he solves every problem/ With a smile, calmly.

The official presidential portrait, with the green and gold sash, distributed throughout the country, did not appeal to the people and certainly not to the minstrels. They preferred the informal photographs and the Getúlio with his arm in the air waving to "his fans," as one troubadour wrote, in the arrivals and departures, in the rallies and soccer fields, where so many saw him. This was what inspired José Vila Nova Primo to write:

> Finally up on the platform/ The happy Vargas arose
> Thanking the people/ Constantly smiling!

Rodolfo Coelho Cavalcanti (in "The Return of Getúlio") is almost prophetic:

> His smile is saying/ I am yours until death.

Describing "The Triumphal Arrival of Getúlio Vargas in Recife" in 1950, Delarme Monteiro da Silva wrote:

> People from every corner/ Of our distinguished state
> Came to see the arrival/ Of Getúlio the long-awaited
> Whose satisfied smile/ Was quite heart-felt. . . .
> He arrived in this land/ The man we so awaited
> The little-big man/ Idolized by one and all
> A man of steely nerves/ Who never makes idle talk.

Vargas's special smile is recalled in this beautiful verse by Minelvino Francisco da Silva, in "The Arrival of Getúlio Vargas in Heaven." Helped by the angels, he is received by Christ and forgiven:

> And he remained in Heaven/ With a smile on his face.

Francisco Sales Areda, in "The Sad Death of President Getúlio Vargas," asks the Eternal Father to admit Vargas to Heaven:

Our God who art on high/ Eternal Father so merciful
Take unto your bosom/ Safe forever
There in your Paradise/ Inspire full of good humor
Our good president Getúlio.

A few would speak directly of Vargas's small stature, though always
with compassion. Here is Minelvino Francisco da Silva again, with "The
Administration of Getúlio and the Problem of Poverty":

He is teeny, he is weeny/ He is a little dandy
Yet no one can match him/ When it comes to action. . . .
The sun of Brazil/ That arose to shine upon
The rich as well as the poor/ He wishes to radiate
Yet when a cloud intrudes/ His rays are deflected
And he is unable to bring clear weather.

One of the most complete portraits, using all the conventions and tricks
of the Northeast, was penned by Rodolfo, entitled "The Victory of Getúlio
Vargas," written shortly after his election in 1950:

Getúlio Dorneles Vargas/ Star that never goes out
He is the sun that illumines/ Zephyr that never dies
Rock that never dislodges/ Ship that never wrecks
Getúlio Dorneles Vargas/ He is the muse who inspires me
He is the image we worship/ He is the air we breathe
He is the song that enlivens/ He is the glory forever. . . .

Getúlio Dorneles Vargas/ He is the flame of heroism
Banner of our history/ Legend of our patriotism
Living symbol of labor/ The consummate Brazilian! . . .

Come Getúlio, come Getúlio/ Our true chieftain
Our great president/ With all reality
Come to save our people/ Who have suffered long.

---

3. Getúlio Vargas: "Workers of Brazil! Here I Am at Your Side!" ◆ Michael L. Conniff

*Politicians must be closely attuned to linguistics—the nuances of sound,
meaning, and impression—in their speeches and progaganda. This passage
shows Getúlio Vargas's evolving relationship with the masses as conveyed
in major pronouncements.*

Reprinted from *Urban Politics in Brazil: The Rise of Populism, 1925–1945*
(Pittsburgh, 1981), 166–67, by Michael Conniff, by permission of the University of
Pittsburgh Press. © 1981 by the University of Pittsburgh Press.

Vargas almost never spoke openly or in private about his political strategies or preferences, leaving contemporaries (and historians) only external evidence from which to reconstruct his thoughts. Presidential addresses are one of the best indications of the growing identification of labor, politics, and publicity during the Estado Novo. Vargas was a skillful speaker according to a contemporary publicity specialist who has compared his radio talks to the Roosevelt fireside chats. I have scanned some thirty speeches Vargas made to labor between 1930 and 1945 for three specific elements: for identification of the "people" in the populist sense that we have used the term; for references to self; and for slogans that indicate a relationship between people and self.

Over the fifteen years of Vargas's first administration, he continually spoke to the working classes about his social and labor programs. The references to labor benefits and social harmony were consistent from the 1930 speech on the Castelo Esplanade until his resignation communiqué in 1945, but the manner in which he identified the beneficiaries of his programs changed noticeably. Through 1938 he addressed his labor speeches to the *povo brasileiro*, or Brazilian people. Only once did he refer to class, and that was in 1932 when he addressed the *classes trabalhadoras*, or laboring classes. It seems clear that he wished to avoid references that might indicate a divergence of interests between classes, a concept that he always explicitly refuted.

In 1938 he began addressing them as *trabalhadores do Brasil*, or workers of Brazil; the first time he gave the term prominence was during an impromptu speech to workers in São Paulo, whom he called *trabalhadores de São Paulo*. By 1940 "workers of Brazil" became his exclusive way of addressing labor, and soon it was rendered an incantation to the masses. It must be recalled that many middle-sector employees—clerks, civil servants, teachers, and so forth—could identify themselves with the masses because they had received substantial benefits from the social legislation in force. Therefore, Vargas created his "people" in the late 1930s from the working class and the lower levels of the middle sectors, from whom he elicited charismatic authority.

Vargas's verbalization of self was also indicative of an emerging populist relationship with the masses. In the early 1930s he chose such institutional terms as "my government," "my acts as head of state," "the acts of the government," "our organization," "our will." The most frequent was "my government." However, in the impromptu speech in São Paulo in 1938 he used "I" several times. Thereafter the singular personal pronoun became more frequent, although the plural never disappeared. In addition, the approximation with the masses was explicit in his press conference statement of early 1944: he wished to eliminate intermediaries between the people and the government and to run an "open door" administration. The culmination of the increasing grammatical proximity between Vargas and the "people" came in his May 1, 1945, speech when he began: "Workers of Brazil! Here I am at your side to join in the commemoration of Labor Day." Although Vargas never recorded his ideas about such matters, it is clear in retrospect that he was creating a new personal self available to the masses as the "father of the poor," to be the recipient of charismatic authority.

The slogans in his various speeches also show Vargas's emerging populism. Nationalism was, of course, always present in his labor addresses. A principal message through 1940, and especially during the authoritarian period, was for the patriotic worker to beware of seduction by insincere politicians and leftist ideologues. Rather, he stressed, the dignity of the citizen came from work. Two slogans of 1940 may be regarded as representative: "Order and work" and "Union and work." By 1944 a new message, that of economic nationalism, had emerged that would infuse his speeches for the next ten years. Typical were the search for "economic emancipation of the country" and the desire to "combat economic colonialism." By extension, Vargas told the working class that by following him it would be assured employment with dignity and just wages and benefits. The threat was no longer foreign ideologies but international monopolies. Vargas was the man who could be trusted to defend the interests of the masses.

---

4. Getúlio Vargas: A Consummate Speech Writer ◆ Lourival Fontes and Glauco Carneiro

Lourival Fontes, Getúlio Vargas's press secretary in the 1940s and 1950s, compiled a book based upon the Brazilian president's notes and instructions for speech writing. He asserts that Vargas was always in control, providing the ideas, editing, rephrasing, polishing, and pacing. Fontes says that the speeches were simple and straightforward, always beginning with the invocation "Brasileiros!" He avoided slang, gallicisms, and stilted wording. He kept his sentences and paragraphs short. "The Forgotten Man was always the target of his creative phraseology . . . and the theme of his encounters with the multitudes." Below are a few notes Vargas sent to Fontes for future speeches, plus critiques of speeches to be delivered to labor audiences.

From Lourival Fontes and Glauco Carneiro, *A face final de Vargas (os bilhetes de Getúlio)* (Rio: Edicões O Cruzeiro, 1966), chap. 15. Translated by Michael Conniff.

There are no superior or inferior races; nor races of masters and slaves.

✦

I am imprisoned by a wall that separates me from the suffering and humble people, who elected me in the hope of a better life. I must fulfill that promise!

✦

I need the support and confidence of the workers, and they in turn will find in me a true friend, ready to help them in their just aspirations. They should avoid being misled by agitators and rabble-rousers. They may come to me without fear, and I will lead them to just and equitable solutions, using the official agencies created to accomplish this.

✦

This is too highfalutin. I don't see here the reference I made to the working classes, as the dynamic element in the social equilibrium and force that is organizing to influence the future, not in a purely political democracy, such as we have, but instead an economic and social democracy. "Workers in the cities and the countryside: those who drive the factories and till the fields. You are the people who follow me and on whom I depend to frighten the hornets waiting to sting me." I wrote that during the scary plane flight. After we arrived, I reread it more calmly. Reduce it to a concept or phrase and send it back for me to look at.

✦

This is all right, but only speak of the cultural part and drop the reference to the worker, the laborer, in the most industrialized city in Brazil. We should say something like, "In this city of São Paulo there are as many thousands of organized and enlightened workers as our dreams of greater economic development, a higher standard of living, and social harmony."

✦

I should appear a victim of persecution.* In the Senate I made a number of speeches showing that the government is following an erroneous financial path and creating a nonexistent crisis. . . . Afterward I suffered all manner of pressures from the government. . . . I came here [to Itu, the ranch in Rio Grande] in silence, I isolated myself, and I waited for time and events to show I was right.

✦

And where's the petroleum? It seems to me that this is a fundamental issue to bring up in Bahia. Did you show João Neves my suggestions? Some of my speeches are incomplete and others are missing.

*These instructions come from Vargas's correspondence with his daughter Alzira, who managed his 1950 election campaign.

I am not very impressed with the tenor of some of these draft speeches that arrived. They are very academic, very correct, but they won't make an impression on the masses [*povo*]. It seems that they are not addressed to the masses. They are more for highbrows. They don't deal with the heart of the social and economic crisis that we are undergoing. The one for São Paulo is good. . . . São Paulo is the largest industrial center and has the largest concentration of workers in the country, yet the speech doesn't deal with the social question: the misery, the high cost of living, the declining wages, the industrial crisis, the lack of bank credit, commodity hoarding, etc. You may say that I can add all that later. But it isn't easy, because I don't have the material. I don't have data to illustrate or even refer to these statements, and it would mean totally rewriting these speeches. And time is short. They are pressuring me to go on the campaign trail and I don't have speeches, I don't have a travel itinerary, and the committee doesn't have money to pay for its activities. PS: Don't work on the São Paulo speech, I already rewrote it.

5. Zé Maria Talks about Getúlio ◆ Robert S. Byars

In the late 1960s, Robert Byars interviewed a forty-seven-year-old Brazilian steel worker in Belo Horizonte, to whom he gave the pseudonym Zé Maria. In the course of talking about citizenship, unions, government, and life in general, Zé Maria warmly remembered Getúlio Vargas.

I think about—when I hear the word "government," I think about leadership—I think about a *person* who is leading the country, y'know?— a person who is governing. When things go wrong, he comes along and takes control of the situation—it doesn't matter if the situation is good or bad.

I think [I would feel comfortable with the late Getúlio Vargas]. I think I even would have enjoyed chatting with him—but, of course, this is no longer possible, right? . . . Getúlio was different. Every time he came here to Belo Horizonte I was right there to see him. I liked him a lot. I don't know why, but I had a special liking for him. I thought he governed well. He was a good man. [He] . . . mixed right in.

I saw Getúlio conversing with the people. He wasn't too proud to speak with any kind of person—even the "lowliest." He appeared honored talking

From Robert S. Byars, "Culture, Politics, and the Urban Factory Worker in Brazil: The Case of Zé Maria," in *Latin American Modernization Problems: Case Studies in the Crises of Change*, ed. Robert E. Scott (Urbana, 1973), 71–72. Reprinted by permission of the University of Illinois Press.

with even the poorest of men—and, it seems he was a very humble man, y'know?—a man who was both humble and intelligent. I don't know if it is just because I am a simple man myself that I liked him—because he spoke just as nicely to the rich as he did to the poor. And, I don't know if it was just a political "technique," y'know? I mean, I was there when he was speaking with a man who was all crippled up—first he put his hand on the man's head, then he gave him an *abraço*. Wherever he went he behaved this way, y'know? I had a tremendous *simpatia* for him. . . .

I think this constant changing of government is responsible for our situation, y'know?—take out one, put in another; cancel the mandate of the first one, then another. It keeps things in a constant state of disorder, y'know? And, so, it upsets the entire country! The poor are suffering, and so are the rich—suffering from this endless changing of governments. . . . When Getúlio Vargas was our president—for some fifteen years—it seems that life was much better, much calmer, more balanced, y'know?

---

6. Catechism of a Getulista ◆ José Barbosa

Parties and politicians have to devote considerable time to indoctrinating followers. Here, José Barbosa, director of the São Paulo chapter of the Brazilian Workers' Party (PTB), invites its members to a seminar in 1948 on what the party stands for—and by extension what it meant to be a Getulista. By then a grass-roots campaign was already under way to draft Vargas as a candidate for the 1950 election.

We are pleased to inform you that we just created a course in labor doctrine that will publicize the basic principles of Laborism, its theoretical and objective elements, among our members.

Every Saturday at 8:30 P.M. in party headquarters we will conduct classes on the major points listed in the agenda below, to be led by specially invited persons within the party or sympathetic to Laborism.

The last Saturday of each month will be dedicated to debates on these themes. Every year in October we will intensify our publicity to mark the anniversary of the 1930 Revolution, led by Getúlio Vargas, the supreme leader of the workers.

The classes in Laborism will be mimeographed and distributed every month to interested parties for five cruzeiros, or free to those unable to pay.

To support this course we created a library of cultural books (Laborism, history, sociology, human geography, economics and finance, ethnography,

From Arquivo Getúlio Vargas, CPDOC, Getúlio Vargas Foundation, Rio de Janeiro. Translated by Michael Conniff.

anthropology, politics, etc.) donated by members. They will be shelved in four collections named after benefactors of Laborism: Getúlio Vargas, Salgado Filho, Marcondes Filho, and Pedro Candia.

The course will follow the themes listed below:

1. World history of Laborism
2. Laborism as part of the socialist ideal
3. Labor and capital, according to Laborism. . . .

Topics of historical significance and debate:

History

1. Politics and society in Brazil before 1930
2. Political and social significance of the National Revolution of 1930
3. Getúlio Vargas and the National Revolution of 1930
4. Creation of the Ministry of Labor and promulgation of labor laws
5. Labor law in Brazil before 1930
6. Social and labor protection under the Constitutions of Brazil
7. Getúlio Vargas and Laborism
8. Laborism in Latin America

Debates

1. Concepts of political party
2. Presidentialism and parliamentarianism
3. Characteristics of Brazilian Laborism
4. Social advances under Getúlio Vargas compared with the current government
5. Labor law
6. Freedom of unionization and the closed shop
7. Union education
8. Laborism and the right to strike
9. Democracy
10. International collaboration
11. Development of welfare and social security protection
12. Ten-year development plans
13. Development of the banking system
14. Financial and fiscal policy
15. Industrial and commercial development

16. Agricultural and cattle-ranching development
17. Improving life in rural areas
18. Agrarian reform
19. Transportation and communication
20. Increased cooperative efforts
21. Public and private education
22. Immigration and colonization
23. Subsoil minerals (petroleum, iron, gold, etc.)
24. Varieties of wage controls and our attitude toward them
25. Trusts, monopolies, and cartels. . . .

These, dear *companheiros*, are the cardinal points that will be developed during the classes and debates in our course in labor doctrine.

We expect your support, solidarity, and stimulus in order to strengthen the PTB, under the wise guidance of our eminent chief Getúlio Vargas, and we will one day establish in Brazil a cohesive, strong, prosperous labor society.

---

7. Adhemar de Barros:
A True Swashbuckler ◆ John Gunther

Born into a wealthy coffee family in the interior of São Paulo in 1901, Adhemar de Barros received a fine education, finishing off a medical degree in Rio with internships in Europe. He dabbled in politics in the 1930s and then was Vargas's surprise pick for governor of São Paulo in 1938. A quick study who copied from European and U.S. leaders, Adhemar adopted the radio, the airplane, and modern publicity techniques to build his popularity. His first major election came in 1947, when he won the governorship. Later he served as mayor of São Paulo and won the governorship again. He ran unsuccessfully for president of Brazil three times.

R ough, large-hewn, capacious, [Adhemar] dominates by bluff, bluster, and sheer weight of personality. . . . We met in Rio, which he happened to be visiting for a weekend, in mildly peculiar circumstances. We had been lunching that day in Petrópolis, the suburb well known as the favorite habitat of the last emperor, when an urgent summons came from Governor Barros giving us an appointment in the evening. We said that this was impossible, because we couldn't get there in time, and the voice said

From John Gunther, *Inside South America* (New York, 1967), 58–59. © 1966, 1967 by John Gunther. Reprinted by permission of HarperCollins Publishers Inc.

explosively, "Come any time!" We arrived at his apartment about 9:30 after a trip through violent rain, and the governor, together with his secretary, an attractive young woman, received us with exuberant goodwill and determination. He wanted very much to be sure we would visit São Paulo.

After lively talk for half an hour we rose to go. Obviously the governor was busy. "Wait!" he commanded. Two men entered, of the type one sees hanging about county courthouses, but I could not tell if they were retainers, journalists, or officials receiving instructions. Barros disappeared with them, returned presently, and announced that we were to stay for dinner. "However," he went on, "there is only enough food for three. But my secretary is a clever woman and will work something out." Again the governor retired to speak to the mysterious retainers and we did not sit down to dinner till 11:30; then seven of us had fish roasted in coconut sauce, curry of chicken, rice, escalopes of veal, the usual attendant vegetables, salad, large quantities of cold sausage, and two desserts. Indeed, the secretary was a clever woman.

---

8. Adhemar de Barros: "He Steals but He Gets Things Done" ◆ Hélio Jaguaribe

In 1954, Brazil witnessed a battle of the titans between populists Adhemar ("He steals but he gets things done") de Barros and Jânio Quadros in the São Paulo gubernatorial election. Jaguaribe used the term populism for perhaps the first time in Latin America to describe this "recent and little-studied political phenomenon." Quadros, whose career was soon called meteoric, won this round and went on to the presidency in 1960. However, he fumbled his opportunity and two years later lost a gubernatorial election to Barros, then positioning himself for the 1965 presidential race. Just as Brazil has had more populists than any other country, São Paulo has been the most sought-after plum for this new-style politician. Most of Jaguaribe's acute observations were later incorporated into the theoretical literature.

Adhemarismo is not a typical manifestation of clientelistic politics, although it uses those methods. To be sure, Adhemarismo in rural areas is structured just like the Social Democratic Party (PSD). Adhemar's rural voters are organized into local committees, headed up by bosses just like the precinct captains of the traditional PSD. And the state committee has old-style rural bosses whose prestige is based on their ability to deliver

From Hélio Jaguaribe, "Qué é o adhemarismo?" *Cadernos do nosso tempo* 2 (January–June 1954): 139–49. Translated by Michael Conniff.

jobs and favors to their constituents. Nevertheless, Adhemar's relations to his rural voters are not at all like those of the PSD bosses. The latter derive their power from the ability to command the loyalty of regional chiefs, who in turn count on municipal leaders, who then make direct contact with the voters.

In Adhemar's case, however, he personally exercises ultimate influence over rural voters. This influence does not derive so much from his constant travels through the region. Rather, it is personal and is articulated by remote control because of his vast popularity. This is very different, then, from the way the PSD operates. Adhemarismo is an emotional appeal that mobilizes the rural masses, while the party merely carries out the mundane tasks of registering the voters Adhemar has already won over, protecting and getting them to the polls, and seeing that they vote for the candidate they prefer.

Thus, while the bosses of the PSD depend heavily on the party to carry out its work, cut political deals, and win over voters, Adhemar himself gives substance to his party. Therefore, instead of his depending on the party, the party depends on Adhemar, and he can exercise a personal and unlimited power that no other leader—except perhaps Getúlio Vargas—is capable of exercising. . . .

The masses are not a class, nor an alliance or association of classes, nor even formally a coalition of classes. The masses are a multitudinous conglomeration of individuals who lack class feelings or conscience. . . .

The general conditions that must prevail for populism to arise are: massification, caused by proletarianization (de facto but not with class identity) of broad sectors of a developing society, disconnecting the individuals from their social origins; and a loss of representativeness by the dominant groups, so they lose their positions of ascendancy. The populist leader may appear who offers himself to the masses and is able to conquer power. His appeal is charisma, legitimacy in a society without defined social relationships.

---

9. Haya de la Torre: Descendant of the Conquistadors ◆ John Gunther

Raised in Trujillo in a respectable middle-class family, Víctor Raúl Haya de la Torre ventured into political realms that no other Peruvian leader had explored. Many-faceted, mystical, perhaps incapable of serving as presi-

From John Gunther, *Inside Latin America* (New York: Harper and Brothers, 1941), 208–14. Reprinted by permission of Jane Perry Gunther.

dent, *Haya nonetheless inspired his people and followers throughout the hemisphere. John Gunther's political travelogue from Latin America in 1940 provides clues to understanding the man's tremendous power and popularity.*

I saw Haya three times, and each time I felt that I was meeting one of the greatest personages of America. The interviews were easy enough to arrange, through the courtesy of friends, though technically Haya is in hiding. He is a refugee, with the police just around the corner; the police certainly know where he is, but they do not arrest him. The reason is, of course, that the government cannot risk the scandal that his overt arrest would cause. It pretends meanwhile to have no knowledge of his whereabouts; it is not officially disclosed whether or not any indictment against him is still in force. But whenever Haya goes to a secret Aprista meeting, his friends may be arrested after he leaves; the organization has no legal right to exist, and any acknowledged Aprista may be clapped in jail at any time.

Haya looks like what he is, a lineal descendant of the *conquistadors*. He is tallow-skinned, of medium height, with broad heavy shoulders. His jet-black hair sweeps into a flying wedge over each ear. His nose is powerfully aquiline; his ears are shaped like stirrups. He has bright olive-brown eyes and a lively sense both of political realities and of humor. He speaks English as well as you or I.

Víctor Raúl Haya de la Torre was born on February 22, 1896, at Trujillo, in northern Peru, one of the very few Peruvian towns with a Spanish rather than an Indian name. His birthday is that of George Washington, which pleases him; it also pleases him that his mother's name was Cárdenas, since he has great admiration for ex-President Cárdenas of Mexico. His father was a journalist, and one of his uncles was a priest. He grew up in a thoroughly respectable, Catholic, bourgeois atmosphere.

As a boy, Haya read Unamuno and Nietzsche, learned French and German, studied the piano, climbed mountains for sport, and noted that of the forty-odd *haciendas* producing sugar in the Trujillo neighborhood when he was a child, only two remained when he was twenty. It was his first lesson in the penetrative power of big business. Then, in his early twenties, three things happened to him; he has never recovered from the three.

First, he visited Cuzco, the ancient capital of the Incas. Young Haya was transfixed—but not just by the ruins. He saw what the old Indians had left, but he also saw their descendants crushed, whipped, and beaten. When he returned to Lima, he wanted to build some kind of monument to Manco Capac, the first Inca, the founder—as he would put it—of Peruvian nationality. (Haya never erected his statue. Many years later, the Japanese colony in Lima did.)

Second, Haya went to the University of Córdoba in the Argentine, and witnessed the social and political fermentation, the "spiritual revolution" as he calls it, going on among the students there. Most of the old universities, like San Marcos in Lima, were cathedrals of reaction, or, in one of Haya's phrases, "viceroyalties of the spirit." Córdoba was different. The young men were emancipating themselves from the Catholic European tradition; they sought to think in terms of Buenos Aires instead of Paris. "In Córdoba, back in 1919, I felt the death of Europe," Haya says. Presently the nationalist "revolt" in Córdoba spread upwards and outwards, to Chile and Peru. Haya brought it to Lima, and became president of the Students' Federation at San Marcos.

Third, Haya was tremendously influenced by the Mexican revolution, then working its turbulent way forward. Mexico showed him something positive: a social revolution attempting to bring freedom to the peasant. Also, the study of Mexico convinced him that all the Latin American states should be a single unity. "Argentina and Mexico are no more different than Vermont and Arizona," he says; he felt that all might become united if the various peoples were released from feudalism. Haya looked to the politicians—and found them wanting. "All the old men were too old," he puts it.

"I was sure of only two things in those days," he told me. "First, that Córdoba was my mother, and Mexico my father. Second, that the Americans must stand together, and that all of us must be different from Europe."

At that time—about 1919–20—Haya had no intention of becoming a politician. He was against all politicians. He wanted merely to observe, to study. But he was impelled by events to a life of action. In 1921 he founded the "Popular Universities" in Lima, where students gave free instruction at night to others too poor to attend regular classes. They shouted *"!Viva la cultura!"* and "Long Live Education!" In a year Haya had 30,000 followers; in two years he could put 60,000 youngsters in the streets. At that time he was only about twenty-five.

Then Haya came into conflict with [President] Leguía and was exiled. There followed eight years of travel, during which Aprismo was born. First, Haya went to Panama, and then to Cuba and Mexico. He was delighted to find his theories confirmed, in that conditions in both countries resembled those in Peru closely. In Mexico he came strongly under the influence of the radical minister of education, José Vasconcelos, whose secretary he became, and of Professor Moisés Sáenz, who was then head of the Mexican Department of Indian Affairs, and who now, by an odd turn of the wheel, is Mexican ambassador in Lima. Haya went on to New York, and then—like all radical intellectuals in those days—to Moscow. He spent four months in Russia, and met Lunacharsky, Trotsky, and Stalin. He did not become a

Communist; indeed, he told Trotsky that communism could never flourish in Latin America. His health broke down, and he spent some months in Switzerland; later he visited Italy and finally England, where he studied at the London School of Economics and Ruskin College, Oxford.

This was the happiest time of his life, he says. He made a living as a journalist, worked in economics and anthropology, and developed the Apra program. He returned to the United States in 1927, lectured at Harvard and Williamstown, and went on to Mexico. He was getting closer to home. He proceeded to Guatemala, and was promptly deported (as he has been deported once from Switzerland); on arrival in Panama he was arrested by Canal Zone police and packed aboard the first boat out. It happened to be bound for Bremen, so Haya, with only tropical clothing, found himself in Germany, penniless, in the middle of winter. He got a job teaching Spanish in Berlin, and stayed there for three years. Then came the 1930 revolution against Leguía in Peru, and Haya reached home at last.

Haya stood for an emancipated Peru in a modern world, as against the hard-bitten conservatism of the old regime. He was a radical; he was called a "Communist" (which he isn't); against him the forces of reaction brought every pressure they could to bear. Haya had no practical political experience, and his long absence from Peru was a handicap. He was a dreamer and an idealist; he abhorred bloodshed and violence; he might have seized power by force of arms, but he would not do so. There is a touch of Gandhi in Haya, and also a touch of Jawaharlal Nehru, that other friend of other Indians.

The government of that fierce little *cholo* Sánchez Cerro did not mind bloodshed, however. After Haya was arrested in 1932—the twenty-seven Aprista deputies were arrested too, some of them on the floor of Congress—the Apristas in Trujillo, Haya's home city, revolted in protest. The army, navy, and police proceeded to clean up Trujillo, and some *six thousand* Apristas, mostly young men, were rounded up and executed. Thousands more were jailed. Even today, under the much milder Prado government, several thousand political prisoners, mostly Apristas, are still in jail, and perhaps a thousand others are in exile. One Aprista exile—the Prado government did not like it much—won a $2,500 Latin American prize novel contest in the United States in 1941.

Practically everyone in Peru, at one time or other, has sought to buy Haya de la Torre, but without success. In 1930, on his way back to Peru, when it seemed certain that he would become president, representatives of big American business offered to bribe him to be "reasonable." In the 1936 election Benavides twice offered Haya "guarantees" if he would drop his opposition to the government candidate, Jorge Prado. Haya demanded freedom for Aprismo first. In 1939 he sent an open letter to all the candidates, suggesting creation of a National Union party under some compromise leader. But the government would pay no attention.

The Aprista program is difficult to sum up, to define. Haya is an idealist, with a long-range view, and though his idealism has remained constant, his views have altered with the years. In general, it may be said that he stands today for three things: First, liberation and education of the Indians, and their incorporation into the life of the state. Second, intra-American unity, close friendship with the United States, and eventual coalescence of Latin America into one country. Third, social progress. Haya is not a Marxist or even a socialist—the Communists detest him and attack him fiercely—but he believes in land reform and restrictions on foreign and local capital.

Haya has always disliked imperialism, and for a long time he was outspokenly anti-American. He felt no bitterness against the American people, but he feared and distrusted North American policy vis-à-vis Latin America. He talked the familiar dreary subject of "Yankee imperialism" and a major tenet in his program was "internationalization of the Panama Canal." Until the canal was made the common property of all the Americans, he felt, the hemisphere states could never be more than puppets of the North American "colossus."

Today—note well—Haya's attitude toward the United States has completely changed. He is no longer anti-American. He explains that it is not he who has altered his convictions but the United States that has transformed its policy. He is an ardent admirer of President Roosevelt, the "Good Neighbor." But whatever is responsible for the shift, it has occurred. Haya and the Aprista movement have undergone conversion. They are no longer anti-United States, but vigorously pro-United States.

One factor in this conversion is, of course, Adolf Hitler and the Nazi menace to Latin America. Haya may not like Yankee imperialism very much, but he has enough political sense to realize that it is far better for Peru than Nazi imperialism would be. The Nazi-Fascist success in Europe opened Aprista eyes. The specter of Hitlerism over Europe, of Hitlerism marching toward South America, frightened the Apristas into common sense. Haya de la Torre is violently anti-Nazi. Therefore, a realist, he is pro-American.

If Haya should ever happen to read this book, he will be annoyed with me because I use the term "Latin America." He prefers a locution that he invented—"Indo-America." This derives from his preoccupation with the Indians, his fondness for the submerged Indian mass. "We should not be ashamed to be called Indo-Americans," he says. He thinks that "Latin America" is a misnomer, and that "Hispano-America" is impossible. Similarly he dislikes the term "Pan-Americanism," which has an imperialist touch that worries him. He prefers "Intra-Americanism."

Haya's philosophy of history derives partly from a belief in continental groups. In the Middle Ages we had small feudal states, he says; then came the emergence and growth of powerful competitive nationalisms; in the future we shall see a *continental* conception of politics, he hopes. Thus comes his vision of a United South America cooperating with the United States to the north. He hates frontiers. He hates limited nationalism. He believes that most frontiers are meaningless, and he points out that almost everywhere in Latin America, frontiers are drawn through uninhabited regions, on empty or nearly empty soil; they exist only as lines on maps, with no human or political reality. He says, "No country is an island." He says, "We must learn to think in *continental* terms."

As to other elements in his program, Haya believes that the Americans must work together for economic betterment. "I am not against capital as such," he told me. "I simply believe that we should control it, instead of letting it control us. I am not even against foreign capital. We must simply make it more useful to us." He thinks that continuation of the Good Neighbor policy is essential, but that no permanent good neighborliness is possible between someone very rich and someone very poor. Therefore we should make every effort, he feels, to build a new and better economic basis between North and South America.

Every time I saw Haya he was at pains to talk about the German, the Italian, and the Japanese menace to the hemisphere, especially to Peru and its close neighbors. He adduced figures and produced maps. He even drew maps. I have one before me as I write, scrawled with his pencil, showing how Iquitos on the Amazon—where Peru, Ecuador, Colombia, and Brazil meet—might become the focus of German penetration. So much for Haya, who is incomparably the most interesting living Peruvian. It is a pity his life is being so largely wasted.

---

10. Arnulfo Arias: The Personality of a Populist ◆ J. Conte Porras

Born into a poor rural family in 1901, Arnulfo Arias managed to get a good education in Panama and eventually graduated from Harvard Medical School. Following in his brother Harmodio's footsteps, he entered politics in the late 1920s and lived them intensely until his death in 1988. The U.S. ambassador wrote, "Politics is in his blood." He ran for president five times, was elected three times, and was deposed by the military three times.

From J. Conte Porras, *Arnulfo Arias Madrid* (Panama: By the author, 1980), 50–55. Reprinted by permission of the author.

He served two and one half years as president, spent two years in jail, and lived in exile for fifteen years. The most successful vote-getter ever to arise in Panama, he was a populist in the mold of Perón, Haya de la Torre, and Velasco Ibarra. His party, called the Panameñista, was little more than a personal vehicle for its leader's career. Yet his credo of Panameñismo struck sympathetic chords in the hearts and minds of a majority of the citizens. This passage is excerpted from a biography that reveals the negative side of the populist leader.

A s to Arnulfo Arias, we should say he was a very unusual specimen. He was raised in the home of rural smallholders yet . . . his education transformed him into a distinguished member of urban society in the capital. We should emphasize that he mimicked and fit in with people associated with the elite Union Club, just like his older brother [Harmodio]. . . .

Upon studying the characteristics of Arnulfo's personality, we could say that at all times he exhibited a great sense of self-confidence, perhaps too much in those moments when threatening signs appeared all around him.

He was unforgiving toward his adversaries, whom he attacked energetically even when he was out of favor, and he did not hesitate to attack them when he was in power. His entire life was a demonstration of fearlessness, daring, and confrontation.

He had the ability to confuse his enemies during moments of crisis, using accusations and provocative statements. His capacity to overcome obstacles rests on his intransigence, which has given him the image and status of a gladiator. Still, his inability to conduct a dialogue kept him from settling conflicts that arose while he was in public office.

In all of his public acts, he displayed a persistent vocation for holding power at any cost, and when he was president he demanded autocratic powers. For many, Arnulfo Arias underwent a mental alteration when he gained power, so much so that he was accused of megalomania and paranoia.

Impulsive, often unthinking, he was not one to hide his passions. His decisions were spontaneous, regardless of the conflicts they might generate. In all his acts as leader he remained unmoved by the enthusiasm of his supporters, yet he could be aggressive and demeaning toward important collaborators.

The people who worked closely with him knew that Arnulfo did not want rivals. His leadership strategy included constant changes in staff.

An outstanding characteristic of his personality was knowing how to make the most out of his condition as persecuted victim. He also denounced administrative disorder.

As an individual, he was convinced of his own predestination for power, and he was able to wait cautiously. He also knew how to strike at his enemies when they were vulnerable.

Arnulfo believed in astrological influences, and because of his mysterious contacts with magicians, witches, and fortune-tellers there emerged a body of fantastic rumors about his private life that, nevertheless, he has been able to incorporate advantageously into his political persona.

Arnulfo was a contradictory man, yet he never worried about these contradictions, nor even about correct pronunciation and grammar.

He was a man of huge talents and a great seismologist of the public mood, who commanded the loyalties of the masses. Neither attribute was based upon his oral abilities, however, because his speeches and statements were often masterpieces of incoherence, despite the usual loud applause they received.

Another characteristic of his strategy was to conduct campaigns "against" certain things, and even when this led to terrible conflicts with other leaders, it usually won the unthinking support of the masses.

---

11. Arnulfo Arias: The Greatest Actor ◆ U.S. Embassy, Panama City

After a strong, probably victorious, showing in the 1948 presidential election in Panama, Arnulfo Arias was eventually sworn in. His tumultuous second term saw the constitution replaced, friends jailed, and unbridled corruption unchecked. He was overthrown by the military in May 1951. The following excerpts from dispatches from the U.S. embassy in Panama City to Washington reveal facets of the leader's personality.

Obarrio [comptroller general] stated that Arnulfo was certainly a most colorful, spectacular, and even charming individual. He thought that if Arnulfo would go to Hollywood, write a book of his life, enter the movies, etc., he would be in his element and would assure himself of a fortune financially. Obarrio referred to Arnulfo as the greatest actor he had ever known or heard of. He said that the courage and control of nerves which Arnulfo showed during the trial on Friday [on charges of murdering a presidential guard] was really beyond the imagination of anyone who was not there to witness his conduct firsthand. He said that Arnulfo was most

From U.S. embassy dispatch to Department of State, June 1951, National Archives, Washington, DC.

self-composed, smiled and spoke to all alike, and even at times when derogatory remarks were being showered at him, or when orange peels and bottle caps were being thrown at him, he showed no concern and kept smiling through it all. Obarrio believes that Arnulfo will some day return to the presidency of Panama with the same glamor and the same support with which he has entered on two previous occasions. . . .

Obarrio said he had worked closely with Arnulfo on many occasions but had never understood him; that there were times when Arnulfo appeared sane and sound and was able to talk man to man and on a very reasonable basis, but that right in the midst of such discussions Arnulfo occasionally appeared to go off on a tangent and take an impossible position and refuse to listen to anyone. Both Obarrio and his wife believe that Arnulfo suffers from a mental defect. They have no evidence to confirm the many rumors going about that Arnulfo has long been a dope fiend. . . .

[A year later Dr. Harmodio Arias] spoke of the role of his brother, Arnulfo. He stated, with obvious sincerity, that he had no information whatsoever with regard to the latter's plans during the electoral period. He then remarked that Arnulfo's surprise move in ordering his followers to boycott the elections had demonstrated an extraordinary degree of discipline among Arnulfo's followers. Indeed, he expressed surprise over the great extent to which they had followed their leader. Though their relations at present are far from close, Dr. Arias spoke with obvious pride of the continuing political authority of his brother. I mentioned to Dr. Arias that I had seen an item in one of the newspapers that Dr. Arnulfo Arias was dedicating his efforts to the eventual calling of a constituent assembly. Dr. Arias appeared quite startled and exclaimed, "That would be very dangerous! A constituent assembly in a country like Panama with all its present passions and hatreds could have terrible consequences."

---

12. Velasco Ibarra: "Give Me a Balcony and I Will Return to the Presidency" ◆ John D. Martz

Colorful, enigmatic, utterly without ideological guile, José María Velasco Ibarra was a constant figure in Ecuadorean politics between the 1930s and 1970s. The political elite faced a dilemma: they could not rule the country with him, yet they could not rule it without him either. Professor Martz

From John D. Martz, *Politics and Petroleum in Ecuador* (New Brunswick, 1987), 76–80, footnotes omitted. © 1987 by Transaction Publishers. Reprinted by permission of Transaction Publishers.

considers his subject a caudillo but, as indicated in this essay, Velasco is best seen as a consummate populist.

From the time of his second presidency in the 1940s, Velasco set a pattern which was difficult to emulate. "His unquestioned talent for building widespread national support has been equaled by an inability to provide constructive leadership once having assumed power. Each time Velasco has aroused popular passions, he has broadened the base of support for the political system, and has then brought progressive disillusionment with both his own leadership and with the efficacy of national government." His populistic technique was described by an eminent Ecuadorean historian during his fourth administration in the following language:

> Velasco possesses the technique of a fighting preacher, with sober movements of the body, mobility in the hands, accusing right index finger, admonishing, penetrating, or brusque movements, a large mouth, his head erect and inclined backwards. When there is a great exaltation, he ends up moving around a flood of words, from which he emerges with difficulty, amid a multiplication of insults at times, but at other times recovering with slow sentences, sudden acceleration, or with triumphal exclamations.

True to our ideologically restricted definition of populism, Velasco was changeable as to program and orientation. He himself gave some measure of his outlook in these words:

> The most important thing that I have tried to do is to create in the Ecuadorean people a pride in being an autonomous, sovereign nation, free and with its banner tested in the forge of battle and ready to endow a collective national entity with its own soul, with its own personality, with dignity and with its own ideas. The most important thing I have done is to try to awaken national optimism, to try to awaken the civic spirit of the nation, to try to convince the Ecuadorean people that they are masters of their own destiny in internal politics and that they are autonomous and sovereign in the realm of international politics.

Consequently, his political stance could and did vary through the years. Quintero's penetrating study demonstrated convincingly that Velasco's initial victory in 1934 was the product of elitist support and votes from traditionalist sources of both Sierra and Coast. "In short, peeling back the populist label to look at the social undergrowth reveals virtually no populism at all."

The leadership role of Velasco from the 1930s on was seen by the oligarchic sectors as a skillful if manipulative means of channeling the urban masses away from social protest. If *Velasquismo* displayed a populist style and appeal, it never constituted a challenge to traditional Ecuadorean power centers. Rather, "it responded to particular conjunctures of economic and political crisis, in which a precarious state of political equilibrium among different sectors of the dominant classes could only be maintained by an 'independent' force that did not openly identify with any one of them." Moreover, this lack of political or economic identification was seen in the absence of clear economic policy. Perhaps most accurately of all, it must be said that Velasco saw Ecuador's problems as not of an economic but of a moral nature.

Velasco consistently reiterated his scorn for political parties throughout his career. He maintained that such organizations were narrow, partisan, and sectarian. Only he could stand aloof as the representative of the entire nation. This attitude permitted him, as during the 1968 presidential campaign, to scorn the adornment of an official platform, which he described as part and parcel of the selfishness of parties. As *El Comercio* remarked shortly before the initiation of his third government, Velasco, as Ecuador's permanent caudillo, was "doubtlessly the man nearest the masses. Like them, he acts emotionally. . . . This is the secret of his success, apart from his extraordinary personal magnetism. On two occasions he has been the Man of Providence for the country. Both times he failed . . . caught in the net of his own contradictions." All of this meant, of course, that the *Velasquista* organization foundered after each electoral campaign.

His first brief term in the 1930s had not been populist, nor was his political appeal seemingly different from that of other national leaders. By 1940, however, he had built a personal following which fed his supporters' fervor. He also insisted that his loss that year to Arroyo del Río was the result of fraud perpetrated by Arroyo's fellow Liberal Andrés F. Córdova, the interim chief of state. Despite incomplete evidence, this claim kept the caudillo's name before the people. His 1944–1947 administration, created through major popular upheaval and massive disturbances, more fully demonstrated his personal appeal. His inconsistencies in policy and program also became apparent, with Velasco responding to sentiment, opinion, and political pressures of the moment. The plethora of works on Velasco and his career have differed somewhat on the question of his doctrine, but the majority have contended that there was no true ideological commitment in his makeup.

If political doctrine is conceived of as incorporating concrete policy commitments, Velasco was not nondoctrinaire. However, the proposals and programs shifted more than once through the years. His 1944–1947 tenure, for instance, began with the backing of the Socialists and other leftists, speaking of major reforms; toward the end he had swung to the Right while unleashing official repression against leftists. His third passage through office (1952–1956) was marked by more traditional pledges to improve education, increase public works, and of course rectify the many alleged shortcomings of his predecessor. In 1960 he again excoriated the outgoing president—his former minister of government, Camilo Ponce—but responded to the coming of the Cuban Revolution by espousing the rhetoric of basic structural transformations. In his fifth term . . . he was overwhelmed from the outset by an array of economic problems which he confronted only on a piecemeal basis. Velasco's own occasional statements that he was a liberal, but attuned to eighteenth-century dogma, did little to clarify his doctrinal position.

If Velasco at different times therefore espoused the rhetoric of both traditionalism and of change, the record itself gave the lie to innumerable promises to liquidate the privileged and to "pulverize the plutocracy." *Velasquista* policies fell well within the parameters of political traditionalism, whatever the distinctive personalistic flair. Generally gaining his greatest electoral support from the Coast—although himself a native *serrano*—Velasco drew ample financial backing from precisely those oligarchical sectors against which he railed in public. During campaigns he brought together a political organization which included affiliates of students, workers, women, and assorted regional groups. Yet his antiparty bias never wavered, and once ensconced in the presidential chair, he ignored organizational matters with cavalier disdain. The political Ecuador he had first known as a young politician was one in which, by stumping the country, he could reach significant numbers of voters.

Despite inconsistencies and contradictions, then, Velasco's qualities included: an antitraditionalist rhetoric which usually defied actual policies; doctrinal shifts and readjustments in light of current opinion; skill at capturing the electorate but an inability to retain its loyalties; administrative incompetence which made delegation of authority impossible; an inability to place his trust in even the closest confidants for more than a brief time; and a personal morality and integrity accompanied by a total blindness to the corruption which enveloped his administrations. A populist in style, whose programs themselves were not effectively populistic and whose career was generously if irregularly funded by oligarchical interests, José María Velasco Ibarra was at his best when standing above the crowds, addressing his beloved *chusma*. His speeches were intended less to be understood rationally than to be shared emotionally. Oratory was intended less to expound ideas than to provoke the emotions. Velasco was less the politician than the providential savior.

An intelligent and well-read visionary, Velasco looked to the future rather than the present, carrying along his audiences. If the present were unpleasant, far better to paint word pictures of what lay ahead. Whereas many *Velasquistas* through the years enriched themselves while in power,

Velasco himself remained a poor man, recognized by the populace for temperamental and political austerity. If he was never the salvation of the people, his messianic public image as a redeemer battling the very interests which in effect he represented and his magnetic public appearances in pretelevision days were unrivaled. His legendary phrase, "Give me a balcony and I will return to the presidency," was more fact than myth. It was to carry him through more than four decades of political prominence, during which time Ecuadorean politics was never free from his moralizing influence and mesmerizing presence.

Suggestions for Further Reading

Cardoso, Fernando Henrique, and Enzo Faletto. *Dependency and Development in Latin America*. Chap. 4. Berkeley: University of California Press, 1979.

Conniff, Michael L., ed. *Latin American Populism in Comparative Perspective*. Albuquerque: University of New Mexico Press, 1982.

Hennesy, Alistair. "Latin America." In *Populism: Its Meaning and National Characteristics*, edited by Guita Ionescu and Ernest Gellner. New York: Macmillan Company, 1969.

Mouzelis, Nicos. "On the Concept of Populism: Populist and Clientelist Modes of Incorporation in Semiperipheral Politics." *Politics and Society* 14:3 (1985): 329–48.

Tella, Torcuato di. "Populism and Reform in Latin America." In *Obstacles to Change in Latin America*, edited by Claudio Veliz. New York: Oxford University Press, 1965.

V

Images of Women

Gertrude Yeager

What image comes to mind when we think of Latin American women? Until the 1960s, Carmen Miranda, a Brazilian singer made famous by Hollywood in the 1940s, sang and danced in a headdress of fruit and defined Latinas for most North Americans. The more sophisticated observer turned to literature rather than to the movies, but here, too, women were reduced to culturally inspired but predictable types—the saintly, suffering mother or the sultry señorita with flashing eyes and garish clothes. In the 1960s a gun-toting Tania, blonde sidekick of Che Guevara, replaced Carmencita for the generation of student revolutionaries. Early serious studies of Latin American women written in the 1970s created a new image in which the haggard peasant woman, victimized not only by sexism but also by international capitalism, became the slave of slaves. Because popular images and stereotypes contain a kernel of truth, they can serve as the starting point for historical investigation.

This essay and the selection of documents that follows suggest not only how such visions came to be but also how women may be incorporated into the region's history, a process that should lead to more complexity and, one hopes, to greater understanding. If the essay is a recipe for Latin American women's history, then consider the documents as the ingredients. They let women tell their own history. And because education has not reached all of them, sometimes they may express themselves in ways that traditional scholarship has ignored.

Latin American history has always included women, provided that they conformed to accepted types. The Spanish conquistador may not, like the Puritan, have brought his wife, but he was not without female companionship. In Mexican history, Malinche, the indigenous translator and mistress of Hernando Cortés, became the symbolic mother of a mestizo race. Sor Juana Inés de la Cruz, a Carmelite nun, long has been recognized as Mexico's first intellectual, while the Virgin of Guadalupe has symbolized and protected the Mexican people since the 1600s. When the wife came (and she did come because the Spanish government instituted laws that were profamily and protected legal wives and heirs), her social class determined her life-style. She frequently presided over a large household that included members of the extended family, servants, slaves, and even her husband's illegitimate offspring. In the absence of male relatives she could manage property and amass wealth; widowhood gave her independence.

Because marriages were arranged and could take place only between persons of equal status, many women did not marry and entered convents whether or not they had a religious vocation (Doc. 4). In the privacy of the cloister they could perfect their spirituality and develop their administrative skills, or, as in the case of Sor Juana, their intellects. Others lived in luxurious apartments and simply amused themselves with theatrical and musical performances. As collective communities the convents wielded large amounts of money, thereby permitting them to play an important role in the colonial economy, although their essential role was to remove excess women from society.

The modern period in Latin American history coincided with the time when women in Western societies had the fewest number of options available to them. The Enlightenment idealized a domestic role for them and glorified the innocent, uneducated heroine. It is little wonder that women spent the next two hundred years enlarging the social space assigned to them. They had to win the right to equal education, for it was the key to the liberal professions and to suffrage. To create public roles, they combined traditional behavior, a model of femininity based on the Virgin Mary, and liberalism, which championed individual freedom and development and took hold in the region with the establishment of republican states.

How is women's history different? The first noticeable difference in the historiography is a lack of watersheds, that is, historically significant dates or events, that clearly mark fundamental change in the lives of Latin American women. A second difference is the nature of the sources. Women left fewer records because they wrote less and had little contact with government bureaucracies, the traditional sources for the historian. While both characteristics are true of women's history in general, they also reflect a paucity of scholarship on the nineteenth century, a result of the generally poor record keeping throughout the region during that period. Thus, the problems in women's history begin with finding documents and establishing issues that could lead to the discovery of historical watersheds and significant debates.

Although political rights eluded them until the midtwentieth century, Latin American women participated in national political life, especially in times of great turmoil, from independence to the present. Despite their considerable efforts and success in carving out social roles, they have remained invisible in traditional historiography until the 1970s. Here is a clear case of how the laws of documentary elitism have kept women out of history because they have not occupied positions of recognized importance, they have not generated records, and records have not been kept on their activities. When women are included, they often become romantic heroines or legendary Amazons (Docs. 1 and 6). The region has produced effective female leaders such as Eva Perón or Rigoberta Menchú who have become international figures, but they are exceptions. To include Latin American women in history often involves the use of nontraditional sources such as the poetry written by promoters of Salvadorean literacy (Doc. 7), or the Chilean *arpilleras* of appliqué and embroidery made by shantytown women in Santiago (see photographs). Protesting with needles and yarn, these anonymous artists depicted the daily life of the people and thus alerted the international community to the inhumanity of the Augusto Pinochet regime, which outlawed the sale of this political handiwork. It also may require a gender perspective to understand why the Mothers of the Plaza de Mayo chose to protest the barbarism of their government when fellow Argentines kept silent (Doc. 8).

The documents included here sample the forms of female political expression in modern Latin America. Political protest divides along class lines. Denied education, women from the popular classes have frequently voiced their concerns through action. Their wants and desires are associated with subsistence issues: food, housing, and protection of the family. Unlike the anonymous heroines of the past, contemporary women have the opportunity to tell their own stories (Docs. 3 and 9). As testimonies become part of the historical record, women should have a better chance of finding their way into history. Educated elite women have used the press effectively since the nineteenth century to pursue a reform agenda based on middle-class values such as expanded educational opportunities, the right to vote, and social reform (Doc. 2). However, they have been ignored until recently for two reasons: their elite status has been problematic for some scholars committed to a history of the oppressed, and their works have not been saved or made available through new editions. Except for Sor Juana, few intellectual histories or literary anthologies include references to female writers. Again, the reason for this omission is lack of education. When coupled to narrow life experience, poor education produced literature deemed unworthy of the national canon.

Restoring women to the region's history began in earnest about fifteen years ago and subsequently has become one of the most important tasks of contemporary scholarship. These early studies introduced analytical concepts

The Soup Kitchen (*arpillera*). Photograph by Harriet Blum; from a private collection, New Orleans

Women United for Democracy (*arpillera*). Photograph by Harriet Blum; from a private collection, New Orleans

that guide subsequent research. Although the history of Latin American women has followed in general the course of women's evolution elsewhere, the area's culture introduced noticeable variants. One is *marianismo*, a strong identification with the symbol of the Virgin Mary and an internalization of the female behavior associated with her. The Marianist model of femininity is that of the mother who protects the weak and offers comfort and refuge. In behavior she is submissive, suffering, and self-sacrificing, but she is also active because the Catholic tradition permitted her to exercise moral and spiritual authority and provided a source of empowerment. Most Catholic countries have similar traditions, but the Latin American version is more pronounced.

Marianismo complements machismo, a culture of exaggerated maleness normally associated with aggressive virility, dominance, and sexual prowess. Concubinage continues to the present day because the Latin American patriarchy permits a man the sexual license to maintain relations with several women in order to validate his manliness. It is not uncommon in many of the region's countries for a man, regardless of social class, to support two or more families. Such relations frequently cross class and racial lines and involve a man of wealth or social position with a woman from humbler origins.

Frequently, Latin American women have become politically active by enlarging or extending the female sphere of influence—the home—to society at large and by assuming the role of mother in the public forum. They essentially "mother" society. In the nineteenth century, Latin American women politicized motherhood and redefined its functions as social and public rather than familial and private. By arguing that mothers were society's first teachers, nineteenth-century women increased available educational opportunities. Recently, Chileans and Argentines used motherhood and moral power derived from the Marianist model to oppose dictatorship. They did not oppose the government for abstract reasons such as "freedom" or "liberty"; they only wanted to know the whereabouts of missing family members. They only wanted a few extra pesos to put food on the table.

Finally, class, the direct result of the continuing presence of social structure based on hierarchy and the historic inequality of income and resource distribution found throughout the region, cannot be divorced from this study. Elite women enjoy all the comforts and benefits of both developed and underdeveloped society. They are often well educated and may work if they wish. In Chile, for example, medicine, dentistry, and architecture traditionally have been professions open to women since the early years of this century because they have a nurturing or artistic dimension and combine nicely with family life. An elite woman goes to work confident that her maid will manage the house, cook the meals, and care for her children. At the other end of the social scale the peasant woman lives without water or other modern conveniences. She takes her children with her to the market or to the field; and because the family needs money, she frequently sacrifices their future to subsist in the present.

Readers should continually test the validity of these existing generalizations upon which these women's history rests and develop new ones. What do women value? Are Latin Americans really different from women elsewhere? Do existing explanations of political phenomena (networking, economic interests, class) exclude women from history as effectively as does the lack of documents? For example, one measure of a political movement is its ability to sustain itself, yet women often leave politics when specific goals have been achieved. Indeed, women in politics complain that their agendas are littered with domestic issues—child care, health care, and education—that ignore larger social concerns.

In the nineteenth century, women in Europe and the Americas organized temperance leagues to protest alcohol abuse because women and children were being beaten by drunken husbands and fathers who spent their salaries on liquor rather than on food (Doc. 5). Today, women have organized Mothers against Drunk Driving (MADD) in much the same spirit. In the case of the Mothers of the Plaza de Mayo and the Chilean *arpilleristas*, they marched and stitched to learn the fate of their children and grandchildren, raise awareness, and earn extra pesos. Their actions easily could become nothing more than future historical anecdotes: interesting but unimportant because of a lack of long-term vision, ideology, or gripping ideas.

---

1. La Pola: Colombian Patriot ◆ María Currea de Aya

This document is doubly interesting. It sketches the life of a Colombian heroine and belongs to a series written by women and designed as a part of the World War II propaganda effort to mobilize female support of President Franklin D. Roosevelt's Good Neighbor policy. Is the depiction of gender roles and the romanticization of La Pola part of the propaganda effort, or do they reflect attitudes about women common in the 1930s? Is she a prototype for female revolutionaries in the twentieth century?

From July 20, 1810, onward, the natives of New Granada, weary of enduring Spanish tyranny, began to organize armies and to undertake a determined and bloody struggle. One of the many enthusiasts for the

From María Currea de Aya, "Policarpa Salavarrieta (Colombia)," *Bulletin of the Pan American Union* (October 1939): 583–85.

patriots' cause was Joaquín Salavarrieta, a Spanish Basque whose surname in the Basque tongue means "House of Beautiful Columns." His parents were Don Francisco Salavarrieta and Doña Eulalia Morales. He married Doña Mariana Ríos, the daughter of Don Francisco Ríos and Doña Bárbara Chamorro, who was of pure Spanish lineage like himself.

We do not know what ambitions, what circumstances or desires moved Joaquín and Mariana to make their home first in the flourishing city of Mariquita and then in Guaduas, a small tropical town where the single street was bordered with humble thatched houses, hidden under the shade of oranges and *guaduas*, the American bamboo which so sways at every impulse of the wind and which has given its name to the town.

There, in a household where the traditions and customs of faraway Spain were kept intact, Policarpa was born on January 26, 1795, and was baptized with the name of one of her Spanish grandmothers. She was one of seven children who, like so many other Spaniards born in the New World, as they grew up felt the desire to free their land from Spanish domination. Policarpa, who was known as "La Pola," passionately embraced the cause of the patriots, and efficiently helped them by carrying messages between the army camps. Already a woman grown, she persuaded many, with her facility of speech and the charm of her race, to take up arms and join the rebels.

In 1816 the Viceroy Sámano resolved to suppress the revolutionary movement with an iron hand. In that year the Salavarrieta family went to Santa Fe de Bogotá; and La Pola, still in communication with the patriots, took advantage of the fact that she was little known in the city to continue her services as courier, accompanied by one of her brothers. On foot and on horseback she used numberless subterfuges and disguises and for a time successfully avoided falling into the enemy's power. She was tall, dark, slender, with large black eyes and a fine provocative mouth; and her wit and intelligence drew the admiration of all who knew her.

A valiant revolutionary, also tall and dark, of Spanish ancestry, fell deeply in love with her and asked her to be his wife. His name was Alejo Sabaraín and La Pola returned his love. But she would not be married until after the victory of the patriot cause. It was a fleeting, idyllic romance, which slipped by in an atmosphere of expectation and of mystery, the two principals knowing the while that they were surrounded by danger and by war, destined to end in tragedy.

Spanish espionage was most active. A certain Iglesia, of whom we know only that he was a fierce and cruel persecutor of the patriots, was a subaltern, but he was offered promotion to an officer's rank if he could find the society or group which, so cleverly organized, was sending communications to the enemy. He suspected La Pola and pursued her with great determination, but for some time was unable to discover her whereabouts.

It was market day. The hilly streets of Bogotá began to fill with people from the country. At the corner of the house which the Salavarrietas occupied was a shop with a great leathern door and a stone post. There, Iglesia hid himself. The wait was not long, for soon there passed the boy who accompanied Policarpa on her trips to the encampments and of whom Iglesia was suspicious. He was told by the shopkeeper that the boy was La Pola's brother and, following him, discovered where they lived. Later he called guards who surrounded the house; he then notified La Pola that she was a prisoner. She, with her usual keenness, made a sign to her brother to burn all her correspondence, thus preventing the names of patriots and secrets of the revolution from falling into Spanish hands.

Her captors took her to the Colegio del Rosario, then converted into a prison. They told her to denounce her companions, which she loftily refused to do. A few days later they read to her the sentence of the Council of War, signed by the Viceroy Sámano, which condemned her to death, together with eight companions, among them Sabaraín, her fiancé. With perfect calmness and serenity she asked that they let her bid him farewell and that they send a priest to her since she wished to receive the last Sacrament. Then, with a woman's coquetry, she begged the grace of not being clad in penitential sackcloth for her execution, as was the custom of the time.

It was dawn on November 17, 1817. The sun, on rising above the hills of Monserrate, shone upon a row of nine scaffolds in the northwest part of the Plaza Mayor, today known as the Plaza Bolívar. In that time of continual executions, the sorrow of the city was increased by the processions of the condemned who, arrayed in black sackcloth, passed through the principal streets, repeating aloud the prayers of the dying, accompanied by the funereal tolling of a multitude of bells.

La Pola had braided her black hair and, having been given permission not to dress in sackcloth, chose the most beautiful of her blouses and a wide skirt which fell in graceful folds. She covered her head with a black triangular shawl and, erect and with perfect naturalness, as if she were just going for a walk, traversed the distance from the prison to the Plaza Mayor. She spoke to the people who sadly crowded about her path and told them that it was necessary to continue the struggle for independence; execrating the Spaniards, she asked vengeance for their victims. She mounted the scaffold and from there sent her last farewell to Sabaraín. She asked for a ribbon and, with a charming gesture of modesty, she tied it about her full skirts in order that neither the wind nor the convulsions of her death agony might disarrange them. It is said that her last words were: "Indolent people! How different your fate would be if you but knew the price of liberty! But it is not too late! See how I, young and a woman, have more than enough courage to suffer death and yet a thousand deaths—and do not forget this example!"

The sacrifice of La Pola caused great disturbance and grief; the desire for liberty was inflamed anew and the patriots fought with even greater determination to attain it, until the battle of Boyacá brought liberty to the country in 1819.

---

2. The Education Debate ◆ Carolina Freyre de Jaimes

With independence won, the political agenda of elite women changed. They picked up their pens and demanded to be educated. Today their methods and demands may seem unexciting, but in the 1850s women who wrote were considered social deviants, which made writing a revolutionary act.

Some used pseudonyms to mask their identities. Others, such as Carolina Freyre de Jaimes and Teresa González de Fanning, saw educational opportunities as so crucial to women's development that they risked scorn and social ostracism to bring their message to the public arena, believing that unless women received the same education as men, they would be denied a social role. Women were considered irrational, emotional, sentimental, and therefore childlike, while the emerging social order prized reason and science. According to prevailing notions, women felt with their hearts, while men thought with their heads.

Some elite women such as the Peruvian Freyre de Jaimes espoused the international political agenda of middle-class females. Freyre de Jaimes wrote for several newspapers in Peru, Bolivia, and Argentina, and her defense of women's rights became more focused and pronounced over time. While in Lima she participated in the literary salons and associated with Juana Manuela Gorritti and Ricardo Palma. The following three selections come from her earliest editorial campaigns in support of education. In the first she considers writing as rebellion. In the second she manipulates the idea of modernization by using comparisons from the United States and Europe, the yardsticks by which Peruvians measured the pace of their own social evolution. She suggests that even Chile, Peru's poor neighbor to the south and its traditional enemy, may be more modern than her own country. And finally, in the last selection, she broadens the context and attacks Peruvian society and the antimodern values upon which it rests.

From *El Correo del Peru* (October 1, 1876; March 1872; January 27, 1872). Translations by Gertrude Yeager.

Writing as Rebellion

Women are not only permitted to write but are invited to the Club Literario (Literary Club) to present their work. No doubt the great majority of men and women have a profound aversion toward the lady writers and ridicule them mercilessly.

Why should it bother men if a woman uses her spare time to write rather than to shop? . . . No one ridicules the lawyer who studies music in his free time; it is recreation for the spirit.

A woman's education limits what she can write about.

Education and Women

Women have been admitted to the University of Vermont, all of its classes, and others in Zurich have become doctors. What do you think, ladies? Woman is weak by nature and soft by character? A woman doctor an absurdity! Education and women have never been incompatible ideas to me. . . . Some believe that to change the poetic mission of women for the prosaic occupation of men may be ridiculous.

But there are places where women exercise influence. In the United States they are teachers, journalists, and are demanding the vote. . . . They say in Chile that women administer the post office and telegraph. We need to raise woman's intelligence to the level of men through education or she will continue to be housebound.

Women are those who are called on to regenerate society; they are messengers of civilization. Lima, a great South American city, presents a very sad contrast from the moral perspective because its women lack education. It is available to those with money while ignorance reigns among the masses. The schools offer a rich and varied curriculum for the elites and intellectual misery for the more numerous poor. To form a free society we must elevate women, amplify their educational opportunities, give them professions if they need employment, and inculcate habits of work, sobriety, and good customs.

Education and Public Morality

Education and material progress make nations great. What is valuable about education in the United States and England is its cultivation of the work ethic and the early creation of independent human beings. They do not follow our vicious system. Here the tutelage of children is prolonged indefinitely. There are young people here who pass their majority without having ever seen any horizon except from their father's house or having considered any other future than that offered by his fortune, however great or little.

What benefits can result in a society where men commonly pass most of their lives, and perhaps their best years, abandoned to habitual laziness that engenders vice and is conducive to such errors as anarchy, the demoralization of the masses, and the prostitution of communities? Work is the basis of morality and order, and a powerful element of social well-being.

In Latin America, men have infinite time to live off the resources of the family. In England rich or poor families require the son to make an independent life and a contribution. The powerful and rich of Peru should follow England's example and give their sons the tools to fashion a life. Our rickety youth in the majority are soft and flabby and can hardly measure up to the forceful manliness that characterizes and distinguishes the Yankee.

---

3. To Educate Is to Liberate ◆
Teresa González de Fanning

González de Fanning, Peru's most famous woman educator, wrote about the need to modernize women's education and make it practical. After her husband died, she became an educator to support herself financially. Initially she had a difficult time making ends meet. She also was well aware of the social prejudice that Peruvians had against private schools. This piece comes from a trilogy of essays written at the end of the century, now considered a pedagogical classic.

Women must be prepared to work; out of ten who wish to marry, we do not believe it is an exaggeration to calculate that at least six will see their first gray hair without having achieved a wedding ring. . . . [Such a woman's] life is truncated and lacks purpose; the only life available is that of a *beata* [lay sister]. Society is cruel to the spinster, and women marry for convenience.

Instruction ought to be related to the aptitudes and needs of the student as well as her social position. . . . If she is rich, teach her how to manage her fortune. If she is poor, teach her how to earn her keep and become an independent person, and above all develop her personality properly so that her knowledge will never serve as an obstacle to marriage. Education for the poor is necessary to conquer life; for the rich it means freedom from long hours of idleness.

From Teresa González de Fanning, *Educación Feminina: Colección de artículos pedagógicos, morales y sociológicos* (Lima, 1898). Translated by Gertrude Yeager.

Many will recall cases of families who fell on hard times, [of women] who without resources became victims of "protectors" in the persons of a brother or priest who spent their fortunes. We must rid society of the erroneous idea that a woman who works loses social status. Work creates good results, and that includes philanthropic work. Once again, to educate women only to marry is erroneous.

---

4. The Problem with Marriage ◆ Carolina Freyre de Jaimes

Freyre de Jaimes also wrote on marriage and its customs. Arranged marriages had been part of Peruvian society from the Spanish conquest. Custom dictated that a fifteen- to twenty-year age difference between bride and groom was ideal. Freyre did not agree and stated her objections plainly in the first selection. She was also anticlerical, as were most liberals. To save the institution of marriage, she attacked the Church's monopoly over it. To her, positivist marriage should be civil or secularly based and rest on mutual respect and love.

Arranged or Forced Marriage

The problem [is] forced marriage between a girl of sixteen and a man of forty. . . . In two years her face is full of anxiety and she suffers from insomnia; he is sad, abject, and pensive. In the past two years neither Carlos nor Ella have had one single instant of happiness. Ella is passionate; she believes that she loves her husband because she is strongly moved when he looks into her eyes.

He loves her truthfully, but with a love that agitates man when trust has died. His vanity tells him that this girl should love him in a pure, disinterested, generous manner. Perish the thought; the only way to have a good marriage between one so young and one so old is if the woman is excessively virtuous and the man has not lost his lust and the purity of his first sentiments.

Marriage and Civil Registry

Marriage suffers because the Roman Catholic Church has a poor and incorrect view of women (who were associated with evil). God also

From *El Correo del Peru* (May 28, 1876; September 16 and 23, 1871; October 14, 1871). Translations by Gertrude Yeager.

created a need for the family. To quote Saint Paul, he who does not give his daughter in marriage is he who would not improve himself. Marriage is necessary according to positivism and progress because it represents the basis of social order.

Marriage is not only enjoyment and pleasure, although without sexual attraction it could not continue to function. It is the fulfillment of God's will that marriage is vital to social organization, to educate, to form an honorable society. Marriage is based on intimacy and identification, confidence, and reciprocal caring.

A man who does not have a legal capacity to marry will look for other forms of diversion. He may become a seducer. He would not love truly because he who dishonors does not love truly.

Marriage is a refuge for children and a relief from obligatory celibacy. It is the behavior of married couples which discredits marriage. The failure to complete vows tends to pervert the institution; lack of love is nothing more than mere selfishness. Adultery breaks vows and divides one flesh, but its greatest offense is that it kills love.

People who do not marry are egoists, mere passengers through life, incapable of understanding love and commitment.

---

5. Against Drunkenness ◆ *Violetas del Anahuac*

Throughout Latin America, elite women began to assume public roles in the nineteenth century. Charity work opened the door to the public sector. Using the moral superiority supplied by the Marianist model, women organized to reform society. Alcoholism was a popular topic in the late 1800s, along with opposition to the white slave trade and efforts for improved housing and sanitation. Although women saw these problems as primarily those of the lower classes, they admitted that the upper classes did not escape the evils of drink. The Violetas del Anahuac, *from which the editorial is taken, was a highly polished women's magazine; although it was published in Mexico, similar reviews appeared throughout the region beginning as early as 1850. Frequently the entire staff was female, and often the actual printing and typesetting were done by lower-class women.*

One of the initiatives that should be adopted in Mexico is the creation, at least in the main urban centers, of workshops where the journeymen who are prevented from entering their regular place of employment because of tardiness or any other reason can go and spend the day productively. In

From *Violetas del Anahuac* (Mexico) 11:7 (February 17, 1889). Translated by Daniel Castro.

Mexico it is well known that the workers whose workday is reduced for any reason spend the time going to different *pulquerías* [place where *pulque*, an alcoholic drink, was consumed]. We believe that the rules and regulations about to be adopted in some European countries could not be more appropriate, and the following ones could be easily adopted in Mexico:

1) The authorization to open a place to sell alcoholic beverages can only be given to people of proven morality, and the locale must meet certain conditions of hygiene, as well as good light and ventilation;

2) The drinking and consumption of spirits by children and young people under sixteen years of age shall be forbidden in these establishments;

3) There should be official vigilance of these establishments and the drinks being sold therein;

4) [There should be] active vigilance to avoid clandestine sales, particularly in second-class establishments; and

5) Drunkenness must be considered a crime and should not be invoked as an attenuating circumstance, under any circumstances, in the commission of a crime.

Do not label us as pretentious, if we add our weak voices to the universal uproar being raised against such a degrading vice. We are only guided by the desire to see women suffer less, because they are the targets of the excesses of their husbands or their children. Let us take the case of the worker's wife who anxiously awaits her spouse to come to the house with a week's worth of wages. In the course of the day, she will build innumerable castles in the air. She will envision thousands of projects which she will rework constantly to make the money go further. She will buy shoes for the oldest child, who is barefoot and is already going to school, and the littlest one needs a coat, because he is cold crawling on the floor (the mother cannot pick him up because of her household chores). The husband desperately needs another shirt, and whatever is left over will be used for the limited weekly budget of the home. For herself? . . . Oh, well! Next time. The hour when the husband normally comes home rolls around. He does not come . . . at half past . . . six o'clock; she feeds the children and puts them to bed, more than anything to avoid the spectacle that the father will provide soon, because undoubtedly he will be drunk, scandalously drunk. It was payday, after all!

Finally the hour arrives, no longer anxiously awaited but feared, when the head of the household appears, but in such a condition. My God! The wife does not dare say a word for fear of unleashing a storm. If she asks for the money, aside from justifying the use he found for it, he will argue that "this is why I work," and it is very much *his* to spend with his friends or in whatever way he wants.

The hapless woman can hardly find a voice to ask him if he wants to eat. He does not even answer. He throws himself on the bed and begins to shake the whole house with his loud snoring. The next day, he gives his wife what remains of his salary and leaves as if nothing had happened, as if he had fulfilled his duty as a husband and as a father.

The next Saturday, there will be a repeat performance until the wife is driven to the limit of her patience, and she will demand with harsh words. Then he will abuse her, because he has spent the week working like a dog, and he is not allowed even a single moment of leisure, and they want him to be there under all circumstances. . . . Come on!

There is a different kind of drunk. These are the middle-class ones in frock coats and top hats. Pity the clothes, as the poor would say. These *gentlemen* do not give a plugged nickel about the death of their ascendants and descendants when they have a bottle and a glass in front of them. These are the ones who drink everything from *maguey* juice to hard liquor.

I have known individuals whose mothers were dying, and, upon being informed of this, they took off running. To see her? you ask. No, to the bar, to get drunker than yesterday, and the day before yesterday, and the day before the day before yesterday. But you must give them their due: Did they not feel bad about their mother's illness?

They make *delightful* husbands. Since they are normally *well educated* people, sooner or later they will catch an unwary soul who will believe their whole story, and know that deep down they are not really bad. Although they are judged badly by the world, [a young woman] believes that she will regenerate him; she is going to become his guardian angel, and the two of them will be happy, very happy. Oh, yes, she tells herself, after studying him in depth, he has good feelings: how much tenderness is evoked by his verses, what delicate phrases he uses to express his love. No, he is not vulgar. Perhaps they have slandered him; that is it. Because he is talented, he inspires envy, and that is that. Nothing to it. I am definitely marrying him, and I shall be the happiest woman. She marries, and in effect she spends a whole year in a *honeymoon* which is the most you can ask for. But this wicked moon is so sweet (after all, it is honey) that it becomes cloying. To her? Of course not: to him. She loves him too much to be bothered by his love. He is the one who begins to be bothered, and to get rid of the cloying sweetness he begins to mix in a little alcohol, and then a bit more, and more, and more, until it happens that there is no sweetness left. Instead, every day he has a more refined taste for alcoholic beverages, and most nights he comes home in worse shape than the aforesaid worker, with a dirty frock coat and his top hat all out of shape.

When the wife sees the stultified expression and the idiotic visage of the tender lover who spoke so idyllically at courtship time, she can hardly recognize him, and she kisses her children and prays to God to free her from wishing her husband ill, but she does not always succeed.

---

6. The *Soldadera* as Mexican Amazon ◆ J. H. Plenn

Because of the absence of documents the story of the soldadera *who fought in the Mexican Revolution (1910–1920) was recorded in nontraditional sources such as legends, ballads, literature, and memories. One decade later she would become a mythic figure who performed acts of supreme heroism and sacrifice, which made her a perfect symbol for oppressed groups in the 1930s: Native Americans, the Mexican popular classes, and feminists. Others were less kind and saw her as camp follower or prostitute, whose bravery was quickly forgotten.*

War, revolution, peace—they mean very much the same thing to the *soldadera*, the heroic "soldier woman" of Mexico who accompanies her man on all his campaigns, lives with him in the barracks and out in the open, and is by his side up to his very last moment in fight, skirmish, or battle. She can easily boast of having no exact counterpart in either of the two hemispheres. Home means the cold stone or dirt floor of any barracks, usually smoky and dimly lighted from the myriad kitchen charcoal fires of the soldiers' women, or the interior or top of a freight car, part of a long, creeping train carrying the men and their women and children across the country.

In time of peace, without the excitement of the flying bullets and shouts of battle, and with no chance defiantly to fire the rifle which her dead or wounded man has dropped, the *soldadera*, maintaining her nerve and deep confident patience in spite of her miserable surroundings, is even more humanly significant in her sorrowful, tragic life, more epic in her anonymity.

Against the background of such a past and present, the future of the "Unknown Woman," following behind her man's weary shuffle or shouting shrill last-minute directions outside the gray barracks or at some forlorn railway station, rises to heroic proportions.

From J. H. Plenn, "Forgotten Heroines of Mexico," *Travel* 66:6 (April 1936): 24–27, 60.

Hardly a country today is without its heroines of war and revolution. Mexico, too, has her "Corregidora" of Independence days, and her sister of Aquiles Serdon of the Madero period, among numerous other celebrated women scattered throughout the country's long dramatic history. Yet, though Mexican women have often been eulogized for their generosity, self-resignation, and maternal kindness, the *soldadera* is one type of woman whose historical and sociological significance in Mexico is only now beginning to receive a small portion of its due recognition. It is precisely her heroic past and present which form the background of the incipient Mexican feminist movement's attempt to stress the important social role that women have played in Mexico.

Women's importance on the bellicose as well as peaceful side of life in Mexico dates back to centuries before the arrival of the white man on this continent. Among the ancient Chichimeca nomad tribes, the women used to gather on some hill and hoist a white flag as a signal that a tribal reunion was to take place there to choose a war chief. This choice of the tribe's leader was left entirely to the women. Similar responsible positions were held by women in the organization of other aboriginal race groups, such as among the Aztecs where the excessive ambition of a priestess-warrior called Malinalxoch caused the first split in the tribe during its migration through the state of Michoacán.

Mexico's colonial period, too, is replete with incidents dealing with the courage and initiative of women during times of stress, among which none is more interesting than that scarcely known, semi-mythical figure, the Mulatto Woman of Córdoba, who is said to have led an uprising of Negro slaves in New Spain during the early part of the seventeenth century. The story handed down through the years of legendary as well as historical tradition tells us that the mulatto girl was a very beautiful daughter of a Negro slave called Yanga and an unknown white woman in Córdoba, Veracruz.

One morning as she was hurrying to the village fountain to draw water before the overseer and his horses might get to it, she was overtaken by the overseer who, angered at the fact that she "presumed" to consider herself better than his horses, struck her across the face with his whip, marring her beautiful features for life. News of the occurrence quickly spread among the Negro slaves who were already chafing under the ill treatment accorded them by the European-born and Mexican-born Spanish landowners, and an insurrection broke out.

Revolt spread to other sectors of the land, including the Tepehuane Indian country in Nayarit and Durango. Although many of the Negroes eventually accepted small land grants and their freedom in return for quitting the field after about twenty-five of them, including four women, had been beheaded and their heads stuck on pikes in the main square of Mexico City, the mulatto woman, mounted on a spirited horse, continued to be the terror of the wealthy people throughout the vast district between the capital and Veracruz. She was finally captured, it seems, and turned over to the Inquisition on a charge of heresy.

Although never heard of again, rumor having it that she was quietly done away with or shipped to the Philippines, she has since become a legendary figure in Mexico, especially among the older present-day generations. She is said to have escaped from the Inquisition cell in the carriage and four [horses] which she drew on the wall, before the very eyes of the astonished jailer! Obviously, a good deal of historical truth can be picked out of the legend. Some serious Mexican historians have even hinted that in the face of the mulatto woman's apparently tragic end, Sor Juana Inés, Mexico's great poetess who was born several years later, took increasing care not to antagonize the Church authorities and abandoned her profane writings, which were admired by the entire world of European culture of that time.

But it was not until the now-famous Mexican Revolution first broke out in 1910 against the regime of Porfirio Díaz and his "Científico" cronies, that the humble Mexican woman's participation in the country's destinies as the ever-present, eternally self-sacrificing mate of the Mexican buck private became carved in bold relief on the panorama of Mexican history. She, the *soldadera*, wearing a coarse blouse and skirt, and a rebozo slung over her back holding a few bare necessities, a kitten or puppy and nearly always a baby, could be seen trudging barefooted by the side of her man, like all the other soldiers' women in the troop, or squatting on the inside or atop of a freight car. It is this type of heroic barefooted woman with the eternally bent back supporting the burden of another newborn child, trudging patiently in the dust raised by the horses' hoofs, that the celebrated contemporary Mexican painter, José Clemente Orozco, has immortalized in his fresco paintings at the National Preparatory School in Mexico City.

Two revolutionary songs which have since become famous sprang up around the theme of the warmhearted, self-resigned *soldadera*. Among Pancho Villa's soldiers, the "Adelita" ballad was a kind of battle hymn, ending with the plaint: "If someday I should battle and fall, I beg you, Adelita, not to forget me." One of the opening verses of this ballad complains: "If Adelita were only my wife, my woman, I'd buy her a dress of silk and dance with her at the barracks." At the same time, in the southern part of the country, Emiliano Zapata's peasant soldiers were singing "La Valentina"— "Here I am at your feet, Valentina: If I'm to die tomorrow, I may as well die now."

But the *soldadera* was more than just a soul mate accompanying her man and father of her child on the long weary marches and through the blood and mud of revolutionary battles. By hook or crook, she managed to get the chickens, turkeys, or pigs for their food, the *pulque* or *aguardiente* that made life seem less horrible, the playing cards to help pass the long hours between the fighting. She hesitated at nothing to get money for their food, even to plundering the dead after every skirmish. There were always a few old *tortillas* to eat, if nothing else. No war correspondent among the Villa correspondents appreciated more the warm human camaraderie prevailing in that tragic complexity than John Reed, who in one chapter of his *Insurgent Mexico* tells us:

> From the tops of the box cars, of the flat cars, where they were camped by the hundreds, the *soldaderas* and their half-naked swarms of children looked down, screaming shrill advice and asking everybody in general if they had happened to see Juan Moñeros or Jesús Hernández or whatever the name of their man happened to be. . . . One man trailing a rifle wandered along shouting that he had had nothing to eat for two days and he couldn't find his woman who made his tortillas for him and he opined that she had deserted him to go with some—of another brigade. . . . The women on the cars said "¡Válgame Dios!" and shrugged their shoulders; then they dropped him down some three-day-old tortillas and asked him, for the love he bore Our Lady of Guadalupe, to lend them a cigarette.

The *soldadera* took care of her man up to the very last minute, that is, if she really loved him. She underwent a thousand trials and hardships, walking in the dust behind her man's horse, occasionally relieving her man of his rifle which he handed down to her to carry once in a while, at times stopping on the road for a day in the company of one or two other women comrades in order to give birth, and arriving at the troop's encampment only to find her man among the newly dead after the previous day's skirmish! In which case, she saw that he was properly buried on the side of the road or in some field, and after a few days of sincere mourning, she went trudging behind someone else's horse in the dust. After all, what else could she do?

The heroism displayed by the *soldaderas* throughout different periods in Mexican history is only too well known in Mexico. Yet the protagonists are nearly always anonymous figures whose bravery and self-sacrifice are remembered over a brief span and then quickly forgotten. Instances of their courage and unselfish initiative are innumerable. One of these takes us back to the latter part of the nineteenth century during the siege of the city of Guadalajara by the famous Nayarit bandit, the "Tiger of Alicia."

General Corona was in charge of the defense of the city at a point called La Mohonera, when it was discovered that there were no more fuses for lighting the old type of cannon used. It looked as if the battle would soon be over, and the "Tiger" and his hordes would enter the country's second largest city to commit every kind of pillage and rape for which they were famous. General Corona could think of nothing to do but swear. The "old women" soon got wind of what had happened, and without a moment's hesitation they undressed and made fuses out of their clothes. It was this action that won the battle and saved the city of Guadalajara. Yet, who were these women? Today they are as unknown as the countless brave *soldaderas* whose actions won numerous battles and skirmishes for the forces with whom their men happened to be fighting during the more recent bloody period of the country's history known as the Mexican Revolution.

It was one of these women whose bravery enabled the Constitutionalist revolutionary army to capture Tampico in 1913 from the Federal troops. Four of the ablest rebel generals led the attack on the port city. But the Federals were well armed and had superior numbers. Shells and machine-gun bullets diminished the rebels' ranks considerably for seven days and nights. On the eighth day, the rebels were still in the outlying swamps, exhausted from the prolonged fighting and the burning sun. Their disheart-ened faces revealed the last depths of misery and hopelessness. Suddenly, one of the *soldaderas* grabbed a banner from a soldier and, raising it above her head with both hands, cried: "We've got to enter Tampico, no matter how. All of you who've got the nerve, follow me!" And she rushed toward the city. Everyone followed. The loss was terrific, but not any more than it had been during the first week of fighting: and Tampico was taken. Today, no one knows the name of that woman; she is simply one of the thousands of "old women" (*viejas*) who went trudging through the dust of thirteen years of fighting in almost every part of the country.

One of the most dramatic and touching examples of the bravery of the *soldadera* is told by Rafael Muñoz, the Mexican writer. The setting is at a railway station in northern Mexico.

> One morning at dawn, when only a few sleepy soldiers had come out of the quarters to squat behind the mesquites, a noisy bunch of rebels, mounted on their little scraggy horses, came racing down the only street of Villa Ahumada, breaking the air with pistol and rifle shots and *vivas* for their leader. In less than five minutes' time, they smashed into the barracks, disarmed two or three soldiers who tried to offer resistance, pumped four bullets into the mustachioed officer, and shut up all the soldiers and women in a boxcar. They stripped the soldiers of their clothes, and fifty rebels were soon wearing the dark blue uniforms and the woolen military caps. . . .
>
> A little before noon, the rebels, dressed in their newly acquired uniforms, came out of the quarters and lined up in single file next to the water tank. . . .
>
> "You know the plan, boys," their leader explained briefly, "only two of you are to get on the engine and grab the engineer. If there's a convoy of Federals on the train, don't move until the rest of us come out of the barracks firing." . . .

From afar off rose the smoke of the engine of the southbound train. The telegraph operator remained at his post under menace of a pistol held next to his face, and the rebels silently held their arms in readiness. The train was not at two kilometers' distance . . . at one . . . at five hundred meters. Suddenly, from out of the quarters a woman came running at full speed. It was Petra, one of the bravest *soldaderas* in the whole regiment. She had removed her red rebozo (shawl) and went running desperately before the oncoming train, waving the red shawl as a signal of danger. A single turn of the wheels would bring the train into the long street.

"The —! . . . Riddle her!"

Half a dozen rebels ran out of the barracks and after her. Together with those lined up in single file next to the water tank, they began to fire at her. The train stopped at the warning of the waving red rebozo and the shots of two hundred men aiming at the woman. Three minutes later, after the shooting had ended, the train moved slowly backward—saved from falling into the hands of the rebels by a brave *soldadera* who lay on the side of the track beneath her red shawl and over a puddle even redder than the rebozo with which she had stopped the train. . . .

"The —! She ruined our combination!"

Two columns—one of smoke, the other of dust—rose above the circling horizon. They came from the train that moved backward and, in another direction, from the rebel group undesirous of awaiting the arrival of more troops.

Villa Ahumada was hushed in silence. A bit later, the soldiers broke open the door of the boxcar, and came out in the open. They were in their underwear. They picked up Petra, and, since there was no cemetery there, they buried her in a corner of the jailyard.

Today the only token of respect to that courageous *soldadera*'s memory is a sign on the jailyard gate bearing the unusual admonition: "Anyone who escapes from here is a ———."

No less remarkable is the story told by the same writer of how a crowd of *soldaderas* helped win a battle for the revolutionary forces in the north by salvaging ammunition for the army's largest piece of artillery, known as the "Baby." The attack on the enemy entrenched about twenty kilometers ahead was scheduled to begin on the following morning. The "Baby" was to bombard the enemy's advance positions and hinder him from improving his entrenchments. The soldiers were away looking for a good position from which to begin the attack.

The women took refuge from the burning June sun underneath the freight cars and platforms of the military train. They fanned their small charcoal fires, clapped the ground corn between the palms of their hands in the preparation of tortillas, and set some beans to boil for their men's meal. Suddenly, the word ran down the long human chain spread between the rails that the "Baby's" ammunition was on fire. The women, several hundred of them, all sprang out from their refuge among the car wheels. Three box-cars—the first in the whole line of trains and containing ammunition for the enormous artillery piece—were wrapped in flames that had no doubt been caused by the kitchen fires improvised by the *soldaderas*.

The fire, rapidly gaining headway through the wooden walls of the box-cars, could never be extinguished by means of pails of water. And the railroad workers were asleep in the caboose coaches. Amid shouts, the women decided to remove the ammunition from the cars before it exploded. Soon the crowd of *soldaderas* was seething about the boxcars. Many climbed into the cars, dodging through the burning doors, and began to remove the boxes of ammunition.

The work was not simple, as each box containing six shells was heavy enough to require the strength of two husky men to carry. The women struggled bravely, madly. Some dragged the boxes to the doors where others would be waiting to carry them on their shoulders. The worst part of the work fell to those who had climbed into the cars. The fire had reached their clothes, singed their hair, and inflicted burns upon their bare arms and perspiring faces.

Two or three were carried away, half asphyxiated from the smoke. Their burning clothes were extinguished with sand. The fight to save the ammunition from exploding grew more and more desperate. Many of the women were almost naked in their burned clothes; others moved about with their hair singed, with blackened faces and smarting red arms. When the men returned with the "Baby," at dusk, the ammunition had been saved, the three boxcars were destroyed, and the *soldaderas* were curing their burns with lard. On the following day, while the soldiers were away driving the enemy before the "Baby's" bombardment, the women recalled the previous day's experiences and built fires away from the rails, even though they were forced to endure the terrific, scorching sun. Thanks to the artillery bombardment, the battle was soon won, and in the joy of welcoming their men back safe and sound, that night the *soldaderas* forgot their own aching bodies covered with burns, forgot their singed hair and the inhuman exertion they had undergone around the three burning freight cars.

Similar accounts of individual and collective heroism on the part of the *soldaderas* could be gathered by the hundreds. One hears of them in the most out-of-the-way spots and at the least expected moment. Undoubtedly, among the poorer people, stories about these women's courage already constitute a subconsciously appreciated tradition. Especially well known are the anecdotes centering around individual figures, most of whom are anonymous, although they have gone down in the annals of this vast oral tradition by some nickname or other. Such is the celebrated "Blonde Colonel," that strange woman whose real name was Ramona Flores and who attained the rank of chief of staff to the Constitutional general, Juan Carrasco, along with numerous special citations for bravery.

The *Coronela* was a stout, red-haired woman in her early thirties who, in spite of her bellicose inclinations, sometimes liked to dress up in black satin, although always with a shining sword at her side. Her husband is said to have been killed while he was an officer during the first (Madero's) revolution, and to have left her a gold mine, with the proceeds of which she raised a regiment and took to the field.

Yet, such cases as that of the "Blonde Colonel" are more or less unusual. The real epic figure of this class of self-sacrificing women is, outwardly, far from glamorous. Miserable living conditions, malnutrition, excessive child-bearing, and a general superabundance of the "slings and arrows of outrageous fortune" soon combine to prematurely age the young, dark-eyed, smooth ebony-haired *soldadera* from some Indian village or the poorer districts of the few large cities. Before long she is a wrinkled, barefooted, bedraggled woman surrounded by undernourished children who soon form part of the sordid army life around them. She can always be seen on her knees before the metate stone, grinding corn to make tortillas for her "man."

Due to the constant transfers, her children are denied the possibility of any schooling. No more heartrending picture could be imagined than a trainload of soldiers and their families filling the interiors of the boxcars and sprawled over the coach tops. Villa was the first man who—for military purposes, however—made inroads on this system of communal life among the soldiers. He often ordered swift, forced marches of bodies of cavalry, leaving the women behind.

Although practically all of the *soldaderas* come from the Indian and the poor mestizo classes, incidents occurring during the 1926 Catholic rebellions in the states of Jalisco and Michoacán in which a number of fanatically religious women of the upper classes participated, would seem to indicate that the heroism and abnegation of which the Mexican woman has given the world such good examples may be racial as well as social class traits.

---

7. The Soldier Woman as Poet

Salvadorean revolutionaries of the 1970s and 1980s expressed their reasons for fighting and their visions of the future in verse. They are even more anonymous than the Mexican soldadera *because the tasks they performed as*

"To You," "To Alphabetize," and "Birthday" from *On the Frontline: Guerrilla Poems of El Salvador*, trans. Claribel Alegría and Darwin J. Flakoll (Willimantic, CT, 1989), 19, 59, 71. Translation copyright Claribel Alegría and Darwin J. Flakoll. Reprinted by permission of Curbstone Press.

health and literacy agents are less dramatic, heroic, and exciting and therefore less memorable. If it were not for these short verses, their participation in the revolution might be overlooked.

To You

Hey, *compa*.
Yes, I'm talking to you
to you who don't know how to read and write.
I invite you to open with me
the door that for so many years
has been closed to you
and move out of that room
of ignorance and blindness
to learn and teach your reality.

You've walked a long road, I know,
but if you learn to read and write
you'll have walked the longest part of the road
because the more you learn
the greater will be the enemy's defeat.
No, don't feel sorry or ashamed.
On the contrary, feel proud
to free yourself and win out
against illiteracy
in the process of the
popular revolutionary war.

–Carmela, literacy teacher of the FMLN

To Alphabetize

We taught the alphabet with our
requisitioned boots and our rifles
and thus we learned the word "enemy."

We taught the alphabet with
revolutionary togetherness
sharing everything when there was nothing
and thus we learned the word "companion."

We learned the alphabet with
silent stubborn teachers
and with errors
through rivulets, pathways, roads, and trails
and thus we learned the word "Guinda."*

Today, August 14, 1984, we teach the alphabet
for the first time with pencil and paper
and we will learn all the words
we have thus far carried in our hearts:
"Victory," "Love."

—Karla, health worker and literacy teacher

Birthday

It's not easy to live 35 years
when death has become so cheap.
Outside, the informer on your trail
assembles your data: age, color of skin,
height, family relations.
Here at the front
an instant of combat
a hard-luck bomb
a rocket
may await you any minute.
Sometimes it's not easy
to pick your way through inner storms
separated from your affections
harmonizing the interests of all
with petty individual interests.
It's not easy to keep on
to love lovingly all corners of all rooms
all the evenings,
but sometimes it is
sometimes when you know you share a huge sun
with all the universe
an irresistible force that demolishes borders
that unites voices in a single hymn,
sometimes it's as easy as can be.

—Lety, political educator

*Guinda: the massive withdrawal of the civilian population in the face of an army "search and destroy" operation.

8. The Politicization of Motherhood: Case 2970 ◆
Inter-American Commission on Human Rights

*At the height of the Dirty War in the late 1970s, when most Argentines
ignored the vanishing of thousands of fellow citizens, a group of women
formed the Mothers of the Plaza de Mayo to protest the disappearance of
their children and grandchildren. Government commando units imprisoned
children or gave those infants born in prison to childless couples who
supported the regime. To call attention to their cause, they marched with
diapers on their heads. The government initially dismissed them as crazy
old women, but they attracted international attention and investigations
began. Why did they march? One woman answered, "When someone takes
away a son or daughter, you don't measure what could happen to you. You
go head first and do whatever you can."**

*This claim, submitted to the Inter-American Commission on Human
Rights, is typical of what motivated the Mothers of the Plaza de Mayo to
protest when most Argentines, including their husbands, simply looked
away.*

Silvia Angélica, of Argentine nationality, twenty-seven years of age,
married. At the time of kidnapping on May 19, 1977, she was two
months pregnant; seven months later the grandmother received the baby girl
born in detention; Mrs. Corazza de Sánchez also has another little girl, four
years old. Her identification card is number 6, 071, 079. She is a housewife
and her address is: Bartolomé Mitre 2637, 2d Floor, 42, Federal Capital.
Date of kidnapping: 5.19.77. Place: "El Clavel" Bar, located Avenue Pavón
across the street from Lanús Station. Time: between 3 P.M. and 5 P.M. On the
date, time, and the place mentioned, the victim was arrested by armed
persons in civilian dress. She worked in a textile factory in the same city. At
the time of the kidnapping she was two months pregnant. After seven
months, she was taken to the home of her mother, accompanied by three
persons, who, although dressed as civilians, belonged to police or security
forces; they had a short meeting during which Mrs. Silvia Angélica handed
her mother a newborn baby girl (five days old), stating that she had had the

From Organization of American States, Inter-American Commission on Human
Rights, *Report on the Situation of Human Rights in Argentina*, General Secretariat,
OAS, Washington, DC, 1980 OEA/Ser L/VII, 49 Doc. 19, corr. 1, April 1980,
original: español, p. 56.

*"Argentines Unite to Gain Information about 'Disappeared' Relatives,"
Christian Science Monitor, July 2, 1981.

baby while in detention and that she had been well treated during delivery. Once the baby was handed over, they left for an unknown destination. Since then nothing further has been heard of the whereabouts of the aforementioned person.

In a note dated September 21, 1978, the government replied as follows: . . .

C. Persons on whom there is no previous record of detention and who are the subjects of a police search under the authority of the Ministry of the Interior:

3. Silvia Angélica CORAZZA DE SANCHEZ

At present the case is being processed in accordance with regulations. However, the Commission considers that the government's reply does not refute the complainant's statements.

9. La Libertad: A Women's Cooperative in Highland Bolivia ◆ Benigna Mendoza de Pariente

In Latin America the popular classes left few records. Their system of learning relied on oral tradition, which stressed listening, recitation, and memorization over writing and reading. Today, scholars record the testimonies of common people and create a valuable data base for writing history. The testimony of Benigna Mendoza de Pariente, a member of La Libertad, a women's savings-and-loan cooperative in Cochabamba, Bolivia, not only relates the facts but also the emotions and tone of her life.

I was born in Totora, about 130 kilometers from here. It was a very peaceful place; my parents have always lived there. I came to Cochabamba when I was about twelve, and I never went back again. I'm afraid of the trip, because you have to go by truck. One time I was on my way for a visit and I saw a truck nearly turn over. It made such an impression on me that I've never traveled anywhere.

I got married when I was very young and had eight children. My eldest girl is already twenty-four. The others came two years apart, down to my youngest daughter, who is eight. Last year two of them finished high school, and this year another one will graduate. I also have a daughter in the *colegio* (junior high school). They all want to go to the university or to a teachers' college. But the teachers' colleges in Bolivia have been shut since last year,

From Robert Wasserstrom, "La Libertad: A Women's Cooperative in Highland Bolivia," *Grassroots Development* 6:1 (1982): 7–9.

and the universities close down without warning. . . . It's a big problem, especially for poor people who already have a lot of insecurity.

Ever since I was very young, I've made *tostados* (roasted corn or rice) to sell in the market. In Cochabamba there really isn't enough work for everyone, and the wages are too low to support a family. You're better off if you have your own little business. Of course, I had a few problems at first— didn't have enough money to get started, and nobody would lend it to me. So I began to join in what we call *pasanaco*. On market days, or sometimes every day, a group of us puts together 100 pesos from whatever we had earned. Let's say that ten people participated. Every week or so a different person would collect the money. That's how I was able to get enough capital to start my business and build my house.

The first thing I did when I got the money was to buy a machine that makes tostados. . . . We started out with a small machine, but it only held a pound of ground corn so I sold it. Then I decided that I could do better if I just bought tostados wholesale and resold them. Now we sell a number of different things like that. . . . The trick is to deal in large quantities if you want to make a profit. Of course, some things are more lucrative than others. You make less from toasted corn—it costs less, and it brings in less. With rice, you need more capital, but you also make more money.

I began living in this part of town eighteen years ago because of an organization called the Tenants' Housing Union. The area used to be part of a huge estate that belonged to three families: the Quirogas, the Sánchez de Losados, and the Gutiérrezes. At first, they didn't want to sell us any land. So we occupied it anyway; we crept in at night and put up our houses by dawn. . . . And once we were here, no one could make us budge.

Not that we got any help, either from the prefect or the mayor. The only person who supported us was a woman who had some position in the ministry. . . . The owners finally agreed to sell us the land because it wasn't really worth much anyway. Then the leaders of the tenants' union bought up everything they could and tried to evict the rest of us. When that happened, we formed another union, and I became one of the officers.

During this time, we clashed several times with the authorities. People here were armed with rocks and sticks; the police used tear gas and even guns. They acted like a bunch of thugs. But they didn't scare anybody. On the contrary, we actually threw them out. Everybody in the union took turns standing guard, just like in the army. If any outsider tried to get through, we set off dynamite. After that, no one dared to bother us.

Not that we didn't have other problems. The community was divided between people who had some money and people who didn't. Eventually, we split into two different groups; the richer group formed their own cooperative. One of the owners figured out what was happening, so he tried to take advantage of the situation. First, he sold land to members of the other cooperative and refused to recognize the union. He also caused a lot of conflict by selling the same lots to different people. Then he exploited the disputes which arose to his own advantage by having people from the cooperative attack union members. For example, one night they came and threw rocks at my house. But we found a very decent lawyer in Sucre, and he convinced the owner to sell us some of the land. If that lawyer hadn't agreed to come here, we might never have reached a settlement. As it was, we fought for twelve years. But when people are united, they can do anything. Unity makes strength!

I joined La Libertad six years ago. I was one of the first members of an organization called COMBASE. They used to give us a monthly allowance for our families. People would go to Don Wilfran, the director of COMBASE, and say, "I'd like money for a stove," or whatever else they needed. And he's ask them, "Why don't you get together and start a cooperative? You could put your money together and do something with it."

At first, I had my doubts. One of my brothers had put his money in a cooperative, and they gave it back to him without a cent in interest! That scared me. I didn't even want to hear the word "cooperative." But Don Wilfran kept telling us that we ought to join forces. He'd say, "Spend a little less on onions and tomatoes. Bring whatever you save and deposit it. Little by little it will add up." After a year, though, I quit. It seemed like such a small amount, and it wasn't enough to get a loan.

I stayed away for a long time. Then one day someone asked me, "Why don't you start coming to the cooperative again? You'll always have something to fall back on. It gives you some security." So I became active again and took out my first loan. And I started to like being able to save a little nest egg. This year I was elected president. First, I was a board member; then I became secretary, then vice president, and now I'm president. We meet every Monday to discuss our business and administer the loan fund. Whenever we can, we approve the requests our members submit. We only reject those people who can't repay.

Suggestions for Further Reading

Andreas, Carol. *When Women Rebel: The Rise of Popular Feminism in Peru*. Westport, 1987.

Arrom, Silvia M. *The Women of Mexico City, 1790–1857*. Palo Alto, 1986.

Barrios de Chungara, Domitila, with Moema Viezzer. *Let Me Speak! Testimony of Domitila, A Woman of the Bolivian Mines*. Translated by Victoria Ortiz. New York, 1978.

Bunster, Ximena, and Elsa Chaney. *Sellers and Servants: Working Women in Lima, Peru*. New York, 1985.

Burgos-Debray, Elisabeth, ed. *I, Rigoberta Menchú: An Indian Woman in Guatemala*. Translated by Ann Wright. New York, 1984.

Carlson, Marifran. *Feminismo: The Women's Movement in Argentina from Its Beginnings to Evita Perón*. Chicago, 1987.

Chaney Elsa. *Supermadre: Women in Politics in Latin America*. Austin, 1979.

De Jesús, Carolina María. *Child of the Dark: The Diary of Carolina María de Jesús*. Translated by David St. Clair. New York, 1962.

Fisher, Jo. *Mothers of the Disappeared*. New York, 1989.

Graham, Sandra Lauderdale. *House and Street: The Domestic World of Servants and Masters in Nineteenth-century Rio de Janeiro*. Austin, 1992.

Guy, Donna. *Sex and Danger: Prostitution, Family, and Nation in Argentina*. Lincoln, 1992.

Hahner, June. *Emancipating the Female Sex: The Struggle for Women's Rights in Brazil, 1850–1940*. Durham, 1990.

Herrera, Hayden. *Frida: A Biography of Frida Kahlo*. New York, 1983.

Jaquette, Jane S., ed. *The Women's Movement in Latin America: Feminism and the Transition to Democracy*. Boston, 1989.

Karasch, Mary. *Slave Life in Rio de Janeiro, 1808–1850*. Princeton, 1987.

Lavrin, Asunción. *Latin American Women: Historical Perspectives*. Westport, 1978.

Lewis, Oscar, et al. *Four women–Living the Revolution: An Oral History of Contemporary Cuba*. New York, 1977.

Martinez-Aller, Verena. *Marriage, Class, and Color in Nineteenth-century Cuba: A Study of Racial Attitudes and Sexual Values in a Slave Society*. Ann Arbor, 1989.

Miller, Francesca. *Latin American Women and the Search for Social Justice*. Hanover, 1992.

Nash, June, and Helen Safa. *Women and Change in Latin America*. New York, 1985.

Patai, Daphne. *Brazilian Women Speak: Contemporary Life Stories*. New Brunswick, 1988.

Pescatello, Ann. *Female and Male in Latin America*. Pittsburgh, 1973.

Stoner, K. Lynn. *From the House to the Streets: The Cuban Women's Movement for Legal Change, 1898–1940*. Durham, 1991.

———. *Latinas of the Americas: A Source Book*. New York, 1989.

VI

The Search for Cultural Identity: Concepts

Leslie Bary

Politics and Culture

The central role given the concept of "culture" in the formation of modern Latin American society will be examined in this chapter. Our texts will demonstrate the importance in Latin American thought of the idea that the region's culture did not develop organically but was—or, according to some, must still be—specifically created. We will see how the imperative, inherited from colonial times, to seek "civilization" and cultural knowledge outside the Latin American continent (an imperative that marks, for instance, the Argentine writer and statesman Domingo Faustino Sarmiento's *Facundo* [Doc. 2]), gives way to a complex search for native cultural models. Peruvian intellectuals and political leaders such as Teodoro Valcárcel, Víctor Raúl Haya de la Torre, and José Carlos Mariátegui created native models based on Indianness and designed to restore the Indian's place at the center of society. But the most recurrent conceptualization of Latin American identity, of which José Martí and José Vasconcelos are among the best-known exponents, posits racial mixture and cultural hybridization as the true bases of Latin American civilization since the beginnings of European colonization.

Cultural and political activity in modern Latin America rarely occupy discrete arenas, and intellectuals consistently and explicitly link the two together. From Independence onward, politicians are often writers, and writers hold positions within the state apparatus. The political writings of such leaders and heads of state as Sarmiento and Simón Bolívar—which, significantly, are now often read as literary and cultural texts—ascribe an integral role to cultural cohesion in shaping the new republics. Literary works such as José Mármol's *Amalia* (1851) or José Hernández's *Martín*

Fierro (1872) are overtly political interventions. Far from being idle fictions, these and other nineteenth-century literary works in fact interpret historical situations, and they address a wide audience in whom they seek to instill a national consciousness. Doris Sommer points out that such works share with historiographical writing the project of actually making history by disseminating specific readings of it. By encouraging readers to identify with the national projects they lay out, this literature shapes readers who not only will accept the history they present but who also will see this history as the nation's common heritage. The sentimental novels of the Brazilian José de Alencar—*O Guaraní* (1857) and *Iracema* (1865), for instance—present idealized love between Indians and Europeans as the founding moments of a unanimous "Brazilianness." Another sentimental novel of this period, the Colombian Jorge Isaacs's *María* (1867), although it seems at first glance to be entirely focused on the private sphere, links the characters' inner life directly to questions of nation-building.[1]

Postcolonial intellectuals often theorize autonomous identities for their societies by asserting a radical difference from the culture of their former colonizers, attempting to recover the difference effaced as the "native" culture was suppressed and subjected to European "reason" through the colonial process.[2] This endeavor is always complex because of the changes colonization makes in the structure of "native" society. It is especially difficult in Latin America because the great variety of cultures brought into contact there during the long colonial period formed a heterogeneous culture. The large-scale decimation of indigenous populations and their displacement from the center of society, along with complex patterns of immigration and miscegenation, made it difficult to differentiate between "native" and "foreign." Paradoxically enough, the post-Independence leaders who first framed the debates on national culture were largely members of white, European-educated, colonial elites, who sought the culture they termed "civilization" in European (and particularly French) models. Cultural identity, then, does not emerge as a given, preexisting "essence" but as an arena for struggle. The concept of identity itself needs constant redefinition as the terms that contribute to it—gender, race, class, nation, continent—come into conflict and shift in relation to one another.

[1]See Gustavo Mejía, "Prólogo," in Jorge Isaacs, *María*, ed. G. Mejía (Caracas: Ayacucho, 1978), ix–xxxii; and Doris Sommer, *Foundational Fictions: The National Romances of Latin America* (Berkeley: University of California Press, 1991), 172–203.

[2]See Seamus Deane, "Introduction," in Terry Eagleton, Fredric Jameson, and Edward W. Said, *Nationalism, Colonialism, and Literature* (Minneapolis: University of Minnesota Press, 1990), 10–11; and Angel Rama, *Transculturación narrativa en América Latina* (México: Siglo XXI, 1982), 12–14.

Unity and Diversity

The search for cultural identity and the struggle for political and economic autonomy functioned jointly in the endeavor of post-Independence Latin American nations to take control of their own futures. As is well known, however, the post-Independence era brought a continued European economic hegemony and increasing political and economic influence from the United States. In the realm of high culture, many Latin American artists and intellectuals still looked to European models, even after Europe's economic power waned. In response to this lingering legacy of colonialism, the concept of cultural union has often been invoked, even long after Independence was formalized. José Enrique Rodó's essay *Ariel* (1900) was ground-breaking in that it affirmed not only the uniqueness but also the value of Latin American culture (Doc. 5). In the 1920s the poet Oswald de Andrade insisted in his *Manifesto Pau-Brasil* ("Brazilwood Manifesto") and *Manifesto Antropófago* ("Cannibal's Manifesto") that his native Brazilian culture is different from, but as valid and as rich as, the European; and Vasconcelos asserted that, since so many cultures have come together in America, it is here that civilization will culminate (Doc. 6).

The unity that such nationalist projects presuppose is real, but the imperative to unity elides "an interior diversity which is a more precise definition of the continent."[3] In a context where cultural identity is linked in so many ways to political power, a key question is who directs the creation of culture and the production of cultural identity. Because the Latin American man of letters is, from Independence to the present day, so often also a man of state, the formulations of identity that have gained the greatest measure of power are closely tied to the social reproduction of the elites. In Brazil and Mexico especially, and in other countries as well, cultural identity now often means identification with an officialized national culture. Even such an oppositional construction of culture as Roberto Fernández Retamar's "Calibán" (1971), written in part to contest the elitist implications of Rodó's *Ariel*, supposes a Latin American unanimity which, although it may be necessary as a strategic position, also elides the question of intracontinental difference (Doc. 7).

Nevertheless, marginalized social groups affirm particular identities which, in some cases, subvert the ideology of the modern nation-state. In the twentieth century, figures such as the black Cuban poet Nicolás Guillén and the Guatemalan Indian leader Rigoberta Menchú insist on particular minority cultural identities as bases for political action and historical consciousness. These struggles, internal to the nation and continent, although

[3]Rama, *Transculturación*, 57.

often overshadowed by the search for a cohesive national and continental identity, are increasingly visible today.

Three Theoretical Concepts

We have been discussing the relationship between culture and political power, the production of culture and cultural identity, and the hybrid nature of "Latin American culture." The recurrence of these topics in debates on cultural identity has given rise to the creation of three theoretical concepts, which are now commonly used to ground discussion of modern Latin American culture and society. These are the *lettered city, imagined communities*, and *transculturation*.

In his book on the social role of the Latin American intellectual, *La ciudad letrada* (1984), Angel Rama develops the concept of the "lettered city" to elucidate the relationship between culture and power structures on the continent from the colony to the twentieth century.[4] Briefly, the lettered city is the urban group composed of educated elites who wield pens to execute the will of viceroys and later, postcolonial rulers. According to Rama, it is this group that determines and enforces society's official order. Rama is careful to emphasize the gap between the "lettered" and "real" city, thus underlining the artificiality or the nonorganic nature of the order imposed by the lettered city and revealing the *letrados'* project as the actual production of society, as opposed to the interpretation and codification of an already existing one. One example of the power of this lettered vision is nineteenth- and twentieth-century *indigenista* narrative, which attempts to depict the reality of indigenous peoples to an urban reading public. Written by non-Indians, this type of narrative often corresponds closely to contemporary government policy and anthropological discourse on the Indian. As such, it is very different from, for instance, the real-life testimony of Menchú (Doc. 8).

The concept of the lettered city is important as a reminder of the close ties between notions of culture and relations of power and between intellectuals and the state, and of the central role that intellectuals played in shaping post-Independence society and educating the public to identify with their vision. An 1868 essay on national literature by the Mexican novelist and poet Ignacio Altamirano is brilliantly illustrative of this. Altamirano writes that "novels are undoubtedly the genre the public likes best. . . . They are the artifice through which today's best thinkers are reaching the masses with doctrines and ideas that would otherwise be difficult to impart."[5]

[4]Angel Rama, *La ciudad letrada* (Hanover, NH: Ediciones del Norte, 1984).
[5]This quotation (in Sommer, 36) is from Altamirano's essay "La literatura nacional," in *La literatura nacional*, ed. José Luis Martínez (México: Porrúa,

Benedict Anderson's study of nationalism, *Imagined Communities* (1983), can help us to see in a more general way how, in fact, the public was brought to identify with the nation. Anderson argues that the modern nation-state (in Latin America and elsewhere) is precisely not an organic but an "imagined" community. By this he means that the consciousness of shared identity and common discourse grounded in that identity which are the bases of nationalist feeling are specifically created, both by historical forces such as the development of print culture, and by ideological interventions such as José de San Martín's 1821 decree that, when Peru's independence had been won from Spain, Native Americans should no longer be called Indians or natives but Peruvians. Anderson emphasizes that identification with a nation cannot be opposed to identification with a "truer" community. Rather, all communities are "imagined," and "communities are to be distinguished, not by their supposed falsity or genuineness, but by the *style* in which they are imagined."[6]

The choice of a style in which to imagine the post-Independence communities was far from obvious, given the heterogeneity of the continent's population and the variety of its cultural roots. The desire for difference from Europe led some nineteenth-century thinkers to see the question of identity in terms of originality. "Aspire to independence of thought," warns the writer and educator Andrés Bello in an 1848 article against the imitation of European philosophies. "Our civilization too will be judged by its works, and if it is seen to copy Europe in a servile manner, what opinion of us will [European thinkers] have?" (Doc. 3).

Understandable though it is after centuries of colonialism and in light of the prestige that French thought had in the early days of Independence, this anxiety of imitation is tied to a cultural debate framed in terms of the dichotomies America and Europe, tradition and modernization, and regional and cosmopolitan or "universal" culture. In contrast, thinkers such as Bolívar and Martí abandon the search for a pure (underived) originality, locating "Latin Americanness" instead in the concept of cultural hybridity. "The blood of our citizens is different; let us mix it to unify it," says Bolívar (Doc. 1). Martí proudly emphasizes the heterogeneous origins of what he called, in a now-famous phrase, "our half-breed [*mestizo*] America," and affirms that the diverse continent possesses a "continental soul" and raises its voice in a "hymn of oneness" (Doc. 4). Yet the concept of hybridization

---

1949), 9–40. Altamirano (1834–1893) was a key figure in the reconstruction of the Mexican republic after the defeat of Maximiliano, and he edited the newspaper *Correo de México* during this period.

[6]Benedict Anderson, *Imagined Communities: Reflections on the Origin and Spread of Nationalism* (London: Verso, 1983), 15 (emphasis added).

does not resolve the question of cultural identity; it merely points out the arena in which the issue may most fruitfully be discussed. Both Bolívar and Martí assume, for instance, that the hybrid space must be a unified one, and they imply that the process of hybridization must be directed from above.

The concept of transculturation introduced by the Cuban anthropologist Fernando Ortiz provides a much clearer analysis of cultural hybridization. Ortiz argues that, although Latin American intellectuals and elite classes may have attempted to derive their thought from Europe's models and to imitate its cultural forms, Latin America as a whole is something other than a replica of Europe. Most important, he views crosscultural contact and the formation of hybrid cultures as an interactive process in which pressure is exerted from below as well as from above.[7]

Ortiz proposed the term as a more accurate description than "acculturation" of the passage from one culture to another. "Transculturation" refers not only to the acquisition of a new culture but also to the partial loss of a preceding one and, importantly, the activity of the subjects of this process, whom Ortiz's model views not simply as receivers of culture but as creators of new cultural phenomena. It is an ongoing process that engages continuing foreign influence, received either directly or mediated through the capital cities (which have the closest connections to such influence, and in which national policy is made), and the selective appropriation, modification, and assimilation of such influence to a preexisting culture, which does not simply fade away but exerts its own influence on the culture received.

Because of its dynamism—its ability to account for and make use of conflict—the concept of transculturation permits us to see hybrid cultures as something more than a repetition of previous ones, reorganized in the form of harmonious syntheses, homogenizing "melting pots" or aggregate "mosaics." This is especially important since some of the best-known presentations of cultural heterogeneity posit it as a new and utopian unity (the "we Mexicans" of Vasconcelos's *La raza cósmica* or the "we Brazilians" of Andrade's poetic and cultural manifestos), which often functions to enhance state power and, hence, the hegemony of the elites.

[7]See Fernando Ortiz, *Contrapunteo cubano del tabaco y el azúcar* (Caracas: Ayacucho, 1978); and related bibliography cited in Rama, *Transculturación*, 32–33.

1. Speech before the Congress of Angostura ◆ Simón Bolívar

Given on the occasion of his installation as president of Venezuela, when independence from Spain had been declared but not entirely won, this speech of February 15, 1819, outlines Bolívar's centralist design for government and his project of national unity and cohesion. Here, he further develops some of the ideas put forth in the well-known "Carta de Jamaica" ("Letter from Jamaica," 1815), in which he distinguished European-descended Americans from the conquistadors, defended the indigenous royalty whom the Spaniards had defeated, and argued passionately for the creation of a single nation of the former Spanish colonies. The Spanish New World, he says in the letter, is culturally unified because it has "one origin, one language, one tradition, and one religion" (p. 104).

The speech at Angostura is often cited because of Bolívar's analysis of the roots of current political difficulties in the colonial situation and his insistence on mestizaje *as the cardinal characteristic of modern Latin American culture. Notable in it as well, however, is his awareness of the difficulty of defining the American culture upon which, he argues, government should be based. The "we" he addresses is easily identified as the creole upper class, and the importance he gives to national unity, and to the control and education of the masses in the service of such unity, fits well with his somewhat authoritarian project of government.*

D o you wish to know the authors of past events and the current order? Consult the annals of Spain, of America, of Venezuela; examine the laws of the Indies, the regimes of former leaders, the influence of religion and of foreign domination: observe the first acts of the republican government, the ferocity of our enemies and the national character. . . . After separating itself from the monarchy, America found itself in the same situation as the Roman Empire when [it fell apart].* Each fragment then formed an independent nation according to its particular situation and background, with the difference that these fragments [returned to their pre-Roman origins].† We do not even maintain vestiges of what once was; we are not Europeans, and we are not Indians, but a mixture of aborigines and

---

From Simón Bolívar, "Discurso ante el Congreso de Angostura," in his *Escritos fundamentales*, ed. Germán Carrera Damas (Caracas: Monte Avila, 1982), 112–45. Translated by Leslie Bary; other quotations from this volume are cited parenthetically.

*The original reads "cuando aquella enorme masa cayó dispersa en medio del antiguo mundo."

†Original: "volvían a restablecer sus primeras asociaciones."

Spaniards. American by birth and European by rights, we are caught in the conflict of disputing ownership of the land with the natives and continuing on in the country in which we were ourselves born; so ours is the most extraordinary and complicated of cases. Furthermore, our lot has always been purely passive, we have had no political existence, and it is thus more difficult for us to attain liberty . . . for not only liberty has been taken from us, but also active, domestic tyranny. . . . [T]he satraps of Persia are Persian. . . . In contrast to this, America received everything from Spain. . . .

Does the *spirit* of laws not say that these should be particular to the people for whom they are made? that it would be a great coincidence if [the laws]* of one nation were appropriate to another? that laws should be relative to the physical aspects of the country, the climate, the nature of the land, its location, its expanse, the way of life of the population? . . . This is the code we should consult, not Washington's! . . .

We must keep in mind that our people are not European or North American; we are a composition of Africa and America, rather than an emanation of Europe; for even Spain itself is non-European because of its African blood, its institutions and its character. It is impossible to say precisely to which human family we belong. The greater part of the indigenous population has been annihilated; the European, the American, and the African have blended together. We are all born of the same mother, but our fathers . . . are foreigners, and all differ visibly in the skin; this dissimilarity carries an obligation of the greatest consequence. . . . The diversity of origins requires an infinitely firm pulse and delicate touch to manage a heterogeneous society whose complex contrivance can be dislocated, divided, dissolved with the slightest disturbance. . . .

A stable government can only be formed on the base of a national spirit which has as its objective a uniform inclination towards two capital points, to moderate the general will and to limit public authority. . . . Unity, unity, unity must be our emblem. The blood of our citizens is different; let us mix it to unify it.

*Original: "las."

---

2. Civilization and Barbarism ◆ Domingo Faustino Sarmiento

Sarmiento—writer, educator, politician, and president of Argentina (1868–1874)—originally published Facundo *(1845) as a serial in the Chilean*

From Domingo Faustino Sarmiento, *Facundo o Civilización y barbarie* (Caracas: Ayacucho, 1977). Translated by Leslie Bary.

newspaper El Progreso *during one of his periods of exile. Written to denounce the tyrant Juan Manuel de Rosas, the book is an interpretation of Argentine history that seeks out the origins of caudillismo and proposes a program for a post-Rosas government. Culture for the historicist Sarmiento is a product of geographical and historical circumstances, and the caudillo Facundo (a precursor of Rosas and often a surrogate for him in this text) is "a manifestation of Argentine life as colonization and the peculiarities of the terrain have made it" as well as a "personification [of] the inner life of the Argentine people" (p. 16). Caudillismo is the expression of a rural and native "barbarism" that "civilization" has not yet extirpated. Sarmiento argues that extensive European immigration and the civilizing effect of the cities will foster long-overdue progress. His (Romantic) admiration of the pampa and its customs as a cradle of Argentine originality is evident, but, like some other North and South American writers of his time, he sees their sacrifice as necessary to progress.**

Facundo is not dead: he is alive in Argentine popular traditions, politics, and revolutions; in Rosas, his heir and complement . . . what in [Facundo] was merely instinct, beginning, [and] tendency, became, in Rosas, system, result, and purpose. In this metamorphosis, the colonial and barbaric nature of the countryside became art, system, and organized policy capable of presenting itself to the world as the character of a people, incarnated in a man who has aspired to take on the airs of a genius who dominates events, men, and things. Facundo, provincial, barbaric, valiant, bold, was replaced by Rosas, son of cultivated Buenos Aires, himself lacking in cultivation, a treacherous, calculating soul who does ill without passion and slowly organizes despotism with all the intelligence of a Machiavelli. . . .

In order to untie this knot which the sword has been unable to cut, [it is necessary] to study in detail the turns of the threads which form it, and to seek their points of origin in [Rosas's] antecedents, in the physionomy of the land, and in popular traditions and customs. . . .

Argentina . . . [has produced] . . . from the depths of its innermost recess, from the intimacy of its heart, Doctor Francia himself in the person of Rosas, but greater, more daring, and more hostile, if this is possible, to the ideas, customs, and civilizations of European peoples. . . . [In him we find] the same rancor against foreign elements, the same conception of the authority of government, the same insolence in defiance of the world's reproaches, added to his savage originality, his coldly ferocious

---

*See Doris Sommer's perceptive chapter on Sarmiento, "Plagiarized Authenticity: Sarmiento's Cooper and Others," in Sommer, *Foundational Fictions* (Berkeley: University of California Press, 1991), 52–82.

character, and his incontractable will. . . . The question is to be or not to be *savage*. . . .*

The illness which afflicts the Argentine Republic is its expanse; the desert surrounds it everywhere; solitude, wilderness without human habitation, are . . . the unquestionable frontiers between provinces. There is immensity everywhere; immense is the plain, immense are the woods and the rivers, the horizon is always uncertain, always blended with the earth among varicolored clouds and tenuous vapors which prevent us from determining that distant point at which the world ends and the sky begins. . . .

[A] notable trait of the physionomy of the country [is] the agglomeration of navigable rivers. . . . But these immense canals excavated by Nature's solicitous hand introduce no change into the national customs. The son of the Spanish adventurers who colonized the country detests navigation, and considers himself imprisoned in the narrow confines of a boat.

When a great river cuts off his passage, he calmly undresses, prepares his horse, and guides it swimming to an islet made out from afar; upon [the islet] the horse and rider rest, and from islet to islet the crossing is finished at last.

Thus the Argentine gaucho disdains the greatest favor Providence has supplied, seeing it as an obstacle to his movements, rather than the most powerful means of making them easy. . . .

The city man wears a European suit and lives a civilized life . . . ; [in the city] there are laws, ideas of progress, means of instruction, municipal organization, regular government, etc. Upon leaving the city's confines, the look of everything changes; the country man wears a different suit, which I shall call American . . . ; his way of life is different, his necessities peculiar and limited; the two societies seem entirely different, like two peoples unconnected with each other. What is more, the country man, far from aspiring to resemble [his urban counterpart], disdainfully rejects his luxuries and courteous manners. . . . Every civilized thing the city has is . . . outlawed there; and anyone who dared appear in a frock coat, mounted in an English saddle, would bring upon himself the jeers and brutal aggression of the peasants.

If from the conditions of country life, such as it has been made by colonization and carelessness, great difficulties for any political organization are born, and many more for the triumph of European civilization, of its institutions and the prosperity and liberty which are their result, it cannot, on the other hand, be denied that this situation has its poetic side, phrases worthy of a novelist's pen. If a sparkle of national literature can shine momentarily in the new American societies, it will arise from the descrip-

*Emphasis in original.

tion of the grandiose natural scenes, and, above all, from the struggle between European civilization and indigenous barbarity, between intelligence and matter; an impressive struggle in America, which gives rise to such peculiar scenes, so characteristic and so far outside the circle of ideas in which the European spirit has been educated, because the [Argentine] dramatic resources are unknown outside the country where they are used; the customs are surprising, and the characters, original. . . .

Does England want consumers, no matter what the government of a country is? But what can six hundred thousand poor gauchos, without industry, almost without necessities, consume, under a government which, extinguishing European customs and tastes, necessarily diminishes the consumption of European products? . . .

When there is a cultured government that cares about the national interest, what business, what industrial movement there will be! . . .

But the principal element of order and the establishment of morals that Argentina possesses today is European immigration, which by itself, and in spite of the lack of security offered it, rushes in daily to the Plate region, and if there were a government capable of directing its movement, it would by itself be enough to cure in no more than ten years all the wounds which the bandits who have dominated the country, from Facundo to Rosas, have inflicted upon it.

---

3. The Role of the University and the Study of History ◆ Andrés Bello

The Venezuelan Andrés Bello, Bolívar's teacher, was perhaps the most influential intellectual and educator of the new Spanish American republics. Bello spent the period from 1810 to 1829 in London on a Venezuelan diplomatic mission, after which, invited by the Chilean government, he went to Santiago to help reorganize the country's educational system. He became rector of the University of Chile in 1843. He was also a member of the Senate for many years and was the author of a code of civil law for Chile. His best-known work is the Gramática de la lengua castellana destinada al uso de los americanos *[Grammar of the Spanish language for the use of Americans] (1847), in which he establishes the continuities between American and Peninsular Spanish. Here he writes: "I consider it important to conserve the language of our forefathers in all possible purity, as a providential medium of communication and a fraternal link among the various nations of Spanish origin spread over the two continents."* *

*Bello, "Prólogo," *Gramática de la lengua castellana destinada al uso de los americanos*: *Obras completas* 4 (Caracas: Ministerio de Educación, 1951), 11.

Bello's leadership in law and government, education and intellectual life, and his work to establish a standard literary Spanish that would link Hispanic peoples, are paradigmatic of the issues of the period. Like his contemporaries, Bello is concerned to affirm American originality in the context of continuity with the humanistic ideals of the European Enlightenment. In the fragments that follow, both dating from 1848, we can see the now-familiar themes of Latin American culture as something that must be created and taught, the need to interpret the local reality on the basis of intellectual models derived from it and not imported from Europe— expressed here in the typically Romantic terms of originality (as opposed to imitation) and "national character."

Speech Given on the Anniversary of the University of Chile

We must not forget that [the University's] organic law, inspired . . . in the soundest and most liberal ideas, has charged the University not only with teaching but with the cultivation of literature and science; it has desired that . . . [the University] contribute to the increase and development of scientific knowledge; that it not be a passive instrument, designed exclusively for the transmission of knowledge acquired in more advanced nations, but rather that it work—as do the literary institutes of other civilized peoples—to increase the common fortune. This purpose appears in each step of the organic law, and does honor to the government and legislature that composed [the law]. Is there anything presumptuous or inopportune in this, anything too difficult for our strength, as some have supposed? Shall we still be condemned to repeat in a servile fashion the lessons of European knowledge, without daring to discuss them, to illustrate them with local applications, to imprint upon them the stamp of our nationality? If we accepted such to be the case, we would be unfaithful to the spirit of European knowledge itself, and would offer European learning a superstitious adoration that it itself condemns. . . .

There are very few fields which, in order to be taught in a suitable way, must not be adapted to us, to our physical nature, to our social circumstances.

Translation mine. This essay has often been reprinted as "El castellano en América" ("Castilian [Spanish] in America"). See Ripoll, *Conciencia intelectual*, 54–62.

From Andrés Bello, *Obras completas*, 15 vols. (Santiago de Chile: Edición oficial del Consejo de Instrucción Pública de Chile, 1881–1893), 8: *Opúsculos literarios y críticos, III* (1885), 371–74. Translated by Leslie Bary. This essay has been anthologized as "Nuestro ideal: la creación de la cultura americana" (Our ideal: The creation of American culture). See, for example, *Bello*, ed. Gabriel Méndez Plancarte (México: Ediciones de la Secretaría de Educación Pública, 1943), 30–33; and Enrique Anderson Imbert and Eugenio Florit, *Literatura hispanoamericana*, 2 vols. (New York: Holt, Rinehart, and Winston, 1970), 1:258–59.

Shall we look for the hygiene and pathology of the Chilean people in European books, and not study the degree to which the organization of the human body is modified by the accidents of the Chilean climate and customs? Can such a necessary study be made elsewhere than in Chile? For medicine, there is a vast field of exploration open in Chile, almost untouched at present, but which will not remain so for long, and whose cultivation is of great interest to physical education, health, life, sanitation, and the increase of population. . . .

I could extend these considerations much further, and give them new strength applying them to politics, morals, poetry, and every genre of literary composition: for, either it is false that literature is the reflection of the life of a people, or it is necessary to admit that every people not sunken in barbarism is called to represent itself in a literature of its own, and to imprint its forms in this literature.

Method for the Study of History

Our youth has anxiously taken up the study of history; we have just seen brilliant proof of their progress in it; and we would like them to be well permeated with the true mission of history to study it with the best results.

We would like above all to prevent them from an excessive servility to the knowledge of civilized Europe.

By a sort of fatality, new nations are subjugated to previous ones. Greece subdued Rome; Greece and Rome, the modern peoples of Europe, when letters were restored to it; and we are now dragged along more than is right by the influence of Europe, whom—at the same time as we take advantage of its learning—we should imitate in its independence of thought. . . .

We must not give too much value to philosophical categories: generalizations which say little or nothing by themselves to whoever has not studied living nature in the paintings of history and, if possible, in the early and original historians. I am not speaking here only of our history, but of all histories. Young Chileans! Learn to judge for yourselves; aspire to independence of thought. Drink from the sources, or at least in the streams closest to them! The very language of the original historians, their ideas, even their obsessions and their fabulous legends, are a part of history, and

From Andrés Bello, "Modo de Estudiar la Historia," in *Obras completas* 19 (Caracas: Ministerio de Educación, 1957), 243–52. Translation mine. Originally published in *El Araucano* 913 (Santiago), February 4, 1848, this essay has often been reprinted as "Autonomía cultural de América" (Cultural autonomy of America). See, for instance, Carlos Ripoll, *Conciencia intelectual de América: Antología del ensayo hispanoamericano* (New York: Eliseo Torres, 1974), 48–54, esp. 53.

not the least instructive and truthful. Do you wish, for instance, to know
what the discovery and conquest of America were? Read the diary of
Columbus, the letters of Pedro de Valdivia and Hernán Cortés. . . . Interrogate
each civilization in its works; ask each historian for his guarantees. This is
the first philosophy we must learn from Europe.

Our civilization too will be judged by its works, and if it is seen to copy
Europe in a servile manner, what opinion of us will a Michelet or a Guizot
have? They will say: America has not yet shaken off her chains; she drags
herself blindfolded in our tracks; not a single thought of her own breathes in
her works, nothing original, nothing characteristic; she imitates the forms of
our philosophy and does not appropriate its spirit. Her civilization is an
exotic plant which has not yet tapped the juices of the land that nourishes it.

---

4. Our America ◆ José Martí

*While still in his teens the Cuban José Martí (born in 1853) was sentenced
to hard labor and then exiled for his participation in the national
independence movement. He studied law in Spain, edited a magazine in
Mexico, taught at the University of Guatemala, and then lived as a writer in
Venezuela and the United States; in all of these countries he sought support
for the cause of Cuban independence. Martí returned to Cuba in 1895 to
join the revolutionary forces and died in battle there the same year.*

*An important theme of his writing is the question of cultural identity; in
contrast to Sarmiento, Martí sees the non-European elements in American
culture as a source of its strength, and he is concerned about the increasing
hemispheric hegemony of the United States. The essay "Nuestra América"
(1891) is famous for its call for continental unity and democracy, its
antiracist stance (although Martí still uses what by today's standards is
racist vocabulary), and its assertion of Spanish America's mestizo culture
as a positive one.*

For in what lands can a man take greater pride than in our long-suffering
republics of America, raised up from among the mute Indian masses by
the bleeding arms of a hundred apostles. . . . Never in history have such
advanced and unified nations been forged in less time from such disordered
elements. The fool in his pride believes that the earth was created to serve
him as a pedestal because words flow easily from his pen, . . . and he charges

From José Martí, "Our America," in *The America of José Martí*, trans. Juan de
Onís (New York, 1968), 138–52. © 1954 by The Noonday Press Inc. Reprinted by
permission of Farrar, Straus and Giroux Inc.

his native land with being worthless and beyond salvation because its virgin jungles do not provide him with means to travel continually abroad, driving Persian ponies and lavishing champagne, like a tycoon. The incapacity does not lie with the nascent country . . . but with those who attempt to rule nations of a unique character, and a singular, violent composition, with laws that derive from four centuries of operative liberty in the United States, and nineteen centuries of French monarchy. A decree by Hamilton does not halt the charge of the *llanero*'s pony. A phrase of Sieyès does nothing to quicken the stagnant blood of the Indian race. One must see things as they are, to govern well; the good governor in America is not one who knows how government is conducted in France or Germany, but one who knows the elements of which his country is composed and how they can be marshaled so that by methods and institutions native to the country the desirable state may be attained wherein every man realizes himself. . . . The spirit of the government must be the same as that of the country. The form of government must conform to the natural constitution of the country. Good government is nothing more than the true balance between the natural elements of the nation.

For that reason, the foreign book has been conquered in America by the natural man. The natural men have vanquished the artificial, lettered men. The native-born half-breed has vanquished the exotic Creole. The struggle is not between barbarity and civilization, but between false erudition and nature. . . . Tyrants in America have risen to power serving those scorned natural elements, and have fallen the moment they betrayed them. Republics have paid in tyrannies for their inability to recognize the true elements of their countries, to derive from them the proper form of government, and govern accordingly. To be a governor of a new country means to be a creator. . . .

To know one's country, and govern it with that knowledge, is the only alternative to tyranny. The European university must give way to the American university. The history of America, from the Incas to the present, must be taught until it is known by heart, even if the Archons of the Greeks go by the board. Our Greece must take priority over the Greece that is not ours: we need it more. Nationalist statesmen must replace cosmopolitan statesmen. Let the world be grafted on our republics; but the trunk must be our own. And let the vanquished pedant hold his tongue. . . .

With the rosary as our guide, our head white and our body mottled, both Indian and Creole, we intrepidly entered the community of nations. . . .

The colony lives on in the republic; and our America is saving itself from its grave errors—the arrogance of the capital cities, the blind triumph of the scorned country people, the influx of foreign ideas and formulas, the wicked and unpolitic disdain in which the aboriginal race is held—through the superior virtue, backed by the necessary conviction, of the republic that struggles against the colony. . . .

We were a strange sight with the chest of an athlete, the hands of a coxcomb, and the brain of a child. We were a masquerade in English trousers, Parisian vest, North American jacket, and Spanish hat. The Indian circled about us in silent wonder, and went to the mountains to baptize his children. The runaway Negro poured out the music of his heart on the night air, alone and unknown among the rivers and wild beasts. The men of the land, the creators, rose up in blind indignation against the scornful city, against their own child. We were all epaulets and tunics in countries that came into the world with hemp sandals on their feet and headbands for hats. The stroke of genius would have been to couple the headband and tunic with the charity of heart and daring of the founding father; to rescue the Indian; to make a place for the able Negro; to fit liberty to the body of those who rose up and triumphed in its name. . . . The European or Yankee book could not provide the answer to the Hispanic-American enigma. Hate was tried, and the countries wasted away, year by year. Exhausted by the senseless struggle between the book and the lance, of reason against dogma, of the city against the country, of the impossible rule by rival city cliques over the natural nation alternately tempestuous and inert, we begin almost without realizing it to try love. The nations stand up and salute each other. "What are we like?" they ask; and they begin to tell one another what they are like. When a problem arises in Cojimar, they do not send to Danzig for the answer. The frock coat is still French, but the thought begins to be American. The youth of America roll up their sleeves and plunge their hands into the dough; it rises with the leavening of their sweat. They understand that there is too much imitation, and that creation holds the key to salvation. "Create" is the password of this generation. The wine is from plantain, and if it proves sour, it is our wine! . . .

There can be no racial hate, because there are no races. . . . [T]heorists juggle and warm over the library-shelf races, which the open-minded traveler and well-disposed observer seek in vain in Nature's justice, where the universal identity of man leaps forth from triumphant love and the turbulent lust for life. The soul emanates, equal and eternal, from bodies distinct in shape and color. . . . But it must not be supposed, from a parochial animus, that there is a fatal and ingrained evil in the blond nation of the continent, because it does not speak our tongue, nor see the world as we do, . . . nor favorably regard the excitable, dark-skinned people, nor look charitably . . . on those less favored by History, who climb the road of republicanism by heroic stages. The self-evident facts of the problem should not be obscured, for it can be resolved, to the benefit of peaceful centuries yet to come, by timely study and the tacit, immediate union of the continental soul. The hymn of oneness sounds already; the present generation carries a purposeful America along the road enriched by their sublime fathers; from the Rio Grande to the Strait of Magellan, the Great Semí [a Taino deity], seated on the flank of the condor, sows the seed of the new America through the romantic nations of the continent and the sorrowful islands of the sea!

---

5. Ariel ◆ José Enrique Rodó

The Uruguayan writer and literature professor José Enrique Rodó's essay Ariel *(1900) is one of the many works produced in Latin America and elsewhere that appropriate elements of Shakespeare's* The Tempest—*itself an allusion to America—to elucidate situations of colonial and postcolonial society and culture.* In this play the magician Prospero rules an island where he has two servants: the agile sprite Ariel, whom Prospero has rescued from the pine tree in which the witch Sycorax, the island's former ruler, had imprisoned him; and the brutish slave Caliban (derived from* cannibal), *Sycorax's son. He releases these servants when, having resolved the political problems that kept him away from the mainland, he leaves the island and returns home to Europe.*

Rodó's Ariel, *which appeared just after the Spanish American War had made Latin Americans acutely aware of the dangers of the United States' increasing imperialism, intends to affirm the common cultural roots of the Spanish American nations. It also affirms the importance of the moral and aesthetic values that Rodó associates with Ariel, as against an excessive admiration of the efficient and "utilitarian" aspects of North American culture that he associates with Caliban. The essay is written as a (fictitious) speech by a wise teacher, Prospero, who, in this final lecture, charges "the youth of America" to be faithful to the ideals that Ariel represents. Thus, Rodó sounds again the themes of teaching and creating culture, of Spanish American unity, and of a unique Spanish American contribution to universal culture.*

S hakespeare's ethereal Ariel symbolizes the noble, soaring aspect of the human spirit. He represents the superiority of reason and feeling over the base impulses of irrationality. He is generous enthusiasm, elevated and unselfish motivation in all actions, spirituality in culture, vivacity and grace

From *Ariel*, pp. 31, 70–71, 93–94, by José Enrique Rodó, trans. Margaret Sayers Peden. © 1988 by the University of Texas Press. Reprinted by permission of the publisher.

*See Roberto Fernández Retamar's discussion of the many versions of *The Tempest*, in Fernández Retamar, *Caliban and Other Essays*, trans. Edward Baker (Minneapolis: University of Minnesota Press, 1988), 6–14.

in intelligence. Ariel is the ideal toward which human selection ascends, the force that wields life's eternal chisel, effacing from aspiring mankind the clinging vestiges of Caliban, the play's symbol of brutal sensuality. . . .

The inextricably linked concepts of utilitarianism as a concept of human destiny and egalitarian mediocrity as a norm for social relationships compose the formula for what Europe has tended to call the spirit of *Americanism*. It is impossible to ponder either inspiration for social conduct, or to compare them with their opposites, without their inevitable association with that formidable and productive democracy to our north. Its display of prosperity and power is dazzling testimony to the efficacy of its institutions and to the guidance of its concepts. If it has been said that "utilitarianism" is the word for the spirit of the English, then the United States can be considered the embodiment of the word. And the Gospel of that word is spread everywhere through the good graces of its material miracles. . . . That powerful federation is effecting a kind of moral conquest among us. . . . Admiration for its greatness and power is making impressive inroads in the minds of our leaders and, perhaps even more, in the impressionable minds of the masses, who are awed by its incontrovertible victories. And from admiring to imitating is an easy step. . . . We imitate what we believe to be superior or prestigious. And this is why the vision of an America de-Latinized of its own will, without threat of conquest, and reconstituted in the image and likeness of the North, now looms in the nightmares of many who are genuinely concerned about our future. This vision is the impetus behind an abundance of similar carefully thought-out designs and explains the continuous flow of proposals for innovation and reform. We have our *USA-mania*. It must be limited by the boundaries our reason and sentiment jointly dictate. . . .

Our Latin America can already boast of cities whose physical grandeur and obvious cultivation will soon qualify them for inclusion among the first cities of the world. We do well to fear, however, that when serene thought draws near to rap upon their lavish exteriors—as upon a sealed bronze vase—no sound will be heard but the disconsolate ring of emptiness. . . .

It is your generation that must prevent this from happening; it is you, our youth, who must rise up, blood and muscle and nerve of the future. . . . I speak to you now with the conviction that you are destined to lead others on behalf of the spirit. . . .

Everything in our contemporary America that is devoted to the dissemination and defense of selfless spiritual idealism—art, science, morality, religious sincerity, a politics of the ideas—must emphasize its unswerving faith in the future. The past belonged entirely to the arm that wages battle; the present, almost completely to the rugged arm that levels and constructs; the future—a future whose proximity is directly related to the degree of will and thought of those who desire it—offers both stability and ambience for the development of the best qualities of the soul.

6. The Cosmic Race ◆ José Vasconcelos

Like Rodó in Ariel, *the Mexican writer, educator, and politician José Vasconcelos envisions in* The Cosmic Race *(1925) a unified Latin America that will lead the world into a new, aesthetically and spiritually oriented era. This essay is famous for its defense of mestizo originality. Vasconcelos's "cosmic race," the child of interracial love and joy, is the mix in which all races will disappear and which will incorporate the positive characteristics of all previous peoples. Didier Jaén argues persuasively that this is more a philosophical than a racial theory.* It is nevertheless important to point out that Vasconcelos held posts in the Mexican government at a time when mestizaje was a state ideology wielded to strengthen citizens' adherence to the nation; that he invokes the cosmic race in terms which make it difficult to distinguish from a master race; and that he ascribes the greatest importance to the European element in the new mix. These traits reveal the gulf between Vasconcelos's mestizo culture and such theories of hybrid cultures as Fernando Ortiz's and Angel Rama's "transculturation."*

Greece laid the foundations of Western or European civilization; the white civilization that, upon expanding, reached the forgotten shores of the American continent in order to consummate the task of recivilization and repopulation. Thus we have the four stages and the four racial trunks: the Black, the Indian, the Mongol, and the White. The latter, after organizing itself in Europe, has become the invader of the world, and has considered itself destined to rule, as did each of the previous races during their time of power. . . . The white race has brought the world to a state in which all human types and cultures will be able to fuse with each other. The civilization developed and organized in our times by the whites has set the moral and material basis for the union of all men into a fifth universal race, the fruit of all the previous ones and [the] amelioration of everything past.

White culture is migratory, yet it was not Europe as a whole that was in charge of initiating the reintegration of the red world into the modality of preuniversal culture, which had been represented for many centuries by the

From José Vasconcelos, *La raza cósmica/The Cosmic Race*, trans. Didier Jaén (Los Angeles, 1979). Reprinted by permission of the Publications Center, Department of Chicano Studies, California State University, Los Angeles.

*See Jaén, "Introduction," in Vasconcelos, *La raza cósmica/The Cosmic Race*, xi–xxxv.

white man. The transcendental mission fell upon the two most daring branches of the European family, the strongest and most different human types: the Spanish and the English. . . .

[W]e, Spaniards by blood or by culture, began by denying our traditions at the moment of our emancipation. We broke off with the past, and some even denied their blood, saying it would have been better if the conquest of our regions had been accomplished by the English. . . . [This] is the same as denying our strong and wise parents when it is we, and not they, who are guilty of our decadence. . . .

Even the pure Indians are Hispanized, they are Latinized, just as the environment itself is Latinized. Say what one may, the red men, the illustrious Atlanteans from whom Indians derive, went to sleep millions of years ago, never to awaken. . . . The Indian has no other door to the future but the door of modern culture, nor any other road but the road already cleared by Latin civilization. The white man, as well, will have to depose his pride and look for progress and ulterior redemption in the souls of his brothers from other castes. He will have to diffuse and perfect himself in each of the superior varieties of the species, in each of the modalities that multiply revelation and make genius more powerful. . . . Perhaps the traits of the white race will predominate among the characteristics of the fifth race, but such a supremacy must be the result of the free choice of personal taste, and not the fruit of violence or economic pressure. The superior traits of culture and nature will have to triumph, but that triumph will be stable only if it is based on the voluntary acceptance by conscience and on the free choice of fantasy. . . .

North Americans have held very firmly to their resolution to maintain a pure stock, the reason being that they are faced with the Blacks, who are like the opposite pole, like the antithesis of the elements to be mixed. In the Ibero-American world, the problem does not present itself in such crude terms. We have very few Blacks, and a large part of them is already becoming a mulatto population. The Indian is a good bridge for racial mixing. Besides, the warm climate is propitious for the interaction and gathering of all peoples. On the other hand, and this is essential, interbreeding will no longer obey reasons of simple proximity as occurred in the beginning when the white colonist took an Indian or Black woman because there were no others at hand. In the future, as social conditions keep improving, the mixture of bloods will become gradually more spontaneous, to the point that interbreeding will no longer be the result of simple necessity but of personal taste or, at least, of curiosity. Spiritual motivation, in this manner, will increasingly superimpose itself upon the contingencies of the merely physical. . . .

In order to express all these ideas that today I am trying to expound in a rapid synthesis, I tried, some years ago, . . . to assign them symbols in the new Palace of Public Education in Mexico. Lacking sufficient elements to do exactly what I wished, I had to be satisfied with a Spanish Renaissance building. . . . On the panels at the four corners of the first patio, I had [allegories carved] representing Spain, Mexico, Greece, and India, the four particular civilizations that have most to contribute to the formation of Latin America. Immediately below these four allegories, four stone statues should have been raised, representing the four great contemporary races: the white, the red, the black, and the yellow, to indicate that America is home to the needs of all of them. Finally, in the center, a monument should have been raised that in some way would symbolize the law of the three states: the material, the intellectual, and the aesthetic. All this was to indicate that through the exercise of [this] triple law, we in America shall arrive, before any other part of the world, at the creation of a new race fashioned out of the treasures of all the previous ones: the final race, the cosmic race.

---

7. Caliban ◆ Roberto Fernández Retamar

The poet and essayist Roberto Fernández Retamar is professor of philology at the University of Havana and director of the publishing house Casa de las Américas. His polemical essay "Caliban" is a key text in contemporary discussions of Latin American cultural identity. In it, he invokes and revises Rodó's use of Shakespeare's Ariel as a metaphor for the Latin American cultural situation. Contesting the Eurocentric presuppositions of Rodó's work, Fernández Retamar draws on Martí's vision of a mestizo culture, which he associates with the figure of Caliban. He discovers Caliban's origins in Columbus's log books, where the Carib Indians are reported to be cannibals, monstrous human beings whose existence threatens civilization and even the notion of "humanity," and shows how this metaphor recurs, in varying guises, in theorizations of Latin American culture from the time of Columbus to the present day. He argues that Sarmiento's dichotomy of civilization and barbarism is a misleading paradigm for Latin American cultural identity and proposes instead the Caliban metaphor. He deploys this metaphor not only to make common cause, as Martí does in "Our America," with Latin Americans who are neither elite nor European-descended, but also to express the situation of an entire culture that lives at the margins of the West, and to accentuate the revolutionary potential which, he says, inheres in a Latin American culture thus conceived.

From Roberto Fernández Retamar, *Caliban and Other Essays*, trans. Edward Baker (Minneapolis, 1988). © 1988 by the University of Minnesota Press. Reprinted by permission of the University of Minnesota Press.

A European journalist, and moreover a leftist, asked me a few days ago, "Does a Latin American culture exist?" We were discussing . . . the recent polemic regarding Cuba that ended by confronting, on the one hand, certain bourgeois European intellectuals (or aspirants to that state) with a visible colonialist nostalgia; and on the other, that body of Latin American writers and artists who reject open or veiled forms of cultural and political colonialism. The question seemed to me to reveal one of the roots of the polemic and, hence, could also be expressed another way: "Do you exist?" For to question our culture is to question our very existence, our human reality itself, and thus to be willing to take a stand in favor of our irremediable colonial condition, since it suggests that we would be but a distorted echo of what occurs elsewhere. This elsewhere is of course the metropolis, the colonizing centers. . . .

While this fate is to some extent suffered by all countries emerging from colonialism—those countries of ours that enterprising metropolitan intellectuals have ineptly and successively termed *barbarians, peoples of color, underdeveloped countries, Third World*—I think the phenomenon achieves a singular crudeness with respect to what Martí called "our *mestizo* America." . . .

[W]ithin the colonial world there exists a case unique *to the entire planet*: a vast zone for which *mestizaje* is not an accident but rather the essence, the central line: ourselves, "our mestizo America." Martí, with his excellent knowledge of the language, employed this specific adjective as the distinctive sign of our culture. . . .

Even in this century, in a book as confused as the author himself but full of intuitions (*La raza cósmica*, 1925), the Mexican José Vasconcelos pointed out that in Latin America a new race was being forged, "made with the treasure of all previous ones, the final race, the cosmic race."

This singular fact lies at the root of countless misunderstandings. . . . Latin Americans are taken at times for apprentices, for rough drafts or dull copies of Europeans, including among these latter whites who constitute what Martí called "European America." In the same way, our entire culture is taken as an apprenticeship, a rough draft or a copy of European bourgeois culture ("an emanation of Europe," as Bolívar said). . . . The confusion lies in the root itself, because as descendants of numerous Indian, African, and European communities, we have only a few languages with which to understand one another: those of the colonizers. . . . Right now as we are discussing, as I am discussing with those colonizers, how else can I do it except in one of their languages, which is now also *our* language, and with so many of their conceptual tools, which are now also *our* conceptual tools? This is precisely the extraordinary outcry that we read in a work by perhaps the most extraordinary writer of fiction who ever existed. In *The Tempest*,

William Shakespeare's last play, the deformed Caliban—enslaved, robbed of his island, and trained to speak by Prospero—rebukes Prospero thus: "You taught me language, and my profit on't/ Is, I know how to curse. The red plague rid you/ for learning me your language!" (1.2.362–64). . . .

Our symbol then is not Ariel, as Rodó thought, but rather Caliban. This is something that we, the *mestizo* inhabitants of these same isles where Caliban lived, see with particular clarity: Prospero invaded the islands, killed our ancestors, enslaved Caliban, and taught him his language to make himself understood. . . .

To assume our condition as Caliban implies rethinking our history from the *other* side, from the viewpoint of the *other* protagonist. The *other* protagonist of *The Tempest* (or, as we might have said ourselves, *The Hurricane*) is not of course Ariel but, rather, Prospero. There is no real Ariel-Caliban polarity: both are slaves in the hands of Prospero, the foreign magician. But Caliban is the rude and unconquerable master of the island, while Ariel, a creature of the air, although also a child of the isle, is the intellectual. . . .

But America has also heard . . . the thesis that was the exact opposite: the thesis of Prospero. The interlocutors were not called then Prospero and Caliban, but rather *Civilization and Barbarism*, the title that Sarmiento gave to . . . his great book on Facundo Quiroga. . . . It [is] not possible to be simultaneously in agreement with *Facundo* and with "Our America." What is more, "Our America"—along with a large part of Martí's entire work—is an implicit, and at times explicit, dialogue with the Sarmiento theses. . . . Martí *rejects* the *false* dichotomy that Sarmiento, falling into the trap adroitly set by the colonizer, takes for granted. . . . The presumed barbarism of our peoples was invented with crude cynicism by "those who desire foreign lands"; those who, with equal effrontery, give the "popular name" of "civilization" to the "contemporary" human being who comes "from Europe or European America." . . .

For Sarmiento, the history of America is the "bands of abject races, a great continent abandoned to savages incapable of progress." If we want to know how he interpreted the maxim of his compatriot Alberdi that "to govern is to populate," we must read this: "Many difficulties will be presented by the occupation of so extensive a country; but there will be no advantage comparable to that gained by the extinction of the savage tribes." That is to say, for Sarmiento, to govern is also to *depopulate* the nation of its Indians (and gauchos). . . .

Our culture is—and can only be—the child of revolution, of our multisecular rejection of all colonialisms. Our culture, like every culture, requires as a primary condition our own existence. I cannot help but cite here . . . one of the occasions on which Martí spoke to this fact in the most simple and illuminating way. "Letters, which are expression, cannot exist," he wrote in 1881, "so long as there is no essence to express in them. Nor will there exist a Spanish American literature until Spanish America exists." . . . Latin American culture, then, has become a possibility *in the first place* because of the many who have struggled, the many who still struggle, for the existence of that "great people" that, in 1881, Martí still referred to as Spanish America but that some years later he would prefer to name, more accurately, "Our America."

But this is not, of course, the only culture forged here. There is also the culture of anti-America, that of the oppressors, of those who tried (or are trying) to impose on these lands metropolitan schemes, or simply, tamely to reproduce in a provincial fashion what might have authenticity in other countries. . . . We can and must contribute to a true assessment of the history of the oppressors and that of the oppressed. But of course, the triumph of the latter will be the work, above all, of those for whom history is a function not of erudition but of deeds. It is they who will achieve the definitive triumph of the true America, reestablishing—this time in a different light—the unity of our immense continent. . . . Such a future, which has already begun, will end by rendering incomprehensible the idle question about our existence.

---

8. I, Rigoberta Menchú ◆ Rigoberta Menchú

Rigoberta Menchú is a Quiché Indian woman from the northwestern province of El Quiché, Guatemala. Born in 1960, she first learned Spanish at the age of twenty, in order to increase her effectiveness as an organizer among the exploited rural workers of Guatemala. In 1992 her name brought worldwide attention when she was awarded the Nobel Peace Prize.

The testimony she presents in I, Rigoberta Menchú *is more than autobiography because, as she says, her "personal experience is the reality of a whole people" (p. 2). Menchú explains that her primary cultural identification is not with a nation or continent but with her particular community. In her narrative, she shows how, through the political work she has undertaken in response to the exploitation of Indian labor and the repression of indigenous peoples in Guatemala—a repression that has included the brutal murder of her parents and some of her siblings by the Guatemalan Army—she expanded this cultural identification. She still carefully positions herself as a member of her own ethnic group but situates herself also as a member of a series of overlapping communities: of indigenous peoples*

From *I, Rigoberta Menchú: An Indian Woman in Guatemala*, ed. Elisabeth Burgos-Debray, trans. Ann Wright (New York, 1984), 1, 2, 15–17, 165, 167, 169–70, 207, 208–9, 246–47. Reprinted by permission of Verso.

nation- and continent-wide, of the women's movement, of the Church, and of the poor.

The text, which narrates Menchú's whole life, is organized principally around the theme of her coming to political consciousness. It includes long sections on the customs of Menchú's community as well as on the political and economic situation of Guatemala's indigenous peoples. The excerpts presented here cannot encapsulate all of this. I have chosen some of the fragments that most directly address cultural identity. Some of the issues that Menchú raises are the tension between the conservation of traditional cultures and the necessity of modernization, the function of folklore, and the connections between politics and culture.

From Chapter I, "The Family"

My name is Rigoberta Menchú. I am twenty-three years old. This is my testimony. I didn't learn it from a book and I didn't learn it alone. I'd like to stress that it's not only *my* life, it's also the testimony of my people. It's hard for me to remember everything that's happened to me in my life since there have been many very bad times but, yes, moments of joy as well. The important thing is that what has happened to me has happened to many other people too: My story is the story of all poor Guatemalans. My personal experience is the reality of a whole people.

I must say before I start that I never went to school, and so I find speaking Spanish very difficult. I didn't have the chance to move outside my own world and only learned Spanish three years ago. . . . I'd like to start from when I was a little girl, or go back even further to when I was in my mother's womb, because my mother told me how I was born and our customs say that a child begins life on the first day of his mother's pregnancy.

There are twenty-two indigenous ethnic groups in Guatemala, twenty-three including the *mestizos*, or *ladinos*, as we call them. Twenty-three groups and twenty-three languages. I belong to one of them—the Quiché people—and I practice Quiché customs, but I also know most of the other groups very well through my work organizing the people. I come from San Miguel Uspuntán, in the northwest province of El Quiché. . . . The towns there all have long histories of struggle. . . . Where I live is practically a paradise, the country is so beautiful. There are no big roads, and no cars. Only people can reach it. Everything is taken down the mountainside on horseback or else we carry it ourselves. So, you can see, I live right up in the mountains.

My parents moved there in 1960 and began cultivating the land. No one had lived up there before because it's so mountainous. But they settled there and were determined not to leave no matter how hard the life was. . . .

They'd been forced to leave the town because some *ladino* families came to settle there. They weren't exactly evicted but the *ladinos* just gradually took over. My parents spent everything they earned, and they incurred so many debts with these people that they had to leave the house to pay them. The rich are always like that. When people owe them money they take a bit of land or some of their belongings and slowly end up with everything. That's what happened to my parents.

From Chapter II, "Birth Ceremonies"

When the baby joins the community, with him in the circle of candles—together with his little red bag—he will have his hoe, his machete, his axe, and all the tools he will need in life. These will be his playthings. A little girl will have her washing board and all the things she will need when she grows up. . . . When the parents do anything they always explain what it means. This includes learning prayers. This is very important to our people. The mother may say a prayer at any time. Before getting up in the morning, for instance, she thanks the day which is dawning because it might be a very important one for the family. Before lighting the fire, she blesses the wood because that fire is going to cook food for the whole family. . . . With the men it's the same. Before they start work every day, whatever hour of the morning it is, they greet the sun. They remove their hats and talk to the sun before starting work. . . . Our people are mainly peasants, but there are some people who buy and sell as well. They go into this after they've worked on the land. Sometimes when they come back from working in the *finca*, instead of tending a little plot of land, they'll start a shop and look for a different sort of life. But if they're used to greeting the sun every morning, they still go on doing it. And they keep all their old customs. Every part of our culture comes from the earth. Our religion comes from the maize and bean harvests which are so vital to our community. So even if a man goes to try and make some money, he never forgets [that] his culture springs from the earth. . . .

The elected fathers of the community explain to us that all these things come down to us from our grandfathers and we must conserve them. Nearly everything we do today is based on what our ancestors did. This is the main purpose of our elected leader—to embody all the values handed down from our ancestors. He is the leader of the community, a father to all our children, and he must lead an exemplary life. Above all, he has a commitment to the whole community. Everything that is done today, is done in memory of those who have passed on.

**From Chapter XXIII, "Political Activity in Other
Communities. Contacts with Ladinos"**

Something I want to tell you, is that I had a friend. He was the man who
taught me Spanish. He was a *ladino*, a teacher, who worked with the CUC.
. . . That *compañero* taught me many things, one of which was to love
ladinos a lot. He taught me to think more clearly about some of my ideas
which were wrong, like saying all *ladinos* are bad. He didn't teach me
through ideas, he showed me by his actions, by the way he behaved towards
me. . . . Anyway, the example of my *compañero ladino* made me really
understand the barrier which has been put up between the Indian and the
ladino, and that because of this same system which tries to divide us, we
haven't understood that *ladinos* also live in terrible conditions, the same as
we do. . . .

Ladinos are *mestizos*, the children of Spaniards and Indians who speak
Spanish. But they are in the minority. There is a larger percentage of
Indians. . . . We don't know the exact number [because] there are Indians
who don't wear Indian clothes and have forgotten their languages, so they
are not considered Indians. And there are middle-class Indians who have
abandoned their traditions. They aren't considered Indians either. However,
this *ladino* minority thinks its blood is superior, a higher quality, and they
think of Indians as a sort of animal. . . . At the same time, there are
differences between *ladinos* too, between rich *ladinos* and poor *ladinos*. . . .
But between these poor *ladinos* and Indians there is still that big barrier. No
matter how bad their conditions are, they feel *ladino*, and being *ladino* is
something important in itself: it's *not* being an Indian. . . .

Sometimes I'd hear how [the] teachers taught and what education was
like in the villages. They said that the arrival of the Spaniards was a
conquest, a victory, while we knew that in practice it was just the opposite.
They said the Indians didn't know how to fight and that many of them died
because they killed the horses and not the people. So they said. . . . Our
people must not think as the authorities think. . . .

We can select what is truly relevant for our people. Our lives show us
what this is. It has guaranteed our existence. Otherwise we would not have
survived.

From Chapter XXIX, "Fiestas and Indian Queens"

Once a year there is a fair . . . and that's when they choose the town's queen.
There has to be an Indian queen and a *ladino* queen. . . .

Later on they hold a big folklore festival in August at the fair in Cobán
with the Indian queens from all the different areas. This fiesta is organized

by the president in power, and important people like senators, foreign personalities, and ambassadors, are invited. . . . Well, the queen who was chosen by each town has to be there. It is obligatory, she has to be there by law. All the queens go with the costumes from the different regions but they have to get to Cobán by their own means. The president (he's always a general) is there in Cobán, so are all the principal deputies, all the important guests, and a lot of tourists. There are always a lot of tourists in our communities, in all the tourist spots in Guatemala. And they take all the photos they want. But for an Indian, taking a photo of him in the street is abusing his dignity, abusing him.

Well, they make these Indian girls parade around, throw kisses, and wave to everyone. They take photos of them and make them behave like the stars of the rich. In Guatemala there are no stars among the poor. Then they parade so that the public will come and see them, more than anything because of their costumes. . . . A friend who was a queen told me that they taught her how to present herself. This *compañera* couldn't speak Spanish very well, so she had to learn the boring little speech she was going to give: greetings for the president, greetings for the most important guests, greetings for the army officers. They made her learn what she was to say. After she'd learned all the movements she had to make, they took her to a cheap hotel, not even to the hotel where the guests were. After the fiesta they told them: "You've played your part, now go home." So they asked to be given a place to stay and they gave them something for a cheap hotel: in Guatemala these are places where just anybody goes, where the drunks go. Well, the *compañeras* had to go to a cheap hotel after the presentation. This is what hurts Indians most. It means that, yes, they think our costumes are beautiful because it brings in money, but it's as if the person wearing it doesn't exist. Then they charge the people who go to the festival a lot for their tickets and get a lot of money from the presentation of the queens. Everyone has to pay to go in. Only people with money can go.

From Chapter XXXIV, "Exile"

Well, my role is now that of a leader. . . . My job is above all carrying papers into the interior or to the towns, and organizing the people. . . . My life does not belong to me. I've decided to offer it to a cause. They can kill me at any time, but let it be when I'm fulfilling a mission, so I'll know that my blood will not be shed in vain, but will serve as an example to my *compañeros*. The world I live in is so evil, so bloodthirsty, that it can take my life away from one moment to the next. So the only road open to me is our struggle, the just war. . . .

This is my cause. As I've already said, it wasn't born out of something good, it was born out of wretchedness and bitterness. It has been radicalized by the poverty in which my people live. It has been radicalized by the malnutrition which I, as an Indian, have seen and experienced. And by the exploitation and discrimination which I've felt in the flesh. And by the oppression which prevents us from performing our ceremonies, and shows no respect for our way of life, the way we are. At the same time, they've killed the people dearest to me. . . . Therefore, my commitment to our struggle knows no boundaries or limits. This is why I've traveled to many places where I've had the opportunity to talk about my people. Of course, I'd need a lot of time to tell you all about my people, because it's not easy to understand just like that. And I think I've given some idea of that in my account. Nevertheless, I'm still keeping my Indian identity a secret. I'm still keeping secret what I think no one should know. Not even anthropologists or intellectuals, no matter how many books they have, can find out all our secrets.

Suggestions for Further Reading

Franco, Jean. *The Modern Culture of Latin America: Society and the Artist*. New York: Praeger, 1967.

———. *Spanish American Literature since Independence*. London: Ernest Benn; New York: Barnes and Noble, 1973.

Freyre, Gilberto. *The Masters and the Slaves*. Translated by Samuel Putnam. New York: Alfred A. Knopf, 1946.

González Echevarría, Roberto. *The Voice of the Masters: Writing and Authority in Modern Latin American Literature*. Austin: University of Texas Press, 1985.

Haberly, David T. "Form and Function in the New World Legend." In *Do the Americas Have a Common Literature?*, edited by Gustavo Pérez Firmat, 42–61. Durham: Duke University Press, 1990.

Johnson, Randal. "Notes on a Conservative Vanguard: The Case of Verde-Amarelo/Anta." *Hispanic Studies* 4, edited by Celso Lemos de Oliveira and María Angélica Lopes, 31–42. Columbia: University of South Carolina, 1989.

Kristal, Efraín. *The Andes Viewed from the City: Literary and Political Discourse on the Indian in Peru, 1848–1930*. New York: Peter Lang, 1987.

Mariátegui, José Carlos. *Seven Interpretive Essays on Peruvian Reality*. Translated by Marjory Urquidi. Austin: University of Texas Press, 1971.

Paz, Octavio. *The Labyrinth of Solitude*. Translated by Lysander Kemp. New York: Grove, 1961.

Picón Salas, Mariano. *A Cultural History of Spanish America from the Conquest to Independence*. Translated by Irving A. Leonard. Berkeley: University of California Press, 1962.

Piedra, José. "Literary Whiteness and the Afro-Hispanic Difference." *New Literary History* 18:2 (1987): 303–32.

Rojas Mix, Miguel. "Reinventing Identity." *NACLA Report on the Americas* 24:5 (1991): 29–33.

VII

The Dilemmas of Development

Peter F. Klaren

"Why is there so much wretchedness, so much poverty in this fabulous land . . . ? Ah, says one—it is the priests' fault; another blames it on the military; still others on the Indian; on the foreigner; on democracy; on dictatorship; on bookishness; on ignorance; or finally on divine punishment." So wrote the distinguished Mexican historian Daniel Cosio Villegas in 1949, alluding to the many explanations that have been put forth over the years for Latin America's chronic underdevelopment.[1]

At nearly the same time the Argentine economist Raúl Prebisch was about to issue his now-famous manifesto for development. His report, *The Economic Development of Latin America and Its Principal Problems*, written for the influential Economic Commission on Latin America (ECLA) of the United Nations in 1950, called for the region's governments to embark upon a systematic program of industrialization in order to close the widening developmental gap that he perceived between the industrialized West, which he called the "center" of the world economy, and Latin America, which he considered the "periphery."

Most governments responded to the call, undertaking extensive import-substitution industrialization programs that had, at least initially, impressive results. This policy, however, had its pitfalls, as did the corrective orthodox, monetarist policies that followed, so that by the 1980s, under the impact of a severe debt crisis and world recession, many Latin American economies were in free fall. By the end of the decade the situation had gotten so bad that many were referring to a "decade of lost development."

The problem, as most specialists had always agreed, was not a lack of natural resources for which the region was well endowed: silver, gold, tin, copper, oil, and a variety of industrial metals, not to mention abundant land.

[1]*Extremos de América*, quoted in Albert O. Hirschman, ed., *Latin American Issues: Essays and Comments* (New York, 1961), 3.

Despite this apparent wealth of resources, Latin America today falls squarely within the underdeveloped Third World, even if most of its countries are labeled by the World Bank as low-middle or middle income. In 1985 annual per capita incomes ranged from $2,248 in Mexico to $320 in Haiti, with most falling between the higher figure and Peru's $1,055.[2]

These averages mask one of the underlying indicators of Latin American underdevelopment: the region's extremely unequal distribution of income. In most countries the top 20 percent of the population earn around 60 percent of the total income, while the poorest 60 percent earn only 16 to 22 percent. Such a polarized income-distribution pattern reflects the generally low standard of living of the majority of the population, which suffers from, among other problems, low literacy levels, high infant mortality, and low life expectancy.[3]

Unequal income distribution also has tended to limit the size of the local market and therefore the potential of domestic manufacturing to contribute to a more balanced economic growth. More seriously, income inequality reflects a hierarchical socioeconomic structure and limited economic and political democracy, which have acted as structural and institutional barriers to the development process.

If income inequality is a major indicator of Latin American underdevelopment, what, we may ask, exactly is development? Lawrence Harrison in *Underdevelopment Is a State of Mind* suggests a basic definition: "Development, most simply, is improvement in human well-being. Most people today aspire to higher standards of living, longer lives, and fewer health problems; education for themselves and their children that will increase their earning capacity and leave them more in control of their lives; a measure of stability and tranquility; and the opportunity to do the things that give them pleasure and satisfaction."[4]

Sociologist James Lang digs deeper in *Inside Development in Latin America*, extracted here (Doc. 1). He argues that in strictly economic terms the region has made significant advances in development since the beginning of the century (in large part due to the intensive industrialization programs called for by Prebisch and ECLA around midcentury). However, he points out that development involves not only certain basic economic rights but also civil and political rights (human rights, civil liberties, political participation): "Combining economic and political rights is the path to freedom; one alone, or neither, leads to tyranny."

[2]James L. Dietz and James H. Street, eds., *Latin America's Economic Development: Institutionalist and Structuralist Perspectives* (Boulder, CO, 1987), 2.
[3]Ibid., 3.
[4]*Underdevelopment Is a State of Mind: The Latin American Case* (Lanham, MD, 1985), 1.

Economist Albert Hirschman turns to the question of how Latin Americans have historically interpreted the causes of their underdevelopment and tried to overcome it (Doc. 2). After Independence (ca. 1825), he says, they were preoccupied with the problem of creating a new political order, so they focused on political rather than economic questions. When, toward the end of the century, a greater degree of political stability evolved, they looked inward and tended to blame their economic backwardness on flaws in the national character as well as supposed traits of racial inferiority.

By the turn of the century, economic doctrines of laissez-faire and free trade dominated the thinking of the elites who stressed integration into the expanding international market via an export-led growth strategy. It was only with the disruptions in international trade caused by World War I and then the economic collapse of the Great Depression that Latin Americans began to find fault with the outside world rather than within themselves for their underdevelopment. As the vulnerability of their one-crop economies to price and demand fluctuations in the West became increasingly apparent, a strong nationalist critique such as that of Peruvian Víctor Raúl Haya de la Torre developed. Anticipating Prebisch and ECLA, he and others advocated a more interventionist and developmentalist state that would actively pursue agrarian reform, income redistribution, and industrialization as a model for development.

During the second half of the twentieth century a wide variety of approaches to political and economic development were suggested and employed in Latin America. They included modernization, Marxism, corporatism, populism, and bureaucratic authoritarianism. Political scientist Abraham Lowenthal briefly discusses these models, where they have been tried, and with what results (Doc. 3). He concludes that the most successful was "reformist democracy," which embodied a modernizationist prescription for underdevelopment. Most of the others proved to have serious flaws.

Modernization theory emphasized the importance of following the Western model of development. It stressed economic growth through the encouragement of foreign investment, technology transfer, and Western values such as practical education and the virtues of hard work. An earlier, embryonic form of modernization was applied at the turn of the century throughout Latin America. Brazilian economist Celso Furtado analyzes in more detail this early form of modernization that emphasized export-led growth and development (Doc. 4). He shows how the development of industry and international trade in the West shaped a new division of labor between the industrializing countries of Europe and the United States (the center) and the primary commodity-producing countries of Latin America (the periphery). In a particularly useful typology of the export economy, Furtado divides Latin America into three primary producing zones—

temperate, tropical, and mining—based on climate, geography, and natural resources.

The 1929 Wall Street crash and ensuing worldwide depression sent the export-dependent Latin American economies into a tailspin. Between 1929 and 1933, as Furtado notes, world exports fell by 25 percent, export prices by 30 percent, and the total value of world trade by over 50 percent. Throughout Latin America the sharp drop in the gross national product (GNP) and the rise in unemployment that followed destabilized governments and intensified the critique by nationalists of the export-led growth strategy long pursued by the ruling elites. Economist Robert Alexander outlines the strategy of import-substitution industrialization (ISI) (Doc. 5), already begun in its initial or "easy" phase as early as World War I in the more advanced South American countries such as Argentina, Brazil, and Chile. ISI accelerated as a consequence of the disruption in international trade caused first by the Great Depression and then by World War II. In effect, Latin Americans were forced to produce the manufactured goods that they needed but could not afford because of an acute shortage of foreign exchange (during the 1930s) and then could not import on account of war (during the 1940s).

The early success of ISI led Prebisch to issue his manifesto (Doc. 6) calling for concerted governmental efforts to promote industrialization. As a rationale he argued that the terms of trade with the West had turned decidedly against primary commodity-producing areas of the world such as Latin America. Prices for imported industrial goods from the West, he pointed out, were steadily rising over time while prices for commodities from the Third World were declining. The region was falling further and further behind in the developmental process.

While ISI policies could reverse this trend, ECLA also argued the need for structural reform to remove societal inefficiencies and inequalities that acted as obstacles to growth and development. Because of this emphasis on basic reform, ECLA's position came to be characterized as "structuralist." These obstacles included agrarian reform (designed to break up the inefficient and unprofitable haciendas) and redistribution of income to the poorer urban sectors of the population. Peasant land ownership and higher urban income, it was believed, would increase demand and enlarge the national market for domestically produced consumer goods.

During the 1950s and early 1960s several Latin American countries, such as Brazil, embarked on vigorous ISI programs. For a time the GNP in these countries grew rapidly (4 to 5 percent annually) while domestic manufacturing as a percentage of GNP grew even faster, diversifying the economy and creating new jobs. Gradually, however, local manufacturing output began to saturate the lower end of the consumer market, reaching the limits of what economists call the "easy" phase of ISI. At the same time, traditional commodity production and exports began to lag (partly because governments tended to neglect the agricultural sector in favor of ISI promotion), creating growing balance-of-payments problems. Finally, protectionism (high tariffs designed to protect domestic manufactured goods from competition from cheap imports) created industrial inefficiencies. By the end of the 1950s and early 1960s these problems combined to stall growth and trigger inflation, producing severe "stagflation" and growing popular unrest throughout Latin America.

This set the stage for the seizure of power by the military, who blamed the growing economic and political chaos on failed ISI policies and on the inability of the civilian politicians to manage the state and the developmental process. This can be seen in the specific case of Brazil, when President Humberto Castello Branco, in an address to the National Congress, describes the situation leading to the military intervention in 1964 (Doc. 7). The turn toward what Argentine political scientist Guillermo O'Donnell has called bureaucratic authoritarianism began with Brazil and Argentina in the mid-1960s and spread to Chile, Uruguay, and again Argentina in the 1970s (Doc. 8). Political scientist Jonathan Hartlyn and economist Samuel Morley summarize the neoliberal approach of the bureaucratic-authoritarian regimes attempting to stabilize and restart the economies of the southern cone countries (Doc. 9).

The structuralist approach to economic development now came under sharp attack by these neoliberals who advocated monetarist and free-market policies of stabilization and development. These, as Hartlyn and Morley state, included measures to reduce fiscal deficits and achieve fiscal balance, thereby reducing runaway inflation. The military governments also moved to open the economy internationally, to reduce the role of the state in the economy, to reform labor legislation in order to weaken unions and make firing easier and cheaper for management, and to eliminate or reduce a wide range of costly government subsidies. Since most of these measures adversely affected the popular classes, the military resorted to political policies designed to demobilize and depoliticize the population. Repression and human-rights violations became widespread.

In order to resolve the acute imbalance of payments that had initiated the crisis, many military governments also resorted to massive foreign loans from banks anxious to recycle the petrodollars that they had accumulated during the 1973 world oil crisis. So began the Latin American debt crisis, which is analyzed by economist Rudiger Dornbusch (Doc. 10). By 1982 the debt crisis had brought the region's economies to a virtual standstill and forced the military back to the barracks, bringing a return to democratic civilian regimes. According to Dornbusch, the military regimes were the victims of massive capital flight, gross mismanagement, and worldwide recession, not to mention massive human-rights violations.

With the return of international recession and stagflation in the 1980s, the governments of Latin America found it increasingly difficult to service their massive international debts, since prices for their exports were declining while interest rates on their loans were rising. The fragile new democratic regimes responded by restructuring their international portfolios and resorting to a second and more radical round of neoliberal stabilization measures designed to halt the new surge of hyperinflation and growth decline. In Venezuela (1989) and Argentina (1990) these measures touched off serious urban rioting. However, elsewhere Latin Americans generally accepted stabilization as a necessary, if unpleasant, price to pay to reduce runaway inflation. Late in the decade the United States under the Bush administration also took two initiatives designed to help resolve the economic crisis: Peter Hakim assesses the problems and prospects for both the Brady Plan and the Enterprise for the Americas in remarks before the U.S. Congress (Doc. 11).

A major consequence of the severe economic crisis of the 1980s has been a marked shift in the nature of the debate over development. According to sociologist Ian Roxborough, "as development has disappeared, so too has development theory. It has been replaced with a debate about stabilization and economic restructuring."[5]

In looking back over a century of Latin American development, there are some reasons to be optimistic, even in the face of the "lost decade" of the 1980s. Despite formidable historical and structural obstacles, the region underwent enormous transformation and growth, particularly during the middle decades of the century. From 1960 to 1980, for example, Latin America's rate of growth was almost twice that of the United States. Industry proved to be the most dynamic sector during this period, with a "rate of growth remarkably comparable to that [which] the United States experienced from 1890 to 1914, during this country's industrial transformation."[6]

Still, high population growth and massive migration to the cities since World War II, as well as the continuing problem of income inequality and the economic downturn of the 1980s, have served as a brake on such progress. Today, as we approach the twenty-first century during a period of

---

[5]"Changing Realities: Changing Theories," in Peter Klaren and T. J. Bossert, eds., *Promise of Development: Theories of Change in Latin America*, 2d ed. (forthcoming, Westview Press).

[6]Abraham F. Lowenthal, *Partners in Conflict: The United States and Latin America* (Baltimore, 1987), 10.

unprecedented world change, the hope and the challenge of Latin America's development lies both in its ability to halt its economic slide and to find ways to take advantage of the emerging new global economic order.

1. Inside Development in Latin America ◆ James Lang

To understand how Latin Americans perceived and confronted their underdevelopment at the grass roots rather than at loftier theoretical or governmental levels, Vanderbilt sociologist James Lang visited community development projects in the Dominican Republic, Colombia, and Brazil. His experiences with ordinary people engaged in the day-to-day struggles for development in these projects led him to conclude that there are "no prepackaged remedies, only localized ones." While economists may theorize and conceive overarching, macroeconomic theories to confront underdevelopment, "a project had a way to work with the poor on the problems they considered of importance; it reached into the neighborhoods where people lived." In the course of these observations, Lang also pro- vides us with a workable definition of development that combines both economic and political rights.

"Lake Titicaca," said Sister Pancretia, "is the highest in the world; it is the lake closest to God." In the fourth grade, we learned simple virtues: to feed the hungry, to care for the sick, to clothe the naked. Experience has overturned the truth of the fourth grade. God's plan was one thing, man's was another.

When John Gunther took a generation *Inside Latin America* in 1941, he described nations that "as everyone knows live by the export of raw materials; they are basically one-crop or one-product countries." His index had no entries for manufacturing, hydroelectric power, or industrialization. To travel through Latin America today is to see a land much changed since Gunther's journey. Brazil is one of the world's top ten automakers, turns out 14 million metric tons of steel a year, and exports jet aircraft to the United States. Brazil can no longer be described by sambas, Carnival, and coffee. And Brazil is not alone. To track the industrial sector in Argentina, Mexico, or Venezuela is to tally petrochemicals, steel output, automobile produc- tion, and cement.

Despite the achievements, aspects of the "old" Latin America Gunther knew persist. "Dictatorship," "poverty," and "illiteracy" were prominent

From James Lang, *Inside Development in Latin America: A Report from the Dominican Republic, Colombia, and Brazil* (Chapel Hill, 1988), xi–xiii, footnotes omitted. © 1988 by The University of North Carolina Press. Reprinted by permis- sion of the publisher and author.

categories in his index: today's Latin America cannot be described without them. Brazil's new democratic government, for example, follows twenty years (1964–1985) of military rule. It has inherited the legacy the old regime left behind: the poorest 40 percent of Brazil's families get by on only 10 percent of the national income; half the country's schoolchildren drop out before the fourth grade. Based on gross national product, Brazil ranks as an upper-middle-income country. Based on infant mortality rates, it belongs in the low-income class.

Gunther's book warned against Nazi infiltration. A new enemy, of course, has replaced the old one. The region's turmoil, however, may still rest on the same basis as before: on recurrent dictatorship, and on persistent poverty and illiteracy. Perhaps ideology is only the symptom. The United Nations Bill of Rights defines an adequate standard of living, basic health care, and education as economic rights. It also specifies civil liberties: the right to security and privacy, freedom from arbitrary arrest and torture, and the liberty of conscience and association. Combining economic and political rights is the path to freedom; one alone, or neither, leads to tyranny.

Regimes in Poland, the Soviet Union, and China cite economic rights as their justification. Rebellion takes the shape of civil liberties. In the United States, the interdependence of both has long been acknowledged, if only implicitly. In the nineteenth century, no country educated ordinary people with the tenacity of the United States. That freedom of the press was an expendable liberty for the illiterate seemed self-evident. The property qualifications states once had for voting also recognized the convergence. People without decent incomes and property of their own provided an unstable basis for democracy. This truth, apparent in the United States, has not been applied to Latin America. South of the Rio Grande, rebellion is premised on economic rights.

In the 1980s most Latin American countries returned to democracy. This has meant the restoration of civil liberties. The task ahead is to address the needs of the majority in a productive fashion. The alternative is familiar enough. Empty promises discredit democracy; inaction rallies the poor against the rich. "Instability" then becomes a pretext for another round of military intervention.

Today, the haves and the have-nots are analyzed in development theory. That was less true in 1940; Gunther's book did not bother to index the concept. One can now take courses in it and choose between textbooks. Some claim that development is impossible because the rich hog everything and run the machinery of state. Others claim that development occurs when a "hidden hand" is allowed to distribute resources. So the poor must wait for revolution or the benefits that are presumed to trickle down. To study orthodox theory is to wade through comparative advantages, competing "engines" of growth, and import-substitution industrialization. Whether people have an education becomes "human capital theory," whether they eat is called "basic needs fulfillment," and whether the sick are cared for is "health delivery." It might be better to stay closer to the fourth grade.

This report does not ask whether exports or domestic demand should be the engine of economic growth. There is no mention of dependency theory, the Kuznets curve, or models that "trade off" growth for inequality. The report does not quarrel with GNP, and it does not attack capitalism, business, or investment. The premise is simply this. In a country like Brazil, functional literacy, decent health care, and gainful employment require more than computer chips and General Motors executives. Regardless of which theories make the economy grow, the benefits do not reach most people fast enough. The hidden hand will not fill the shopping carts in Santo Domingo, Bogotá, or Rio de Janeiro any time soon. This does not mean Brazil should abandon the computer. It means that for poorer citizens "development" has to be something more than superhighways and petrochemicals.

This report is about what that "something more" is. It tells the story of health and rural development projects in the Dominican Republic, Colombia, and Brazil. Gunther interviewed politicians; this book talks with physicians and agronomists, with farmers and midwives. My part was to listen. People explained what they did in community health and rural extension, how they organized their work, and why they did it. I asked questions and wrote down what they told me. I file this report more as a journalist than as a political analyst. I do not know how to end inequality or how to reconcile liberty with economic rights. The people I met did not know either. Nonetheless, they had set out to do what they could, where they were, and with what they had.

They offered no prepackaged remedies, only localized ones. That is a small truth for modern times when solutions must be big ones. Still, how they accomplished things preserved peoples' dignity and strengthened their self-respect. A project had a way to work with the poor on the problems they considered of importance; it reached into the neighborhoods where people lived. Community development was a good school for self-reliance, and a good way to turn democracy from promise to practice.

The people I met believed in such truths. The lesson was not just for Latin America either. In the United States, social policies have been short on consistency and self-reliance. If the United States worked with the poor in the spirit of the Dominican Republic's Plan Sierra, it might find new possibilities within itself and understand better the contentious Third World at its borders.

Twenty-five years later, I did get to Lake Titicaca. It was as deep, blue, and clear as Sister Pancretia promised.

2. Ideologies of Economic Development ◆
Albert O. Hirschman

The distinguished developmental economist Albert Hirschman analyzes how Latin Americans have perceived and interpreted their underdevelopment over the course of two centuries. Preoccupied after Independence in 1825 with the problem of how to reorganize politically after their separation from Spain, Latin American intellectuals did not really confront the problem until a measure of political stability was finally achieved toward the end of the nineteenth century. Then they tended to blame their backwardness on flaws in their own character as well as on what they saw as their racial inferiority. At that time, racist explanations for underdevelopment were common in the West. Once the Great Depression exposed the vulnerability of their export-dependent economies, however, they turned to other explanations for their condition, blaming the legacy of imperialism for most of their ills.

From Independence to the First World War:
The Age of Self-Incrimination

Some of the best-known ideologies of economic development have arisen or have become prominent and influential in countries whose economic progress was seriously lagging behind that of the industrial leaders. *Relative economic backwardness* is thus an important concept which Alexander Gerschenkron has used with powerful effect to explain the specific characteristics of the successive forward surges of France, Germany, and Russia in the 19th century and to show how every one of these thrusts was accompanied by a specific set of ideals about the cause and cure of the lag that was to be overcome. With respect to these countries it appears that the greater the lag the more radical and exalted were the theories which fired the effort at catching up.

Unfortunately, this suggestive generalization does not seem to hold in Latin America (or, for that matter, in the other countries which are today considered to be underdeveloped). The lag of the Latin American countries behind the industrial and general economic progress of Europe in the 19th century did not then give rise to any indigenous theories, ideas, or views about the nature of Latin America's development problem. The reason may

From Albert O. Hirschman, "Ideologies of Economic Development in Latin America," in *Latin American Issues: Essays and Comments*, ed. Albert O. Hirschman (New York, 1961), 4–12, footnotes omitted. © 1961 by the Twentieth Century Fund.

be that for many decades after the wars of independence the problems of survival, organization, and consolidation of the South American states in the midst of border disputes, internal revolts, and civil wars stood in the center of public attention so that the "ideologues" concentrated first on the problem of political organization.

This is not the place to retrace the development of Latin American political thought. But it should perhaps be briefly recalled that the constitutions which were adopted by the new Latin American states were largely inspired, if not copied, from that of the United States while the "generous ideas of the French Revolution" served as the ideological foundation for the new republics. With the constitutions being continually violated, suspended, and rewritten by the numerous military dictators and with the actual political, social, and economic conditions being extraordinarily far removed from Liberty, Equality, and Fraternity, there developed in Latin America that characteristic divorce between ideology and reality which has been well characterized by Octavio Paz in his incisive essay on Mexico, *El laberinto de la soledad*:

> The liberal and democratic ideology, far from expressing our concrete historical situation, obscured it. The political lie installed itself almost constitutionally among our countries. The moral damage has been incalculable and reaches into deep layers of our character. Lies are something we move in with ease. During more than a hundred years we have suffered regimes of brute force, which were at the service of feudal oligarchies, but utilized the language of liberty.

This permanent and painful "collision between theory and practice, between words and action, between content and form" has been described by virtually all observers of the Latin American scene; and we shall see that, far from dead, it has invaded new territories, such as economic and social policy-making.

The inability of the political system to provide basic requisites of law and order, the spectacle of the strides made by Europe and the United States, and the defeats and humiliations suffered (mainly by Mexico) at the hands of the Colossus of the North did lead, in the course of the 19th century, to considerable soul-searching on the part of Latin American intellectuals. They turned away from the revolutionary ideals and dreams which had served their countries poorly and became willing to settle for less than utopia. In the second half of the century, many came to preach "a practical sense of life," "an inquiring, experimental and practical mind," "rigorous scientific method," and "clearly defined, positive ends." This state of mind found its most curious expression in the ideological support many of Mexico's outstanding educators and intellectuals gave to the long dictatorship (1884–

1911) of Porfirio Díaz, the "honest tyrant" who was to bring order out of chaos and prosperity out of stagnation and misery. It is well to recall that Díaz was admired not only by Mexican intellectuals; Tolstoy among others hailed him as a "modern Cromwell" who used autocratic methods in guiding his country toward democracy. Thus, under Porfirio Díaz, Mexico experimented with an idea that today has wide currency and application in the Middle East and Asia: namely, that one-man military rule can play a positive, tutelary role in a new country by ridding it of corruption, by giving it a vacation from disruptive political strife, and by guiding it firmly and efficiently toward modernity.

One reason why educators such as Justo Sierra threw their support to Díaz was their strong feeling that much time and patient work was needed to remedy Mexico's ills. Indeed, faced with the incapacity of Latin American societies to achieve stable, just, and progressive governments, they concluded that nothing less than a complete transformation of Latin American "character" and society was required, and this was evidently a long-term task. The structure of society was to be improved through the formation of a middle class, and patient education was needed thoroughly to reshape the Latin American character.

In this latter respect, feelings ran to an astonishingly high pitch. At the beginning of this century, some of the most widely read works by Latin Americans about themselves and their society consisted of little more than a seemingly endless and remarkably pitiless recitation of their vices and failures. Outstanding among these works were Bunge's *Nuestra América* [Buenos Aires, 1903] and Bomfim's *O parasitismo social e evolução: A América Latina* (Rio de Janeiro, 1903). Strongly influenced by the then-fashionable determinism based on race and heredity, both books barely stop short of proclaiming the irreparable racial inferiority and progressive degeneration of all Latin America. Bunge's work, which is highly entertaining and which went through six editions, contains many valuable insights and in particular a masterful portrait of the *cacique*, but his whole analysis is built on the proposition that the three basic constituents of the Latin American character are laziness, sadness, and arrogance!

Another highly interesting work in this category which deals specifically with economics is *Nuestra inferioridad económica: Sus causas, sus consecuencias* (Santiago, 1912) by the Chilean historian Francisco Encina. To him the principal reasons for the inadequate progress of Chile's economy are certain pervasive character traits such as lack of initiative, of perseverance and of morality, inability to cooperate, ostentatiousness, etc. These traits, in turn, are due to poor heredity and the wrong kind of education.

Today, when we are more aware of the hypersensitive nationalism sometimes encountered in Latin America, it is worthwhile to recall this extraordinary orgy of self-denigration, self-laceration, and pessimism which can be traced back to Simón Bolívar and to his famous statement that in Latin America "treaties are pieces of paper, constitutions are books, elections are fights, liberty is anarchy, and life a torment."

How was this "sick continent" and this "ill people" to be cured? The Argentinians [Domingo Faustino] Sarmiento and [J. B.] Alberdi, writing respectively in the middle and late 19th century, advised imitation of the U.S. model. Sarmiento wrote: "Let us achieve the stage of development of the United States. Let us be the United States." Alberdi gave much the same advice several decades later: "In economics even more than in politics the best example for Americans to follow is America herself. In economics North America is the great model for South America."

But the economic doctrines that were prevalent among the more prominent Latin American writers on social and economic affairs were even more strongly influenced by the British free trade and noninterventionist doctrines. Perhaps the successive governments were either too weak or too tyrannical for anyone to think of advising that they take on additional functions. Also, as Celso Furtado suggests, Latin American 19th-century writers had their social roots among the large landholders and slave owners and may therefore have shown little interest in building up a manufacturing establishment. In this context it becomes significant that Alberdi failed to advocate industrialization for Latin America even though he hit on the idea that latecomers possess certain advantages—an idea which has been invoked elsewhere as a persuasive argument for industrialization:

> By preventing the rise of industry in her American colonies Spain benefited industrial Europe and handed to her a rich territory which now has to buy from the most advanced industrial nations. On the other hand the very backwardness of South America is an advantage. Instead of inheriting a bad industry, South America has at her disposal the most advanced European industry of the 19th century.

It appears that in spite of his insight about the advantages of backwardness, Alberdi is happy enough with the existing state of affairs which makes it possible for Latin America to acquire quality manufactures in Europe.

The Interwar Period and the Rise of Anti-imperialism

Up to the first decade of the 20th century this literature with its passionate self-criticism and its advocacy of laissez-faire and a social and economic system similar to that of the advanced industrial nations was perhaps dominant. In the next phase we encounter a greater tendency to find fault with the outside world rather than with oneself. Correlatively, a search begins for specifically Latin American solutions to the area's economic problems. United States' interventionism in Panama, the Caribbean, and Mexico, the loss of face of Europe as a result of the First World War, and the Russian and Mexican revolutions all contributed to this change. Yet cohesive theories of social and economic reform were slow to emerge. The Mexican Revolution was remarkable in that it wholly belied the Napoleonic maxim that a revolution is an idea that has found bayonets—here it was rather the revolution which found its ideas as it proceeded with varying speed and over a large number of years along its pragmatic road.

Paradoxically, the most ambitious attempt at revolutionary theorizing about Latin American society arose in a country that up to this day at least has gone through a minimum of social change: I am speaking about Peru and the writings of [Victor Raúl] Haya de la Torre and [José Carlos] Mariátegui.

Haya de la Torre formulated his thinking in the early twenties, in an intellectual climate dominated by the October Revolution. He soon felt the need to differentiate himself from orthodox communism and set out to discover the peculiar character of Latin America's problems. Thus, he considered Lenin's definition of imperialism as the last stage of capitalism and noted that for the nonindustrial countries, imperialism was rather *their first* experience with capitalism. For this reason, Haya de la Torre maintained that a revolution in Latin America could not be undertaken by the weak and submerged proletariat but must also rely on the intellectuals and the middle classes, which, according to him, were endowed with far more fighting spirit in Latin America than in Europe.

Under these conditions, the struggle must be conducted under an anti-imperialist rather than an anticapitalist banner. Action against imperialism was the first point of Haya's five-point program, the others being: political unity of Latin America, nationalization of land and industries, internationalization of the Panama Canal, and solidarity with the oppressed people and classes everywhere. But like some of these latter points (e.g., nationalization) Haya's anti-imperialism was subject to interesting qualifications. For Haya explicitly recognized Latin America's need for foreign capital, but, so he argued, if only Latin American countries stopped competing for foreign capital, and united in an anti-imperialist coalition, they could obtain it under far more favorable conditions since capitalist countries have a compelling need to export capital:

> The naive thesis of our feudal rulers, vassals of imperialism, proclaims "every capital is good" while the antithesis of our passionate radicals says "we don't need foreign capital." The Aprista synthesis holds that as long as the present economic order lasts, some capital flows are necessary and good and others unnecessary and dangerous; and that only the anti-imperialist state should

control capital investment under strict conditions. The latter can be imposed in view of the compulsion to emigrate, which is felt by the excess capital of the big industrial centers. *In our countries, the capitalist stage must therefore unfold under the leadership of the anti-imperialist State.*

Stripped of rhetoric, this simply means that the state should exercise control over the direction of investment—a condition which is today frequently demanded by the foreign (e.g., World Bank) capital itself, rather than imposed upon it.

Haya's search for an "Indoamerican way" rests upon closer inspection essentially on the desire for economic development without some of the disruptions and injustices that have marked the process elsewhere:

> Why not build into our own reality "as it really is" the bases of a new economic and political organization which will accomplish the educational and constructive task of industrialism but will be free of its cruel aspects of human exploitation and national vassalage?

Attribution of backwardness to imperialist exploitation, direction of economic development by the state, avoidance of the excesses that have marked the early stages of capitalist development in the West, and the community of interests of all of Latin America—these are basic ingredients of Haya's thought which as we shall see have left a deep mark on Latin American economic thinking.

A final element is the search for elements in the Indian or primitive past of Latin America that are not only worth preserving but that can be used in building a better social and economic order. Haya speaks eloquently about the dualism of the Peruvian economy and about the need to preserve and to build a new agrarian society on the collectivist tradition of the Indian economy. In the work of another influential Peruvian, the Socialist José Carlos Mariátegui (1895–1930), the preservation of the communal *ayllu* (corresponding to the Aztec-Mexican *calpulli-ejido*) and the call for its victory over the *latifundio* are principal themes. Actually, U.S. anthropologists who have done field work in Peru have expressed serious doubts about the vigor of the communes and about the extent to which they still hold land in common, engage in reciprocal labor, etc. Nevertheless, the continuing belief among intellectuals that it may be possible to build on the Indian past is in itself of interest. It is part of the attempt to find an "own" way to economic progress and social justice.

Whether or not the currents thus far reviewed qualify as economic theories, knowledge of this background is important to an understanding of contemporary thinking. For, essentially, the debate is still defined by two principal questions: One, where lies the responsibility for our lag? In ourselves or in the outside world which exploits us? Two, how can we make progress? By imitating others (the West or Russia) or by fashioning our own way?

---

3. Various Approaches to Political and Economic Development ◆ Abraham Lowenthal

Political scientist Abraham Lowenthal reviews the major approaches to development undertaken in the last quarter century. He concludes that both bureaucratic authoritarianism, with its monetarist "free-market" approach, and socialism, with its dependency critique and Marxist approach in Cuba and Nicaragua, were largely failures. Mexico's one-party corporatist state was more successful for much of the twentieth century but now shows serious signs of unraveling. Only democratic reformism in Colombia, Venezuela, Costa Rica, and the Dominican Republic seems to have been relatively successful in achieving a measure of development.

In the early 1960s, when the "modernization" paradigm and theories about the "stages of economic growth" still had great influence, many scholars and practitioners assumed that economic growth, social equity, expanded popular participation, and political stability all went hand in hand. Countries were assumed to be moving together, at different times and paces, through a series of phases. Economic development brought with it a series of other positive trends: the erosion of oligarchical social and political structures, the expansion of the middle class and its influence, an increase in political involvement, and the strengthening of institutions.

Argentina, with its perpetually stormy politics, was then the one exception. It was a relatively prosperous country, and had been for decades, but it could not seem to keep its political act together. It was a largely middle-class nation, yet it was torn by class strife. Political participation in Argentina always seemed to threaten institutions rather than to strengthen them.

In 1973, Guillermo O'Donnell, an Argentine social scientist, suggested that his country's experience might not be exceptional but, rather, an advanced case of a new paradigm. Drawing mainly on the cases of Argentina and Brazil, O'Donnell argued that relatively high levels of modernization and the limits of import-substitution industrialization together place severe

From Abraham F. Lowenthal, *Partners in Conflict: The United States and Latin America in the 1990s*, rev. ed. (Baltimore, 1990), 20–24. Reprinted by permission of Johns Hopkins University Press and the author.

strains on democratic institutions. These pressures facilitate authoritarian rule by technocrats, allied with the military, as a way of protecting middle-class privileges against rising popular demands.

O'Donnell's analysis of intensified social conflict, stalemate, and an eventual move to institutional "bureaucratic authoritarian" rule aptly described not only developments in Argentina and Brazil but also subsequent events in Chile and Uruguay. His thesis helps explain the cruel paradox that those countries with the highest level of social mobilization were precisely the ones that became the most brutally repressive during the 1970s. In fact, the most salient approach to political and social organization in Latin America during those years was neither constitutional democracy nor leftist revolution, but authoritarian rule by military and civilian technocrats of the Right.

Most of these authoritarian regimes were characterized not only by exclusionary political demobilization but also by a monetarist approach to economic policy. To varying degrees, they enshrined market capitalism in its relatively pristine version, revising the public policies of previous decades in order to integrate national economies more fully into the international capitalist system. Import and exchange controls were dropped or made substantially less restrictive, prices were decontrolled, and unemployment was allowed to rise to help bring inflation levels down.

Neither the political nor the economic approach of "bureaucratic authoritarianism" succeeded, however. Not even in Brazil, by far the least doctrinaire and the most dynamic of these countries, did the authoritarian approach wear well; its appeal eroded steadily for a decade, fueling the pressures for *abertura*. The coalition of social and political forces which helped bring authoritarian governments to power in Argentina, Chile, and Uruguay also disintegrated in each case, albeit in different ways and to different degrees. The military has already left office in Argentina, Brazil, and Uruguay. Chile's Pinochet regime has scant support outside the military.

Despite initially positive indications, it has also become clear that the monetarist "free-market" approach has failed, perhaps in direct proportion to the purity and inflexibility with which it was administered. Nowhere was its failure more dramatic than in Chile. National production fell 14 percent in 1982, urban unemployment rose to more than 20 percent, and workers receiving only a twenty-dollar monthly minimum wage accounted for another 13 percent of the population. The situation in 1983 was even worse, and recovery in Chile since then has been slow and incomplete. Chile's foreign debt has swelled from $5.5 billion in 1979 to about $20 billion in the mid-1980s, almost 300 percent of export earnings.

In sum, enthusiastic talk of the Brazilian and Chilean "miracles"— unjustified early tributes to the apparent early economic success of the authoritarian regimes—has long since ended. The bureaucratic-authoritarian path turned out to be a dead end.

A second approach to development has been the military populism epitomized by Peru's experiment, tried briefly also in Bolivia, and proposed by military officers and civilian ideologues in several other countries. These regimes paralleled the "bureaucratic authoritarian" ones in their reliance on military leadership and technocratic expertise and in their deep distrust of political parties. They differed, however, because they tended to empower previously disenfranchised or less powerful groups. They were more open to socialist or quasi-socialist forms of organization, less repressive in their means of social control, and less closely tied to the United States and to multinational corporations.

None of these military populist regimes survived into the 1980s. On the whole, they left behind them disappointment, political rejection, and economic disaster. The military governments were unable either to mobilize popular support for their programs or to manage the economy successfully, and none gained lasting legitimacy. For the foreseeable future, the reformist military path in Latin America has been discredited.

A third generally unsuccessful approach in Latin America has been the socialist path. This course has been followed since 1960 in Cuba, in Chile under Allende from 1970 to 1973, since 1979 (with interesting variations) in Nicaragua, and in Grenada from 1979 to 1983. St. Lucia also flirted briefly with socialism, and Jamaica, Guyana, and Suriname experimented with it to a very limited extent.

The Allende period in Chile, cut short by the Pinochet coup, underlined the difficulties of implementing a socialist approach in precisely the highly mobilized and relatively modern settings that Soviet strategists previously had thought most conducive to socialism. Polarization, internal sabotage, and international pressures combined to reveal the narrow constraints within which an elected socialist regime must work in Latin America.

In Cuba, a highly personal autocracy has gradually been institutionalized as the roles of the party and the government bureaucracy have expanded. Means have been developed over the years to allow for some public involvement in decision making, at least on local issues. Economic organization slowly evolved in the 1970s to provide for private incentives and rewards, largely as a response to admitted failures in various sectors, but these experiments are apparently being abandoned in the late 1980s, as they, too, have proved disappointing.

Heavily subsidized for a quarter-century by the Soviet Union, Cuba has been a poor showcase for socialism. The Mariel incident of 1980 (in which more than 125,000 Cubans emigrated within a few weeks) revealed the high level of dissatisfaction that persists there after a generation. Although Cuba still has some influence in Central America and the Caribbean, it is not as appealing a model in any country of South America as it was in 1960. A few student activists and other would-be revolutionaries still advocate following the Cuban path, and Fidel Castro's personal stature remains high in some quarters (in part, perhaps, because of the David and Goliath relationship between Cuba and the United States), but the Cuban approach is widely regarded as unpromising.

The Sandinistas in Nicaragua and, until 1983, the New Jewel Movement in Grenada have made efforts—apparently heeding Cuba's advice—to keep political leadership collective and allow scope for private sector economic activity, if not for much autonomous political expression. Neither country has prospered, however, in any case. Jamaica experienced seven successive years of negative growth and gathering social unrest under Manley, though the subsequent experience of the Seaga regime has made it clear that there is no easy path to growth in Jamaica. Guyana and Suriname, too, have had negative experiences with socialism. St. Lucia abandoned its socialist program almost before it began. In short, socialism has been consistently unsuccessful in Latin America. Persistent and sometimes intense U.S. opposition may be one of the reasons for this record, but it is not the only or the main one.

Mexico's system of one-party dominance is the fourth approach tried in Latin America during the past twenty-five years. A generation of import substitution, followed by the discovery and rapid development of major petroleum and natural gas deposits, enabled Mexico to grow, with some setbacks, until 1982. Then a number of simultaneous reverses forced the country into a severe liquidity crisis. But even before Mexico's financial difficulties emerged, the country was facing serious problems: widening income disparities, incipient inflation, and political violence. Mexico was able partially to address these problems during the 1970s with a series of political reforms which broadened the scope for opposition, and the bonanza of oil wealth temporarily obscured the nation's economic difficulties. In the 1980s, however, Mexico has been facing severe economic problems, and opposition to the dominant party is growing. The Mexican path has proved far from satisfactory.

The most successful Latin American experience during the past quarter-century has been with reformist democracy, which was practiced throughout the entire period in Colombia, Venezuela, and Costa Rica, and since 1966 in the Dominican Republic. All these nations have placed some limits on the democratic contest for power, whether through a strong two-party system or by reaching agreement, explicit or tacit, on the rules of politics. These four countries have gone at least a generation in each case without a coup, and they have maintained generally favorable records on human rights in recent years. The Venezuelan and Colombian economies have been stimulated, and to some extent distorted, by massive injections of capital—from petro-dollars in Venezuela and the profits of the massive drug trade and periodic coffee booms in Colombia. All four countries have felt increased strains: economic and financial problems, some political violence, and incipient military restlessness in Venezuela and Colombia; side effects of the Central American turmoil and the impact of recession in Costa Rica; and the social effects of prolonged and painful austerity in the Dominican Republic. In all these nations, the centrist consensus underlying institutional stability is still fragile. But by continental standards, all have done well in managing internal tensions and sustaining some economic advance.

---

4. The Transformation of International Trade in the Second Half of the Nineteenth Century and Its Impact on Latin America ◆ Celso Furtado

The distinguished Brazilian economist Celso Furtado was an early contributor to what came to be known as the dependency theory of Latin American underdevelopment. He explains how a new international division of labor emerged from the nineteenth-century industrial advance in Europe, powered mainly by Great Britain which, at one time, accounted for over 70 percent of world trade. Latin America, a commodity- and natural resource-rich part of the world, would specialize in the production and export of foodstuffs, fibers, and minerals, which were in great demand in industrializing countries to feed urban workers and provide raw materials for the factories. Furtado shows how the idea of comparative advantage worked to specialize the region's commodity production into specific ecological zones, which he identifies as temperate, tropical, and highland. This export, or outward-oriented, development produced accelerated economic growth from 1880 down to World War I, but it was severely disrupted by the onset of the Great Depression of the 1930s.

Typology of Economies Exporting Raw Materials

The Latin American countries began to enter the channels of expanding international trade in the 1840s. The primary exporters involved in this process tended to fall into three groups: 1) countries exporting temperate agricultural commodities; 2) countries exporting tropical agricultural

From Celso Furtado, *Economic Development of Latin America*, 2d ed., trans. Suzette Macedo (Cambridge, 1976), 129–33, footnotes omitted. Reprinted by permission of Cambridge University Press.

commodities; 3) countries exporting mineral products. In each case, foreign trade helped to establish a distinctive economic structure whose characteristic features should be borne in mind when studying its subsequent evolution.

The first group is composed essentially of Argentina and Uruguay. In this case, exportable agricultural production was based on the extensive use of land and was destined to compete with the domestic production of countries undergoing rapid industrialization. Extensive use of good agricultural land made it possible to achieve high profitability from the start. On the other hand, the very extensiveness of the agriculture practiced and the sheer volume of freight involved necessitated the creation of a widespread transportation network which indirectly led to the rapid unification of the domestic market, focusing on the major ports of shipment. This group of countries displays the characteristics of regions . . . constituting an expanding frontier of the industrializing European economy. This frontier, to which European agricultural technology was transplanted in the early stages, soon became an important center for developing new agricultural techniques of its own. Both the techniques of farming vast open spaces and of large-scale transportation, storage, and shipment of cereals originated in the United States. In sum, the countries in this group, precisely because they competed with the domestic production of countries at a more advanced stage of development and with regions of recent European settlement enjoying a high standard of living, were from the start integrated into a productive sector of the world economy characterized by constant technological advance. Throughout the phase of expansion in their foreign trade, these countries achieved high rates of growth.

The second group, consisting of countries exporting tropical agricultural products, includes more than half the Latin American population. It includes Brazil, Colombia, Ecuador, Central America, and the Caribbean, as well as certain regions of Mexico and Venezuela. Countries in this group entered international trade in competition with colonial areas and the southern region of the United States. Sugar and tobacco remained typically colonial products until the last years of the nineteenth century. It was the rapid expansion of the world demand for coffee and cacao from the midnineteenth century onwards that enabled tropical commodities to play a dynamic role in integrating the Latin American economy into world trade during the period under consideration. In this case, structural changes in the British economy had less direct impact, since the British market continued to be abundantly supplied by colonial regions where labor was plentiful and wages were low. The role of dynamic center fell to the United States and, to a lesser extent, to the European countries. On the whole, tropical commodities were of little significance as a factor in development, although they did involve the opening up of large areas for settlement. On the one hand, their prices continued to be influenced by the low wages prevailing in colonial regions, which had long been traditional tropical commodity producers. On the other, they did not usually require the creation of a complex infrastructure: on the contrary, in many regions traditional means of transport continued to be used. Finally, since they were produced in areas lacking the capacity to develop new techniques for themselves, tropical products tended to remain within the framework of the traditional economies. Nonetheless, in certain regions, tropical export agriculture did manage to play an important role in development. The most notable instance is probably that of the coffee region of São Paulo, in Brazil. Here the physical and chemical qualities of the soil permitted extensive coffee planting over large areas. The relatively high productivity of labor and the vast size of the area planted favored the creation of an infrastructure and promoted home market expansion. The special nature of this case becomes evident when we recall that at the end of the nineteenth century the São Paulo highlands supplied two thirds of the total world coffee output.

The third group, consisting of countries exporting mineral products, includes Mexico, Chile, Peru, and Bolivia. Venezuela entered this group in the 1920s as an exporter of petroleum. By creating a rapidly expanding market for industrial metals, the transport revolution of the midnineteenth century brought about a radical change in Latin American mining. In the first place, precious metals, notably silver, rapidly lost their importance. Second, small-scale mining operations of the artisan or quasi-artisan type were gradually replaced by large-scale production controlled by foreign capital and administered from abroad. The considerable rise in the world demand for nonferrous metals coincided with major technological progress in production methods which permitted or required the concentration of production in large units. This process of concentration, carried out initially in the major producing country—the United States—soon spread to other areas, where local producers were marginalized by American organizations with heavy financial backing and the technical "know-how" required to handle low-grade ores. Thus, the development of the export mining industry entailed not only denationalization but the establishment of a productive sector which, given its marked technological advance and high capital intensity, tended to become isolated and to behave as a separate economic system or, rather, as part of the economic system in which the decision center controlling the production unit belonged. Foreign control of a highly capitalized activity, employing a small labor force, meant that the major share of the flow of income generated by this activity was deflected from the domestic economy. In these circumstances its value as a factor for inducing direct change in the domestic economy was practically nil. Moreover, since the infrastructure created to serve export mining industries is highly specialized, the resultant external economies are minimal or non-existent for the economic system as a whole. Finally, since this type of mining activity called for specialized imports and created a limited flow of wage income, it made no significant contribution to the creation of a domestic market. Its potential as a dynamic factor became evident only when the State intervened, obliging mining companies to acquire part of their inputs locally and collecting, in the form of tax revenue, a significant share of the flow of income traditionally remitted abroad. . . .

Export Expansion Phase

The three decades preceding the First World War were a period of rapid economic development and intense social change for Latin America as a whole: in Mexico, where the Porfirio Díaz administration created the conditions for a large inflow of foreign capital directed mainly into mineral production; in Chile, whose victory in the War of the Pacific against Bolivia and Peru enabled her to monopolize the sources of nitrate; in Cuba, where, even before independence was attained in 1898, the country's increasing integration into the United States market had brought about a dramatic expansion in sugar production; in Brazil, where the spread of coffee over the São Paulo highlands and the influx of European immigrants hastened the collapse of the slave economy; finally, in Argentina, where the economy and society underwent drastic changes under the impact of the great wave of immigration and the penetration of substantial foreign capital.

A closer look at the three largest countries reveals the importance of the changes that occurred during this period. In Mexico, the population increased from 9.4 million in 1877 to 15.2 million in 1910. In the last decade of the Porfirio Díaz administration (1900–1910), the annual average growth rate of the real per capita product was 3.1 percent. During this decade the production of minerals and petroleum, the country's basic export sector, grew at an annual rate of 7.2 percent, that is, twice as fast as manufacturing production and nearly three times as fast as agricultural production. In Brazil, the population increased from 10.1 million in 1872 to 17.3 million in 1900. In the last decade of the nineteenth century, the rate of population increase in São Paulo was over 5 percent a year, while for the country as a whole it was under 2 percent. Nearly all the 610,000 immigrants entering Brazil during this decade went to the State of São Paulo. Between 1880 and 1910, the total length of railways increased from 3.4 to 21.3 thousand kilometers. Coffee exports, which amounted to around 4 million 60-kilogram bags in 1880, rose to almost 10 million in 1900 and to over 16 million on the eve of the First World War, a total seldom surpassed in later years. In the same period, exports of cacao rose from 6,000 to 40,000 tons, and rubber exports from 7,000 to 40,000 tons. However, it was in Argentina that the changes brought about in this phase were most marked. Between the periods 1890–1904 and 1910–1914, Argentina's population doubled, increasing from 3.6 to 7.2 million; the country's railway network was extended from 12.7 to 31.3 kilometers; cereal exports rose from 1,038,000 to 5,294,000 tons; and exports of frozen meat rose from 27,000 to 376,000 tons.

In short, during the period under consideration, Latin America became an important component of world trade and a key source of raw materials for the industrialized countries. In 1913 the Latin American share in world commodity exports was as follows: cereals—17.9 percent; livestock products—11.5 percent; coffee, cocoa, and tea—62.1 percent; sugar—37.6 percent; fruit and vegetables—14.2 percent; vegetable fibers—6.3 percent; rubber, furs, hides, and leather—25.1 percent.

---

5. Import-Substitution Industrialization ◆ Robert J. Alexander

Economist Robert Alexander describes how World War I and the Great Depression served to activate import-substitution industrialization (ISI) in Latin America by cutting off access to imported goods and forcing the region to produce its own manufactures. In time the first, "easy" phase of ISI reached a point of exhaustion, so that measures had to be taken by the state to amplify the existing market. Expanding the income of urban and rural workers (the latter through agrarian reform) would, it was believed, serve to increase mass purchasing power and hence create a larger national market for domestic goods.

The second stage of economic development, in conformity with the import-substitution process, arose as a result of interference with the export-import pattern established earlier. The first such shock came during World War I, when it became exceedingly difficult for the economically dependent, or "colonial," countries to obtain the manufactured goods they were by then accustomed to receiving from Europe and the United States. As a result, the people of these nations either had to do without these goods or produce them domestically. In many of the underdeveloped countries, consequently, the process of industrialization really received its first great impetus during World War I.

Reprinted from the *Journal of Economic Issues* 1 (December 1967): 119–20, 125–27, by special permission of the copyright holder, the Association for Evolutionary Economics.

Once World War I was over, many of these early industries could not meet the competition coming from European and North American manufacturers. However, soon after the war came the Great Depression, during which the same phenomenon occurred as had taken place a decade earlier, only in an exaggerated form. It was the depression which convinced public opinion in the underdeveloped countries which were politically independent that there was need for a conscious policy of industrialization and general economic development.

World War II, following hard on the heels of the depression, confirmed this belief. As former colonies achieved their independence in the postwar period, their leaders were imbued with the same conviction of the need for rapid economic development and, most important of all, for industrialization. Hence, since the Great Depression and particularly since the war, the governments of the underdeveloped nations have been following policies, such as protectionism, the building of social capital, and even the financing of new manufacturing industries, which make the import-substitution mode of development possible. . . .

Sooner or later the import-substitution strategy of development reaches a point of exhaustion. A point is reached at which an economy has installed virtually all those kinds of industries which can produce commodities formerly imported. At this juncture, the nature of the development problem changes. Instead of being the largely physical one of mounting industries to produce goods for which there is already a market, it becomes one of amplifying existing markets—if the process of development and growth is to continue. . . .

From the point of view of the industrial sector as a whole, new conditions will now demand a new outlook and new policies. With the virtual completion of the import-substitution phase of industrialization, it will be to the advantage of the manufacturing firms as a group to bring about an increase in the purchasing power of large segments of consumers who have been in the market but whose incomes have been so low as to permit them to buy only relatively small amounts of goods, and to bring into the market those parts of the population which have hitherto been outside of it.

The first problem will involve particularly the urban wage earners who constitute a substantial proportion of the market for consumer goods. Although their real-income levels have been substantially higher in the import-substitution phase than the incomes of most rural workers, they have generally remained well below comparative wages in the older industrialized countries. An increase in their real wages can constitute an important increase in existing markets. The increase in the real purchasing power of this group will require both an increase in their productivity and a rise in their share of the returns from what they produce. The laborers' need for greater productivity makes the increased concern for costs and quality, which we noted as being to the advantage of each individual firm, to the advantage of the industrial sector as a whole. The laborers' need for a larger share of their product will require a change in the psychology of the industrial entrepreneur, who has tended in the import-substitution phase of development to stick rather too closely to the habit of the traditional merchant of turning out relatively small amounts of product at a large markup per unit. The psychology of mass production will contribute considerably to the possibility of mass consumption.

The need for bringing into the market those elements which heretofore have been largely out of it will require fundamental changes in agriculture. An agrarian reform now becomes of great importance, both as a means of bringing new consumers into the market—the large numbers of rural workers, sharecroppers, tenant farmers who have not been in the market—and of laying a basis for an increase in domestic agricultural output, thus making it possible for agriculture to produce more adequately the raw materials and foodstuffs required by the urban sector.

In addition, it becomes important at this point to have heavy investment in agriculture, in terms both of providing equipment and machinery, and of developing more adequate marketing and storage facilities and providing fertilizers, credit, extension services, experimental stations, and the like. Large investments will also be required to develop adequate transportation facilities, not only in terms of major highways and perhaps occasional railroads but also neighborhood roads permitting the agriculturalists to get their products to the main transportation arteries. . . .

So far, few of the underdeveloped countries have reached the third phase in the import-substitution strategy of economic development. Virtually all of the developing countries in Asia and Africa, as well as most of those in Latin America, would seem to be still at a stage in which their industrialization is proceeding on the basis of building industries which can produce import substitutes. However, there are a few Latin American countries—notably Brazil, Chile, Mexico, and Argentina, as well perhaps as Venezuela, Colombia, and Peru—which have completely or nearly exhausted import-substitution possibilities, at least as a major impetus to further development.

6. Economic Development and Its Principal Problems ◆ Raúl Prebisch

*In his widely influential analysis of Latin American developmental prob-
lems in 1950, Argentine economist Raúl Prebisch argued that the presumed
benefits of comparative advantage and specialization of labor to commodity
producers such as Latin America simply had not materialized, as the
neoclassical economists, beginning with Adam Smith, had so firmly believed. Rather, incomes and standards of living in the industrializing countries
had moved up faster than those of the commodity-exporting regions. The
only way for Latin Americans to remedy the adverse terms of trade experienced by the latter was to industrialize their economies systematically. This
virtual manifesto for industrialization, coming from the prestigeous Economic Commission for Latin America of the United Nations, propelled
governments in the region to embark on concerted programs of import-
substitution industrialization during the 1950s and 1960s.*

In Latin America, reality is undermining the out-dated schema of the
international division of labor, which, after acquiring great importance in
the 19th century, continued to exert considerable academic influence until
very recently.

Within this framework, the specific task which fell to Latin America, as
part of the periphery of the world economic system, was that of producing
food and raw materials for the great industrial centers.

There was no place in this schema for the industrialization of the new
countries. It was nevertheless forced upon them by events. Two world wars
in one generation and a great economic crisis between them have shown the
Latin American countries their possibilities, pointing the way to industrial
activity.

The academic discussion, notwithstanding, is far from ended. In economics, ideologies usually lag behind events or else outlive them. It is true
that the economic advantages of the international division of labor cannot
be denied logically, but the fact is usually overlooked that this schema is
based upon an assumption which has been conclusively proved false by
facts. According to this assumption, the benefits of technical progress are
passed on to the community either by lowering prices or raising incomes.
The primary producing countries obtain their share of these benefits through

From Raúl Prebisch, *The Economic Development of Latin America and Its
Principal Problems* (E/CN.12/89/Rev.1), 1–2. New York, 1950. United Nations
publication, Sales No. 1950. II. G. 2.

international trade and therefore have no need to industrialize. On the contrary, their lower efficiency would make them lose the classic advantages of trade.

The flaw in this assumption is the attribution of general validity to a process which in itself is very limited. If community refers to the great industrial countries, it is indeed true that the benefits of technical progress are gradually passed on to all groups and classes. If the concept is extended to include the periphery of world economy, the generalization comprises a serious error. The enormous benefits resulting from increased productivity have not reached the periphery in proportion to those obtained by the population of those great countries. This explains the outstanding differences found in the standard of living of the masses of these two groups and the manifest discrepancies in their capacity to capitalize, since the margin of saving depends on increased productivity.

There is therefore an evident disequilibrium, a fact which, whatever its origin or justification, destroys the basic assumption of the schema of the international division of labor; hence the fundamental importance of the industrialization of the new countries. Industrialization is not an end in itself, but is the only means at their disposal of obtaining a share of the benefits of technical progress and of progressively raising the standard of living of the masses.

7. Speech to the Brazilian National Congress ◆ Humberto Castello Branco

As Brazilian President Castello Branco noted in his message to the National Congress, at the opening of the 1967 session, for a time the growth led by import-substitution industrialization was substantial, amounting to an average annual increase of 5.8 percent between 1947 and 1961. However, Castello Branco, in an effort to justify the seizure of power by the armed forces in 1964, goes on to summarize just how far economic conditions had deteriorated as ISI reached its limits. These conditions worsened under the populist Goulart government (1964), leading to widespread popular unrest and the generally chaotic political and social situation that, according to Castello Branco, precipitated the military coup.

From "Speech by Humberto Castello Branco, 1967," in *The Politics of Antipolitics: The Military in Latin America*, 2d ed. (revised and expanded), 228–30, ed. Brian Loveman and Thomas M. Davies, Jr., trans. Cecilia Ubilla. © 1978, 1989 by the University of Nebraska Press. Reprinted by permission of the University of Nebraska Press.

A s an unavoidable consequence, there occurred a decline in the efficiency of all aspects of national activity. Confronted with the need to reveal the implications of such a situation in relation to national development, we shall now undertake a brief analysis of the Brazilian situation as of March 1964, focusing especially on the socioeconomic aspects.

Despite the various structural limitations that tended to conspire against self-sustained and rapid development, the Brazilian economy experienced satisfactory performance in the period from World War II to the year 1961, and especially between the years 1947–1961. During that period the gross domestic product grew at an average annual rate of 5.8 percent (equivalent to 3 percent per capita). The . . . expansion of the industrial sector through the substitution of domestic products for imported goods was the most important stimulus.

However, this process of development took place against the backdrop of a social and economic structure unfavorable to lasting economic progress. Alongside the rapid growth of the manufacturing sector, the conditions of the agrarian sector—in which more than 50 percent of the national population existed at a low standard of living—remained almost unchanged, victim of the reigning technical backwardness in the rural sector and of the unsatisfactory levels of education, health, and hygiene.

Likewise, an archaic financial structure, highly sensitive to inflationary pressure, persisted along with a lack of basic services (transportation, energy, silos and warehouses, and communications), aggravated over and over by incorrect economic policies. An opportunistic and myopic view of the economic relations of the country with the rest of the world led to neglect of exports, which constituted the main determining element of the external purchasing power of the country. As a consequence, the Brazilian capacity to import stagnated.

Finally, during the entire above-mentioned period, that is, from after the war to 1961, the Brazilian economy developed within an atmosphere of continuous inflation of variable but bearable intensity, to the point of having permitted the satisfactory evolution of the gross domestic product, at least until 1961. In the meantime, the presence of those inflationary pressures, with partial control by government officials, was harmful enough to produce undesirable distortions in the system of relative prices and to give way to speculative activities, one consequence of which was the weakening of the money and capital market and the rates of savings and exports. The extraordinary growth of the Brazilian population and the resulting increase in the demand for new jobs, linked to the vulnerability of the public administration to political pressure, encouraged the transformation of employment in the public sector into "political spoils." This undermined operational efficiency and generated increasing deficits. The consolidated deficits of the government in turn were traditionally financed with currency issues, a source of new inflationary pressures. It ended in a vicious circle. . . .

Starting in 1962, several circumstances tended to increase the government expenses, independent of the comparative increase in the fiscal revenues, with a consequent progressive evolution of deficits in the case of the National Treasury and an increase of the rate of inflation. There were also serious signs of a worsening of the balance-of-payments situation and the reduction of import capacity. The deficiency of the economic infrastructure became more acutē, creating a climate of uncertainty and uneasiness. As a consequence, the level of investments and the growth rate of the economy declined, and the weaknesses of the national economy became more evident.

As a result of all this, increases in the general level of prices, which had reached an average of 15 percent per year between 1941 and 1946 [and] rose to 20 percent in the period from 1951 to 1958, suffered a rapid acceleration starting in 1959. The rate of increase in the cost of living rose in that year to 52 percent in Guanabara, and, after going down in 1960, started rising progressively until reaching 55 percent in 1962 and 81 percent in 1963. In the first quarter of 1964, it reached 25 percent and, given its rate of acceleration, it could have very well reached 150 percent by the end of the year. . . . The social and political atmosphere of the previous administration could not have been more unfavorable; the following factors should be underlined: the constant political tension created by the disharmony between the federal executive on the one hand and the National Congress and the state governments on the other, distrustful of the anticonstitutionalist intentions and desires of the old regime [to maintain itself in power]; a penchant toward state property and control that created a continuous discouragement and threat to private investors; the communist infiltration, generating apprehensions about the overthrow of the social and economic order; the successive paralysis of production by the "strike commands." Not only did urban activities suffer, but also investment in farming and cattle raising were discouraged. . . . Political instability and administrative improvisation prevailed, producing a lack of national direction . . . the entrepreneurial classes suffered from a crisis of distrust; the working classes found themselves frustrated because of the impossibility of their realizing the demagogic promises; finally, certain more restless groups, such as the students, not finding an outlet for their idealistic impulses, slipped into the error of subversive solutions. . . .

To summarize, when this government took power, the financial and economic situation was truly gloomy. To the structural deficiencies of the national economy had been added temporary troubles which underscored these [deficiencies], disrupted internal markets, pushed the increase in prices to the verge of extreme inflation, generated a crisis of confidence

[and] a slowdown in the flow of investments and in the rate of economic development. [These troubles also] increased the level of unemployment, and, finally, they damaged the country's credit abroad. The most urgent task, therefore, was to contain the extraordinary rise of the general level of prices, to recover the minimum necessary order for the functioning of the national economy, to overcome the crisis of confidence, and to return to the entrepreneurs and to the workers the tranquility necessary for productive activities.

8. The Bureaucratic-Authoritarian State ◆ Guillermo O'Donnell

Political theorist Guillermo O'Donnell outlines the main characteristics of his bureaucratic-authoritarian state. The government was controlled by the military, whose social base was the "upper bourgeoisie." Its twin aims were "the restoration of 'order' in society by means of the political deactivation of the popular sector [or repression], on the one hand, and the normalization [or stabilization] of the economy, on the other." The regime, he emphasized, was both politically and economically exclusionary, by which he means that its harsh repressive and stabilizing measures adversely affected the majority. By opening the economy to the world market, the bureaucratic-authoritarian state also allowed foreign "transnational" companies to penetrate and therefore "denationalize" the economy.

The bureaucratic-authoritarian [(B-A) state has the following principal characteristics:]

1. It is, first and foremost, guarantor and organizer of the domination exercised through a class structure subordinated to the upper fractions of a highly oligopolized and transnationalized bourgeoisie. In other words, the principal social base of the B-A state is this upper bourgeoisie.

2. In institutional terms, it is [composed] of organizations in which specialists in coercion have decisive weight, as well as those whose aim it is to achieve "normalization" of the economy. The special role played by these two groups represents the institutional expression of the identification, by its own actors, of the two great tasks that the B-A state is committed to accomplish: the restoration of "order" in society by means of the political

From Guillermo O'Donnell, "Tensions in the Bureaucratic-Authoritarian State and the Question of Democracy," in *The New Authoritarianism in Latin America*, ed. David Collier (Princeton, 1979), 280–82, footnotes omitted. © 1979 by Princeton University Press. Reprinted by permission of Princeton University Press.

deactivation of the popular sector, on the one hand, and the normalization of the economy, on the other.

3. It is a system of political exclusion of a previously activated popular sector which is subjected to strict controls in an effort to eliminate its earlier active role in the national political arena. This political exclusion is achieved by destroying or capturing the resources (especially those embodied in class organizations and political movements) which supported this activation. In addition, this exclusion is guided by a determination to impose a particular type of "order" on society and guarantee its future viability. This order is seen as a necessary condition for the consolidation of the social domination that B-A guarantees and, after achieving the normalization of the economy, for reinitiating a highly transnationalized pattern of economic growth characterized by a skewed distribution of resources.

4. This exclusion involves the suppression of citizenship, in the twofold sense defined above. In particular, this suppression includes the liquidation of the institutions of political democracy. It also involves a denial of *lo popular* [relating to "the people," or *pueblo*]: it prohibits (enforcing the prohibition with coercion) any appeals to the population as *pueblo* and, of course, as class. The suppression of the institutional roles and channels of access to the government characteristic of political democracy is in large measure oriented toward eliminating roles and organizations (political parties among them) that have served as a channel for appeals for substantive justice that are considered incompatible with the restoration of order and with the normalization of the economy. In addition, B-A appears as if placed before a sick nation—as expressed in the rhetoric that derived from the severity of the crisis that preceded its implantation—whose general interest must be invoked; yet, because of the depth of the crisis, B-A cannot claim to be the representative of that sick nation, which is seen as contaminated by innumerable internal enemies. Thus, B-A is based on the suppression of two fundamental mediations—citizenship and *lo popular*. In an ambiguous way it may evoke the other mediation—the nation—but only as a "project" (and not as an actual reality) which it proposes to carry out through drastic surgical measures.

5. B-A is also a system of economic exclusion of the popular sector, inasmuch as it promotes a pattern of capital accumulation which is highly skewed toward benefiting the large oligopolistic units of private capital and some state institutions. The preexisting inequities in the distribution of societal resources are thus sharply increased.

6. It corresponds to, and promotes, an increasing transnationalization of the productive structure, resulting in a further denationalization of society in terms of the degree to which it is in fact contained within the scope of the territorial authority which the state claims to exercise.

7. Through its institutions it endeavors to "depoliticize" social issues by dealing with them in terms of the supposedly neutral and objective criteria of technical rationality. This depoliticization complements the prohibition against invoking issues of substantive justice as they relate to *lo popular* (and, of course, class), which allegedly introduces "irrationalities" and "premature" demands that interfere with the restoration of order and the normalization of the economy.

8. In the first stage that we are considering here, the political regime of the B-A state—which, while not formalized, is clearly identifiable—involves closing the democratic channels of access to the government. More generally, it involves closing the channels of access for the representation of popular and class interests. Such access is limited to those who stand at the apex of large organizations (both public and private), especially the armed forces and large oligopolistic enterprises.

---

9. The Neoliberal Prescriptions of the Bureaucratic-Authoritarian State ◆ Jonathan Hartlyn and Samuel A. Morley

Political economists Hartlyn and Morley summarize the measures taken by the bureaucratic-authoritarian regimes to stabilize the economy. These measures included: 1) steps to allow the market rather than the state to allocate resources, 2) efforts to control inflation and correct the imbalance of international payments, and 3) government incentives to improve export and agricultural production. The overall approach was orthodox neoliberalism designed to lower inflation by removing government subsidies and balancing the budget while opening the economy to the international market in hopes of restarting economic growth.

Bureaucratic-authoritarian regimes were established in Argentina in 1966 and again in 1976, in Brazil in 1964, and in Chile and Uruguay in 1973. These regimes, particularly those initiated in the 1970s, pursued a common set of economic policies. First, they all believed in price mechanisms and a free market, which was expressed in a desire to let profit incentives and prices, rather than government planners, determine the allocation of resources in the economy. The Chileans were far more orthodox and rigid in this

Reprinted by permission of Westview Press from Jonathan Hartlyn and Samuel A. Morley, "Bureaucratic-Authoritarian Regimes in Comparative Perspective," in *Latin American Political Economy: Financial Crisis and Political Change*, ed. Jonathan Hartlyn and Samuel A. Morley, p. 39. Published by Westview Press, 1986, Boulder, Colorado.

regard than the Brazilians, whose B-A regime created a host of large state enterprises at the same time that the Chileans were selling state enterprises inherited from the Allende regime.

Second, each of the B-A regimes was dedicated to controlling inflation and correcting the balance of payments. In large measure, these regimes came into power because of economic crises, reflected by rising or repressed inflation and foreign exchange shortages, that civilian governments had been unable to control. The military response to these two problems was to cut government deficits by such measures as raising taxes, reducing the expansion of the money supply, suppressing wage demands in order to reduce cost-push pressures on prices, and devaluing the currency to make exports more competitive and to correct the balance-of-payments deficit. In short, what these B-A regimes did was to impose a classic, orthodox stabilization program of the sort generally demanded by the International Monetary Fund.

Subsequently, when the immediate balance-of-payments and inflation crises were overcome, the long-run economic characteristics of the regimes became clearer. The two most important were a greater orientation toward both exports and agriculture. The regimes tended to reverse the more extreme import-substitution policies—domestic industrial promotion at the expense of agriculture—that had been followed by their predecessors. They lowered tariffs and established the crawling-peg exchange rate so that exporters would not have to worry about overvaluation. They also established a variety of subsidies for exports, both industrial and agricultural. Finally, they all held out a welcome mat for foreign direct investment, which they hoped would join in a constructive partnership to develop their countries and, not incidentally, help shore up the kind of political and social order they were hoping to establish.

---

10. Anatomy of the Debt Problem ◆ Rudiger Dornbusch

To stabilize their economies and spur renewed growth, the military regimes of the 1970s, particularly after the 1973 oil embargo, turned increasingly to foreign banks for loans. This policy led to a rapid and excessive buildup of foreign debt, which, as MIT economist Rudiger Dornbusch states, together

Reprinted by permission of Westview Press from Rudiger Dornbusch, "The Latin American Debt Problem: Anatomy and Solutions," in *Debt and Democracy in Latin America*, ed. Barbara Stallings and Robert Kaufman, pp. 7–10, footnotes omitted. Published by Westview Press, 1989, Boulder, Colorado.

with poor management and the onset of world recession, precipitated the
debt crisis of the 1980s.

The Latin American debt crisis now is six years old and growing. When
Mexican debts trade at 50 cents on the dollar, and those of Peru at less
than a dime, the debt crisis is obviously unresolved. Far from improving
their creditworthiness, the debtors are falling behind. Debt ratios are far
above the 1982 level, and debtor countries' economies are showing the
strains of debt service in extremely high inflation, a deep drop in income,
and an unsustainable cutback of investment. The debtors cannot afford to
pay, nor can they afford to walk out on the system.

On the side of creditors, reserves are built up to provide a cushion
against potential losses. In the meantime, creditor banks are unanimous in
their reluctance to continue lending in a situation where the debts are
obviously deteriorating. Increasingly, the World Bank is filling the gap left
by the debtor countries' inability to pay and the banks' unwillingness to
lend. Former Treasury Secretary Baker's "muddling through" remains the
Reagan administration's strategy, a treadmill of pretense and make-believe
in which both debtors and creditors are falling behind. There is a major
public interest in changing the course and breaking the deadlock. . . .

Origins of the Debt Crisis

Debt crises are common in a broader historical perspective. The last
worldwide crisis was that of the 1930s when all of Latin America, with very
few exceptions (most notably Venezuela and Argentina), went into
moratorium for many years. Even as the 1930s defaults got fully under way,
Winkler wrote:

> The fiscal history of Latin America . . . is replete with instances of government
> defaults. Borrowing and default follow each other with perfect regularity.
> When payment is resumed, the past is easily forgotten and a new borrowing
> orgy ensues. This process started at the beginning of the past century and has
> continued down to the present day. It has taught us nothing.

The cleanup of debtor-creditor relations occurred in the 1950s. Borrowing resumed in the 1960s when first Mexico and then all of Latin America
made new forays into the world capital market.

Sporadic debt difficulties occurred throughout the 1970s, but the system-
wide problems only emerged in 1982 when Mexico, and soon most of Latin
America, had to reschedule its external debt. Three factors account for the
generalized debt problem: poor management in the debtor countries, the
world macroeconomy that took a singularly bad turn, and initial overlending.

In the late 1970s exchange rates in most Latin American countries were massively overvalued. This was a popular policy because it helped limit or bring down inflation with recession. But the cure was very shortlived, since the resulting loss of competitiveness soon led to large trade deficits and capital flight. The extent of overvaluation is apparent from some data for the period 1977 to 1981. Argentina experienced a real appreciation of 85 percent, Brazil 36 percent, Chile 57 percent, and Mexico 30 percent. The resulting trade imbalance was financed by borrowing in world capital markets. Moreover, when capital flight became important, especially in Argentina and Mexico, external loans financed this exodus of private capital. It was a curious spectacle when a central bank borrowed in New York to obtain the dollars that it sold to private citizens who in turn deposited them in Miami.

There is considerable uncertainty about the precise extent of capital flight. One recent study, published by the Institute of International Economics, gives estimates for various countries over the period 1976–1982. It shows Argentina with capital flight of $22.4 billion, Brazil $5.8 billion, Mexico $25.3 billion, and Venezuela $20.7 billion. To put these data on capital flight in perspective, it is important to judge them relative to the stock of debts outstanding. In the case of Argentina, for example, the 1982 stock of external debt was $44 billion. Thus, capital flight accounted for no less than half of the accumulated debt.

The second element in the debt crisis was the sharp deterioration of the world economy. Under the impact of tightening U.S. monetary policy, with other industrial countries following suit, world interest rates skyrocketed, economic activity declined, and real commodity prices plummeted. Table 1.1 shows the relevant data.

Each element in world macroeconomic development was unfavorable for debtors. Higher interest rates implied increased debt service burdens, while lower commodity prices and reduced activity in center countries implied a sharp drop in export earnings. Thus, between increased debt service and reduced export earnings, a large foreign exchange gap resulted. Table 1.2 shows the deterioration in debt and debt service ratios between 1979 and 1982.

Without the banks' eagerness to lend, the debt crisis would obviously not have occurred in the first place. In hindsight, why did banks not use more caution? That question is asked in the aftermath of each wave of default, and the answer has not yet been found. The most plausible explanation is that of Guttentag and Herring, who argue that banks have "disaster myopia"—they underestimate the true probability of infrequent events. The combination of overindebtedness and a sharp world deterioration is one such case. The combination makes for pervasive defaults, but it is a rare event.

Table 1.1
Aggregate World Macroeconomic Indicators, 1970–1987

	Real Commodity Prices (1980=100)[a]	*LIBOR[b] (%)*	*Inflation[c] (%)*	*Growth Rates[d] (%)*
1970–79	115	8.0	11.4	3.4
1980	100	14.4	13.0	0.0
1981	96	16.5	-4.1	-7.0
1982	89	13.1	-3.5	-3.3
1983–87	84	8.5	4.0	3.2

[a]Measured in terms of manufactured export prices of industrial countries
[b]London Interbank Offered Rate, base interest rate for most Latin American loans
[c]Rate of increase of industrial countries' unit export values
[d]Industrial production
Source: IMF and Economic Commission for Latin America

Table 1.2
Debt and Debt Service Ratios,[a] 1979–1982

	1979	*1980*	*1981*	*1982*
Debt[b]	165	152	186	241
Interest and Amortization[b]	27.9	25.4	32.9	40.3
Interest[b]	11.1	13.1	18.6	24.2

[a]Countries with recent debt service problems
[b]As percent of exports of goods and services
Source: IMF

The banks' role in the debt crisis went beyond the initial overlending. An essential element was the halt on all lending once the debt service difficulties of lenders became apparent. Each bank's attempt to pull out of further lending, seeking recovery of principal at the expense of other creditors, had all the appearances of a bank run. Suddenly, debtors could no longer roll over their interest payments and borrow to finance current account imbalances; they had to adjust. The main feature of the debt crisis was precisely that abrupt halt to all lending. Debtors frozen out of the world capital market learned firsthand the old banking truth: "It is not speed that kills, it is the sudden stop."

---

11. The United States Responds: The Brady Plan and the Enterprise for the Americas Initiative ◆ Peter Hakim

In March 1991, Peter Hakim, staff director of the Inter-American Dialogue, appeared before the Subcommittee on Foreign Operations of the House Appropriations Committee. After assessing the dire economic straits confronting Latin America as a consequence of debt and depression, he described two U.S. initiatives designed to help resolve the crisis. The Brady Plan, designed by President George Bush's secretary of the treasury to alleviate the debt crisis, essentially called for debt relief by Latin America's principal creditors. Hakim criticized the plan (for being too little and of benefit only to the better-off rather than to the weakest countries in the region) and then made specific suggestions for its strengthening. As for the Enterprise of the Americas, it proposed further debt relief from the U.S. government, the establishment of a $100-million investment fund, and the creation of a free-trade zone throughout the Americas that would give Latin America greater access to U.S. markets for its goods.

I want to thank the subcommittee for this opportunity to testify on the two most important U.S. policy initiatives toward Latin America in recent years. The first is the so-called Brady Plan, launched just two months after President Bush took office in 1989 and offering a new strategy for dealing with Latin America's accumulated debt burdens. The second, the Enterprise for the Americas Initiative, was announced by President Bush last June and called for a combination of measures to help strengthen Latin America's economies and foster more productive long-term economic relationships between the United States and the region. The proposed free-trade agreement with Mexico is vital to this second initiative.

From Peter Hakim, "External Debt and Free Trade in the Americas: Statement to the Subcommittee on Foreign Operations, Committee on Appropriations, U.S. House of Representatives, Washington, DC, March 1991," in *New Directions in U.S.-Latin American Economic Relations* (Washington, DC: Overseas Development Council/Inter-American Dialogue, 1991), 11–21. Reprinted by permission.

Let me start by emphasizing several crucial points:

First, Latin America's deep economic and social problems are still a long way from solution. Since 1982, Latin America has been mired in its worst depression ever, one that has affected virtually every country in the region. And the cumulative effects of that depression now pose severe obstacles to economic recovery in all but a very few countries. Some figures will reveal Latin America's economic straits:

- The region's debt burdens are enormous. Its aggregate debt exceeds $420 billion, $100 billion greater than in 1982 when the debt crisis first struck. Interest payments on that debt, amounting to some $35 billion a year, deprive the region of the resources it needs for investment and crucial imports; they also keep budget deficits high, fuel inflation, and sap private investor confidence.

- Latin America is plagued by record levels of inflation. Average inflation for the region as a whole last year was 1500 percent, ten times what it was in 1980.

- Eight years of low investment have left most Latin American nations with deteriorated physical plants, outdated technologies, and a lagging ability to compete internationally.

- More people than ever are trapped in poverty. Unemployment stands at historic highs in many countries; wages have deteriorated badly, by 50 percent or more in some places; and the quality of housing, health care, and education has steadily worsened.

Second, Latin America's economic hardships present a grave danger to the region's still fragile democratic institutions. Latin America has made impressive strides toward democratic rule in recent years. Every country in the region, except Fidel Castro's Cuba, is now governed by elected civilian leadership. Yet the practice of democracy remains very uneven throughout the region and, in fact, is floundering in many countries. No easy relationship can be drawn between economics and politics in the region, but economic distress has consistently undermined the credibility of democratic leaders and is frustrating the development of vibrant democracies. In some places, persistent economic crisis may yet lead to a return to authoritarian rule.

Third, I believe that Latin America, with its population of 400 million people, is important to the economic well-being of the United States. Even in the midst of depression, Latin America is a $50-billion-a-year market for U.S. exporters—larger, for example, than the Japanese market. An economically healthy and growing Latin America could absorb some $20 to $30 billion more in U.S. exports each year, an amount equivalent to what we now export to Germany. Of every dollar Latin America spends on imports, 50 cents comes to the United States. There is nowhere else in the world where we enjoy that kind of advantage.

Fourth, although each Latin American country must take responsibility for its own economic reconstruction, U.S. policy toward Latin America does make a difference. Trade policy matters because Latin America sends one half of its exports to the United States; even more striking, increased sales to U.S. buyers represented more than 75 percent of Latin America's export growth in the 1980s. Debt policy matters, not only because U.S. government agencies and U.S. banks hold some 30 percent of Latin American debt, but also because the international debt strategy followed by all of Latin America's creditors is largely shaped in Washington. And the U.S. government retains predominant influence in the formulation of the lending policies of the major international financial institutions that serve Latin America.

The two pillars of U.S. economic policy toward Latin America are now the Brady Plan and the Enterprise for the Americas Initiative. The first of these essentially looks backward; it was designed to help resolve a devastating problem—Latin America's debt crisis—that had been festering for many years. The second, the Enterprise Initiative, in contrast, looks forward to the future; it offers a vision—still vague but nonetheless exciting—of a new economic (and perhaps political) relationship between the United States and Latin America.

In the remainder of my testimony, I will try to answer three central questions about each of these initiatives: What have they accomplished so far? What do they currently promise? And what can be done to make them more effective in achieving their aims?

The Brady Plan

The Brady Plan offered a crucial innovation in U.S. debt strategy (and hence in the strategy pursued by Latin America's European and Japanese creditors as well). It reversed long-standing U.S. policy calling for Latin American countries fully to repay their loans. The Brady Plan acknowledged that Latin America's debt could not, in fact, be paid in full and called upon the commercial banks to reduce their Latin American debt claims (which accounted for some two thirds of all outstanding obligations). In exchange, the banks were to be offered some guarantees that their remaining claims would be paid. Backing up those guarantees were public resources made available largely through the IMF and World Bank.

Overall, the amount of debt reduction to date has been small. Indeed, in the two years since the Brady Plan was announced, Latin America's aggregate debt has actually increased, not declined. Out of twenty heavily indebted Latin American countries, four—Mexico, Venezuela, Costa Rica, and Uruguay—have negotiated reductions with their creditor banks. And three others—Chile, Colombia, and Bolivia—each for different reasons, are not currently in need of debt relief.

Two main problems have emerged in the implementation of the Brady Plan. First, the amount of debt reduction being offered to qualifying countries may not be sufficient to allow the countries both to resume growth and make good on their remaining obligations. This means that new relief packages may have to be negotiated at some point in the future—or that public resources will have to be used to cover the guarantees. Second, the Brady strategy is not helping those countries in greatest economic difficulty and most in need of debt relief.

Costa Rica has so far obtained the most generous debt reduction arrangement, reducing its commercial debt by 60 percent, but its overall debt declined by only 25 percent. Mexico's debt payments have been reduced by only about 12 percent. The fact is that a rise of one or two percentage points in international interest rates could wipe out the entire value of the debt reduction provided so far.

There are also, however, indirect benefits from debt relief. Debt reduction agreements—coupled with economic policy reforms—can help to restore business confidence and thereby may help to mobilize other sources of capital. Mexico seems to have benefited in this way, although it is too soon to determine whether the benefits will endure over time.

The countries that have had their debts reduced are among the strongest economic performers in Latin America. The dozen or so Latin American countries in greatest economic distress now appear unlikely to qualify for relief under the Brady Plan, at least not any time soon. Most of them are already deeply in arrears to their commercial creditors—and very few have managed to make much headway in reforming their economies. The problem in many cases can be traced to the weakness of political authority—which, in a vicious cycle, is often a consequence of economic failure. But whatever the cause of their distress, the Brady Plan offers these countries no relief.

Three specific steps are now needed to make the Brady Plan work more effectively:

First, the amount of debt reduction should no longer be left entirely to negotiations between the countries and the banks. Either the World Bank or

International Monetary Fund should be charged with establishing a debt-reduction target for each country seeking a Brady Plan agreement, and perhaps be called on to serve as a mediator in the actual negotiations. The objective would be to assure that adequate relief is provided to eligible countries and that debt repayment guarantees do not exceed the amount that each country can, in fact, pay back and, thereby, put public resources at risk.

Second, the initiation of debt-reduction negotiations should not be delayed until a country has satisfied all the requirements for reaching an agreement. Several major countries, most prominently Brazil and Argentina, do not yet qualify for debt relief. They are in arrears on their commercial debt and their economies are being battered by hyperinflation and large budget deficits. Currently, negotiations for Brady Plan relief can only begin when these problems are brought under control. Yet massive debts and mounting arrears compound the problems, because they are a source of uncertainty that frightens investors and contributes to capital flight and financial speculation. This is the "Catch 22": the countries' efforts to put their economies in order are frustrated by their debt burdens; but they can expect no relief from the burdens until they manage to reorder their economies.

This cycle could be broken if the commercial banks and debtor countries like Brazil and Argentina undertook—perhaps with World Bank and IMF mediating help—to establish the basic framework and objectives of a debt-reduction agreement that would be refined and implemented when the countries fulfilled the appropriate conditions for doing so. By reducing future uncertainties, such a framework agreement could serve as a crucial incentive for the countries to persist in their reform efforts and would reassure investors that debt would not be an insurmountable obstacle to continued recovery and growth.

Third, the Brady Plan must be made relevant to the large group of countries that need massive and immediate relief but cannot hope to meet the conditions for such relief in the foreseeable future because of the sad state of their economies. These countries—including Peru, the Dominican Republic, Honduras, and Nicaragua, among others—have not been paying interest for some time, and probably will never be able to meet more than a very small fraction of their debt obligations. If these countries are ever to get back on their feet, most, if not all, of their debt will have to be forgiven. Together, they account for only a small portion of outstanding debt, so the cost of relief should not be burdensome to creditors. Such relief should clearly be restricted to those countries that are pursuing economic reform programs under the aegis of the World Bank or the IMF.

The Enterprise for the Americas Initiative

The Enterprise for the Americas Initiative proposes to reduce the official bilateral debts Latin American countries owe to the United States. As such, it complements the Brady Plan's provision for commercial debt relief. Although the amount of U.S. official debt is limited—totaling only about $12 billion, or less than 3 percent of the region's overall debt—some smaller countries of Central America and the Caribbean do stand to obtain meaningful benefits. And the benefits could be considerably greater if the United States is able to convince Japan and Europe to join in official debt reduction efforts in Latin America. Moreover, the funds that would be made available for environmental programs could be of major significance in a region suffering severe ecological problems.

The second leg of the Enterprise Initiative—calling for the establishment of a special investment promotion fund—will also be of only modest value to most Latin American countries. The proposed $100 million in U.S. support a year will just not go very far, even if Europe and Japan each agree—as they have been asked to do—to contribute similar amounts.

The Enterprise Initiative's enthusiastic welcome in Latin America is mostly explained by its trade provision—specifically its proposal for the eventual establishment of a free-trade zone throughout the Americas. Access to the U.S. market—which now absorbs some $60 billion in Latin American exports each year—is what is crucial to the region's prospects for recovery and growth. Expanded trade with the United States can help Latin America build a dynamic export sector and attract a steady flow of foreign investment.

The timing of the Enterprise Initiative—as well as President Bush's subsequent visit to Latin America last December—was propitious. Latin Americans have been concerned that their region would be ignored in a post-Cold War world, as U.S. attention turned to Eastern Europe, to the economically dynamic countries of Asia, and to the Middle East. That concern has been compounded by the uncertainties surrounding the Uruguay Round of GATT negotiations and the apparent trend toward the creation of regional trading blocs from which Latin America might be excluded. Both the Enterprise Initiative and the president's visit signaled that, despite the dramatic global changes taking place, Latin America was still considered a significant area for U.S. attention.

Just as important, the Initiative focused exclusively on economic policy issues, which Latin Americans have long felt should be at the center of their relationship with the United States. Washington finally seemed ready to place commercial and financial ties, not security and drugs, at the core of its relations with Latin America. Finally, Latin Americans appreciated the

Initiative's emphasis on multilateralism, a welcome change from the unilateral and bilateral approaches that have long dominated U.S. policy in the region.

All told, the Enterprise Initiative has created the potential for constructively recasting U.S.-Latin American relations. The new relationship would be based on the mutual interests and longer-term priorities of both sides; it would no longer be defined mainly by the concerns of Washington or respond only to situations of crisis in the region.

The challenge for the United States and the countries of Latin America is how to give substance and definition to the Initiative, particularly to its proposal for free hemispheric trade, and thereby sustain what momentum has been generated and avoid dashing the expectations that have been created.

Latin American countries do not expect to achieve special trade arrangements with the United States overnight. They recognize that Washington's first priorities are the successful completion of the Uruguay Round and the establishment of a free-trade agreement with Mexico, far and away the major U.S. trading partner in the region. But as the United States proceeds on these fronts, Latin Americans want clear signals that Washington will subsequently move forcefully toward hemisphere-wide free-trade negotiations.

The United States has already taken a first step by signing bilateral "framework agreements" with a number of Latin American countries. By specifying the key issues and problems for trade negotiations and creating bilateral mechanisms for discussing them, these agreements are a helpful, albeit modest, starting point. Four other steps should now be taken:

First, the United States should move quickly to implement the non-trade provisions of the Enterprise Initiative. Although the likely benefits from these provisions—i.e., the bilateral debt reduction and the creation of an investment promotion fund—are small, so is their cost to the United States. Yet action on them would provide reassurances of Washington's commitment to the Initiative overall, as would concerted U.S. efforts to secure the participation of Japan and Europe.

Second, the United States should continue to encourage Latin American countries to reach their own subregional trade arrangements. Such arrangements are crucial in building toward a genuine hemispheric free-trade area that would get beyond bilateral trade deals between the United States and individual Latin American countries.

Third, the United States should promote the establishment of a new regional organization—along the lines of the Americas Commission proposed by Richard Feinberg—that would help to structure and facilitate trade negotiations in the hemisphere. Such an institution, if properly staffed and organized, would serve all countries as a crucial forum for trade discussions, a source for continuing analysis and information on trade matters, and eventually as a mechanism for dispute resolution.

Fourth and finally, Washington . . . should seek to accelerate debt relief in Latin America, primarily by making the Brady Plan work for all countries in the region ready to pursue needed economic reforms. Maintaining the fiction that unpayable debt will somehow and at some time be paid does no one any good—not the commercial banks, the Latin American countries, or the U.S. taxpayers. Latin American countries are already major trading partners with the United States. They will become far more important and stronger partners once they regain their economic health, and debt relief is a crucial element in their recovery.

No one expects the United States to resolve Latin America's economic problems. That is mainly up to the Latin American countries themselves. What they want and need from us is not aid but expanded opportunities to compete for sales and investment capital in U.S. markets. In exchange, they have made clear that they are willing to open up their markets to U.S. exporters and investors. This is precisely the kind of mutually beneficial relationship we should be seeking to establish with the region.

Selected Bibliography

Annis, Sheldon, and Peter Hakim, eds. *Direct to the Poor: Grassroots Development in Latin America*. Boulder: Lynne Rienner, 1988.

Cardoso, Fernando Henrique, and Enzo Faletto. *Dependency and Development in Latin America*. Translated by Marjory Urquidi. Berkeley: University of California Press, 1979.

Dietz, James L., and James H. Street, eds. *Latin America's Economic Development: Institutionalist and Structuralist Perspectives*. Boulder: Lynne Rienner, 1987.

Foxley, Alejandro. *Latin American Experiments in Neo-Conservative Economics*. Berkeley: University of California Press, 1983.

Harrison, Lawrence E. *Underdevelopment Is a State of Mind: The Latin American Case*. Lanham, MD: Madison Books, 1985.

Hirschman, Albert O. *A Bias for Hope: Essays on Development and Latin America*. New Haven: Yale University Press, 1971.

———, ed. *Latin American Issues: Essays and Comments*. New York: Twentieth Century Fund, 1961.

Johnson, John J. *Political Change in Latin America*. Stanford: Stanford University Press, 1958.

Klaren, Peter F., and Thomas J. Bossert, eds. *Promise of Development: Theories of Change in Latin America*. Boulder: Westview Press, 1986.

Love, Joseph L. "Raúl Prebisch and the Origins of the Doctrine of Unequal Exchange." *Latin American Research Review* 15:1 (1980): 45–72.

Lowenthal, Abraham F. *Partners in Conflict: The United States and Latin America*. Baltimore: Johns Hopkins University Press, 1987.

Roxborough, Ian. *Theories of Underdevelopment*. London: Macmillan and Company, 1979.

Valenzuela, J. Samuel, and Arturo Valenzuela. "Modernization and Dependency: Alternative Perspectives in the Study of Latin American Underdevelopment." *Comparative Politics* 10:4 (July 1978): 535–57.

Wiarda, Howard J., ed. *Politics and Social Change in Latin America: The Distinct Tradition*. Amherst: University of Massachusetts Press, 1974.

VIII

Revolutionary Movements in Central America

Hugo F. Castillo

This chapter focuses on the emergence and development of revolutionary movements in Central America in the second half of the twentieth century. In simple terms the questions are: Why did revolutionary movements emerge? What historical conditions have led political groups and movements to resort to force of arms as a means of self-defense, opposition to the government, or access to power? The answers to these questions are complex, and we must look for clues to the historical development of sociopolitical and economic structures of the region, to the specifics of social conflict, to the forms of exercising power in each of these countries, and to the intimate relations between the dominant groups in the region and the United States. These are factors that have led to a structural crisis of enormous proportions. The documents that follow sample the perceptions, reactions, experiences, and analyses of individuals and organizations that have participated actively in the revolutionary struggle in Central America.

The Central American crisis that began to build in the early 1960s has been the subject of innumerable studies and has generated a great number of interpretations, some of them clearly contradictory. It is possible, however, to establish some basic characteristics of regional historical development that will help us to understand the roots of the present crisis and the practical difficulties in resolving it. The crisis is comprehensive because it affects economic, sociopolitical, and ideological structures. Politically, the narrow control that oligarchical and entrepreneurial groups have exercised over the state in conjunction with the army has been characterized by a general strengthening of repressive forms of government and the exclusion of vast sectors of the population from the political process. Given these conditions, the lack of popular endorsement for those who retain power has been one of the most clearly discernible sources of tension. The meager legitimacy and flexibility exhibited by dominant groups have tended to deepen the contradictions within the system and increase the levels of social and political confrontation. Furthermore, the direct and indirect obstruction of channels for the expression of popular demands contributed to the resentment among groups excluded from power. Finally, active U.S. intervention in the region has resulted in defining the anti-imperialistic character of the Central American revolutionary struggle.

In the last third of the nineteenth century the dynamic expansion of export agriculture, such as coffee and sugar, accelerated. This process adversely affected the peasants who had been deprived of their lands, forcing many to become rural wage laborers or to emigrate. The impoverishment and uprooting of the peasant sector occurred at variable levels of intensity across the region and over time, but the result has been everywhere the same. The concentration of population in urban areas, plus the slow increase in sources of employment, have created tremendous contrasts between the poor suffering hardships and the privileged enjoying riches and prosperity. The creation of the Central American Common Market in the 1960s and the process of import-substitution industrialization facilitated the birth of an urban working class in the most important cities, but the artisan sector, although in decline from the competition of imported products, continues to be important. Finally, expansion of the service sector, both public and private, and of light industry has permitted the growth of professional groups and the middle class in general. These new groups have organized and expressed their demands through political parties, mass organizations, and social movements. Social and economic injustices perpetuated by the existing order, together with a lack of the possibility of reform through democratic mechanisms and the repression of those who raise their voices to denounce abuses and injustices, have provoked a sharpening of the crisis and the development of new forms of social mobilization and political struggle, including armed struggle.

Throughout the history of Latin America, urban and peasant insurrections and rebellions have expressed resentment in a violent manner, rejecting as unacceptable certain forms of dispossession, control, or exploitation, and questioning political order that did not offer prospects for betterment. However, the type of armed struggle that interests us now, while certainly a part of that long tradition of insurrectional movements and rebellions, exhibits unique elements and characteristics associated with social revolutions. Armed struggle is distinguished by the political alliances that it endorses and by the methods used to bring about political and social change. This process of change involves the removal from power of those groups who have controlled the country. The tactics include mass mobilization, grass-roots activism and resistance, and different forms of armed struggle. Let us examine, then, the background of social revolution in Central America.

To begin, we must distinguish between guerrilla war as a political-military movement and guerrilla war as a military tactic. Guerrilla war, in contrast to conventional warfare, has been employed generally by a weaker group who must persist in combating an enemy with far superior forces and resources. Guerrilla movements and insurrections are not confined to particular countries or to a specific historical period; rather, they have emerged in periods of crisis or under repressive regimes. In the Central American context, guerrilla groups constitute political-military movements which combine different tactics as the means to gain power. Armed struggle is therefore an extension of and complement to political struggle in times of prerevolutionary or revolutionary crisis. The political-military activities of the guerrilla have to demonstrate that the regime in power is vulnerable, that it is possible to defeat it, or at least create conditions to negotiate a political way out of the crisis.

Attempts at social revolution had begun all over Latin America by the middle of the twentieth century. The Cuban Revolution of 1959 shook the entire continent by opening new perspectives and establishing an important historical precedent that was studied and debated passionately in the Latin American political arena. The Cuban revolutionary experience showed clear differences from those of the Russians and Chinese, especially in Cuba's strong reaction against its historic domination by the United States. The novel experiences of the Cuban Revolution provided some insights into the preconditions and tactics of successful revolutionary struggle. These insights were synthesized in the now-classic essay by the Argentine revolutionary leader, Ernesto "Che" Guevara, on the theme of guerrilla war (Doc. 1).

The impact of the Cuban Revolution among leftist Latin American parties and among student groups was enormous, giving rise to an intense political and ideological debate over the character of Latin American revolution, political and social alliances, and the validity of the armed struggle. The political strategy of the Communist party, which emphasized electoral participation and broad "popular front"-style coalitions, now was subject to intense criticism by leftist groups who questioned its proposed political alliance between the working and middle classes. Guerrilla movements began to appear in greater force in many countries in the 1960s and 1970s with the clear intention of accelerating the revolutionary process. The preconditions of the revolutionary crisis were present: tremendous economic and social inequalities deepened by the economic expansion since World War II and accentuated by intransigence on the part of the ruling oligarchies.

In Central America various guerrilla movements emerged at the beginning of the 1960s, and they quickly initiated armed propaganda and military actions, presenting new political and military challenges to the dictatorships of the region. In Nicaragua and Guatemala guerrilla groups, influenced by the Cuban experience, began to develop bases of support in the countryside. Students in Nicaragua and army officers in Guatemala constituted the initial nucleuses. These attempts at organizing armed struggle ended in military defeat and forced the survivors to retreat and reexamine their strategies.

In 1967, Cuba hosted a conference of the Organization of Latin American Solidarity (OLAS), to which most of the region's revolutionary parties and organizations sent representatives, to discuss problems of tactics and strategy. The final declaration of this meeting (Doc. 2) addresses the possibilities and perspectives of a continental revolution.

Along with guerrilla activity in rural areas, guerrilla movements with an urban base appeared in various countries. Urban areas offered the advantages of large concentrations of population and of material and human resources in a small area. Urban guerrillas emerged in Venezuela, Brazil, and, later, in Argentina and Uruguay. One of the best-known leaders in Brazil was Carlos Marighella, who prepared a manual containing basic guidelines for urban guerrilla operations. Document 3 is an extract from this pamphlet, in which Marighella instructs militants on the importance of security.

Often, urban and rural guerrillas did not receive the assistance they hoped for and became politically isolated. This isolation made them vulnerable to government attacks. The capture and execution in 1967 of Guevara, one of the brightest and most experienced leaders, reflected the political and tactical problems confronting insurgent movements during this period. At the end of the 1960s the great majority of guerrilla groups had been destroyed or contained and isolated. During this period the primacy given to the military aspect of the struggle determined, in great measure, the internal organization of the movements and the tactics they employed. The emphasis on preventing infiltration led to the neglect of political activities in dealing with popular groups, a problem that played an important role in the guerrillas' isolation and defeat.

Some movements were characterized by their adherence to Marxism, an orientation reflected in the structural changes that they proposed to implement at such time as the revolution might triumph. Usually, however, considerations of a political and practical nature have obliged revolutionaries to be flexible in matters of doctrine, thus opening the possibility of tactical alliances and joint strategies with other social sectors. Less doctrinaire movements more easily establish diverse levels of coordination between military action and political parties and mass organizations. This type of coordination makes tasks of social and political control more difficult for anti-insurgency forces.

Two Central American revolutionary movements took stock and clarified their programs in 1969. Document 4, presented at the Fifth Plenary Session of the Honduran Communist Party in 1969, is a good example of Marxist analysis of the political situation in Honduras in the late 1960s. It defines the character of the revolution in that country and outlines its principles. Also in 1969 the Sandinista National Liberation Front (FSLN) of Nicaragua clarified its methods of struggle and program objectives, expanding its campaign against the Somoza dictatorship in the early 1970s. The interaction between the FSLN and the popular insurrectional mobilization in the revolutionary crisis of Nicaragua in 1978–1979 is explained in an interview with Humberto Ortega, one of the best strategists of the Sandinista Front (Docs. 5 and 6).

In the early 1970s the Guatemalan guerrilla struggle was renewed by the organization of the Edgardo Ibarra Front. This group constituted the base of the future Guerrilla Army of the Poor (EGP), one of the strongest movements in the country. Document 7 offers a peasant's perspective as well as the story of the first woman to be incorporated into the struggle of the EGP.

The rise of grass-roots organizations able to make their demands heard and to press for the implementation of certain reforms and for respect for their rights reflects an important change in the balance of social and political power in Central America. Among the strongest supporters of the grass-roots organizations are church groups. Beginning with the Vatican II Council (1962), and continuing with the Archbishops' Conference at Medellín (1968) and at Puebla (1979), elements within the Catholic Church have sided with the poor and the oppressed, thus opening a new chapter in the history of the Latin American church. The organization of Christian Base Communities, which analyzed and discussed the Biblical message and worked to find its relevance for the problems of the weak and dispossessed, contributed to arousing social conscience and a level of political mobilization without precedent in the history of the region. These Christian groups joined the struggle of the masses and endorsed the development of grass-roots organizations. The testimony of Rigoberta Menchú, a Guatemalan Indian woman, tells of her participation in one of these groups and explains how she linked the examples and teachings of the Bible to the problems and duties of the present (Doc. 8).

Through years of the crisis in El Salvador, popular organizations have achieved high levels of development, while the enormous economic destruction and political erosion occasioned by the war have encouraged both parties to seek a negotiated settlement. The program issued by the

FDR-FMLN (Doc. 9) offers a political analysis of the conflict and formulates proposals to achieve peace and establish a democratic system. The diary of an FMLN combatant (Doc. 10) gives an unusual perspective on life in a Salvadorean guerrilla camp. After 1989 the FMLN softened its position and made substantial political concessions. The army also became more willing to talk, thus opening the possibilities for a political solution for the civil war, which culminated in the signing of a peace treaty in January 1992. In Guatemala and Honduras the struggle continued to take its toll in human lives, suffering, and dislocation.

In the early 1990s all Central American countries are headed by conservative presidents, and U.S. security concerns in the region are vanishing with the breakdown of the Soviet Union and the end of the Cold War. Furthermore, years of protracted war did not result in a clear military victory for either side, thus raising some fundamental questions about the prospects and viability of revolutionary movements or the effectiveness of the army in winning the war. Under these circumstances, political negotiation and diplomacy became the most effective means to end the cycle of violence and war and bring peace to the region. The disarmament of the guerrillas and their incorporation into political and economic life pose some difficult problems, such as allocation of land and other forms of aid and training for the former combatants. The restructuring of the police and the reduction in the size of armies also require some difficult adjustments. But the most difficult challenges of the postwar period will be building mutual trust and a real commitment to democratic institutions, along with the implementation of economic and social policies that promote economic development and a more fair distribution of wealth. Until social and economic transformations occur, the underlying causes of revolution in Central America will remain.

1. General Principles of Guerrilla Fighting ◆ Ernesto "Che" Guevara

Ernesto Guevara, born in Argentina in 1928 and killed while trying to organize a guerrilla movement in Bolivia in 1967, was one of the most influential and inspiring revolutionary figures in Latin America in the 1960s. His ideas and example had great impact in Cuba and in the rest of the region. Guerrilla Warfare, *published in 1960, condenses the experiences*

From Che Guevara, *Guerrilla Warfare*, with intro. by Major Harries-Clichy Peterson, USMCR (New York: Praeger, 1961; 1962), 1–10.

learned in Cuba and offers practical advice to revolutionaries. This extract is from the section, "Essence."

The armed victory of the Cuban people over the Batista dictatorship has been recognized throughout the world as an epic triumph. It has revised old dogmas about the behavior of Latin American masses and has proved the people's ability to free themselves from an oppressive government through guerrilla warfare.

We believe that the Cuban revolution revealed three fundamental conclusions about armed revolution in the Americas:

I)   Popular forces can win a war against an army.
II) One does not necessarily have to wait for a revolutionary situation to arise; it can be created.
III) In the underdeveloped countries of the Americas, rural areas are the best battlefields for revolution.

The first two conclusions refute the do-nothing attitude of those pseudo revolutionaries who procrastinate under the pretext that nothing can be done against a professional army. They also refute those who feel the need to wait until, in some perfect way, all the required objective and subjective conditions are brought about through their own efforts. These undeniable truths were discussed in Cuba and are probably being discussed in Latin America now. Of course, not all the prerequisites for a revolution are going to be created solely by guerrillas. Certain minimum preconditions are needed to kindle the first spark. The people must be shown that social wrongs are not going to be redressed by civil means alone. And it is desirable to have the oppressor, wittingly or not, break the peace first.

Under these conditions, popular discontent assumes increasingly positive forms, creating a state of resistance that, provoked by the attitude of the authorities, can easily lead to an outbreak of fighting.

If a government has come to power through some form of popular vote, whether fraudulent or not, and if that government maintains at least the appearance of constitutional law, a guerrilla uprising cannot be brought about until all possible avenues of legal procedure have been exhausted.

The third conclusion is strategic, to convince those who want to center the revolution on urban masses not to overlook the tremendous role of rural people in underdeveloped America. We do not wish to underestimate the importance of armed resistance conducted by organized workers, but in the cities, armed revolt can all too easily be smothered when customary civil liberties are suspended or ignored, thus forcing resistance movements to act clandestinely, without arms, and against enormous dangers. This does not hold true in rural areas where guerrillas and inhabitants cooperate closely, beyond the reach of oppressor forces.

We place the above-mentioned three conclusions at the head of this work despite the detailed analysis to follow, for they constitute the basic contribution of the Cuban experience.

Guerrilla warfare, the basis of the people's fight for liberation, has many different characteristics and facets. It is obvious—and all who have written about it concur—that war is subject to certain strategic laws, and those who violate these laws will be defeated. Guerrilla warfare, a phase of general warfare, must be governed by all these laws; but in addition it has its own laws, and this unique set of rules must be followed if it is to succeed. Of course, different geographic and social factors in individual countries may call for different methods and forms of guerrilla warfare, but the basic laws apply to all guerrilla campaigns.

It is our task here to present these basic considerations, to develop a theory, to define and draw conclusions from our experience for the benefit of other peoples fighting for freedom.

Who are the combatants in guerrilla warfare? On one side, we have the oppressive oligarchy with its agent, the professional army, well armed and disciplined and frequently the recipient of foreign aid. Allied with the army are pampered bureaucracies. On the other side stand the people of the nation or region concerned. Guerrilla warfare is a fight of the masses, with the guerrilla band as the armed nucleus. The bands need not be considered inferior to the opposing army. Rather, the contrary is true: One resorts to guerrilla warfare when oppressed by superior numbers and arms. For the individual guerrilla warrior, then, wholehearted help from the local population is the basis on which to start. Popular support is indispensable. Let us consider the example of robber bands that roam a certain region. They possess all the characteristics of a guerrilla band—homogeneity, respect for their leader, bravery, familiarity with the terrain, and frequently even thorough understanding of tactics. They lack only one thing: the support of the people. And inevitably, these bands are caught and wiped out by police forces.

Why does the guerrilla fight? He is a social reformer. He takes up arms in response to widespread popular protest against an oppressor, impetuously hurling himself with all his might against anything that symbolizes the established order. . . .

When we analyze the tactics of guerrilla warfare, we see that the guerrilla must possess a highly developed knowledge of the terrain on which he operates, avenues of access and escape, possibilities for rapid maneuver, popular support, and hiding places. All this favors rural areas. Moreover, here the guerrilla can represent the desires of the great mass of poor farmers to possess their own land, animals, and all that makes up their life from cradle to grave. In other words, the guerrilla is—above all else—an agrarian revolutionary. So, for an up-to-date understanding of guerrilla warfare, what we are interested in is an armed group that fights the existing government, whether colonial or not, that acts on its own initiative, is rural in character, and economically is based on the desire to hold land. Mao Tse-tung's China began as workers' uprisings that were defeated and almost wiped out. It recovered only when it took seat in rural areas and adopted the cause of agrarian reform. Ho Chi-minh's victory in Indochina was based on poor rice farmers oppressed by French colonists. In Algeria, Arab nationalism is bolstered by oppressive conditions of sharecropping imposed by French colonists. In Puerto Rico, special conditions so far have prevented a guerrilla outbreak, but nationalism is arising because the poor farmers want their land back from the Yankee invader. This same craving drove the farmers of Eastern Cuba to fight, ever since Batista first came to power thirty years ago, for the right to hold land.

This type of hostility feeds on itself, and eventually transforms guerrilla warfare into positional warfare as the strength and number of fighting units increase. The possibility for such transformation is as great as the chance to destroy the enemy whenever encountered. Therefore, never undertake any fight that cannot be won.

There is a saying: "The guerrilla is the maverick of war." He practices deception, treachery, surprise, and night operations. Thus, circumstances and the will to win often oblige him to forget romantic and sportsmanlike concepts. Military strategy and tactics represent the way the group conceives its objectives of taking full advantage of the enemy's weak points. Individual combat is much the same in guerrilla warfare as at the squad level in conventional warfare. When trickery does not work, it's only because the enemy is alert and cannot be caught off guard. However, because the guerrilla band commands itself and because the enemy cannot forever guard all areas, surprise is always possible. It is the guerrilla's duty to exploit it!

Some disparaging people call this "hit and run." That is exactly what it is! Hit and run, wait, stalk the enemy, hit him again and run, do it all again and again, giving no rest to the enemy. Perhaps this smacks of not facing up to the enemy. Nevertheless, it serves the goal of guerrilla warfare: to conquer and destroy the enemy.

It is obvious that guerrilla warfare is a preliminary step, unable to win a war all by itself. What happens is that the guerrilla army swells in size until it becomes a regular army. Only then will it be ready to deliver a knock-out blow.

Just as a division commander no longer has to sacrifice himself out front leading his troops, the guerrillas—each one his own commander—do not have to sacrifice themselves in battle. A guerrilla is willing to give his life to realize an ideal, not merely to defend it.

Thus, the essence of guerrilla warfare is the miracle by which a small nucleus of men—looking beyond the immediate tactical objective—becomes the vanguard of a mass movement, achieving its ideals, establishing a new society, ending the ways of the old, and winning social justice. Considered in this light, guerrilla warfare takes on a true greatness, a sense of destiny, without the need for further rhetoric. Likewise, an unfaltering will to fight and persistence against immense obstacles are the greatness of the guerrilla.

---

2. General Declaration of the First Conference ◆ Organization of Latin American Solidarity

The first OLAS Conference, held in Havana in 1967, was an important event in the history of those Latin American leftist parties and movements that thought a continental revolution was possible. Armed struggle as a means to achieve revolutionary change, the relentless fight against imperialism, and solidarity with the Cuban Revolution were among the main topics of analysis and discussion. (Ernesto "Che" Guevara did not attend; he was in Bolivia trying to spark revolution.) On August 10 the OLAS proclaimed the following:

1 That making the Revolution constitutes a right and a duty of the peoples of Latin America.

2. That the Revolution in Latin America has its deepest historical roots in the liberation movement against European colonialism of the 19th century and against imperialism of this century. The epic of the peoples of America and the great class battles that our peoples have carried out against imperialism in earlier decades constitute the source of historical inspiration of the Latin American revolutionary movement.

3. That the essential content of the Revolution in Latin America is to be found in its confrontation with imperialism and the bourgeois and landowner oligarchies. Consequently, the character of the Revolution is the struggle for national independence, emancipation from the oligarchies, and the socialist road for its complete economic and social development.

4. That the principles of Marxism-Leninism guide the revolutionary movement of Latin America.

From *Tricontinental* (Cuba) (May-August 1967): 33–34.

5. That armed revolutionary struggle constitutes the fundamental course of the Revolution in Latin America.

6. That all other forms of struggle must serve to advance and not to retard the development of this fundamental course which is armed struggle.

7. That, for the majority of the countries of the continent, the problems of organizing, initiating, developing, and crowning the armed struggle at present constitutes the immediate and fundamental task of the revolutionary movement.

8. That those countries in which this task has not yet been undertaken nevertheless will regard it as an inevitable sequence in the development of revolutionary struggle in their countries.

9. That the historic responsibility of furthering revolution in each one of these countries belongs to the people and to their revolutionary vanguards in each country.

10. That the guerrilla is the nucleus of the liberation armies, and guerrilla warfare constitutes the most effective method of initiating and developing the revolutionary struggle in most of our countries.

11. That the leadership of the Revolution demands, as an organizational principle, the existence of a unified politico-military command as a guarantee of success.

12. That the most effective solidarity that the revolutionary movements may practice among themselves is the furthering and the culmination of their own struggle in their respective countries.

13. That the solidarity with Cuba and the collaboration and cooperation with the armed revolutionary movement is an undeferrable international duty of every anti-imperialist organization of the continent.

---

3. Minimanual of the Urban Guerrilla ◆ Carlos Marighella

Carlos Marighella, born in Bahia, Brazil, in 1911, was a brilliant and experienced militant of the Brazilian Communist party who had been active in politics since the 1920s, traveled to China in the early 1950s, and spent long years in prison for his activism. In the mid-1960s he had some open disagreements with the leadership of the party in regard to the tactics of the organization. In 1967, Marighella, against specific orders from the secretary-general of the party, attended the OLAS Conference in Havana. A few months later, in 1968, he founded the Action for National Liberation, a

From Carlos Marighella, *Minimanual of the Urban Guerrilla*, App. G (Washington, DC: Government Printing Office, 1983).

revolutionary organization that would wage an urban guerrilla war against the Brazilian military regime. He was killed by security forces in November 1969.

Marighella wrote the Minimanual of the Urban Guerrilla *to instruct the revolutionaries on the practical aspects of this irregular warfare. Here, he discusses security.*

The urban guerrilla lives in constant danger of the possibility of being discovered or denounced. The chief security problem is to make certain that we are well hidden and well guarded, and that there are secure methods to keep the police from locating us or our whereabouts.

The worst enemy of the urban guerrilla and the major danger we run is infiltration into our organization by a spy or an informer.

The spy trapped within the organization will be punished with death. The same goes for those who desert and inform to the police.

A good security is the certainty that the enemy has no spies and agents infiltrated in our midst and can receive no information about us even by indirect or distant means. The fundamental way to ensure this is to be cautious and strict in recruiting.

Nor is it permissible for everyone to know everyone and everything else. Each person should know only what relates to his work. This rule is a prudent point in the ABCs of urban guerrilla security.

The battle that we are waging against the enemy is arduous and difficult because it is a class struggle. Every class struggle is a battle of life or death when the classes are antagonistic.

The enemy wants to humiliate us and fights relentlessly to find us and destroy us, so that our great weapon consists in hiding from him and attacking him by surprise.

The danger to the urban guerrilla is that he may reveal himself through imprudence or allow himself to be discovered through lack of class vigilance. It is impossible for the urban guerrilla to give out his own or any other clandestine address to the enemy or to talk too much. Annotations in the margins of newspapers, lost documents, calling cards, letters or notes, all these are clues that the police never underestimate.

Address and telephone books must be destroyed and one must not write or hold papers. It is necessary to avoid keeping archives of legal or illegal names, biographical information, maps, and plans. The points of contact should not be written down but simply committed to memory.

The urban guerrilla who violates these rules must be warned by the first one who notes his infraction and, if he repeats it, we must avoid working with him.

The need of the urban guerrilla to move about constantly and the relative proximity of the police, given the circumstances of the strategic police net which surrounds the city, force him to accept variable security methods depending on the enemy's movements.

For this reason it is necessary to maintain a service of daily news about what the enemy appears to be doing: where his police net is operating and what gorges and points of strangulation are being watched. The daily reading of police news in the newspapers is a great fount of information in these cases.

The most important lesson for guerrilla security is never, under any circumstances, to permit the slightest sign of laxity in the maintenance of security measures and regulations within the organization.

Guerrilla security must be maintained also and principally in cases of arrest. The arrested guerrilla can reveal nothing to the police that will jeopardize the organization. He can say nothing that may lead, as a consequence, to the arrest of other comrades, the discovery of addresses and hiding places, the loss of arms and ammunition.

---

4. The Road of the Honduran Revolution ◆ Honduran Communist Party

The Communist Party of Honduras was founded in 1927 and then restructured in 1954; after that, the party experienced several divisions due to internal disagreements regarding strategy, leadership, and means of struggle. In the 1980s the party reaffirmed its commitment to armed struggle and coordinated its actions with other movements involved in the same effort. This excerpt is from a document prepared for the party's Fifth Plenary Session in April 1969.

Considering a series of factors, we can say that in Honduras the guerrilla struggle is the most appropriate form of popular action, the form that most closely responds to the needs of the revolutionary movement and that holds the greatest possibility for further development and complete success. Guerrilla war will be the chief form that the people's war of liberation takes in our country. Guerrilla war will be a catalyst for popular discontent and will give impetus to other mass actions, sharpening the social contradictions, raising the moral and spiritual opposition of the people, and accelerating the demise of the ruling classes. Through guerrilla warfare, whose principal terrain will be the mountains, the revolutionary forces will gradually alter the balance of forces which, though unfavorable at the beginning, will eventually match those of the enemy and will conquer and defeat him. This

From *Tricontinental* (Cuba) (November-December 1969): 35–38.

will be a process requiring large numbers and the patient work of accumulating those forces over a long period; it will be a prolonged war.

Guerrilla warfare, because of its many effects on the social and political life of the country, will be a factor contributing to the maturation of the revolutionary situation and to the development of all those objective and subjective conditions necessary for the triumph of the people's revolution.

In our country there are certain conditions that are particularly appropriate to the armed revolutionary process. There is a violent structural crisis. Since the military coup of October 1963, the crisis of the reactionary state has entered a particularly sharp phase. The possibility of change through peaceful means has been ended not only for the revolutionary forces but for other opposition forces as well. Popular discontent has increased, as has been proved by the willingness of certain groups to engage in direct action. These conditions are what make possible the beginning and the development of armed struggle. These objective conditions and not the "despair of the petite bourgeoisie" are what has made possible the guerrilla uprisings that have occurred sporadically since the third of October and which, despite their defeat, have taught the revolutionary movement some important lessons.

But, on the other hand, subjective conditions are actually moving counter to our objectives. This can be explained, as we have already seen, and in no way argues against the thesis of a popular war of liberation. It is certain that armed actions should not be undertaken if the minimum subjective conditions do not exist—that is to say, a certain level of organization and a mass consciousness sufficient to ensure the consolidation and development of the armed movement. But it is false to expect the full maturity of these conditions in a country such as ours, because the joining of objective and subjective conditions are necessities of the final battle for the immediate seizure of power, but are not essential to begin and develop an armed guerrilla struggle operating in the mountains, in an agricultural, semifeudal, and dependent country such as ours.

In Honduras the objective conditions are sufficiently developed so that they can be joined with minimum subjective conditions which will be created by organization, propaganda, agitation, and elevation of mass political consciousness, which our Party and other revolutionary organizations have undertaken. This will permit the beginning of an armed revolutionary process which will be strengthened as it fights the enemy and embarks on the formation of a people's liberation army—a guerrilla army—a revolutionary instrument through which it will be possible to destroy the bureaucratic military apparatus of the oligarchic and proimperialist state.

A prolonged people's armed revolutionary struggle is our country's specific path. It is the most certain road to the people's victory over imperialism and its internal allies. The Communist Party has no reason to exist other than as the revolutionary vanguard of the masses and their instrument for seizing state power; it must develop its work in this direction because it is the only way to accomplish the great changes so necessary if Honduras is to become a completely free and truly democratic and sovereign nation.

The Object of Our Revolution

After the triumph of the democratic revolution for national liberation which removes state power from the forces of imperialism and the bourgeois landowning oligarchy—enemies of the people's rights, progress, and national independence—a revolutionary government of workers, peasants, and urban petite bourgeoisie will come to power. It will be a patriotic, popular, democratic, and independent government supported by the people and entrusted with making those changes necessary to free our country from imperialist dependency, liquidate the remnants of feudalism, and end the economic and social backwardness that exists today. The most important immediate tasks of the revolutionary government will be the following:

1) Democratic agrarian reform. The great landholdings will be confiscated and handed over with land titles to the peasants who have no land or not enough land. The so-called national and common lands will also be distributed among the peasants. The revolutionary government will give the peasants technical assistance and credit on easy terms and with low interest, will help them to obtain tools, seeds, and fertilizers, and will assure them a market for their products, will cancel their rental debts to landowners and speculators and whatever other onerous loans or financial pressures they may have.

A minimum plot of land will be left for any national landowner to cultivate and to live on. The large commercial farms will not be divided. The state will keep this land and will utilize it to organize state farming in which the workers will have favorable working conditions.

The government will encourage the organization of peasant cooperatives and will give them every facility for obtaining machinery and all kinds of help through which they can increase their productivity and improve themselves as an economic agricultural collective.

2) Recuperation of all national wealth from Yankee imperialists. The revolutionary government will nationalize all the agricultural, industrial, mineral, commercial, electricity, and transport plants now in the hands of North American monopolies. The factories of the capitalists of other countries will not be nationalized nor will those of the national capitalists, but they will be obliged to abide by the new rules of the revolution.

3) Industrialization of the country. The revolutionary government will develop national industry according to the needs of the country. It will create the necessary state organizations for research, for the development of projects, and the establishment of new factories according to existing possibilities. It will expand the national market and open new markets abroad for its national products. It will bring electricity to all parts of the country.

4) The revolutionary government will immediately undertake to teach the entire population to read and write, will reform all levels of the educational system, will facilitate the entrance of the children of workers, peasants, and poor families into secondary schools and universities; will educate new technicians and new intellectuals in the service of the revolution; will energetically combat counterrevolutionary ideological reaction; will lend its patronage to art, literature, and all the expressions of national culture while opposing reactionary deformation of culture; will indoctrinate the people with a true revolutionary spirit of constant vigilance against imperialist dangers and the conspiracies of native reaction, and will develop in them a high level of international consciousness and solidarity with the peoples of the world.

5) The private banks will be nationalized. The Central Bank of Honduras, National Bank for Development, [and] Autonomous Municipal Bank will be democratized. The state will be responsible for all banking functions. Insurance companies will also be nationalized.

6) The revolutionary government will annul all sales taxes and all other taxes onerous to the people. It will institute tax reform, replacing in-direct taxes with proportionate taxes levied according to the level of investments.

7) It will fix a basic wage for all urban and farm workers which meets their vital needs. The government will take all measures possible to improve the conditions of the people's lives.

8) It will build hospitals and health centers in every part of the country where they are necessary. It will give free medical treatment to the people.

9) It will pass new protective maternity and child welfare laws. It will improve and extend social welfare throughout the country.

10) It will lower rents for houses. It will develop plans for the construction of housing for poor families on a grand scale.

11) The revolutionary government will base its foreign policy on national sovereignty. It will denounce the military pact signed with the United States and all others which are not in the national interest. It will expel from the country the Yankee missions and advisers who have intervened in Honduran affairs. In the international camp, it will wage an intransigent battle against imperialism and colonialism and will maintain friendly and mutually beneficial relations of fraternal solidarity with the socialist countries, the countries

that have won their national independence, and with the peoples of the world.

With respect to the peoples of Central America the government will follow a policy of anti-imperialist collaboration and solidarity, seeking unity when conditions make that possible, so that the five countries of Central America become one sole democratic nation.

12) Under the revolutionary government, Honduras will extend its commercial relations to include all the countries of the world who wish to establish trade on conditions of equality and mutual benefit.

As it carries out the work of democracy and national liberation, the revolutionary government, at the same time, will undertake the task of constructing a socialist society in Honduras.

---

5. Nicaragua: The Historic Program of the FSLN ◆ Sandinista National Liberation Front

The Sandinista National Liberation Front (FSLN) is a political movement founded in July 1961 and named after César Augusto Sandino, who waged a guerrilla war against U.S. troops occupying Nicaragua between 1927 and 1933. Inspired by the example of the Cuban Revolution, the founders of the FSLN incited rural guerrilla warfare against the Somoza regime. It took them more than a decade to build an effective, well-trained guerrilla force that could stand up to the National Guard. In 1969 the FSLN defined and made public its political program, which follows.

The Sandinista National Liberation Front (FSLN) arose out of the Nicaraguan people's need to have a "vanguard organization" capable of taking political power through direct struggle against its enemies and establishing a social system that wipes out the exploitation and poverty that our people have been subjected to in past history.

The FSLN is a politico-military organization, whose strategic objective is to take political power by destroying the military and bureaucratic apparatus of the dictatorship and to establish a revolutionary government based on the worker-peasant alliance and the convergence of all the patriotic anti-imperialist and antioligarchic forces in the country.

From Tomas Borge et al., *The Sandinistas Speak: Speeches and Writings of Nicaragua's Leaders* (New York, 1982), 13–22. © 1982 by Pathfinder Press. Reprinted by permission of Pathfinder Press.

The people of Nicaragua suffer under subjugation to a reactionary and fascist clique imposed by Yankee imperialism in 1932, the year Anastasio Somoza García was named commander in chief of the so-called National Guard (GN).

The Somozist clique had reduced Nicaragua to the status of a neocolony exploited by the Yankee monopolies and the country's oligarchic groups.

The present regime is politically unpopular and juridically illegal. The recognition and aid it gets from the North Americans is irrefutable proof of foreign interference in the affairs of Nicaragua.

The FSLN has seriously and with great responsibility analyzed the national reality and has resolved to confront the dictatorship with arms in hand. We have concluded that the triumph of the Sandinista people's revolution and the overthrow of the regime that is an enemy of the people will take place through the development of a hard-fought and prolonged people's war.

Whatever maneuvers and resources Yankee imperialism deploys, the Somozist dictatorship is condemned to total failure in the face of the rapid advance and development of the people's forces, headed by the Sandinista National Liberation Front.

Given the historic conjuncture, the FSLN has worked out this political program with an eye to strengthening and developing our organization, inspiring and stimulating the people of Nicaragua to march forward with the resolve to fight until the dictatorship is overthrown and to resist the intervention of Yankee imperialism, in order to forge a free, prosperous, and revolutionary homeland.

I. A Revolutionary Government

The Sandinista people's revolution will establish a revolutionary government that will eliminate the reactionary structure that arose from rigged elections and military coups, and the people's power will create a Nicaragua that is free of exploitation, oppression, backwardness: a free, progressive, and independent country.

The revolutionary government will apply the following measures of a political character:

A. It will endow revolutionary power with a structure that allows the full participation of the entire people, on the national level as well as the local level (departmental, municipal, neighborhood).

B. It will guarantee that all citizens can fully exercise all individual freedoms and it will respect human rights.

C. It will guarantee the free exchange of ideas, which above all leads to vigorously broadening the people's rights and national rights.

D. It will guarantee the freedom for the worker-union movement to organize in the city and countryside; and freedom to organize peasant, youth, student, women's, cultural, sporting, and similar groups.

E. It will guarantee the right of emigrant and exiled Nicaraguans to return to their native soil.

F. It will guarantee the right to asylum for citizens of other countries who are persecuted for participation in the revolutionary struggle.

G. It will severely punish the gangsters who are guilty of persecuting, informing on, abusing, torturing, or murdering revolutionaries and the people.

H. Those individuals who occupy high political posts as a result of rigged elections and military coups will be stripped of their political rights.

The revolutionary government will apply the following measures of an economic character:

A. It will expropriate the landed estates, factories, companies, buildings, means of transportation, and other wealth usurped by the Somoza family and accumulated through the misappropriation and plunder of the nation's wealth.

B. It will expropriate the landed estates, factories, companies, means of transportation, and other wealth usurped by the politicians and military officers, and all other accomplices, who have taken advantage of the present regime's administrative corruption.

C. It will nationalize the wealth of all the foreign companies that exploit the mineral, forest, maritime, and other kinds of resources.

D. It will establish workers' control over the administrative management of the factories and other wealth that are expropriated and nationalized.

E. It will centralize the mass transit service.

F. It will nationalize the banking system, which will be placed at the exclusive service of the country's economic development.

G. It will establish an independent currency.

H. It will refuse to honor the loans imposed on the country by the Yankee monopolies or those of any other power.

I. It will establish commercial relations with all countries, whatever their system, to benefit the country's economic development.

J. It will establish a suitable taxation policy, which will be applied with strict justice.

K. It will prohibit usury. This prohibition will apply to Nicaraguan nationals as well as foreigners.

L. It will protect the small and medium-size owners (producers, merchants) while restricting the excesses that lead to the exploitation of the workers.

M. It will establish state control over foreign trade, with an eye to diversifying it and making it independent.

N. It will rigorously restrict the importation of luxury items.

O. It will plan the national economy, putting an end to the anarchy characteristic of the capitalist system of production. An important part of this planning will focus on the industrialization and electrification of the country.

II. The Agrarian Revolution

The Sandinista people's revolution will work out an agrarian policy that achieves an authentic agrarian reform: a reform that will, in the immediate term, carry out massive distribution of the land, eliminating the land grabs by the large landlords in favor of the workers (small producers) who labor on the land.

A. It will expropriate and eliminate the capitalist and feudal estates.

B. It will turn over the land to the peasants, free of charge, in accordance with the principle that the land should belong to those who work it.

C. It will carry out a development plan for livestock raising aimed at diversifying and increasing the productivity of that sector.

D. It will guarantee the peasants the following rights:

1. Timely and adequate agricultural credit
2. Marketability (a guaranteed market for their production)
3. Technical assistance.

E. It will protect the patriotic landowners who collaborate with the guerrilla struggle, by paying them for their landholdings that exceed the limit established by the revolutionary government.

F. It will stimulate and encourage the peasants to organize themselves in cooperatives, so they can take their destiny into their own hands and directly participate in the development of the country.

G. It will abolish the debts the peasantry incurred to the landlord and any type of usurer.

H. It will eliminate the forced idleness that exists for most of the year in the countryside, and it will be attentive to creating sources of jobs for the peasant population.

III. Revolution in Culture and Education

The Sandinista people's revolution will establish the bases for the development of the national culture, the people's education, and university reform.

A. It will push forward a massive campaign to immediately wipe out illiteracy.

B. It will develop the national culture and will root out the neocolonial penetration in our culture.

C. It will rescue the progressive intellectuals, and their works that have arisen throughout our history, from the neglect in which they have been maintained by the anti-people's regimes.

D. It will give attention to the development and progress of education at the various levels (primary, intermediate, technical, university, etc.), and education will be free at all levels and obligatory at some. . . .

IV. Labor Legislation and Social Security

The Sandinista people's revolution will eliminate the injustice of the living and working conditions suffered by the working class under brutal exploitation, and will institute labor legislation and social assistance.

A. It will enact a labor code that will regulate, among other things, the following rights:

1. It will adopt the principle that "those who don't work don't eat," of course making exceptions for those who are unable to participate in the process of production due to age (children, old people), medical condition, or other reasons beyond their control.
2. Strict enforcement of the eight-hour work day.
3. The income of the workers (wages and other benefits) must be sufficient to satisfy their daily needs.
4. Respect for the dignity of the worker, prohibiting and punishing unjust treatment of workers in the course of their labor. . . .

V. Administrative Honesty

The Sandinista people's revolution will root out administrative governmental corruption, and will establish strict administrative honesty. . . .

VI. Reincorporation of the Atlantic Coast

The Sandinista people's revolution will put into practice a special plan for the Atlantic Coast, which has been abandoned to total neglect, in order to incorporate this area into the nation's life. . . .

VII. Emancipation of Women

The Sandinista people's revolution will abolish the odious discrimination that women have been subjected to compared to men; it will establish economic, political, and cultural equality between woman and man.

A. It will pay special attention to the mother and child.

B. It will eliminate prostitution and other social vices, through which the dignity of women will be raised.

C. It will put an end to the system of servitude that women suffer, which is reflected in the tragedy of the abandoned working mother.

D. It will establish for children born out of wedlock the right to equal protection by the revolutionary institutions.

E. It will establish day-care centers for the care and attention of the children of working women.

F. It will establish a two-month maternity leave before and after birth for women who work.

G. It will raise women's political, cultural, and vocational levels through their participation in the revolutionary process.

VIII. Respect for Religious Beliefs

The Sandinista people's revolution will guarantee the population of believers the freedom to profess any religion.

A. It will respect the right of citizens to profess and practice any religious belief.

B. It will support the work of priests and other religious figures who defend the working people.

IX. Independent Foreign Policy

The Sandinista people's revolution will eliminate the foreign policy of submission to Yankee imperialism, and will establish a patriotic foreign policy of absolute national independence and one that is for authentic universal peace. . . .

X. Central American People's Unity

The Sandinista people's revolution is for the true union of the Central American peoples in a single country. . . .

XI. Solidarity among Peoples

The Sandinista people's revolution will put an end to the use of the national territory as a base for Yankee aggression against other fraternal peoples and will put into practice militant solidarity with fraternal peoples fighting for their liberation. . . .

XII. People's Patriotic Army

The Sandinista people's revolution will abolish the armed force called the National Guard, which is an enemy of the people, and will create a patriotic, revolutionary, and people's army.

XIII. Veneration of Our Martyrs

The Sandinista people's revolution will maintain eternal gratitude to and veneration of our homeland's martyrs and will continue the shining example of heroism and selflessness they have bequeathed to us.

---

6. Nicaragua: The Strategy of Victory ◆ Humberto Ortega

In this 1980 interview the Sandinista leader analyses the political context in which the Nicaraguan people engaged in different forms of opposition to the Somoza dictatorship, including insurrectionary tactics and armed struggle. He also discusses the interactions between the FSLN and the mass movement in Nicaragua.

M. Harnecker: When did the masses begin to join the insurrectional process?

H. Ortega: The operations of October 1977 gave a big boost to the mass movement, but it wasn't until after the assassination of Pedro Joaquín Chamorro that they came out in full force and made crystal clear their potential, their determination, and their Sandinista will to join the armed struggle.

I would like to make it clear [that] the uprising of the masses as an aftermath to Chamorro's assassination was not led exclusively by the FSLN.

M. Harnecker: Was it a spontaneous action?

H. Ortega: It was a spontaneous reaction on the part of the masses which, in the end, the Sandinista Front began to direct through its activists and a number of military units. It was not a mass movement responding to a call by the Sandinistas; it was a response to a situation that nobody had foreseen.

Now then, our capacity for introducing ourselves into that mass movement was still limited at the time and was aimed at reaffirming our

From Humberto Ortega, interview by Marta Harnecker, "Nicaragua: The Strategy of Victory," *Granma* (Cuba), January 27, 1980.

political and military presence among the masses, but not yet from a concrete organic standpoint because we didn't have the necessary cadres.

In October we began to take steps in that direction: the activists, the mechanisms . . . and new permanent forms of mass organization began to take shape quickly: the neighborhood committees, the work done in a number of factories and in the student movement. Furthermore, the United People's Movement was already beginning to take shape even before October. This was the result of the Sandinistas' efforts to regroup the revolutionary organizations around their program in order to fight against Somoza's regime and gradually lead the people in our process of national and social liberation.

When the bourgeois opposition sectors began to retreat during the strike, the FSLN made its presence felt with the armed actions of February 2. This is why we decided to capture Granada, Rivas, and the antiguerrilla camp in Santa Clara, Nueva Segovia.

The capture of the antiguerrilla camp was led by Germán Pomares, Victor Tirado, and Daniel Ortega. Camilo, our younger brother, led the attack on Granada, and the capture of Rivas was led by Edén Pastora and the priest Gaspar García Laviana.

It was the first really serious blow dealt in the crisis. These large-scale actions redoubled the masses' enthusiasm and their determination to fight Somoza. They now saw a strengthened vanguard capable of fighting, of dealing blows to the enemy, of capturing cities. In other words, the masses saw a considerable advance from the operations in October to these operations, in the same way they considered the operations in October to be a considerable advance over the previously defensive position of the Sandinistas. Therefore, we were gaining momentum, for the operations in February were superior to those in October.

M. Harnecker: Wouldn't the fact that you had to withdraw from the captured cities be considered a failure?

H. Ortega: No, not at all, because we took the cities, seized the weapons of the National Guard, overpowered them, harassed the enemy, and kept on hitting them every chance we got. Everybody stayed in or around the cities.

By then the Carlos Fonseca Column was operating in the northern part of the country, without having suffered a single tactical defeat.

At the same time, the guerrilla forces of the Pablo Ubeda Column, operating in the mountain areas, were able to get back together due to a respite in the intense pressure that the National Guard had been putting on them. The guerrilla movement in Nueva Segovia had much more effect on the vital economic, social, and political centers because it was operating nearer to them. But it was the traditional guerrilla movement and the movement in the mountains that made possible the growth and the moral and political hegemony of the Sandinista movement until October.

In other words, October was the continuation of the armed struggle mainly in the mountains because that was what the existing operational conditions called for, but the time came when the armed struggle had to be transferred to zones of greater political importance.

It wasn't a question of storing away what we had accumulated, but of reproducing it. If we remained there we'd be holding on to what we had, but if we moved to other zones we'd be reproducing ourselves.

The greatest expression of the impact of the February actions is the insurrection of the Indians in Monimbó. It was the first of its kind, organized and planned ahead of time by the Indians and Sandinistas who were there. The battle lasted for almost a whole week, until February 26. The enemy crushed that uprising, which was partial. . . .

M. Harnecker: You mean it was the only one in the whole country?

H. Ortega: Yes, but at the same time, that partial uprising was the soul of the masses on a nationwide scale and became the heart of the insurrection that was to take place throughout the country.

M. Harnecker: When you were planning the Monimbó uprising, weren't you aware of the limitations of an isolated action?

H. Ortega: But we didn't plan the uprising. We just took the lead in the action that was decided upon by the Indian community.

The Monimbó uprising began around February 20 and continued for about a week. The capture of several cities (Rivas and Granada, for example) and the action carried out by the Northern Front had aroused a feeling of great expectation, of agitation among the masses, and the insurrectional propaganda spread by the FSLN beginning in October through pamphlets, etc., distributed throughout the country was beginning to bear fruit. The vanguard, however, hadn't been able to make contact in a more organic form with those sectors of the masses with the greatest political awareness. The actions of that sector, encouraged by the telling blows dealt the National Guard by the FSLN, in the midst of the Somoza regime's political crisis and the country's social and economic problems, surpassed the vanguard's capacity to channel all that popular agitation.

The neighborhood of Monimbó, which is a district of Masaya with some 20,000 inhabitants and both urban and rural zones, began in a spontaneous fashion to prepare for the insurrection. They began to organize block by block, set up barricades around the whole district, and take over the key spots. They also began to execute henchmen of the regime, to apply people's justice for the first time. They began to work as a Sandinista unit when they still lacked the organized leadership of the Sandinista movement.

And this doesn't mean that there were no Sandinistas there. There certainly were, and that is precisely why Camilo Ortega went to Monimbó, with contacts we had there, to try to lead the uprising, and he was killed in the fighting.

M. Harnecker: I understand now. Therefore, it was not an uprising that you had planned. Now then, would you have stopped it if you had been able to do so?

H. Ortega: It would have been very difficult to do that, because the uprising responded to the objective development of the community. Of course, in keeping with our plans, maybe we would have postponed it or planned it differently. Maybe we wouldn't have organized an armed insurrection but rather some other kind of mass activity, but that's the way things turned out. This was the way this Indian sector responded immediately to the incentive provided by the capture of the cities by the FSLN several days before.

In late February the organization of the vanguard was still limited and we didn't have the cadres to channel the determination and fighting spirit that existed among the masses.

M. Harnecker: An isolated uprising like that one meant that the enemy could concentrate all its forces against it?

H. Ortega: Exactly, and that's something we learned by experience.

M. Harnecker: Then it's important to know about other historical experiences in order to avoid making mistakes?

H. Ortega: Of course. We, the vanguard, knew of those historical experiences, but the masses didn't.

M. Harnecker: So it was actually a lesson for the people?

H. Ortega: Yes. We, the vanguard, knew it from the classics. The principle of concentration of forces has been one of the basic principles in warfare since ancient times.

What's important is that, in our case, we went through that experience in spite of the vanguard. The vanguard was certain that the uprising would be a setback, but a setback that would be transitory, because the decision of Monimbó contributed to raising the morale of the rest of the people who joined the uprising.

To what extent can the action be considered to have been a historical mistake? To what extent was the action an error on the part of the people, or was it simply their only option at that time? The fact remains that that example contributed both nationally and internationally to the development and ultimate triumph of the insurrection. Perhaps without the painful step which entailed great sacrifice it would have been more difficult to achieve that moral authority, that arousal among the country's masses, that spirit of support for one another that came from having witnessed how they had sacrificed themselves to win the support of the whole world for a people that were waging a struggle singlehanded. Perhaps without that example it would have been more difficult to speed up the conditions for the uprising.

That was an experience we and the people learned from.

With the experience we had acquired from October to Monimbó we were able to verify that the masses were willing to stage an uprising, but they needed more military organization, more mass organization. There was a need for riper political conditions and there was a need for more agitation, for better means of propaganda, such as a clandestine radio station.

It was necessary to mobilize the masses for war through the most elementary forms of organization.

M. Harnecker: You began to consider the matter of the radio station then?

H. Ortega: We'd been thinking about it since October but we hadn't been able to set it up. We had a radio set that the first anti-Somoza fighters had used in 1960, but it was old and we weren't able to put it in working order at that time.

However, we managed to fix it later and we put it in operation in those months of 1978. It was heard in Rivas, but very faintly. By then we were fully aware of the need for a radio station, of a way to communicate with the masses in order to prepare them for the insurrection.

But to get back to the idea I was developing. A gradual strengthening of forces was achieved amidst an enormous amount of activity that included the execution of Gen. Regualdo Pérez Vega, chief of the general staff of the National Guard, the capture of the palace in August, and winding up the first stage of this insurrectional movement that had begun in October 1977, with the nationwide uprising in September 1978.

---

7. Testimony of a Rural Worker from the Quiché Region in Guatemala ◆ María Lupe

María Lupe joined the revolutionary Guerrilla Army of the Poor (EGP), founded in 1972, early in the history of this movement. The EGP recruited supporters among landless peasants and squatters, and it has been particularly strong in Guatemala's northern department of El Quiché. María recounts her experiences as a rural worker, activist, and combatant.

From María Lupe, "Testimony of María Lupe: A Rural Worker," *Latin American Perspectives*, issue 36, vol. 10, no. 1 (Winter 1983): 105. Reprinted by permission of Sage Publications.

B efore, my husband and I were very poor. We worked for the rich on a plantation. I took care of the young people; I cooked and cleaned from one in the morning until ten o'clock at night. Since there was no electricity everything was done manually. My husband earned $.50 per day, and I was paid in meals only. Later, we bought a house and a little bit of land, but things became very bad for us and we were always in debt.

About twelve years ago we decided to go and see what we could find in the north, in Ixcan, but there it was even harder for us. There was nothing there, the store was four days from the road. We spent four months eating only *atol* [a drink made from corn] and tortillas. One of the local children died of malnutrition. I was pregnant with my third daughter, and I was very pale and undernourished. She was born in the seventh month, very thin, and I almost lost her. Later the engineers came and they gave us a little plot of land. During that time many people arrived and things improved a little. The people that came were from all over the country, from the coast, from the mountains, from all over.

After two years the first members of the Guerrilla Army of the Poor arrived. I remember just when it was because there wasn't even any corn at that time. I was scared, because I didn't know any better, and because all I had been told by the government was that the guerrillas only came to rob and to rape our daughters. Even one of my kids was scared, one who is now a guerrilla himself, and he ran and hid the radio.

The compañeros helped everyone to build a house, and it was the first time that we had worked collectively. Later, they explained to us that they were poor too and that they were fighting so that the poor could live a better life and that we were going to win. How are they going to win, I thought, when the towns are all so far apart? But now I see how the struggle has developed all over the country.

We were one of the first families that began to collaborate. I liked to raise chickens and pigs and I sold them at a good price to the compañeros and also gave some to them. Later, we gave them information and bought things for them that they needed. Others took advantage of them; they sold them things at very high prices, but when they realized what the compañeros were doing, that their purpose for being there was to help us and themselves, then these people stopped taking advantage and began to collaborate also.

All the families collaborated although there were times when we could only speak to the woman or only to the man in a family, and then later the one would try to convince the other; but sometimes they could not agree. Many times the men who were participating did not want their women working with the other men in the group, because of jealousy. So we arranged it so that other women worked with them instead. The women organized the preparation and serving of [food]; they brought it to my house, and then we would take it to the mountains where the compañeros were training.

After a year spies began to appear, and later the army placed a military commissioner there. There was a lack of secrecy, so everyone knew about those of us who were collaborating, especially those first families. My husband and oldest daughter, twelve years old, went to train in the mountains, and there my daughter learned to read and write. They stayed there three months and then they returned. But after a month they had to return to the mountains for good because the army was pursuing them. At the time Luis Arenas was executed, a very repressive landowner who was called the "Tiger of Ixcan." This was made public by the organization and then the repression really began.

I continued alone with my six children. I said that I could not work on the plantation, but later they had me doing everything. Since I was aware, I continued collaborating. Information and food were collected from people in the entire area. It was a rare individual who did not know of the compañeros. Since people live far from one another, we began to support one another, working collectively among twenty families or so, forming a network.

Those of us who were organized were given classes, the women and the men separately. A compañera spoke to us about the discrimination against women, about why we had not been able to mix and work with the men, about the lack of trust they had in us. We knew about discrimination within a marriage, apart from the exploitation by the rich; husbands who say we can only be in the home, that we can't do certain things, and generally women, not being conscious of anything else or of any other way of life, believed this to be natural.

The first element we dealt with in our meetings was the problem of women being hit by their husbands. It was very hard to change this custom. At the same time as we were discussing it, the compañeros were explaining to the men how a woman is not a slave and that she should not be beaten. But to stop this practice is very difficult and in some cases impossible. It was also necessary to fight for a woman's right to participate in political work. There were times when she would have to go out at night, for example, and her husband would not want her to leave. Later, they understood that it was because of lack of trust in the relationship that he would not allow her to go out. My husband and I never had problems like this.

Other customs were even harder to change. For example, among landowners like ourselves, we marry at fifteen years of age and older, but we marry freely. But amongst the Indian population it is different. Some Indian people who lived close by came and offered to buy my twelve-year-old daughter. It was their custom that if this is what our daughter wanted, then it was okay, but if not, then no. They accused us of discriminating against them because they were Indians. We spoke about this with the compañeros of the organization, and they spoke with the Indians later, but one cannot simply change the customs of a people so easily. Finally, the Indian man bought another young woman, an Indian woman. They remained hostile towards us. Later, the young man became a guerrilla, and our two families worked together, but it is very hard to change these customs. It is even harder for the Indian woman than it is for the Indian, because of the hard life she leads. Sometimes when the compañeros of the organization come to their homes, the women hide. They are very timid and since the compañeros do not speak their dialect, they cannot communicate with them.

I was the first compañera to arm herself, because I was pursued by the army; they came to take me away. I left the children with another woman, but she really couldn't care for them well. I had to come down from the mountains into the town, where the army knew me and was looking for me, and take my children away with me. We did this like a military operation, and we went back to the mountains with the children. We lived several months like that, in the encampment, and sometimes I was there alone with the children.

Later, because of security precautions, I left the encampment and went to live in another town. Then I lost contact with the organization. I had very little money and no one from the organization made contact with me. So, with the children, I worked washing other people's clothes and selling tortillas. My oldest daughter worked as a babysitter to make some money. How we survived I don't know. We lived that way for five months, with me telling everyone that my husband had left us, that he was a wretched man, and they believed me.

Already in the encampment they were doing everything: training, studying, going out to the towns and speaking with the people, making necessary purchases, etc. If the men went into the towns alone, the people did not trust them, but if the women also went they saw that there were women participating, women carrying arms, women equal to the men.

We gave talks to the people in the towns about simple things, comparing the growth of the organization to the growth of the corn. The women in the organization gave talks to the women, and the men to the men.

8. Testimony of a Guatemalan Indian Woman on the Formation of Christian Base Communities ◆ Rigoberta Menchú

Rigoberta was in her early twenties when she narrated her experiences to anthropologist Elisabeth Burgos-Debray, in an unlikely place: Paris. Rigoberta's commitment to the defense of the rights of her people cost her persecution and exile but won her the Nobel Peace Prize in 1992. In this part of her account she talks about what it is like to read the Bible through the eyes of the oppressed. Such people found in the Bible a source of inspiration and strength to rise against oppression and to assert their dignity as human beings and Christians.

We began to study the Bible as our main text. Many relationships in the Bible are like those we have with our ancestors, our ancestors whose lives were very much like our own. The important thing for us is that we started to identify that reality with our own. That's how we began studying the Bible. It's not something you memorize, it's not just to be talked about and prayed about, and nothing more. It also helped to change the image we had, as Catholics and Christians: that God is up there and that God has a great kingdom for us the poor, yet never thinking of our own reality that we were actually living. But by studying the scriptures, we did. Take "Exodus" for example, that's one we studied and analyzed. It talks a lot about the life of Moses who tried to lead his people from oppression and did all he could to free his people. We compare the Moses of those days with ourselves, the Moses of today. "Exodus" is about the life of a man, the life of Moses.

We began looking for texts which represented each one of us. We tried to relate them to our Indian culture. We took the example of Moses for the men, and we have the example of Judith, who was a very famous woman in her time and appears in the Bible. She fought very hard for her people and made many attacks against the king they had then, until she finally had his head. She held her victory in her hand, the head of the king. This gave us a vision, a stronger idea of how we Christians must defend ourselves. It made us think that a people could not be victorious without a just war. We Indians do not dream of great riches, we want only enough to live on. There is also the story of David, a little shepherd boy who appears in the Bible, who was able to defeat the king of those days, King Goliath. This story is the example

From *I, Rigoberta Menchú: An Indian Woman in Guatemala*, ed. Elisabeth Burgos-Debray, trans. Ann Wright. (Verso/NLB, London and New York, 1984), 131–36. Reprinted by permission.

for the children. This is how we look for stories and psalms which teach us how to defend ourselves from our enemies. I remember taking examples from all the texts, which helped the community to understand their situation better. It's not only now that there are great kings, powerful men, people who hold power in their hands. Our ancestors suffered under them too. This is how we identify with the lives of our [Mayan] ancestors [who] were murdered and tortured because they were Indians. We began studying more deeply and, well, we came to a conclusion: that being a Christian means thinking of our brothers around us, and that every one of our Indian race has the right to eat. This reflects what God himself said, that on this earth we have a right to what we need. The Bible was our principal text for study as Christians and it showed us what the role of a Christian is. I became a catechist as a little girl and I studied the Bible, hymns, the scriptures, but only very superficially. One of the things Catholic Action put in our heads is that everything is sinful. But we came round to asking ourselves: "If everything is sinful, why is it that the landowner kills humble peasants who don't even harm the natural world? Why do they take our lives?" When I first became a catechist, I thought that [it was] God's will that we should live in suffering, that God did not give us that destiny, but that men on earth have imposed this suffering, poverty, misery, and discrimination on us. We even got the idea of using our own everyday weapons, as the only solution left to us.

I am a Christian and I participate in this struggle as a Christian. For me, as a Christian, there is one important thing: that is the life of Christ. Throughout his life, Christ was humble. History tells us he was born in a little hut. He was persecuted and had to form a band of men so that his seed would not disappear. They were his disciples, his apostles. In those days, there was no other way of defending himself or Christ would have used it against his oppressors, against his enemies. He even gave his life. But Christ did not die, because generations and generations have followed him. And that's exactly what we understood when our first catechists fell. They're dead, but our people keep their memory alive through our struggle against the government, against an enemy who oppresses us. We don't need very much advice, or theories, or documents: life has been our teacher. For my part, the horrors I have suffered are enough for me. And I've also felt in the deepest part of me what discrimination is, what exploitation is. It is the story of my life. In my work I've often gone hungry. If I tried to recount the number of times I'd gone hungry in my life, it would take a very long time. When you understand this, when you see your own reality, a hatred grows inside you for those oppressors that make the people suffer so. As I said, and I say it again, it is not fate which makes us poor. It's not because we don't work, as the rich say. They say: "Indians are poor because they don't work, because they're always asleep." But I know from experience that we're outside ready for work at three in the morning. It was this that made us decide to fight. This is what motivated me, and also motivated many others. Above all, the mothers and fathers. They remember the ones they would like to have with them now but who died of malnutrition, or intoxication in the fincas, or had to be given away because they had no way of looking after them. It has a long history.

And it's precisely when we look at the lives of Christians in the past that we see what our role as Christians should be today. I must say, however, that I think even religions are manipulated by the system, by those same governments you find everywhere. They use them [either] through their ideas or through their methods. I mean, it's clear that a priest never works in the fincas, picking cotton or coffee. He wouldn't know what picking cotton was. Many priests don't even know what cotton is. But our reality teaches us that, as Christians, we must create a Church of the poor, that we don't need a Church imposed from outside which knows nothing of hunger. We recognize that the system has wanted to impose on us: to divide us and keep the poor dormant. So we take some things and not others. As far as sins go, it seems to me that the concept of the Catholic religion, or any other religion more conservative than Catholicism, is that God loves the poor and has a wonderful paradise in Heaven for the poor, so the poor must accept the life they have on Earth. But as Christians, we have understood that being a Christian means refusing to accept all the injustices which are committed against our people, refusing to accept the discrimination committed against a humble people who barely know what eating meat is but who are treated worse than horses. We've learned all this by watching what has happened in our lives. This awakening of the Indians didn't come, of course, from one day to the next, because Catholic Action and other religions and the system itself have all tried to keep us where we were. But I think that unless a religion springs from within the people themselves, it is a weapon of the system. So, naturally, it wasn't at all difficult for our community to understand all this and the reasons for us to defend ourselves, because this is the reality we live.

As I was saying, for us the Bible is our main weapon. It has shown us the way. Perhaps those who call themselves Christians, but who are really only Christians in theory, won't understand why we give the Bible the meaning we do. But that's because they haven't lived as we have. And also perhaps because they can't analyze it. I can assure you that any one of my community, even though he's illiterate and has to have it read to him and translated into his language, can learn many lessons from it, because he has no difficulty understanding what reality is and what the difference is between the paradise up above, in Heaven, and the reality of our people here

on Earth. We do this because we feel it is the duty of Christians to create the
kingdom of God on Earth among our brothers. This kingdom will exist only
when we all have enough to eat, when our children, brothers, [and] parents
don't have to die from hunger and malnutrition. That will be the "Glory," a
kingdom for we who have never known it.

I'm only talking about the Catholic church in general terms because, in
fact, many priests came to our region and were anticommunists, but
nevertheless understood that the people weren't communists, but hungry;
not communists, but exploited by the system. And they joined our people's
struggle too, they opted for the life we Indians live. Of course, many priests
call themselves Christians when they're only defending their own petty
interests, and they keep themselves apart from the people so as not to
endanger these interests. All the better for us, because we know very well
that we don't need a king in a palace but a brother who lives with us. We
don't need a leader to show us where God is, to say whether he exists or not,
because, through our own conception of God, we know there is a God and
that, as the Father of us all, he does not wish even one of his Children to die,
or be unhappy, or have no joy in life. We believe that, when we started using
the Bible, we began studying it in terms of our reality; it was because we
found in it a document to guide us. It's not that the document itself brings
about the change; it's more that each one of us learns to understand his
reality and wants to devote himself to others. More than anything else, it
was a form of learning for us. Perhaps if we'd had other means to learn,
things would have been different. But we understood that any element in
nature can change man when he is ready for change. We believe the Bible is
a necessary weapon for our people. Today I can say that it is a struggle
which cannot be stopped. Neither the governments nor imperialism can stop
it, because it is a struggle of hunger and poverty. Neither the government
nor imperialism can say: "Don't be hungry," when we are all dying of
hunger.

To learn about self-defense, as I was saying, we studied the Bible. We
began fashioning our own weapons. . . . Perhaps I shouldn't talk of weapons
[which] were very simple. And at the same time, they weren't so simple
when we all started using them, when the whole village was armed. As I
said before, the soldiers arrived one night. Our people were not in their
homes. They'd left the village and gone to the camp. They made sure that
we hadn't abandoned the village altogether but thought it would be better to
occupy it in the daytime. So sometime later, when we weren't expecting
them, about fifteen days later, our lookouts saw the army approaching. We
were in the middle of building houses for our neighbors. We needed some
more huts there. We had two lookouts. One was supposed to warn the
community and the other had to delay or stop the soldiers [from] entering.

They were aware that they might have to give their lives for the community. At a time like this, if someone can't escape, he must be ready to accept death. The army arrived, and the first two to enter wore civilian clothes. But our children can easily recognize soldiers, by the way they walk, and dress, and everything about them, so the lookouts knew they were soldiers in disguise. They asked the names of certain compañeros in the community so they could take them away, kidnap them. One of the lookouts got away and came to warn the village that the enemy was nearby. We asked him if he was sure and he said: "Yes, they are soldiers, two of them. But as I was coming up here I saw others coming, farther off, with olive green uniforms." The whole community left the village straightaway and gathered in one place. We were very worried because the other lookout didn't appear. They were capable of having kidnapped him. But he did turn up in the end and told us how many soldiers there were, what each one was like, what sort of weapons they had, how many in the vanguard and the rearguard.

This information helped us decide what to do, because it was daytime and we hadn't set our trap. We said: "What are we going to do with this army?" They came into the village and began beating our dogs and killing our animals. They went into the houses and looted them. They went crazy looking for us all over the place. Then we asked: "Who is willing to risk their lives now?" I, my brothers, and some other neighbors immediately put up our hands. We planned to give the army a shock and to show them we were organized and weren't just waiting passively for them. We had less than half an hour to plan how we were going to capture some weapons. We chose some people—the ones who'd go first, second, third, fourth, to surprise the enemy. How would we do it? We couldn't capture all ninety soldiers who'd come to the village, but we could get the rearguard. My village is a long way from the town, up in the mountains. You have to go over the mountains to get to another village. We have a little path to the village just wide enough for horses . . . and there are big rivers nearby so that the path isn't straight. It bends a lot. So we said, "Let's wait for the army on one of those bends and when the soldiers pass, we'll ambush the last one." We knew we were risking our lives, but we knew that this example would benefit the village very much because the army would stop coming and searching the village all the time. And that's what we did.

9. A Broad-based Provisional
Government ◆ Salvadorean FDR-FMLN

*The Democratic Revolutionary Front-Farabundo Martí National Liberation
Front (FDR-FMLN) of El Salvador was a broad coalition of more than
twenty political parties, unions, mass organizations, and revolutionary
groups founded in 1980 with the purpose of bringing effective democracy
and social justice to the country. This broad-based alliance was strong
enough to present a real opposition (political as well as military) to the
rightist alliance—military-oligarchy—that had controlled the government
since the 1930s. Here, the FDR-FMLN sets forth its 1984 integration
proposal and platform for a broad-based provisional government.*

This platform establishes the basic guidelines and necessary measures to
be adopted by the broad-based provisional government, with the contributions and advice of several organizations, sectors, and citizens. It will
become a government that seeks solutions to the most urgent development
problems in this country.

First of all, we propose a package of measures to be applied immediately.
Second, there are some measures and guidelines to enhance the broad-based
provisional government's action during its administration. Immediate
measures:

1. Dissolution of the 1983 constitution and its replacement by a
constitutional decree regulating the broad-based provisional government's
activities.

2. Dissolution of the state of siege and all the decrees issued since 1980
which violate individual and social liberties.

3. Freedom for all political prisoners and missing persons and the
annulment of all sentences issued based on repressive and special decrees.

4. Full guarantees for the exercise of collective and individual democratic rights and freedoms. A provisional statute should be issued to regulate
agrarian, livestock, and state workers' rights to organize labor unions. The
unions will be indemnified for damage done to their property through
repression since 1979. The organization of the people's power will be
legitimized; this was created during the war in various zones of the country.

From "FDR-FMLN, Integration Proposal and Platform for a Broad-based
Provisional Government by the Salvadorean FDR-FMLN, 1984," Foreign Broad-
cast Information Service, Latin America, February 10, 1984 (Washington, DC:
Government Printing Office).

5. Elimination of security corps, death squads, and their political arm, the ARENA [Nationalist Republican Alliance] party; creation of a civil police corps under the Interior Ministry.

6. Withdrawal of U.S. or any other country's military advisers, intervention, and military aid; an end to all supplies of weapons.

7. Purging of the government Armed Forces. Once this is achieved, its leaders should be organized within the broad-based provisional government's structures.

8. Investigation and trial of civilians and military officers responsible for genocide, political crimes, torture, disappearances, and the illegal deprivation of individual liberties. The deaths [caused by] FMLN fighters and of Army soldiers and officers in combat do not constitute a crime.

9. The Supreme Court of Justice would investigate and pass judgment on crimes against human rights. It must also purge and reorganize the judicial branch. Nongovernment human rights organizations, which have defended the people during the dictatorship's regime, would be asked to cooperate in this task.

10. The return of exiles and refugees and the implementation of an emergency program to reintegrate and care for returning refugees, those who have been dismissed from the Armed Forces, and the families and persons who, as a result of the war, have been left without protection. The broad-based provisional government will request the cooperation of international agencies and nongovernment organizations for these tasks.

11. Implementation of an emergency program to reconstruct the economic, educational, and health infrastructures which have been either destroyed or damaged by the war.

12. The establishment of a moratorium on debts to benefit small and middle businessmen. This would include a rapid and timely finance program to benefit the industrial, agricultural, and livestock sectors so as to promote economic reactivation.

13. Price setting and control of staples consumed by the people to improve the people's real incomes. The marketing and distribution of staples must also be reorganized and controlled.

14. Renegotiation of the foreign debt, acknowledging the financial commitments acquired by previous governments.

15. The reestablishment of the autonomy of the National University of El Salvador and the allocation of sufficient resources for its reorganization and operation. The university campus would be put at the disposal of its legitimate authorities immediately.

16. There would be a massive literacy campaign and an adult training program in the areas of health, education, agricultural and livestock production, and community organization.

17. The development of a massive employment program through the promotion of state and private investment in those sectors that produce jobs. An emergency program would be implemented to acquire the raw materials and tools necessary for economic reactivation. Producers would be guaranteed adequate marketing channels and frameworks.

18. The promotion and development of a popular organization program through the organization and consolidation of municipalities, communities, and state institutions, which must participate in the planning, implementation, and evaluation of programs that benefit the community.

19. The development of a massive communications program, with the creation and use of popular mass media means for local consumption.

20. The creation of an electoral organization that, on the basis of an agreement among the concerned parties, would prepare free general elections and a reliable electoral registry.

Economic and Social Reforms

1. The establishment of the requirements for the full implementation of the agrarian reform program, ensuring the free participation of farm workers in this implementation. The development of a cooperative organization program that would involve individual small farm owners.

2. The establishment of the requirements for the full nationalization of the country's banks and financial system to place both credit and finance organizations at the service of the majority.

3. The construction of the foundations for a complete reorganization of our foreign trade, including the control of primary export products: coffee, cotton, sugarcane, maritime products, and meat. This would also include control of the import of raw materials, input products, spare parts, and technology needed for our national production.

4. The construction of the foundations for an adequate solution to the housing problems of low-income sectors; the progressive expansion of social security services; and the reorientation of foreign investments for an effective contribution to the fulfillment of social needs.

Foreign Policy

The broad-based provisional government would develop its foreign policy on the basis of the following criteria:

1. The broad-based provisional government would pursue a policy of world relations for peace, in opposition to a rash arms buildup and nuclear weapons. It would defend the principles of peaceful coexistence, self-determination, and nonintervention; thus, it would join the Nonaligned Movement and, consequently, carry out a struggle against colonialism,

neocolonialism, Zionism, racial discrimination, and apartheid. It would comply with pledges undertaken at international organizations and would encourage active participation at international forums for the discussion and solution of problems arising from economic relations between countries. It would reaffirm its Bolivarian traditions and would consequently seek to promote and participate in regional forums that could strengthen the Latin American countries' positions on regional political, diplomatic, financial, and social problems.

2. In regard to its relations with the United States:

A. It would propose that agreements not be concluded that guarantee both countries' national security. Thus, the broad-based provisional government would pledge not to permit the installation of foreign military bases and/or missiles in its territory. Also, the U.S. Government must pledge that it will not carry out, promote, or encourage actions of destabilization against the broad-based provisional government or the government that is elected during this process. The Salvadorean Government would not endanger its national territory with activities seeking to destabilize governments in neighboring countries, nor would it allow the movement of weapons and foreign troops through its territory. It would promote the conclusion of pacts of nonaggression and nonintervention in the area's internal affairs.

B. The Salvadorean Government's relations with the United States and Central America would be reoriented and based on unconditional respect for the rights of self-determination, independence, and national sovereignty, and on mutual cooperation and interdependence. Thus, it would seek to achieve Morazán's ideal of Central American unity and would strive to free our region of foreign military forces. It would not participate in military alliances; consequently, it would withdraw from the CONDECA [Central American Defense Council]. It would actively participate in the promotion and development of regional organizations that can guarantee political solutions to international controversies with the conclusion of agreements that promote economic, social, and political unity.

---

10. Party in a Guerrilla Camp in El Salvador ◆ An FMLN Combatant

The daily life in any camp is rough and uncertain. There are few occasions for relaxation. This extract from the diary of an FMLN guerrilla gives

From "Camp J-15: Diary of an FMLN Combatant," excerpt taken from *Venceremos*, reprinted in *The Alert!* (July-August 1988): 5.

unique insight into life among the compas and describes one of the rare opportunities for insurgent fighters to enjoy themselves.

There was going to be a party at the camp at sundown. The forces were dispersed to get everything needed. Pepe and a little kid went looking for some of the compas (*compañeros*, or companions) from the special forces who have the best music tapes: the Rolling Stones, the Crusaders, break dances, and the ever present cumbias of Aniceto Molina. We had seen the compas pass by and knew we would find them on a hillside somewhere. We designated the sharpest of kids for that mission. It had to be guaranteed; without music there is no partying.

Roberto would go looking for "Michael Jackson." Everyone called him by that name. He's a compañero whose body is all splintered by bomb fragments. On one occasion he put together a little theater in his workshop camp and ran it for several months. Furthermore, he's a genius at home repairs: radios, lighters, tape recorders, and jackknives. He was even able to make the hospital's X-ray machine work after six months of futile attempts. When you would yell out to him, "What's up, Michael Jackson?", an enormous laugh would come out of him and he would show his smile, all toothless. "That damned thing [the bomb] almost killed me—it left only my eyes untouched!" And certainly he is pretty deaf, when he sets up his tape player speakers and the music is heard for 20 miles around. And he says, "Since the reconnaissance planes have no ears yet, there is no problem with my invention."

The first underground pharmacy had just been built. Camp J-15 had to celebrate. That morning during formation, Azeal was told, "Look, compa, we go through life digging—digging *tatus* (underground bomb shelters); it's about time we threw a party, the best of parties." This camp draws the attention of whoever goes by; it has a guerrilla collective and family life. There are twelve people in Camp J-15. Mama More is a little old woman who has been helping the compas since the beginning. In her small house and with her cornfields she fed all those who went by, always passing on information on the whereabouts of the soldiers. One day, when things turned ugly, her husband told her, "I'm leaving this place. We're going to get killed." And she answered, "So, go on. . . . I think that even if I just make tortillas for the compas, I'll be of some help to them." And it has been that way for all these years.

Then there was Don Ricardo. He was ahead of her since he was already in his seventies, but never a burden. He cut wood for the kitchen, he went to literacy classes, he would bring us avocados, and he was tireless when it was time to talk about how things were going for us in the war. One day he told me, "We've got to win soon; I want to see our victory day."

Those who work in the pharmacy and build the shelters are all caught up in the work right now, trying to cut the last branches to cover the first underground pharmacy. It's an underground shed; it's not bombproof, but it's rainproof, and that's no small thing.

Everyone comes by here. It's a health center and pharmacy and a strategic encampment and, as such, well guarded. But that doesn't make it an isolated and quiet place; the combatants, the health-care workers, and the popular clinics in the zone all have access to it.

It is an art, doing the many things that we do here—an art of motivation, sense of responsibility, tenderness to the compas, always mixed in with disorganization and solutions, or with the situation that the enemy gets us into. From that unruly commotion no structure can be safe. It's the positive way of thinking and the confidence of victory that is able to transform the disorder into a functioning camp.

Living in Camp J-15 can sometimes be hard. There are a multitude of tasks with the resulting fatigue from which you see no immediate results. In the combat units you fight face to face with the enemy; in the hospital, as the compas recuperate, life and death challenges accompanied by flirting between nurses and combatants show one of the most tender sides of the struggle. In the workshops, it's putting thorough thinking into turning inside out the seized weapons to see how they work. In J-15: medicines, underground passages, and files; files, underground passages, and medicines. "My God, may the triumph be ours soon," Neto often says.

At night, there is a tradition of chatting while listening to the radio. Although it may seem laughable, the radio and the clocks are the most sophisticated things we have here. To have possession of them is a privilege. They are windows to the world of time and space. The radio assures us long conversations at night with the BBC or Radio Holland, Radio Havana, Radio Spain; we know them all—time and exact frequency. The news broadens the horizons beyond the mountains a little. It gives us back that fraternity across frontiers that maintains us here; it brings us closer to that broad and alien world, and, above all, it allows us to hear about our own struggle through the broadcasts of Radio Farabundo Martí and Venceremos.

So there was a party in this camp. A party with sweet bread and tamales. A party with a little coffee and maybe some Delta cigarettes. It was a big party! Compas came from all directions. The women were wearing their best clothes; the men arrived and the big dance started. We put on rock, at first, till some complained and asked for the cumbias. And so it goes on, repeating over and over the same ten tapes throughout the six or seven hours of the party.

We danced them all. When you are dancing, you forget about being tired and everything else. There are moments when the war shows a sweet face . . . but later comes that large feeling of loss, when weeks go by without seeing the many now-foggy faces of that night, or feeling the more serious embraces and the shared loves. Tomorrow by five we'll be in our respective camps. It's no disco—it's a party among combatants of the FMLN. There are no psychedelic lights, but instead the consistent shout: "Turn out that lamp or you'll be seeing the A-37's bombs at dawn!" It's more than entertaining; it's coming together with human beings, sharing and going through the daily concerted tasks that surround our lives.

Selected Bibliography

Gott, Richard. *Guerrilla Movements in Latin America*. Garden City: Anchor Books, 1972.

Guevara, Ernesto. *Guerrilla Warfare: Introduction and Case Studies*. Edited by Brian Loveman and Thomas M. Davies, Jr. Lincoln: University of Nebraska Press, 1985.

Kohl, James, and John Litt, eds. *Urban Guerrilla Warfare in Latin America*. Cambridge: MIT Press, 1974.

Mercier Vega, Luis, ed. *Guerrillas in Latin America*. Translated by Daniel Weissbert. New York: Praeger, 1969.

Pomeroy, William J. *Guerrilla Warfare and Marxism*. New York: International Publishers, 1968.

Wickham-Crowley, Timothy P. *Exploring Revolution: Essays on Latin American Insurgency and Revolutionary Theory*. New York: M. E. Sharpe, 1991.

Wright, Thomas C. *Latin America in the Era of the Cuban Revolution*. New York: Praeger, 1991.

IX

Inter-American Relations

Joseph S. Tulchin

The end of the Cold War was greeted by Latin Americans with mixed emotions. On the one hand, there was relief that the specter of nuclear holocaust was lifted from their daily lives as well as hope that the end of the superpower confrontation would make the United States less likely to interpret everything that happened in the hemisphere in terms of the potential threat to its own security and less likely to intervene in their internal affairs. There was optimism that the new era, marked symbolically by the celebration of the Columbian Quincentenary in 1992, would bring the nations of the hemisphere greater freedom to define their own identities in the international system. The fact that, for the first time in history, nearly all were governed by a civilian, democratic regime was further cause for optimism.

There were dark spots, however, on the rosy picture. Although all the governments in the hemisphere, with the exception of Cuba, were ostensibly democratic, some were less democratic in practice than in form. More generally, in the aftermath of the debt crisis that had caused most of the economies of the region to stagnate for most of the 1980s, virtually every country suffered cruel social problems that threatened to undermine its political democracy. Poverty was more widespread in some countries than at any time in their history. Nationalists in the military rumbled and grumbled about selling out to external forces.

In this crisis, development was more important than ever. The desperate inequality would be relieved and the democracies strengthened only by the resumption of growth with equity. And, as at so many critical junctures in the past, the development of the nations of Latin America was inextricably tied to the world economy and to their relations with the United States. Would they be competitive in the world economy? Would they—could they, should they—form part of the emerging free-trade area of which

President George Bush had spoken in announcing the Enterprise for the Americas Initiative (Doc. 13), in which the United States obviously would play the dominant role? People spoke of the relative decline in the world of the United States in the face of rising Japanese power and the emergence of a European common market, and its defensive posture in forming a hemispheric trading bloc, but no one in the hemisphere doubted that the United States was the dominant force in the region and, for the first time, unopposed in its paramountcy, except by the government of Fidel Castro.

It was not always thus. To understand inter-American relations we must look back in time beyond the assumption of U.S. hegemony in the hemisphere. Throughout the nineteenth century, Great Britain was the dominant foreign power in Latin America. The British eschewed formal dominance; they preferred to leave local politics to locals and exercised their control through trade and investment. This informal empire established only loose guidelines for international behavior: payment of debts and protection of foreigners.[1]

From the first stirrings of the movements for independence there was some discussion of hemispheric brotherhood and unity. While it never enjoyed commercial or political influence to rival Great Britain, the United States was always present in Latin American thinking as a model, a potential ally or brother. Americans, North and South, saw themselves as part of the brave new world. There were energetic people in the North such as Henry Clay, who saw Latin America as a fruitful field for cooperative enterprise, as part of a great American System (Doc. 1). At the same time, however, Simón Bolívar expressed a common regional attitude when he said, alluding to the North Americans' expansionist tendencies, that the United States "seem[s] destined by Providence to plague America with torments in the name of freedom."[2] The same tension exists today between an urge toward Latin American integration and collaboration as protection *against* the United States and an urge toward closer collaboration with Washington as protection *by* the United States (Doc. 2). At stake, as it has been since independence, are the nations' sense of identity, their self-respect, and their ability to defend their own interests in the face of an external power or powers that defined the code of behavior in the international system.

---

[1]J. Gallagher and R. Robinson, "The Imperialism of Free Trade," *Economic History Review* 6 (1953): 1–15; D. C. M. Platt, *Finance, Trade, and Politics in British Foreign Policy, 1815–1914* (New York: Oxford University Press, 1968).

[2]Bolívar to Colonel Patrick Campbell, British chargé d'affaires, Bogotá, August 5, 1829, in *Selected Writings of Bolivar*, comp. Vicente Lecuna, ed. H. A. Bierck, Jr. (New York: Colonial Press, 1951), 2:731–32.

The United States adopted a cautious policy during the Latin American struggle for independence and directed its diplomatic efforts at preventing European nations from exploiting Spain's weakness in the hemisphere by a concerted intervention or in any manner that might endanger its own security. The nation's leaders were preoccupied with U.S. weakness and vulnerability—especially until the end of the War of 1812. The purpose of President James Monroe's message to Congress on December 3, 1823, better known as the Monroe Doctrine (Doc. 3), was to keep European powers out of the western hemisphere. It established a pattern that would be followed for many years: that U.S. Latin American policy would be formulated in response to the needs of domestic politics and to events outside the hemisphere, generally in Europe, and not with reference, primarily, to events in Latin America.

In the years following 1823 the European threat receded and the United States concentrated its energies on westward expansion. In the course of the movement across the continent, its people spoke of their "manifest destiny" at the expense of those whom they considered less powerful and less worthy. One nation, Mexico, suffered the very real and painful consequences of American expansion: the loss of one half of its national territory (Docs. 4 and 5). Frightened by American bellicosity, the Latin American nations were torn between their fear and hatred of the United States as a grasping predator and their admiration and need for their northern neighbor as a model and protector. Colombia went so far as to sign a defense treaty with the United States to guarantee the neutrality of the Isthmus of Panama (the Bidlack Treaty of 1846). Other nations in the region, while copying the U.S. Constitution or otherwise using the United States as a model, preferred to keep Washington at a distance. Predictably, when faced with an external threat, many Latin Americans referred to the teachings of Bolívar and sought protection in unity, but without significant results. External threats also had the curious effect of inhibiting the Latin American nations from using force to settle their international differences. If they feared outside intervention, they were inclined to settle disputes with their neighbors by peaceful means. International relations in South America during this period have been characterized as a balance of power.[3]

The situation changed when the United States emerged from a period of internal consolidation following the Civil War. Americans began to concern themselves more insistently with events outside their boundary. Secretary of State James G. Blaine participated energetically in hemispheric diplomacy in trying to end the War of the Pacific (involving Chile, Peru, and

[3]Robert N. Burr, "The Balance of Power in Nineteenth-century South America: An Exploratory Essay," *Hispanic American Historical Review* 35 (1955): 37–60.

Bolivia) and to mediate several Central American boundary disputes. He also took the initiative in calling the Pan American Conference, which met in Washington in 1889, to encourage hemispheric trade (Doc. 6). A few years later, in an 1895 note to the British government demanding a peaceful settlement of the boundary dispute between the British colony of Guiana and Venezuela, Secretary of State Richard B. Olney expressed a new aggressiveness in dealing with European nations interfering with hemispheric affairs when he declared that the United States "is practically sovereign on this continent, and its fiat is law upon the subjects to which it confines its interposition."[4]

Americans were ready for overseas expansion at the end of the nineteenth century. They trumpeted many arguments in its favor, and historians ever since have debated their relative importance.[5] As Blaine's scheme for a Pan American Customs Union makes plain, the government was anxious to help businessmen make deeper incursions into the Latin American market. New foreign markets were vital to the nation's well-being. Race and religion figured prominently in the writings of those who justified imperialism on the grounds that the United States had a civilizing mission, a duty to help "inferior peoples."

Pulling all of these arguments together, Captain Alfred Thayer Mahan of the U.S. Navy, in a series of influential magazine articles, outlined his concept of national security based on sea power. Mahan saw a strong fleet, secure lines of communication, and control over certain strategic points (for example, an interoceanic canal) as the operational links of a commercial empire by which the United States would exert its civilizing force in the world. Spain's inability to put down a revolt in Cuba, only ninety miles from the Florida coast, was the opportunity that the expansionists wanted. The United States won the war easily and gained control over Puerto Rico, Guam, the Philippines, and Cuba, with the self-imposed obligation of helping Cuba to its independence.

In the years following the war with Spain, the United States slowly came to define its new status as the paramount power in the Caribbean. With rather unseemly enthusiasm, President Theodore Roosevelt welcomed the

---

[4]Olney to Minister Thomas F. Bayard, July 20, 1895, U.S. Department of State, *Papers Relating to the Foreign Relations of the United States* (Washington, DC: Government Printing Office, 1896), 1:585.

[5]For a detailed discussion of the issues see Walter LaFeber, *The New Empire* (Ithaca: Cornell University Press, 1963); Ernest R. May, *American Imperialism: A Speculative Essay* (New York: Atheneum, 1968); and David Healy, *U.S. Expansionism: The Imperialist Urge in the 1890s* (Madison: University of Wisconsin Press, 1970).

opportunity presented in 1903 by the revolt of the Colombian province of Panama to recognize the independence of the new isthmian republic. With one stroke he realized one of Mahan's cardinal objectives of national security by signing the Hay-Bunau-Varilla Treaty, which gave the United States exclusive rights to construct a canal across the isthmus. Roosevelt believed that strong nations had the right and the duty to teach the benefits of civilization—good government and fiscal responsibility—to weaker and less fortunate ones. He acquiesced in an Anglo-German blockade of Venezuela in 1902–1903 for the purpose of collecting debts, apparently in the belief, as expressed to a German friend in 1901, that "if any South American state misbehaves toward any European country, let the European country spank it." During the blockade he wrote to his friend Albert Shaw that "nothing England and Germany have done . . . has in any way conflicted with . . . the Monroe Doctrine."

Roosevelt gradually changed his stance. First, American public opinion surprised him with the intensity of its opposition to the joint blockade. Second, the negotiations between Venezuela and the blockading powers, in which a representative of the United States participated, revealed that, while an intervening power might forswear territorial acquisition, the mere act of intervention accorded a degree of influence over the intervened nation that was as dangerous to U.S. interests in the Caribbean as the acquisition of territory. Finally, the Hague Tribunal, to which the Venezuelan dispute was referred, awarded preferential treatment to the blockading powers. This decision put a premium on efforts to collect debts by force. Roosevelt's response, worked out in the course of a dispute between European creditors and the Dominican Republic in 1904, and known as the Roosevelt Corollary to the Monroe Doctrine, was to assume the role of policeman in the hemisphere. He did not question the right of powerful creditors to force weaker nations to behave responsibly. To avoid European intervention in the Caribbean, he would have the United States serve as Europe's bill collector (Doc. 7). "Civilized nations," as the great powers called themselves, behaved according to an international code of acceptable behavior. Less civilized nations would be held to that code, by force if necessary.

The presence of a policeman did not by itself put an end to disorder and fiscal irresponsibility. As the problems persisted, William Howard Taft, Roosevelt's successor, thought that stability in Latin America would be more likely if the nations' economies were strengthened. He proposed massive doses of capital—Dollar Diplomacy—as the means to avoid the unpleasant and unwanted U.S. interventions in the domestic affairs of the nations in the Caribbean Danger Zone. In spite of some initial successes, Dollar Diplomacy led to more interventions, not fewer, and to no great increase in stability. President Woodrow Wilson took a new tack. He worked toward the same goals—political stability and fiscal responsibility to forestall European intervention—but was loath to use private capital as the instrument of U.S. policy. He preferred to teach the Latin Americans the virtues of democracy and constitutional government. But this too failed, and during Wilson's administration U.S. troops were sent into Mexico, Cuba, Nicaragua, Haiti, and the Dominican Republic to drive home the lessons of democracy. The terms of the debate were set for the next seventy years: Could the United States impose stability on the nations of the hemisphere and promote the well-being of their peoples by exporting democracy and capitalism, even if the export were done by coercion or imposition?

Latin Americans, especially those farther to the south, had never been happy with U.S. pretensions to dominance. The struggle against the United States began as soon as it made its first aggressive claims to leadership. At the First Pan American Conference in 1889, the Argentine delegation led the opposition to measures for hemispheric cooperation sponsored by the United States and for the next hundred years tried to block or frustrate U.S. hegemony.[6] José Enrique Rodó's classic, *Ariel*, became the bible of idealists who opposed the wanton exercise of U.S. power in the hemisphere. Critics questioned the benefits of civilization at the end of a bayonet (Doc. 8). The voices raised against U.S. intervention—and they were not restricted to those who chafed under direct U.S. control—swelled to a crescendo at the Sixth Pan American Conference at Havana in 1928. There, only dramatic and brilliant oratory by the chief delegate of the United States, Charles Evans Hughes, frustrated a motion to condemn any and all interventions by one state in the affairs of another (Doc. 9).

Ironically, events already had made Hughes's arguments academic. Changes wrought by World War I in the security position of the United States, together with increasing disillusionment with the fruits of formal responsibilities in the Caribbean, led to efforts to withdraw from existing interventions and to avoid new ones. The war eliminated the possibility that European nations might make a grab for territory in the hemisphere. At the same time, however, the war had forced the United States to expand its concept of strategic necessity to include such items as petroleum (fuel), cables (communications), and bank loans (finance capital). Its policy after the war was directed at establishing informal influence over Latin America, based on trade and investment, in a redefinition of its paramountcy.[7]

---

[6]On the century of conflict see Joseph S. Tulchin, *Argentina and the United States: The History of a Conflicted Relationship* (Boston: Twayne, 1990).

[7]See Joseph S. Tulchin, *The Aftermath of War* (New York: New York University Press, 1971).

As the United States approached its strategic objectives in fuel, communications, and finance capital, it became less hostile to the Latin American position on nonintervention and juridical equality of sovereign states. At first, American acceptance was hesitant and inconsistent. President Herbert Hoover reiterated it in a series of public statements at the end of the 1920s, and President Franklin D. Roosevelt gave it the fortunate appellation, the Good Neighbor. The Good Neighbor policy was defined in resolutions at the Pan American Conferences at Montevideo (1933) and Buenos Aires (1936), and worked out during the 1930s in a series of episodes testing the limits of U.S. willingness to allow the Latin American nations to act as they saw fit, even though such action might conflict with traditional interpretations of international law or might prejudice U.S. interests. Revisionist historians question the idealism of the Good Neighbor policy, preferring to see it as another effort by Washington to blunt the force of Latin American nationalism and as mere rhetorical flourish to cover U.S. efforts to expand its markets in the region.[8] Whatever the motives behind the Good Neighbor policy, there is no question that most Latin Americans approved of it (Doc. 10).[9] More important, the confidence engendered by the Good Neighbor policy lent legitimacy to U.S. leadership during the next war.

World War II drew most of the nations of the hemisphere together. The United States needed Latin American support and got it. Latin Americans needed U.S. protection and got it, although many were unhappy with the sudden escalation of U.S. control over their economies and asked repeatedly for some assurance of postwar cooperation to relieve them of the oppressive burden of dependence on external markets. The tension and bitterness inherent in the love-hate relationship between the paramount nation and its client states surfaced during the conference at Chapultepec in 1945. The United States steadfastly refused to concede to Latin Americans' demands for regional agreements to protect their primary products or to aid them in meeting the high costs of industrialization. Instead, it was preoccupied with the shape of the postwar world and insisted on fitting its relations with Latin America into that broader framework.

Instead of improving when the war ended, inter-American relations deteriorated badly. The Cold War distracted the United States from hemispheric events. In a bipolar world, the government in Washington saw

[8]For different interpretations of this period see David Green, *The Containment of Latin America* (Chicago: Quadrangle Books, 1971); and Bryce Wood, *The Making of the Good Neighbor Policy* (New York: Columbia University Press, 1961).

[9]Donald M. Dozer, *Are We Good Neighbors? Three Decades of Inter-American Relations, 1930–1960* (Gainesville: University of Florida Press, 1959), 1–70.

Latin America as just another region, another potential victim of Communist subversion, whose problems merited consideration as possible weak points in the struggle against communism (Doc. 11). Even the Alliance for Progress, in some ways a high-minded and revolutionary enterprise, was a response to the Cold War. If the Alliance proved a success, it would offer a satisfactory alternative to the socialist revolution led by Fidel Castro in Cuba. Latin America had to follow the path to progress indicated by the United States.[10] The disaster at the Bay of Pigs (1961) and the attitude toward the socialist regime of Salvador Allende in Chile (1970–1973) indicated the limits of U.S. tolerance for change and the rigidities of Cold War policy. Most Latin Americans were unhappy with their status as pawns in the Cold War (Doc. 12).

The debate in the United States over the struggle for development and change in Latin America—to which the nations of the region were at once witnesses and subjects—was whether the sources or the causes of the impulse for change were internal and legitimate or external and subversive. The extreme view, expressed during the administration of Ronald Reagan, that all unrest in the region was caused by the Soviet Union (the "Evil Empire," he called it) or its puppets, robbed Latin America of its humanity as well as its capacity for independent action and was clearly counter to reality. The extreme view collapsed along with Soviet power. But what of the future? The administration of George Bush responded to the sudden shift in strategic threat together with a preoccupation with the growing threat of world-trade blocs and the relative decline of U.S. power by proposing a hemispheric free-trade area that would reach from Alaska to Tierra del Fuego. This was the Enterprise for the Americas Initiative (Doc. 13). The Latin American response was enthusiastic. Some hailed the initiative as the most important U.S. policy since the Alliance for Progress. Others, perhaps cynically, were convinced that the United States was the only alternative left for Latin Americans, so that it was necessary to align themselves with the government in Washington. Whatever the reason, it appeared that every country in the hemisphere was convinced, at least for the moment, that its future lay in moving toward more pluralistic politics and more capitalistic economies with the leadership of the United States.

[10]See, for example, Gregorio Selser, *Alianza para el Progreso: La Mal Nacida* (Buenos Aires: Ediciones Iguazu, 1964).

1. U.S. Recognition of the Republics of Latin America ◆ Henry Clay

U.S. Representative Clay of Kentucky, a former war hawk and advocate of energetic participation by the federal government in developing the nation's resources, argues here against the Monroe administration's cautious policy. (He is referred to in the third person by an anonymous scribe.) In this 1820 address to Congress, Clay speaks from genuine conviction in favor of an American System. He is spurred on also by his rivalry with Secretary of State John Quincy Adams. Later, Clay would serve as secretary of state in President Adams's cabinet.

After the return of our Commissioners from South America; after they had all agreed in attesting the fact of independent sovereignty being exercised by the Government of Buenos Ayres, the whole nation looked forward to the recognition of the independence of that country as the policy which the Government ought to pursue. . . . Two years ago, Mr. C. [Henry Clay] said, would in his opinion, have been the proper time for recognizing the independence of the South. Then the struggle was somewhat doubtful, and a kind office on the part of this Government would have had a salutary effect. Since that period, what had occurred? Anything to prevent a recognition of their independence, or to make it less expedient? No; every occurrence tended to prove the capacity of that country to maintain its independence. . . .

Here Mr. C. quoted a few passages from the work of the Abbé de Pradt, recently translated by one of our citizens, which, he said, though the author was not very popular among Crowned heads, no man could read without being enlightened and instructed. These passages dwelt on the importance of the commerce of South America, when freed from its present restraints, &c. What would I give, exclaimed Mr. C., could we appreciate the advantages which may be realized by our pursuing the course which I propose! It is in our power to create a system of which we shall be the center, and in which all South America will act with us. In respect to commerce, we should be most benefited; this country would become the place of deposits of the commerce of the world. Our citizens engaged in foreign trade were at present disheartened by the condition of that trade; they must seek new channels for it, and none so advantageous could be found as those which the trade with South America would afford. . . .

From *The Annals of Congress*, 16th Cong., 1st sess. (May 10, 1820), 2225–28.

But however important our early recognition of the independence of the South might be to us, as respects our commercial and manufacturing interests, was there not another view of the subject, infinitely more gratifying? We should become the center of a system which would constitute the rallying point of human wisdom against all the despotism of the Old World. Did any man doubt the feelings of the South towards us? In spite of our coldness towards them, of the rigor of our laws, and the conduct of our officers, their hearts still turned towards us, as to their brethren; and he had no earthly doubt, if our Government would take the lead and recognize them, that they would become yet more anxious to imitate our institutions, and to secure to themselves and to their posterity the same freedom which we enjoy.

On a subject of this sort, Mr. C. asked, was it possible we could be content to remain, as we now were, looking anxiously to Europe, watching the eyes of Lord Castlereagh, and getting scraps of letters doubtfully indicative of his wishes; and sending to the Czar of Russia, and getting another scrap from Count Nesselrode? . . . Mr. C. deprecated this deference for foreign Powers. . . . Our institutions, said Mr. C., now make us free; but, how long shall we continue so, if we mould our opinions on those of Europe? Let us break these commercial and political fetters; let us no longer watch the nod of any European politician; let us become real and true Americans, and place ourselves at the head of the American system.

---

2. Two Letters in Favor of a Hemispheric Confederation ◆ Simón Bolívar

Bolívar was imbued with the notion of a league of Spanish American republics to bolster the fragile security of the new nations. During the period covered by these two letters (1824–1826), Bolívar's thinking on the Confederation had evolved to the point where he believed that Argentina was not likely to become a useful member. Later, at the end of his life, the Liberator would become disillusioned with the entire scheme.

To José Sánchez Carrión, Colombian Minister of Foreign Affairs, Lima, December 7, 1824

After fifteen years of sacrifices devoted to the struggle for American freedom in order to secure a system of guarantees that will be the

From *Simon Bolivar, Selected Writings, 1810–1830*, comp. Vicente Lecuna, ed. Harold A. Bierck, Jr., trans. Lewis Bertrand (New York: Colonial Press, 1951), 2:456–59, 567–70.

shield of our new destiny in peace and war, it is time [that] the interests and ties uniting the American republics, formerly Spanish colonies, possessed a fundamental basis to perpetuate, if possible, these governments.

To initiate that system and to concentrate the power of this great political body calls for the exercise of a sublime authority, one capable of directing the policy of our governments, whose influences should maintain a uniformity of principles and whose very name alone should put an end to our quarrels. . . .

In 1822, profoundly imbued with these ideas, I, as president of the Republic of Colombia, invited the governments of Mexico, Peru, Chile, and Buenos Aires to form a Confederation and to hold at the Isthmus of Panama, or at some other point agreed upon by the majority, a congress of plenipotentiaries from each state "that should act as a council during periods of great conflicts, to be appealed to in the event of common danger, and to be a faithful interpreter of public treaties when difficulties arise, in brief, to conciliate all our differences. . . ."

To defer any longer the meeting of the General Congress of the plenipotentiaries of the republics that, in fact, are already allied, in order to await the decision of the others would be to deprive ourselves of the advantages which that assembly will afford from its very beginning. . . .

The day when our plenipotentiaries exchange their credentials will mark an immortal epoch in the diplomatic history of the world.

A hundred centuries hence, posterity, searching for the origin of our public law and recalling the compacts that solidified its destiny, will finger with respect the protocols of the Isthmus. In them will be found the plan of the first alliances that will have marked the beginning of our relations with the universe. What, then, will be the Isthmus of Corinth compared with that of Panama?

To José Rafael Revenga, Colombian Minister of Foreign Affairs, Magdalena, February 17, 1826

I have before me your letters of October 21, November 6, and November 21, in which you write at length respecting the Confederation of the Isthmus and the amendments that you have proposed to its members. I am writing an official letter to the vice president, giving my opinion of these addenda, and I should like herein to discuss them with you at greater length.

An alliance with Great Britain would give us great prestige and respectability. Under her protection we would grow, and we would later be able to take our place among the stronger civilized nations. Any fears that powerful England might become the arbiter of the counsels and decisions of the assembly, that her voice, her will, and her interests might determine the course of its deliberations, are remote fears; and, should they one day materialize, they cannot outweigh the positive, immediate, and tangible benefits that such an alliance would give us at this time. First, the Confederation must be born and grow strong, and then the rest will follow. During its infancy we need help so that in manhood we will be able to defend ourselves. At present the alliance can serve our purpose; the future will take care of itself. . . .

I believe as you do that, if the plan were to be adopted by all America and by Great Britain, it would represent an enormous bulwark of power which would inevitably result in stability for the new states. . . .

I shall now add a few words regarding Buenos Aires and Chile. The former will never join the Confederation in good faith. She will in every way attempt to hinder and impede it and will place every possible obstacle in the path of the assembly. This is a foregone conclusion, considering her present organization and the temperament and principles of her ungovernable inhabitants. As for Chile, if she sends plenipotentiaries, she will do so in the best of good faith, and she will be more amenable and useful to the Confederation.

---

3. Message to Congress ◆ James Monroe

After an intensive period of high-level discussion, Secretary of State John Quincy Adams and President Monroe combined to draft the sections of the annual message to Congress on December 3, 1823. Two important principles of policy were enunciated: noncolonization and, after an interval of forty paragraphs on miscellaneous subjects, the doctrine of two spheres. The first arose out of consideration of conflicting claims on the northwest coast of North America, and the second out of the apparent threat by the Holy Alliance to intervene on the side of Spain in the Latin American struggle for independence.

In the discussions to which this interest [in the northwest] has given rise and in the arrangements by which they may terminate, the occasion has been judged proper for asserting, as a principle in which the rights and interests of the United States are involved, that the American continents, by the free and independent condition which they have assumed and maintain, are henceforth not to be considered as subjects for future colonization by any European power. . . .

From James D. Richardson, comp., *Messages and Papers of the Presidents*, 20 vols. (New York: Bureau of National Literature, 1897–1922), 2:209–19.

In the wars of the European powers in matters relating to themselves we have never taken any part, nor does it comport with our policy so to do. It is only when our rights are invaded or seriously menaced that we resent injuries or make preparation for our defense. With the movements in this hemisphere we are of necessity more immediately connected, and by causes which must be obvious to all enlightened and impartial observers. The political system of the allied powers is essentially different in this respect from that of America. This difference proceeds from that which exists in their respective Governments; and to the defense of our own, which has been achieved by the loss of so much blood and treasure, and matured by the wisdom of their most enlightened citizens, and under which we have enjoyed unexampled felicity, the whole nation is devoted. We owe it, therefore, to candor and to the amicable relations existing between the United States and those powers to declare that we should consider any attempt on their part to extend their system to any portion of this hemisphere as dangerous to our peace and security. With the existing colonies or dependencies of any European power we have not interfered and shall not interfere. But with the Governments who have declared their independence and maintained it, and whose independence we have, on great consideration and on just principles, acknowledged, we could not view any interposition for the purpose of oppressing them, or controlling in any other manner their destiny, by any European power in any other light than as the manifestation of an unfriendly disposition toward the United States. In the war between those new Governments and Spain we declared our neutrality at the time of their recognition, and to this we have adhered, and shall continue to adhere, provided no change shall occur which, in the judgment of the competent authorities of this Government, shall make a corresponding change on the part of the United States indispensable to their security. . . .

If we compare the present condition of our Union with its actual state at the close of our Revolution, the history of the world furnishes no example of a progress in improvement in all the important circumstances which constitute the happiness of a nation which bears any resemblance to it. . . .

The expansion of our population and accession of new States to our Union have had the happiest effect on all its highest interests. That it has eminently augmented our resources and added to our strength and respectability as a power is admitted by all. But it is not in these important circumstances only that this happy effect is felt. It is manifest that by enlarging the basis of our system and increasing the number of States the system itself has been greatly strengthened in both its branches. Consolidation and disunion have thereby been rendered equally impracticable. . . . To what, then, do we owe these blessings? It is known to all that we derive them from the excellence of our institutions. Ought we not, then, to adopt every measure which may be necessary to perpetuate them?

---

4. The United States Prepares for War with Mexico ◆ James Buchanan and James K. Polk

The United States had its eye on the territory of California and sought to acquire it, as it had Texas, by indirection and without violence. President Polk, however, was determined to press relentlessly U.S. claims against Mexico. The first selection is from the State Department's instructions in 1845 to its consul in Monterey, California, Thomas O. Larkin, setting forth the bases for Washington's rather delicate policy. After negotiations with Mexico had failed to settle the differences between the two nations to the satisfaction of the United States, a clash between armed forces at the disputed boundary prompted Polk's demand for war, as seen in the second selection.

Secretary of State Buchanan to Thomas O. Larkin, October 17, 1845

I feel much indebted to you for the information which you have communicated to the Department from time to time in relation to California. The future destiny of that country is a subject of anxious solicitude for the Government and people of the United States. The interests of our commerce and our whale fisheries on the Pacific ocean demand that you should exert the greatest vigilance in discovering and defeating any attempts which may be made by foreign governments to acquire a control over that country. In the contest between Mexico and California we can take no part, unless the former should commence hostilities against the United States; but should California assert and maintain her independence, we shall render her all the kind offices in our power, as a sister Republic. This Government has no ambitious aspirations to gratify and no desire to extend our federal system over more territory than we already possess, unless by the free and spontaneous wish of the independent people of the adjoining territories. The exercise of compulsion or improper influence to accomplish such a result, would be repugnant both to the policy and principles of this Government. But whilst these are the sentiments of the President, he could not view with indifference the transfer of California to Great Britain or any other European

From Buchanan to Larkin, October 17, 1845, *Diplomatic Correspondence of the United States: Inter-American Affairs*, sel. and arr. William R. Manning, 8 vols. (Washington, DC: Carnegie Endowment for International Peace, 1932–1939), 8:189.

Power. The system of colonization by foreign monarchies on the North American continent must and will be resisted by the United States. It could result in nothing but evil to the colonists under their dominion who would naturally desire to secure for themselves the blessings of liberty by means of republican institutions; whilst it must prove highly prejudicial to the best interests of the United States. Nor would it in the end benefit such foreign monarchies. On the contrary, even Great Britain, by the acquisition of California, would sow the seeds of future war and disaster for herself; because there is no political truth more certain than this fine Province could not long be held in vassalage by any European Power. The emigration to it of people from the United States would soon render this impossible.

Whilst the President will make no effort and use no influence to induce California to become one of the free and independent States of this Union, yet if the people should desire to unite their destiny with ours, they would be received as brethren, whenever this can be done without affording Mexico just cause of complaint.

President Polk's Message to Congress, May 11, 1846

The grievous wrongs perpetrated by Mexico upon our citizens throughout a long period of years remain unredressed, and solemn treaties pledging her public faith for this redress have been disregarded. A government either unable or unwilling to enforce the execution of such treaties fails to perform one of its plainest duties.

Our commerce with Mexico has been almost annihilated. It was formerly highly beneficial to both nations, but our merchants have been deterred from prosecuting it by the system of outrage and extortion which the Mexican authorities have pursued against them, whilst their appeals through their own Government for indemnity have been made in vain. Our forbearance has gone to such an extreme as to be mistaken in its character. Had we acted with vigor in repelling the insults and redressing the injuries inflicted by Mexico at the commencement, we should doubtless have escaped all the difficulties in which we are now involved.

Instead of this, however, we have been exerting our best efforts to propitiate her good will. Upon the pretext that Texas, a nation as independent as herself, thought proper to unite its destinies with our own, she has affected to believe that we have severed her rightful territory, and in official proclamations and manifestoes has repeatedly threatened to make war upon us for the purpose of reconquering Texas. In the meantime we have tried every effort at reconciliation. The cup of forbearance has been exhausted even before the recent information from the frontier of the Del Norte. But now, after reiterated menaces, Mexico has passed the boundary of the

United States, has invaded our territory and shed American blood upon American soil. She has proclaimed that hostilities have commenced, and that the two nations are at war.

As war exists, and, notwithstanding all our efforts to avoid it, exists by the act of Mexico herself, we are called upon by every consideration of duty and patriotism to vindicate with decision the honor, the rights, and the interests of our country. . . .

The most energetic and prompt measures and the immediate appearance in arms of a large and overpowering force are recommended to Congress as the most certain and efficient means of bringing the existing collision with Mexico to a speedy and successful termination.

---

5. Two Mexicans View the War with the United States ◆ Carlos Bosch García and Luis G. Zorilla

In the 1840s, Mexico was awake to the danger of U.S. aggression but powerless to forestall it. The Mexican government was at once outraged by the annexation of Texas, anxious to resolve its differences with the United States (but not at a cost to the national honor), mired in severe financial embarrassment, and rendered virtually impotent by internal bickering. Such a combination made for highly emotional responses to events. The war with the United States was a national trauma for Mexico, and, like an old wound, the scars still smart. The following excerpts are taken from two works on U.S.-Mexican diplomatic relations. Both historians, Carlos Bosch García and Luis G. Zorilla, strive for objectivity. Three dry diplomatic documents as paraphrased by Bosch García appear even drier. Nevertheless, the message is clear: Mexicans were outraged and impotent in the face of U.S. expansion. Succeeding generations in Mexico continue to resent U.S. aggression and the failure of their forebears to act decisively to block it.

Carlos Bosch García

May 30, 1844, Mexico. J. Bocanegra, Mexican Minister of Foreign Affairs, to B. E. Green, U.S. Minister

Upon hearing from Green of the decision to annex Texas to the United States, Bocanegra sent the American a long, vigorous dispatch. In it, he advanced all the considerations due to nations which held territories, the

From Carlos Bosch García, *Material para la Historia Diplomática de México (México y los Estados Unidos, 1824–1848)*, trans. Christopher Hunt (México: Escuela Nacional de Ciencias Políticas y Sociales, UNAM, 1961), 424–25, 462, 543.

rights by which governments and enlightened men ought to live. He ignored completely the political motives with which Green justified the American action.

Bocanegra commented upon the behavior of the United States during the evolution of the conflict, upon legal titles, and upon the concept of "first settlers" of a region. He asserted that Mexico had always claimed posssession of Texas, and that it had never intended to give up the territory. Bocanegra further noted that while Mexico had not intervened to any great extent during the development of the Texan independence movement, the United States had helped the movement in order to assure its success. As for Green's announcement of the annexation decision, which had been intended as an American gesture of respect toward Mexico, Bocanegra observed that it did no more than reveal a consummated, irrevocable act.

Finally, Bocanegra emphasized that Mexico was prepared to defend what it considered its own, and he reminded Green that the dispatch of August 28, 1843, was still in effect. Mexico's only remaining hope, he concluded, was that the American Senate would exercise better judgment and refuse to ratify a treaty which violated reason, law, and justice. Otherwise, Mexico would be forced to proceed according to its international rights.

January 1845, Mexico. Congressional decree in response to the annexation

The Mexican Congress reacted to the annexation of Texas by denouncing it as a monstrous usurpation of foreign territory, a violation of the sovereignty of nations, and therefore a grave threat to world peace. In its decree, the Congress accused the United States of treacherously planning the annexation over a long period of time, during which it proclaimed its cordial friendship with Mexico. The appropriation of Texas violated Mexico's rights; besides insulting its national dignity, the annexation threatened Mexico's independence and its very political existence. Furthermore, it violated the spirit of all treaties going back before 1832. The American law of annexation, the decree continued, had no effect upon Mexican rights to Texas, which the country was prepared to defend. The injustice of the plundering of Texas gave Mexico the right to retaliate with all its resources; accordingly, the Congress called all citizens to the defense of Mexican independence. The government would put its entire military force under arms.

December 3, 1845, Mexico. Article in La Voz del Pueblo

In announcing the arrival in Mexico of [John] Slidell, the newspaper *La Voz del Pueblo* violently attacked the American envoy and his government, which it accused of mendacity. It attributed to the United States responsibility for every possible kind of villainy in the international field, and commented that there was only one serious offense which the American government had failed to commit. This last insult would be delivered by Slidell, who had come on the frigate *Saint Mary* to arrange for the purchase of Texas, New Mexico, and the Californias. The newspaper warned Mexicans that in a few months they would have no country, for the United States would have taken it from them. The article concluded by asking if such an atrocity could be contemplated impassively.

Luis G. Zorilla

An idea of the claims which were so persistently protected by the government in Washington, and which had fallen into the hands of speculators, is given by Ambassador Waddy Thompson in a letter to the secretary of state, dated that same November 20: "[As to] the claims of W. J. Parrott, the Union Land Company, the Trinity Land Company, and Gilbert L. Thompson . . . I have examined them thoroughly, and do not hesitate to say that 2 percent on the amount claimed would be a large allowance, and more than they will ever receive by the decision of any impartial tribunal." All other claims, continues Thompson (who negotiated the treaty), together do not exceed $200,000.00. "I would most gladly have avoided the responsibility of the negotiation. I am thoroughly convinced that much the larger portion of these claims will be rejected by any impartial tribunal," he insists further on in the letter. After the treaty failed to gain ratification, negotiations for a settlement on the claims were dropped, for the poor diplomatic relations between the two countries were aggravated by the arrival of an American naval squadron off Verde Island at Veracruz in June 1844, and were finally broken off. . . .

The failure of Mexican negotiations over Texas caused the Congress to accuse the administration of José Joaquín de Herrera of negligence, and to refuse to authorize a loan of 15 million pesos which the president had requested in order to begin the war. Despite the country's moral and economic collapse caused by the small clique which had seized power, Herrera managed to build an army of 6,000 men. . . .

Paredes headed north, but on December 14, 1845, he declared that he and his troops, who were supposed to defend the nation, were in rebellion against the government. Turning his back on the foreign enemy, he returned

From Luis G. Zorilla, *Historia de las Relaciones entre México y los Estados Unidos de América, 1800–1958*, trans. Christopher Hunt (México: Editorial Porrua, 1965), 1:177–82, 209–10. Reprinted by permission of the publisher.

to the capital, to assume the presidency which had twice eluded him. At first there were no protests; Paredes gained much support, and the press revived the idea of establishing a monarchy to save the country from chaos. Unrest spread as the enemy advanced across national territory to the banks of the Bravo; there was a series of revolts and military uprisings in Oaxaca, Puebla, Sonora, and other places.

Paredes saw his own course of action imitated: the forces he had sent to defend the Californias, under General Rafael Tellez, declared their opposition to the new president in Mazatlán on May 20, 1846; they appropriated ships and provisions, leaving California undefended. Rebellion spread to Guadalajara under General Yanez, who, in league with Gómez Farías and López de Santa Ana from his exile abroad, convinced the garrison in the capital to join its chief, Mariano Salas, in revolt as soon as Paredes departed to put down the uprising in Guadalajara. Salas became interim president, and while both quarreling factions appealed to him to save the fatherland, [Zachary] Taylor and 10,000 men dug in at Matamoros, where, since the end of March, they had been building Fort Brown.

Toward the end of 1847 . . . as the political disaster demoralized both liberals and conservatives, our country experienced its most painful moments. Our downfall and disintegration seemed an endless nightmare. The goal of all efforts was the immediate protection of partisan interests. The uprisings of Paredes and the *polkos*, which pretended to be patriotic, were most anti-Mexican in their results, not realizing that actions—not the words which attempt to disguise them—are decisive.

In 1847 the United States of America had more than 21 million inhabitants and natural resources which were superior to Mexico's in every respect. The Mexican population surely did not exceed 8 million, and the country's past was marked by irreconcilable factionalism in both domestic and international affairs, and by thirty-seven years of internal strife. Knowing what we do about the intentions of the government in Washington, and the maneuvers planned and executed by its officials, we need not argue over which country was the aggressor in this war. Although Mexico played into the hands of the United States by accepting its challenge to fight, war was preferable to the only other recourse: handing over without resistance everything that Washington demanded. Conditions for peace such as those offered by [President James K.] Polk are never accepted by a nation—they must be imposed by force of arms. Furthermore, the march of the American army to the Mexican capital was not as glorious as contemporaries pretended; the maneuvers of the State Department were far more brilliant.

Amid such calamities, the greatest of which was the irresponsibility of many of its leaders, it is heartening to see that Mexicans nonetheless put up a resistance.

6. Act Authorizing the President to Call a
Pan American Conference ◆ U.S. Congress

Secretary of State James G. Blaine's initial attempt to bring the nations of the hemisphere together in 1881 was frustrated by the assassination of President James A. Garfield and Chester A. Arthur's subsequent reversal of policy. Seven years later, Blaine was back in office and succeeded in 1889 in realizing his plan for a hemispheric gathering that would facilitate the expansion of U.S. trade and influence.

An act authorizing the President of the United States to arrange a conference between the United States of America and the Republics of Mexico, Central and South America, Hayti, San Domingo, and the Empire of Brazil, which is in words and figures as follows, to wit:

Be it enacted by the Senate and House of Representatives of the United States of America, in Congress assembled, That the President of the United States be, and he is hereby, requested and authorized to invite the several Governments of the Republics of Mexico, Central and South America, Hayti, San Domingo, and the Empire of Brazil to join the United States in a conference to be held at Washington, in the United States, at such time as he may deem proper, in the year eighteen hundred and eighty-nine, for the purpose of discussing and recommending for adoption to their respective Governments some plan of arbitration for the settlement of disagreements and disputes that may hereafter arise between them, and for considering questions relating to the improvement of business intercourse and means of direct communication between said countries, and to encourage such reciprocal commercial relations as will be beneficial to all and secure more extensive markets for the products of each of said countries. . . .

Sec. 2. That in forwarding the invitations to the said Governments the President of the United States shall set forth that the Conference is called to consider—

First. Measures that shall tend to preserve the peace and promote the prosperity of the several American States.

Second. Measures toward the formation of an American customs union, under which the trade of the American nations with each other shall, so far as [is] possible and profitable, be promoted.

From Senate Executive Doc. No. 231, 51st Cong., 1st sess., *Minutes of the International American Conference* (Washington, DC: Government Printing Office, 1890), 1–3.

Third. The establishment of regular and frequent communication between the ports of the several American States and the ports of each other.

Fourth. The establishment of a uniform system of customs regulations in each of the independent American States to govern the mode of importation and exportation of merchandise and port dues and charges, a uniform method of determining the classification and valuation of such merchandise in the ports of each country, and a uniform system of invoices, and the sanitation of ships and quarantine.

Fifth. The adoption of a uniform system of weights and measures, and laws to protect the patent rights, copyrights, and trade-marks of citizens of either country in the other, and for the extradition of criminals.

Sixth. The adoption of a common silver coin, to be issued by each Government, the same to be legal tender in all commercial transactions between the citizens of all the American States.

Seventh. An agreement upon the recommendation for adoption to their respective Governments of a definite plan of arbitration of all questions, disputes, and differences that may now or hereafter exist between them, to the end that all difficulties and disputes between such nations may be peaceably settled and wars prevented.

Eighth. And to consider such other subjects relating to the welfare of the several States represented as may be presented by any of said States which are hereby invited to participate in said Conference.

---

7. The Burdens of Policeman in the Caribbean ◆ Theodore Roosevelt

The Hague Tribunal award in 1904 in the Venezuelan debt case had immediate repercussions. It was feared in Washington that the award, as a precedent, might threaten American security through developments in the Dominican Republic, where European creditor nations were rumored to be planning an intervention on the grounds that the country was in default on its debts. The letters from President Roosevelt and his discussion of foreign policy in his message to Congress reveal his thinking before and after the decision of the Hague Tribunal on the Venezuelan claims and show the steps by which he arrived at the decision to intervene.

From Elting E. Morison, ed., *The Letters of Theodore Roosevelt*, 8 vols. (Cambridge: Harvard University Press, 1951), 4:723–24, 734–35, 801; the president's message to Congress is reprinted from *Papers Relating to the Foreign Relations of the United States, 1904* (Washington, DC: Government Printing Office, 1905), xli–xlii.

February 10, 1904, TR to Theodore Roosevelt, Jr.

Santo Domingo is drifting into chaos, for after a hundred years of freedom it shows itself utterly incompetent for governmental work. Most reluctantly I have been obliged to take the initial step of interference there. I hope it will be a good while before I have to go further. But sooner or later it seems to me inevitable that the United States should assume an attitude of protection and regulation in regard to all these little states in the neighborhood of the Caribbean. I hope it will be deferred as long as possible, but I fear it is inevitable.

February 23, 1904, TR to Joseph Bucklin Bishop

I have been hoping and praying for three months that the Santo Domingans would behave so that I would not have to act in any way. I want to do nothing but what a policeman has to do in Santo Domingo. As for annexing the island, I have about the same desire to annex it as a gorged boa constrictor might have to swallow a porcupine wrong-end-to. Is that strong enough? I have asked some of our people to go there because, after having refused for three months to do anything, the attitude of the Santo Domingans has become one of half chaotic war towards us. If I possibly can, I want to do nothing to them. If it is absolutely necessary to do something, then I want to do as little as possible. Their government has been deviling us to establish some kind of a protectorate over the islands, and take charge of their finances. We have been answering them that we could not possibly go into the subject now at all.

May 20, 1904, TR to Elihu Root, a public letter read at a banquet in New York

Through you I want to send my heartiest greetings to those gathered to celebrate the second anniversary of the Republic of Cuba. I wish that it were possible to be present with you in person. I rejoice in what Cuba has done and especially in the way in which for the last two years her people have shown their desire and ability to accept in a serious spirit the responsibilities that accompany freedom. Such determination is vital, for those unable or unwilling to shoulder the responsibility of using their liberty aright can never in the long run preserve such liberty.

As for the United States, it must ever be a source of joy and gratification to good American citizens that they were enabled to play the part they did as regards Cuba. . . .

All that we desire is to see all neighboring countries stable, orderly, and prosperous. Any country whose people conduct themselves well can count upon our hearty friendliness. If a nation shows that it knows how to act with decency in industrial and political matters, if it keeps order and pays its obligations, then it need fear no interference from the United States. Brutal wrongdoing, or an impotence which results in a general loosening of the ties of civilized society, may finally require intervention by some civilized nation, and in the Western Hemisphere the United States cannot ignore this duty; but it remains true that our interests, and those of our southern neighbors, are in reality identical. All that we ask is that they shall govern themselves well, and be prosperous and orderly. Where this is the case they will find only helpfulness from us.

December 6, 1904, TR's Annual Message to Congress

[After talking about the need for force and manliness in foreign affairs, and the concept of a righteous war, the president continued:] Chronic wrongdoing, or an impotence which results in a general loosening of the ties of civilized society, may in America, as elsewhere, ultimately require intervention by some civilized nation, and in the Western Hemisphere the adherence of the United States to the Monroe Doctrine may force the United States, however reluctantly, in flagrant cases of such wrongdoing or impotence, to the exercise of an international police power. If every country washed by the Caribbean Sea would show the progress in stable and just civilization which with the aid of the Platt amendment Cuba has shown since our troops left the island, and which so many of the republics in both Americas are constantly and brilliantly showing, all question of interference by this Nation with their affairs would be at an end. Our interests and those of our southern neighbors are in reality identical. They have great natural riches, and if within their borders the reign of law and justice obtains, prosperity is sure to come to them. While they thus obey the primary laws of civilized society they may rest assured that they will be treated by us in a spirit of cordial and helpful sympathy. We would interfere with them only in the last resort, and then only if it became evident that their inability or unwillingness to do justice at home and abroad had violated the rights of the United States or had invited foreign aggression to the detriment of the entire body of American nations. It is a mere truism to say that every nation, whether in America or anywhere else, which desires to maintain its freedom, its independence, must ultimately realize that the right of such independence cannot be separated from the responsibility of making good use of it.

8. An Argentinian Speaks Out against
Imperialism ◆ José Ingenieros

*Many people in Latin America were unhappy with the suffocating prepon-
derance of the United States in hemispheric affairs. Groups in the protectorate nations spoke bitterly against U.S. intervention. And in spite of
assurances from Washington that states in South America were "different"
(not subject to the same policing as Caribbean nations), there were many
whose nations had not been intervened who criticized Yankee imperialism.
This selection by José Ingenieros (1877–1925), an Argentine writer and*
pensador, *is taken from a speech delivered on October 11, 1922, at a dinner
honoring the Mexican man of letters José Vasconcelos. Ingenieros's major
works include* Sociología argentina, La evolución de las ideas argentinas,
and El hombre mediocre.

We must recognize that in the few years of this century, events have
occurred in Latin America which demand serious, even gloomy
reflection. And we hope that these words, spoken to this warm fraternal
gathering of Argentine writers in honor of a Mexican colleague, will be
echoed among the intellectuals of the continent, so that an insistent concern
for the future will be awakened in all.

We are not, we no longer wish to be, we no longer can be pan-
Americanists. The famous Monroe Doctrine, which for a century seemed to
be the guarantee of our political independence against the threat of European
conquests, has gradually proved to be a declaration of the American right to
protect us and to intervene in our affairs. Our powerful neighbor and
meddlesome friend, having developed to its highest level the capitalist
mode of production, during the past war has attained world financial hegemony. This development has been accompanied by the growth in voracity
of the American privileged caste, which has increasingly pressed for an
imperialist policy, and has converted the government into an instrument of
its corporations, with no principles other than the capture of sources of
wealth and exploitation of the labor of a population already enslaved by an
amoral, nationless, inflexible financial elite. Among the ruling classes of
this great state, the urge to expand and conquer has grown to the point where
the classic "America for the Americans" actually means "America—our
Latin America—for the North Americans." . . .

From Miguel Hidalgo et al., *Hispanoamérica en lucha por su independencia*,
trans. Christopher Hunt (México: Cuadernos Americanos, 1962), 217–25. Reprinted
by permission of the publisher.

This at least is the implication of recent American imperialist policy, the course of which is alarming for all of Latin America. Since the war with Spain, the United States has taken possession of Puerto Rico and imposed upon Cuba the vexatious conditions of the shameful Platt Amendment. It lost little time in amputating from Colombia the Isthmus of Panama, through which the country would join its Atlantic and Pacific coasts. Later, the United States intervened in Nicaragua to secure for itself the route of another possible interoceanic canal. It threatened the sovereignty of Mexico in the unfortunate Veracruz adventure. Under puerile pretexts, it militarily occupied Haiti. Soon afterwards, the United States shamefully occupied Santo Domingo, offering the usual excuse of pacifying the country and restoring its finances. . . .

Only yesterday, and now, as I speak, the United States cripples and dissolves the Central American Federation, knowing that its prey is easy to devour if it is first divided into small bites. Only yesterday, and now, as I speak, it refuses to recognize the constitutional government of Mexico unless it first signs treaties which favor foreign capitalism over national interests. Only yesterday, and now, as I speak, it insults Cuba by imposing on it General Crowder as titular intervenor.

I see on many faces the old objection: Panama is the natural limit of expansion, and capitalist imperialism will stop there. Until a few years ago, many of us believed this; we should admit it, even though this feeling of collective egotism does not honor us. The most distant nations—Brazil, Uruguay, Argentina, and Chile—felt safe from the clutches of the eagle, thinking the torrid zone would arrest its flight.

Lately, some of us have admitted that we were wrong. . . . We know that some governments—we will spare feelings by not naming them—live under a de facto tutelage, quite similar to the disgrace sanctioned by law in the Platt Amendment. We know that certain recent loans contain clauses which assure American financial control and imply to some extent the right of intervention. And finally, we know that during the past few years American influence has been felt with increasing intensity in all political, economic, and social activities in South America. . . .

The danger does not begin with annexation, as in Puerto Rico, nor with intervention, as in Cuba, nor with a military expedition, as in Mexico, nor with tutelage, as in Nicaragua, nor with territorial secession, as in Colombia, nor with armed occupation, as in Haiti, nor with purchase, as in the Guianas. In its first phase, the danger begins with the progressive mortgaging of national independence through loans destined to grow and to be renewed endlessly, under conditions which are progressively detrimental to the sovereignty of the beneficiaries. . . .

For the peoples of Latin America, the issue is quite simply national defense, although many of our rulers often ignore or hide it. American capitalism seeks to capture the sources of our wealth, with the right to intervene in order to protect its investments and to assure returns on them. In the meantime, we are allowed only an illusion of political independence. As long as a foreign state expressly or surreptitiously possesses the right to intervene, political independence is not effective; as long as it refuses to recognize any government which does not support its policy of privilege and monopoly, it threatens national sovereignty; as long as it does not clearly show that it renounces such policies, it cannot be considered a friendly country. . . .

[Ingenieros proposed a Latin American Union, actually founded in 1925, whose purpose and norms would be:]

To develop in Latin American countries a new consciousness of national and continental interests, promoting all ideological developments which lead to the effective exercise of popular sovereignty, and fighting all dictatorships which oppose reforms inspired by the desire for social justice. . . .

The Latin American Union affirms its commitment to the following principles:

Political solidarity among all Latin American countries, and concerted action in all questions of world interest.

Repudiation of official pan-Americanism, and suppression of secret diplomacy.

Arbitration, by exclusively Latin American jurisdictions, in any litigation between Latin American nations, and reduction of national armament to the minimum compatible with the maintenance of internal order.

Opposition to any financial policy which compromises national sovereignty, and particularly to the acceptance of loans which sanction or justify the coercive intervention of foreign capitalist states.

Reaffirmation of democratic principles, in accordance with the latest judgments of political science.

Nationalization of sources of wealth, and abolition of economic privilege.

Opposition to any influence of the Church on public life and education.

Extension of free, obligatory secular education, and thorough university reform.

9. A Defense of the U.S. Position ◆
Charles Evans Hughes

By the end of the 1920s the United States was coming under increasing attack for its interventions and, from several nations in Latin America, for its protectionist economic policies that hurt inter-American trade. The Sixth Pan American Conference at Havana in 1928 was the forum for the first open debate on interventionism. The State Department was aware of the criticism and had instructed the U.S. delegation to the conference to avoid the subject. When that proved impossible, Charles Evans Hughes, the leader of the delegation, defended his country's policy and prevented any action by the conference that might have been embarrassing to the United States. Hughes won debater's points. He did not succeed in settling any issues or stilling the voices of criticism. This account is taken from a memorandum on the conference by Henry C. Beerits, Hughes's private secretary.

In 1927 an International Commission of Jurists had met in Rio de Janeiro to determine the items on public international law to be submitted for consideration at the Sixth Pan American Conference. One of the proposals of the commission had been that no American country had the right to intervene in the affairs of any other American country. Hughes did not want to oppose the proposal, but its intent precluded U.S. intervention even to protect American life and property in Latin America. After discussion in a subcommittee of which Hughes was chairman, Dr. Honorio Pueyrredón, chief of the Argentine delegation, suggested reluctantly that the proposal be dropped because of irreconcilable differences, and it was agreed finally to reconsider the matter at the next Pan American Conference, which was to be held in five years. Pueyrredón stalked out of the Conference in disgust. On the last day of the plenary session of the Conference when the proposal of the Committee on Public International Law came up, that the subject of intervention be considered at the next Pan American Conference, Dr. Laurentina Olascoaga of Argentina leapt to his feet and argued in favor of nonintervention.

At once the atmosphere of the Great Hall changed as though a current of electricity had run through it, and the air became charged with tense

From Henry C. Beerits memorandum, "Latin American Conference," pp. 13–14. Papers of Charles Evans Hughes, Manuscript Division, Library of Congress, partially reprinted in David J. Danelski and Joseph S. Tulchin, eds., *The Autobiographical Notes of Charles Evans Hughes* (Cambridge, 1972). © 1972 by the President and Fellows of Harvard College. Reprinted by permission of Harvard University Press.

excitement. Delegate after delegate arose to affirm the ideas of the Argentine delegate. Then Guerrero [of El Salvador], who had promised to drop the matter, arose and said [that] if the Conference were unanimous, as it appeared to him it was, he saw no reason why it should not go on record on the subject of intervention. [Without making a formal motion he proposed the following:]

> The Sixth Conference of the American Republics, taking into consideration that each one of the Delegates has expressed his firm decision that the principle of nonintervention and the absolute juridical equality of States should be roundly and categorically stated, resolves: No State has the right to intervene in the internal affairs of another.

At this the Cubans in the gallery broke into thundering applause.

At this point the Great Hall was invaded by the dignitaries of the University, gorgeously gowned, and for an hour learned doctors of law, science, and philosophy delivered long speeches. But while the doctors were speaking the delegates were whispering. Fernandes of Brazil and Olaya of Colombia came to Mr. Hughes and protested that this action by Guerrero was a breach of honor, and that it was impossible that it be tolerated. Mr. Hughes replied that he could not be put in the position of stopping discussion on the matter. He sent word to Dr. Antonio Sánchez de Bustamente (Judge of the Permanent Court of International Justice), who was chairman of the Conference, on no account to adjourn the session until the matter was settled.

The interruption in the proceedings of the Conference served only to increase the fierce flame of excitement. After the dignitaries had concluded their addresses, the delegates launched forth into a fierce debate on the non-intervention proposal. It was as tense and exciting a meeting as Mr. Hughes ever witnessed. Maúrtua of Peru arose and attacked Guerrero. One of the Nicaraguan delegates defended the United States. Fiery speech followed upon fiery speech, and the air was becoming more and more tense. Dr. Bustamente at one point found it necessary to call the meeting to order so as to prevent a heated personal exchange between Jesús M. Yepes of Colombia and Guerrero from reaching a stage where nothing but pistols for two would have been acceptable to wounded Latin American honor.

While all this discussion was taking place, the position of Mr. Hughes was a very delicate one. If the votes were there to defeat the nonintervention resolution, it was better that he did not appear to prevent its passage. If, on the other hand, the votes were not there to prevent its passage, it was essential that he speak in an attempt to defeat it. It was an exceedingly tense experience for him and he never felt more strongly his responsibility for America.

The Great Hall was ringing with violent applause and excited cries each time one of the delegates spoke in favor of the nonintervention proposal. Mr. Hughes finally decided that the time had come when he must speak.

Immediately, the room became hushed with eager expectancy. Mr. Hughes started speaking with firm and measured tones. He gave the history of the decision to postpone discussion of the question, in view of the fact that unanimity on the question could not be then attained. Then he took up with great candor the question of intervention, and explained very frankly the policy of his country with respect to this matter. In conclusion he stated:

Let us face the facts. The difficulty, if there is any, in any one of the American Republics, is not of any external aggression. It is an internal difficulty. . . . From time to time there arises a situation most deplorable and regrettable . . . in which sovereignty is not at work, in which for a time in certain areas there is no government at all. . . .

Those are the conditions that create the difficulty with which at times we find ourselves confronted. What are we to do when government breaks down and American citizens are in danger of their lives? Are we to stand by and see them killed because a government in circumstances which it cannot control and for which it may not be responsible can no longer afford reasonable protection? I am not speaking of sporadic acts of violence, or of the rising of mobs, or of those distressing incidents which may occur in any country however well administered. I am speaking of the occasions where government itself is unable to function. . . .

Now it is a principle of international law that in such a case a government is fully justified in taking action—I would call it interposition of a temporary character—for the purpose of protecting the lives and property of its nationals. I could say that that is not intervention. One can read in textbooks that that is not intervention. . . . Of course, the United States cannot forego its right to protect its citizens. No country should forego its right to protect its citizens. International law cannot be changed by the resolutions of this Conference. . . . The rights of nations remain, but nations have duties as well as rights. . . . This very formula, here proposed, is a proposal of duty on the part of a nation. But it is not the only duty. There are other obligations which courts, and tribunals declaring international law, have frequently set forth; and we cannot codify international law and ignore the duties of states, by setting up the impossible reign of self-will without any recognition upon the part of the state of its obligations to its neighbors. . . .

I am too proud of my country to stand before you as in any way suggesting a defense of aggression or of assault upon the sovereignty or independence of any State. I stand before you to tell you that we unite with you in the aspiration for complete sovereignty and the realization of complete independence.

I stand here with you ready to cooperate in every way in establishing the ideals of justice by institutions in every land which will promote fairness of dealing between man and man and nation and nation.

I cannot sacrifice the rights of my country but I will join with you in declaring the law. I will try to help you in coming to a just conclusion as to the law; but it must be the law of justice infused with the spirit which has given us from the days of Grotius this wonderful development of the law of nations, by which we find ourselves bound.

Mr. Hughes never had greater success in his life. When he finished speaking, the galleries rang with applause. A marked change had taken place in the tempo of the audience while he spoke. As the New York *Times* put it, "as Mr. Hughes sat down there was a sudden tension over the whole chamber. It seemed as if everyone realized that the resolution for an immediate decision on the question of intervention was beaten. Mr. Hughes had beaten it by the sheer force of his personality, his eloquence and deep sincerity."

The result was that the Conference voted to postpone consideration of the question of intervention until the meeting of the Seventh Pan American Conference, to be held five years later. Thus the stormy session adjourned, and the delegates finally appeared for their dinner at 10:30 that night.

Mr. Hughes by his masterly speech had prevented the Conference from ending on a harsh note of discord, and thus had saved Pan Americanism from suffering a setback. This was the first Conference at which every one of the twenty-one members of the Pan American Union was represented. It resulted in many tangible achievements, but perhaps its greatest achievement was an increase in Pan American understanding and good will.

---

10. An Appreciation of the
Good Neighbor Policy ◆ Francisco Cuevas Cancino

Focusing on the motives behind the Good Neighbor policy, as many North American historians have done, obscures the fact that most Latin Americans responded warmly to President Franklin D. Roosevelt's initiatives. The image of the United States in the region did improve. Latin Americans applauded the New Deal and were encouraged by an attitude which they thought would make possible a community of equals. This selection is taken from the work of a Mexican scholar who is not always friendly toward the United States.

A s the heir to and principal exponent of an established attitude of sympathy toward Latin America, Franklin Roosevelt cannot justify his claim of having originated the policy of the Good Neighbor. He more than

From Francisco Cuevas Cancino, *Roosevelt y la Buena Vecindad* (México: Fondo de Cultura Económica, 1954), 120, 161–63, 231–32, 466–67. Translated by Joseph S. Tulchin. Reprinted by permission of the publisher.

compensates for this, however, with that magnificent, innovative ethical element which forms the essence of his Good Neighbor policy and distinguishes so many of his decisions. This ethical factor is more evident in his policy toward Latin America than in his attitude toward any other part of the world. One could even assert that while the principles of Good Neighborhood only slightly affect Roosevelt's general decisions in foreign policy, they dominate his program toward Latin America.

There is another, equally essential element which has not been sufficiently emphasized. Latin American peoples, so frequently governed by corrupt oligarchies, believe in democracy as a system which is personified by a caudillo who identifies himself with their aspirations. For them, the ostensible symbol of democracy is a commander who pulls together popular aspirations, an incorruptible leader who will set the political machinery in motion for the benefit of the disinherited.

The austere figure of [Herbert] Hoover, with his ties to financial magnates, could not possibly fit the South American ideal. The words which Hoover spoke during his tour of our continent seemed to come from an impassive heart. Latin Americans were wary of such a cold man; they saw his good deeds as exceptions, and remembered only his mistakes. He did not represent democracy, and consequently even in the best of circumstances his Latin American policy could achieve only limited success.

Roosevelt is the antithesis of Hoover. The conditions under which he reached the White House seem to prove him the champion of the American masses, which like the Latin American people are exploited by an overdeveloped capitalism. And the brilliant beginning of his administration, which shows Roosevelt's commitment to improving conditions for the poor, will surely have profound repercussions in Latin America. His speeches, filled with fiery images, touch the hearts of the countries south of the Bravo [called the Rio Grande in the United States], and earn Roosevelt the allegiance of their workers and rural masses. His words seem to spring from a love for mankind, and the affection is returned to him not only by his fellow citizens. The bond of friendship between Roosevelt and Latin America is very strong; it is the fundamental novelty of the Good Neighbor policy, for before Roosevelt, no American statesman was able to capture the imagination of our continent. Thus it is hardly a surprise that when he visited Rio de Janeiro and Buenos Aires on the occasion of the opening of the Inter-American Conference of 1936, he was received with cries of "Long live Democracy!" He remembered this greeting affectionately and with deep understanding, for it represents his popular support. It typified his leadership of the disinherited masses of both the United States and the rest of America. . . . Here, in his ability to be seen, both at home and abroad, as the democratic leader par excellence, lies Roosevelt's political genius. . . .

[The Buenos Aires Inter-American Conference was important because] for the first time our two civilizations worked together toward continental solidarity. United by democratic aspirations, all the American republics aligned themselves behind a common leader, reaffirming the principle of peace and making possible the agreements which enabled the nations to stand together against aggression: the declaration of Lima and Panama; the meetings of diplomats; and our current pan-Americanism, which could only be built upon the foundation of spiritual unity laid so masterfully by Roosevelt at Buenos Aires. Because of its foresight, and the role it played in the development of pan-Americanism, the Buenos Aires Conference must be counted among the most important meetings ever to take place on this continent. . . .

There is something more profound than mere policy in the Good Neighbor program, and it is here that Roosevelt's scheme is vulnerable to criticism. Its principles are of such ethical plentitude that the program cannot avoid violating, to an extent, its own spirit. For as long as man pursues concrete, immediate ends, he can follow a fixed, coherent course of action; but when he aspires to principle, his doubts about directions to follow, individual decisions to make, and the possibility of error begin to grow, even though he remains as eager and purposeful.

Roosevelt's initial formulation of the Good Neighbor policy confirms this opinion. The fundamental axis of the program is each country's self-respect. If this principle is adopted with conviction, then each action which violates it—whatever the immediate, external results—is harmful to the nation which takes it. Acceptance of this premise will assure respect for the rights of other countries, the moral bases of which limit the action of each nation. . . .

In his inaugural address, Franklin Roosevelt fixed limits for his international policy. In perfectly simple terms, he raised his people above everyday cares and, steeped in moral feeling, explained his policy by means of universals. The relation of his Good Neighbor program to the actions his country would take was clearly outlined. Under Roosevelt, an entire nation accepted the primacy of the great natural laws and, without misunderstanding concrete problems, attempted to resolve all questions ethically. Thus a new international attitude grew as a splendid flower.

Roosevelt's inaugural speech constituted a first, essential step, but it did not in itself transcend all problems. Similar declarations have been made and have proved meaningless; they have been no more than expressions of individual convictions, which the world has heard attentively, but which have not gained the force of law. The case of the Good Neighbor policy, however, has been different. On numerous occasions, Roosevelt's declaration has been respected, and international problems have been approached in the light of its high standards. The policy has become a reality; the paths down which Roosevelt has guided his country have not been those of mere political accommodation.

The behavior of one country is not in itself strong enough to spread new customs; there are many isolated practices which have not affected the rules which govern the international community. Each member of this community must recognize the freshness and virtue of the new attitude, adopt it as a regulatory norm for its own conduct, and agree to enforce it. This was the final step in the evolution of the Good Neighbor policy: following the American example, other countries—first a group, then all the rest—agreed that the program encompassed more than policy, that it belonged among the highest rules which guide international conduct. From Roosevelt's declaration in 1933, to its application to American policy, to its acceptance as an international principle, there is an unbroken line of continuity.

---

11. The United States and Latin America in the Cold War ◆ John Foster Dulles, John F. Kennedy, and Thomas C. Mann

The Cold War began almost before the peace had been made to end World War I. In the Western Hemisphere the Rio Defense Treaty (1947) was directed against the Soviet Union, and the United States made its hostility to communism clear on numerous occasions, as evidenced by the following selections.

When the U.S. government determined that the regime in Guatemala was "about to go Communist" and thus would constitute a threat to the United States, it acted both openly and clandestinely to bring about that government's fall. Secretary of State John Foster Dulles traveled to Caracas in March 1954 to attend the Tenth Inter-American Conference to line up the Organization of American States (OAS) behind U.S. efforts to oust the Guatemalan government. The selections that comprise Part I of this document are taken from Dulles's address at the Second Plenary Session, March 4; the statement he made introducing the U.S. draft resolution on Communist intervention, March 8; and the final text of the resolution (XCIII) known as the Caracas Declaration.

From Department of State, Publication 5692, Tenth Inter-American Conference, *Report of the Delegation of the United States of America with Related Documents* (Washington, DC: Government Printing Office, 1955), 44–55, 156–57; State Department *Bulletin* 44, #1141 (May 8, 1961), 659–61; and Department of State, *Press Release* No. 241, October 12, 1965.

Part I. John Foster Dulles

From Dulles's Address at the Second Plenary Session

We here in the Americas are not immune from that threat of Soviet communism. There is not a single country in this hemisphere which has not been penetrated by the apparatus of international communism acting under orders from Moscow. No one of us knows fully the extent of that conspiracy. From time to time small parts are detected and exposed. . . .

None of us wants to be maneuvered into the position of defending whatever Communists attack. We do not carry on political warfare against ideas or ideals. But equally we must not be blind to the fact that the international conspiracy I describe has, in 15 years, been primarily responsible for turning what were 15 independent nations into Soviet colonies and they would, if they could, duplicate that performance here. . . .

From the earliest days of the independence of our countries, we have all stood resolutely for the integrity of this hemisphere. We have seen that integrity would be endangered unless we stood resolutely against any enlargement here of the colonial domain of the European powers. We have made our position in this matter so clear that it is known to, and accepted by, all the world. What was a great danger has thus receded.

We have not made it equally clear that the integrity of this hemisphere and the peace, safety, and happiness of us all may be endangered by political penetration from without, and that we stand resolutely and unitedly against that form of danger.

Because our position has not been made clear, the danger mounts. I believe that it is time to make it clear with finality that we see that alien despotism is hostile to our ideals, that we unitedly deny it the right to prey upon our hemisphere, and that if it does not heed our warning and keep away, we shall deal with it as a situation that might endanger the peace of America.

What I suggest does not involve any interference in the international affairs of any American Republic. There is ample room for natural differences, and for tolerances, between the political institutions of the different American states. But there is no place here for political institutions which serve alien masters. I hope that we can agree to make that clear.

Statement by the Secretary of State Introducing the
U.S. Draft Resolution on Communist Intervention

It may next be asked whether this international Communist apparatus actually seeks to bring this hemisphere, or parts of it, into the Soviet orbit. The answer must be in the affirmative.

I shall not here accuse any government or any individuals of being either plotters, or the dupes of plotters. We are not sitting here as a court to try governments or individuals. We sit rather as legislators. As such, we need to know what will enable us to take appropriate action of a general character in the common interest.

Within all the vast area, now embracing one-third of the world's people, where the military power of the Soviet Union is dominant, no official can be found who would dare to stand up and openly attack the Government of the Soviet Union. But in this hemisphere, it takes no courage for the representative of one of the smallest American countries openly to attack the government of the most powerful.

I rejoice that that kind of freedom exists in the Americas, even if it may be at times abused. But [it is] essential . . . that there be a relationship of sovereign equality. We of the United States want to keep it that way. We seek no satellites, but only friendly equals. We want none who come to this table to speak as the tools of non-American powers. We want to preserve and defend an American society in which even the weak may speak boldly, because they represent national personalities which, as long as they are free, are equal.

Declaration of Solidarity for the Preservation of the Political Integrity of the American States against the Intervention of International Communism [The Caracas Declaration]

Whereas: The American republics at the Ninth International Conference of American States declared that international communism, by its antidemocratic nature and its interventionist tendency, is incompatible with the concept of American freedom, and resolved to adapt within their respective territories the measures necessary to eradicate and prevent subversive activities;

The Fourth Meeting of Consultation of Ministers of Foreign Affairs recognized that, in addition to adequate internal measures in each state, a high degree of international cooperation is required to eradicate the danger which the subversive activities of international communism pose for the American States; and

The aggressive character of the international communist movement continues to constitute, in the context of world affairs, a special and immediate threat to the national institutions and the peace and security of the American States, and to the right of each state to develop its cultural, political, and economic life freely and naturally without intervention in its internal or external affairs by other states,

The Tenth Inter-American Conference

I

Condemns:

The activities of the international communist movement as constituting intervention in American affairs;

Expresses:

The determination of the American States to take the necessary measures to protect their political independence against the intervention of international communism, acting in the interests of an alien despotism;

Reiterates:

The faith of the peoples of America in the effective exercise of representative democracy as the best means to promote their social and political progress; and

Declares:

That the domination or control of the political institutions of an American State by the international communist movement, extending to this Hemisphere the political system of an extracontinental power, would constitute a threat to the sovereignty and political independence of the American States, endangering the peace of America, and would call for a Meeting of Consultation to consider the adoption of appropriate action in accordance with existing treaties.

II

Recommends:

That, without prejudice to such other measures as they may consider desirable, special attention be given by each of the American governments to the following steps for the purpose of counteracting the subversive activities of the international communist movement within their respective jurisdictions:

1. Measures to require disclosure of the identity, activities, and sources of funds of those who are spreading propaganda of the international communist movement or who travel in the interests of that movement, and of those who act as its agents or in its behalf; and
2. The exchange of information among governments to assist in fulfilling the purpose of the resolutions adopted by the Inter-American Conferences and Meetings of Ministers of Foreign Affairs regarding international communism.

III

This declaration of foreign policy made by the American republics in relation to dangers originating outside this Hemisphere is designed to protect and not to impair the inalienable right of each American State freely to choose its own form of government and economic system and to live its own social and cultural life.

Part II. John F. Kennedy

The Alliance for Progress seemed to mark a significant change in U.S. policy. President Kennedy devoted more attention to Latin America than any president since Franklin Roosevelt. The idealistic tone of his speeches, his willingness to put his government's seal on the call for sweeping social and economic changes written into the Charter of Punta del Este (1961), and the State Department's diplomatic interventions in favor of democratic regimes won many supporters in Latin America. But through it all ran the same preoccupation with the Cold War, as this speech shows, delivered to the Society of Newspaper Editors on April 20, 1961, just after the tragic debacle at the Bay of Pigs in Cuba.

The Lesson of Cuba, Address by President Kennedy

The President of a great democracy such as ours, and the editors of great newspapers such as yours, have a common obligation to the people: an obligation to present the facts, to present them with candor, and to present them in perspective. It is with that obligation in mind that I have decided in the last 24 hours to discuss briefly at this time the recent events in Cuba.

On that unhappy island, as in so many other areas of the contest for freedom, the news has grown worse instead of better. I have emphasized before that this was a struggle of Cuban patriots against a Cuban dictator. While we could not be expected to hide our sympathies, we made it repeatedly clear that the armed forces of this country would not intervene in any way.

Any unilateral American intervention, in the absence of an external attack upon ourselves or an ally, would have been contrary to our traditions and to our international obligations. But let the record show that our restraint is not inexhaustible. Should it ever appear that the inter-American doctrine of noninterference merely conceals or excuses a policy of nonaction—if the nations of this hemisphere should fail to meet their commitments against outside Communist penetration—then I want it clearly understood that this Government will not hesitate in meeting its primary obligations, which are to the security of our Nation.

Should that time ever come, we do not intend to be lectured on "intervention" by those whose character was stamped for all time on the bloody streets of Budapest. Nor would we expect or accept the same outcome which this small band of gallant Cuban refugees must have known that they were chancing, determined as they were against heavy odds to pursue their courageous attempts to regain their island's freedom. . . .

Meanwhile we will not accept Mr. Castro's attempts to blame this Nation for the hatred with which his onetime supporters now regard his repression. But there are from this sobering episode useful lessons for all to learn. Some may be still obscure and await further information. Some are clear today.

First, it is clear that the forces of communism are not to be under-estimated, in Cuba or anywhere else in the world. The advantages of a police state—its use of mass terror and arrests to prevent the spread of free dissent—cannot be overlooked by those who expect the fall of every fanatic tyrant. If the self-discipline of the free cannot match the iron discipline of the mailed fist—in economic, political, scientific, and all the other kinds of struggles as well as the military—then the peril to freedom will continue to rise.

Second, it is clear that this Nation, in concert with all the free nations of this hemisphere, must take an even closer and more realistic look at the menace of external Communist intervention and domination in Cuba. The American people are not complacent about Iron Curtain tanks and planes less than 90 miles from our shores. But a nation of Cuba's size is less a threat to our survival than it is a base for subverting the survival of other free nations throughout the hemisphere. It is not primarily our interest or our security but theirs which is now, today, in the greater peril. It is for their sake as well as our own that we must show our will.

The evidence is clear—and the hour is late. We and our Latin friends will have to face the fact that we cannot postpone any longer the real issue of the survival of freedom in this hemisphere itself. On that issue, unlike perhaps some others, there can be no middle ground. Together we must build a hemisphere where freedom can flourish and where any free nation under outside attack of any kind can be assured that all of our resources stand ready to respond to any request for assistance.

Third, and finally, it is clearer than ever that we face a relentless struggle in every corner of the globe that goes far beyond the clash of armies or even nuclear armaments. The armies are there, and in large number. The nuclear armaments are there. But they serve primarily as the shield behind which subversion, infiltration, and a host of other tactics steadily advance, picking off vulnerable areas one by one in situations which do not permit our own armed intervention.

Power is the hallmark of this offensive—power and discipline and deceit. The legitimate discontent of yearning peoples is exploited. The legitimate trappings of self-determination are employed. But once in power, all talk of discontent is repressed—all self-determination disappears—and the promise of a revolution of hope is betrayed, as in Cuba, into a reign of terror. Those who staged automatic "riots" in the streets of free nations over the effort of a small group of young Cubans to regain their freedom should recall the long roll call of refugees who cannot now go back to Hungary, to North Korea, to North Vietnam, to East Germany, or to Poland, or to any of the other lands from which a steady stream of refugees pour forth, in eloquent testimony to the cruel oppression now holding sway in their homelands.

We dare not fail to see the insidious nature of this new and deeper struggle. We dare not fail to grasp the new concepts, the new sense of urgency we will need to combat it—whether in Cuba or [South Vietnam]. And we dare not fail to realize that this struggle is taking place every day, without fanfare, in thousands of villages and markets—day and night—and in classrooms all over the globe.

The message of Cuba, of Laos, of the rising din of Communist voices in Asia and Latin America—these messages are all the same. The complacent, the self-indulgent, the soft societies are about to be swept away with the debris of history. Only the strong, only the industrious, only the determined, only the courageous, only the visionary who determine the real nature of our struggle can possibly survive.

No greater task faces this Nation or this administration. No other challenge is more deserving of our every effort and energy. Too long we have fixed our eyes on traditional military needs, on armies prepared to cross borders or missiles poised for flight. Now it should be clear that this is no longer enough—that our security may be lost piece by piece, country by country, without the firing of a single missile or the crossing of a single border.

We intend to profit from this lesson. We intend to reexamine and reorient our forces of all kinds—our tactics and other institutions here in this community. We intend to intensify our efforts for a struggle in many ways more difficult than war, where disappointment will often accompany us.

For I am convinced that we in this country and in the free world possess the necessary resources, and all the skill, and the added strength that comes from a belief in the freedom of man. And I am equally convinced that history will record the fact that this bitter struggle reached its climax in the late 1950s and early 1960s. Let me then make clear as President of the United States that I am determined upon our system's survival and success, regardless of the cost and regardless of the peril.

Part III. Thomas C. Mann

After President Kennedy's death in 1963, the Cold War line seemed to harden, as shown in this speech by Undersecretary of State Mann delivered before the annual meeting of the Inter-American Press Association on October 12, 1965.

It has been suggested that non-intervention is thought by some to be an obsolete doctrine.

I know of no Washington officials who think this way. On the contrary, I believe unilateral intervention by one American state in the internal political affairs of another is not only proscribed in the OAS Charter, but that non-intervention is a keystone of the structure of the inter-American system. American states have a treaty as well as a sovereign right to choose their political, social and economic systems free of all outside interference. . . .

Latin Americans do not want a paternalistic United States deciding which particular political faction should rule their countries. They do not want the United States to launch itself again on what one scholar described as a "civilizing mission," no matter how good its intentions are. This explains why, in the case of the Dominican Republic, we refrained, during the first days of violence, from "supporting" the outgoing government or "supporting" either of the factions contending for power.

It explains why we and others thought it best to work for a cease-fire and to encourage the rival Dominican factions to meet together and agree on a Dominican solution to a Dominican problem. It explains why, to use a phrase of international law, we offered our good offices rather than attempting to preside over a meeting for the purpose of proposing political solutions with a "made in USA" label on them.

The second area of confusion concerns the response which an American state, or the Organization of American States as a whole, can make to intervention. When, in other words, a Communist state has intervened in the internal affairs of an American state by training, directing, financing and organizing indigenous Communist elements to take control of the government of an American state by force and violence, should other American states be powerless to lend assistance? Are Communists free to intervene while democratic states are powerless to frustrate the intervention?

This is not so much a question of intervention as it is of whether weak and fragile states should be helped to maintain their independence when they are under attack by subversive elements responding to direction from abroad.

Surely we have learned from the October 1962 missile crisis that the establishment of Communist military bases in this hemisphere threatens the security of every American state. Surely we have learned that political control of an American state by Communists is but the prelude for use of that country as a base for further aggressions.

A number of juridical questions deserve consideration—not in an atmosphere of crisis, demanding an immediate decision, but in an atmosphere of calmness and objectivity. As illustrative of the kind of questions that ought to be considered, I pose these two:

What distinctions ought to be made, on the one hand, between subversive activities which do not constitute an immediate danger to an American state and, on the other, those which, because of their intensity and external direction, do constitute a danger to the peace and security of the country and the hemisphere?

Second, assuming that, as I have suggested, certain subversive activities do constitute a threat to the peace and security of the hemisphere, what response is permitted within the framework of the inter-American system?

I do not offer precise answers to these questions at this time. I only wish to say that the problem of Communist subversion in the hemisphere is a real one. It should not be brushed aside on a false assumption that American states are prohibited by inter-American law from dealing with it.

I turn to a political question: How seriously should we regard Communist subversion in this hemisphere?

I will not take your time to remind you of the expansionist history of the Communist countries in recent years in Eastern Europe and in Asia. The history and the tactics used are well-known. . . .

It is difficult to understand the precise reasons why some appear to be less concerned than others about attempts to expand, by force and violence, areas of Communist domination in this hemisphere.

What we can be certain of is that the greatest danger to freedom and to peace will come when the free world is confused, uncertain, divided and weak—when expansionistic communism comes to believe that new aggressions can be committed without risk.

[Mann went on to clarify some "misconceptions about particular United States actions in the recent Dominican crisis" and concluded with a ringing defense of the American revolutionary traditions and the U.S. commitment to reforms.]

12. Three Latin Americans View the United States ◆ Leopoldo Zea, Alonso Aguilar, and Osvaldo Sunkel

The selections that comprise this document are intended to represent a wide spectrum of opinion. While the three scholars differ markedly in their vision of the world and their hopes for the future, they share certain assumptions about the United States that should interest U.S. readers.

The first selection is by Leopoldo Zea, a renowned Mexican teacher and scholar. He has taught for many years at the National University of Mexico (UNAM) and published several books on Latin American thinkers and philosophy. His best-known work in translation is The Latin American Mind *(1963).*

Part I. Latin America and the World ∞ Leopoldo Zea

The shape that relations between Latin America and the United States will inevitably take is appearing above the horizon. On one side is the North America admired by Latin American nations endeavoring to achieve their greatest worth; on the other is the North America repudiated by those same nations who have seen it scheming with forces representative of a past unresigned to being past. On the one side is admiration for the North America that stands for freedom; on the other is repudiation for the North America that incites and supports those who impede freedom in Latin America. Both admiration and repudiation are henceforth going to characterize relations of the two. These attitudes are unrelated to the disputes arising between the United States and the U.S.S.R.; indeed, they are antecedent to them. Problems in relations between Latin America and North America should be resolved with reference to circumstances uncomplicated by those ensuing from the cold war that followed World War II. . . .

I am firmly convinced that our America can greatly assist this emerging world [of developing nations]. Situated between two worlds—the West and the non-West—we continue our efforts to deal with conditions growing out of anxieties we have long experienced and now have in common with many countries. If the countries which provoked these anxieties by their expansion could understand them, then a more responsible and stable world would result. The nations that have learned the lessons of the West now seek to participate in such a world and to find a place of responsibility in it. . . .

From Leopoldo Zea, *Latin America and the World*, trans. Frances K. Kendricks and Beatrice Berler (Norman, 1969), 28–30, 54–58, 96–99. © 1969 by the University of Oklahoma Press. Reprinted by permission of the University of Oklahoma Press.

What is going to happen in Latin America? Will there be the pretexts offered by the cold war for maintaining the status quo which suits the interests of the United States in this part of the world? Everybody knows— and I emphasize—that the problems discussed in Latin America are the old ones that antedate those growing out of the cold war and, on the whole, antedate the organization of communism as a militant doctrine. The problems of Latin America in its relations with the United States are as old as its history—they appeared almost as soon as the countries of this continent had declared independence. . . .

[Zea goes on to describe Simón Bolívar's attitude to the United States.]

The cold war between the United States and the U.S.S.R. has been a marvelous pretext for justifying North American intervention in Latin America in defense of, or for expanding, the interests of its investors. Any action incompatible with these interests is interpreted as an expression of Communist intervention in America and, on that account, a menace to the security of the continent. Efforts that Latin American countries make to improve their economic condition necessarily come up against interests already established or being established by United States investors, provoking the reaction which interferes with the success of those efforts. These countries not only have to struggle against those national interests opposed to any change which would affect their predominance but, what is more, have to face the pressure imposed on them by the representatives of foreign investors whose interests could be affected. Thus a problem as old as that of the land in Latin America is converted into one linked with the cold war which the great powers sustain. Those who resist any agrarian reform will be hailed as supporters of freedom and democracy, while those who dare to proclaim that the land should belong to those who work it will be considered opponents of those principles. . . .

[Zea appeals for hemispheric solidarity to protect the interests of the individual Latin American nations.]

The Iberian community—or Latin America—could be a point of departure for the creation of a world in which the voice of our countries would be effective and would count decisively in world destiny. More than an association, it would be a community of those having something in common— not a society of those uniting their efforts through fear. This community would aim to achieve or to maintain freedom and other human values no less noble; it would not be merely an association necessary for survival. It would be a great community founded through the free will and sovereignty of countries with a common destiny—not an association of frightened sardines that obey the shark, as Arévalo said, for fear of being devoured by the shark or at least postponing the destiny the shark has indicated for them. . . .

Can we realize this dream now that distances have been shortened, now that the interests of all—both the strong and the weak—are closely linked? Can all the Latin American countries create a community that will permit them to enter into discussions and to balance interests with their powerful neighbor of the north as equal with equal in the search for solutions of problems of both our continents? Will the Latin American community, on its part, be effective in finding solutions for all world problems, with its efforts joined by that of other groups, united not by reason of tongue, religion, or culture but by the situation resulting from the common impact of Western influence? Will the Latin American community, united with other groups formed for the same reasons—the Arabs, the Africans, and the Asiatics—have sufficient weight to form another even more powerful group and thus be able to balance their interests with those of the primary powers?

Bolívar held that a community of our countries could be the basis for a wider community that could be extended to the countries of Asia and Africa, in order to make them free and to destroy the yokes that Europe—that is, the Western world—had established over them, in order to form, with all those countries and of course with the others that make up the earth, a new and powerful union that would be comparable only to the one that Iberia dreamed of expanding throughout the world in order to create a great united Christian world in which all men could be equal. "In the march of centuries," said Bolívar, "it might, perhaps, be possible to find only one nation covering the entire earth."

II. Pan-Americanism ∞ Alonso Aguilar

Alonso Aguilar is professor of economic planning and Latin American economic development in the School of Economics of the National University of Mexico. He has participated in many international and political meetings, lectured at universities in Mexico and abroad, and written extensively in his field. In the book from which this document is excerpted, his point of view is Marxist, harshly critical of the United States and frankly revolutionary. However, his is by no means an extreme or radical statement of the Latin American position.

On April 28, 1965, the President of the United States, Lyndon B. Johnson, ordered the landing of 400 Marines in Santo Domingo in order to forestall the imminent triumph of the people in overthrowing a weak and unpopular military dictatorship. It is possible that many Latin Americans,

From Alonso Aguilar, *Pan-Americanism, From Monroe to the Present: A View from the Other Side* (New York, 1968), 152–53. © 1968 by Monthly Review Inc. Reprinted by permission of Monthly Review Foundation.

although naturally concerned about this development, were momentarily unable to gauge its significance and grave implications. But only a few days sufficed—one week, actually—for the aggressive policy of the United States to be exposed and for Latin America to realize that imperialism was still imperialism despite the rhetoric of the foreign ministers of the OAS and despite the good intentions, wishful thinking, and repeated pronouncements endorsing the principles of self-determination and nonintervention.

When the 400 Marines sent to "protect the lives and property of U.S. citizens residing in the Dominican Republic"grew into an aggressive force of almost 40,000 fully armed troops, Mr. Johnson's hypocrisy no longer deceived anyone. His motivations, in fact, were basically the same as those which had prompted Mr. Blaine (Secretary of State during President Harrison's Administration) to propose the first Pan-American Conference; which caused Theodore Roosevelt to invent a "revolution" in Panama in order to seize control of the Isthmus; which led President Taft to use the American flag to protect United States monopolies seeking raw materials and markets outside their own country; and the very same which Calvin Coolidge defended in repeated declarations to the effect that the rights of United States investors, and the obligation of the government in Washington to protect them, stood above the principles of self-determination and respect for national sovereignty.

The aggression against the Dominican Republic together with the so-called Johnson Doctrine, which purports to be its rationale, have high-lighted the profound crisis which the inter-American system is undergoing, revealing in a single stroke that the policy of anti-Communism inherited from Churchill and Truman, instead of serving the national interests of Latin America or safeguarding the security of the continent, constitutes a grave threat to the sovereignty of these nations and is no more than a crude device for maintaining the status quo.

Anti-Communism, favorite weapon of the Pentagon strategists, the U.S. State Department, representatives to the Organization of American States, and the Latin American oligarchies and "gorillarchies"—its most recent form is the Johnson Doctrine—is not an instrument against armed aggression by a foreign power. It is, rather, the principal weapon being used by imperialism and its allies to hold back social or political progress in Latin America and other parts of the world where the people seem ready to transform present socioeconomic conditions.

For almost a century and a half, the United States had used the Monroe Doctrine to prevent European countries from exporting their political systems to the Americas. By extension, under the Johnson Doctrine, the nations of Latin America are prevented from choosing their form of government and so do not even control their own destinies. As events have dramatically shown in the Dominican Republic and before that in Brazil, Cuba, and Guatemala, Latin Americans are in a sorry plight. If a Latin American nation, in the full exercise of its sovereignty, chooses a government or type of social organization unfavorable to United States interests or unacceptable to privileged local minorities, the result is either violent unilateral intervention by the United States or the emergence of a politician or army officer disposed to betray his people by crying out for Pan Americanism to enter into immediate action in defense of the indefensible.

[The third Extraordinary Inter-American Conference was convened at Panama in 1966 to consider possible reforms of the OAS charter.]

It was easy to see that two different positions confronted one another; on the one side, the governments wanted to endow the OAS with more effective means of combating "Communist subversion"; on the other, the nations which, though recognizing the "reality of the Communist threat," insisted on incorporating into the Charter of the Organization the principles of the Alliance for Progress and of the World Conference of Trade and Development which had been held in Geneva in 1964. Within a few days, the original and vague agreement of the majority of the Latin American delegates regarding the problems of development became the first draft of a plan for reforms and additions to those articles of the Charter which contained certain measures tending to accelerate economic growth and to obtain more favorable conditions in international trade. But, unlike other meetings at which the United States accepted various economic demands in exchange for greater political subordination, this time, at Panama, the United States rejection was immediate and flat. The preliminary draft was criticized as "unnecessary," "too long and wordy," and "too far removed from the spirit of inter-American equality of the Charter." And, in a less conventional tone in which his annoyance was evident, Senator Jacob Javits explained his country's rejection by saying, "The United States cannot sign any old piece of paper handed it by the Latin Americans."

While discouragement pervaded Panama and Buenos Aires (where there was at that time a meeting of the Inter-American Economic and Social Council at which the same flat rejection by the United States delegation was to be forthcoming), in Washington, April 14th was declared "Pan-American Day," and Congressman Armistead Selden exhorted the governments of the continent to strengthen the OAS, using the same vehemence with which he had proposed a resolution months before that raised intervention by one country in the affairs of another to the rank of a "right" of United States imperialism to trample the sovereignty of other nations. He declared: "I urge you to recognize that the ultimate objectives of the Alliance for Progress can only be attained if the OAS is ready to meet face to face the constant hostility emanating from the Communist bases in Cuba."

Congressman Dante Fascell, a southern colleague of Selden's, also exhibited his government's absolute lack of understanding of the problems of Latin America, as well as its proverbial ability to see spooks behind every bush, with his statement that the celebration of Pan American Day in Washington "serves to demonstrate to Latin America that the United States is wholeheartedly on its side in the struggle against Communist usurpation."

Between 1962 and 1966 alone—that is, during the first four years of the "decade of progress"—constitutional law and order in Latin America was broken from eight to ten times by military forces bent on combating Communism and assuring "representative democracy." Frondizi in Argentina; Ydígoras in Guatemala; Arosemena in Ecuador; Bosch in the Dominican Republic; Villeda Morales in Honduras; Goulart in Brazil; and shortly after, Arturo Illía in Argentina, were all to topple, one after the other, charged with ineptitude and leniency toward Communism. Their removal from office was a reflection of the hard line of Thomas Mann and others in the State Department, who advocated supporting Latin American military dictatorships as long as they were anti-Communist and protected United States investors.

While the last Panama Conference was in session, Senator William Fulbright, Chairman of the Senate Foreign Relations Committee, said in a speech at the University of Connecticut: "Possibly, it would be more advisable for us to concentrate on our own democracy instead of trying to impose our version of it on all those unfortunate Latin Americans who stubbornly oppose their northern benefactors instead of fighting the real enemy we so graciously found them."

How right he was!

Part III. National Development Policies and External Dependence in Latin America ∞ Osvaldo Sunkel

Osvaldo Sunkel is professor of economic development at the Economics Faculty and research fellow of the Institute of International Studies of the University of Chile. He was formerly with the UN Economic Commission for Latin America (ECLA) and the Latin American Institute for Economic and Social Planning. This document is excerpted from a revised version of a lecture delivered on November 17, 1966, at the University of Chile during the series of Inaugural Lectures of the Institute of International Studies. Professor Sunkel's tone is more objective and his posture more "scientific"

From Osvaldo Sunkel, "National Development Policies and External Dependence in Latin America," *Journal of Development Studies* 6, no. 1 (1966): 23, 30–31, 43–46. Reprinted by permission of the *Journal of Development Studies*, published by Frank Cass & Company Limited, 11 Gainsborough Road, London E11, England. © Frank Cass & Co., Ltd.

than Aguilar's. He seems to be describing reality, nothing more. The North American reader should realize, however, that every Latin American understands that the references to an unnamed "dominant power" mean the United States and that Latin America is dependent upon the United States.

The influence which external relations exercise on national development policy derives from the fact that the Latin American countries are enmeshed in the system of international relations of the capitalist world. This system is characterized by the presence of a dominant power, a series of intermediate powers, and the underdeveloped countries ascribed to it. Like the domestic situation, this system is also essentially dynamic. Significant variations are experienced both because of changes inside the countries and as a result of the confrontation with the other principal system of international relations, that of the socialist world. Variations in this worldwide confrontation also affect the limits within which national development policy may move.

As a result of the stagnation of traditional agriculture, the structure of foreign trade, the type of industrialization, and the function which the State is fulfilling . . . our countries are, from the point of view of the structure and functioning of the economy, entirely dependent on their foreign economic relations. . . . This extreme dependence is rooted in several conditions: the vulnerability and structural deficit of the balance of payments; the type of industrialization and the form of exploitation of the export sector which have not permitted our countries—with a few exceptions—to acquire the ability to adapt and create their own technology; the fact that an important and probably growing part of industry and of the export activities are either foreign owned or depend on licenses and foreign technical assistance, all of which weighs heavily on the availability of foreign exchange; and the fact that both the fiscal sector and the balance of payments persistently tend to deficit, which leads to the necessity of foreign financing. In certain conditions this foreign financing can mean the accumulation of such considerable debts and such a structure of maturities that the very servicing of the debt requires resort to additional foreign financing—a genuine vicious circle. It is this aspect—the overbearing and implacable necessity to obtain foreign financing—which finally sums up the situation of dependence; this is the crucial point in the mechanism of dependence. . . .

There remains, however, a last fundamental question: to what extent will the limitations imposed by the web of international relations within which our countries exist, permit us to adopt policies and strategies of national development such as those suggested? Or, in other words, given the repercussions which a policy of national development would necessarily have on the nature of our external relations, would the affected foreign and domestic interests be sufficiently powerful to block these policies?

I believe that, with respect to this, we are in a better position than a few years ago. From the domestic point of view it has already been suggested that conditions could be such that ideas of this nature might form part of a program, a strategy, and an ideology of development. With respect to the capitalist world, within which we are, the adoption of strategies and institutional forms such as those which have been suggested would probably have been unacceptable up to eight or ten years ago. But today it is possible to air these problems openly and new solutions seem feasible. There have been fundamental changes in the international scene. These changes relate to the relationship between the two principal world blocs and in particular to the relationship between the two superpowers. Since the Cuban crisis made clear that the direct influence of one of the great powers in the sphere of influence of the other carried the risk of nuclear war, they have arrived at a kind of détente. The nuclear balance of power has eliminated the immediate danger of war between the two great powers. This threat having disappeared, the hegemonic powers have lessened their rigid control and the perfect alignment which each had demanded from the intermediate powers and the underdeveloped countries inscribed within their spheres of influence. This has permitted the rise of intermediate countries relatively free of their respective hegemonic powers, and the adoption of important innovations in the development policy of these countries designed to arrive at forms most suited to national conditions. This is the case of the transformations which have occurred in the socialist economies of Eastern Europe and of the reorientation of the policy of international cooperation which the Alliance for Progress represents for Latin America. . . .

The program of the Alliance for Progress, at least in its original conception and in the vestiges which remain, approved of this desire to try new formulae. The adoption of positive attitudes towards change in the underdeveloped countries is without doubt linked to the fact that direct nuclear confrontation between the great powers is impossible. What then are the forms in which this confrontation can take place? Obviously one is the ideological struggle, particularly at the level of development policy, each side showing the world that development can best be achieved in a capitalistic or, conversely, a socialist way. Therefore it is now in the interest of the dominant powers, even though they are conscious of running certain risks, to try out formulae which might lead to rapid and satisfactory development *without rupturing the prevailing political system*. This is in fact the argument given by both the U.S. and the U.S.S.R. to justify Santo Domingo and Czechoslovakia. Situations like these are clearly possible, but I believe that they are only temporary and partial setbacks in the context of a long-term process of liberalization; internal pressures for liberalization and for decreasing the world-wide commitments of superpowers continue, and nationalistic voices are mounting in the satellite nations and everywhere.

This process has had the effect not only of a thaw within each system, but also led to the rapid proliferation of relationships between the countries of each bloc. The last five or six years show a clear evolution in this direction, both in international trade, in political relations, and also in international cultural relations. The countries of the underdeveloped world, each of which was before directly and exclusively affiliated with its own hegemonic power, have now wider possibilities of international trade, foreign aid, cultural contact, technical assistance and consultation, ideological discussion, exchange of students and professors, and of research, with the countries of the other bloc. . . .

[Because of the nuclear stand-off] revolutionary movements in an underdeveloped country cannot count on open and declared economic or military support from the respective great power, while the government of the country in question will be able to count on massive and declared support from its respective hegemonic power. In other words, the possibility of guerrilla movements expanding and converting themselves into victorious revolutionary movements seems remote, at least in Latin America. Would this mean the maintenance of the status quo? I think not. The possibility of implementing progressive policies in Latin America will obviously depend, in the first place, on the social structure and political forces, the degree of national integration, the legitimacy of the government, and other internal circumstances. But when positive circumstances are present to a greater or lesser extent, the limits of development policy can, in my opinion, expand considerably beyond the traditional boundaries.

The principal considerations which support this thesis are: [that the danger of internal revolutionary change has been practically eliminated; that tensions in Latin America have their origin in the economic and social structure of these countries; that contact between all nations has been expanding; and that the hegemonic power will try to avoid prerevolutionary situations and promote development].

Finally, then, given the changes in the international political scene, it seems to me that the possibility of carrying out a national development policy depends fundamentally on the domestic situation, that is to say, the degree of differentiation of the social structure, the degree of political participation, and the existence or possible formation of new political movements which would constitute a functional response to the concrete socio-political problems in terms of a program, a strategy, and an ideology of national development.

To summarize what I have wanted to suggest in these reflections—the only aim of which is to stimulate a more positive debate on these matters than that which we have had up to now—what I have tried to do is the following: to accept that *national* development is the fundamental objective of the policy of development; second, to indicate that the fulfillment of the objective of reducing external dependence requires very important reorientations in traditional development strategy, particularly relating to agrarian policy, integration, foreign relations, and industrial policy; third, to indicate that in some countries of Latin America economic, social, and political changes and transformations have been occurring which seem to indicate the possibility that such new policies could be formulated and applied; fourth, to suggest that in these particular cases, the changes in the international situation would seem to have created conditions which are sufficiently tolerant and flexible to permit the application of policies of national development.

---

13. Speech Announcing the Enterprise for the Americas Initiative ◆ George Bush

In this 1990 speech to administration officials and members of the business community, President Bush introduces his three-part plan to encourage a new economic partnership with the democracies of Latin America. This partnership, with its focus on "trade, not aid," will bring hemisphere-wide, free-market reform to the countries of North, Central, and South America.

In the past twelve months every one of us, from the man in the White House to the man on the street, has been fascinated by the tremendous changes, the positive changes taking place around the world. Freedom has made great gains, not just in Eastern Europe, but right here in the Americas. We've seen a resurgence of democratic rule, a rising tide of democracy never before witnessed in the history of this beloved hemisphere. And with one exception, Cuba, the transition to democracy is moving toward completion. We can all sense the excitement that the day is not far off when Cuba joins the ranks of world democracies and makes the Americas fully free.

A new leadership has emerged, backed by the strength of the people's mandate—leadership that understands that the future of Latin America lies

From speech given at the White House, Washington, DC, June 27, 1990. See U.S. Department of State, Bureau of Public Affairs, Office of Public Communications, *Current Policy* No. 1288, June 1990.

with free government and free markets. In the words of Colombia's courgeous leader Virgilio Barco—President Barco: "The long running match between Karl Marx and Adam Smith is finally coming to an end" with the "recognition that open economies with access to markets can lead to social progress."

Back in February [1990], I met in Cartagena with heads of the three Andean nations. And I came away from that meeting convinced that the United States must review its approach not only to that region but to Latin America and the Caribbean as a whole.

All signs point to the fact that we must shift the focus of our economic interaction toward a new economic partnership because prosperity in our hemisphere depends on trade, not aid. I've asked you here today to share with you some of the ideas, some of the ways we can build a broad-based partnership for the 1990s to announce the new Enterprise for the Americas Initiative that creates incentives to reinforce Latin America's growing recognition that free-market reform is the key to sustained growth and political stability.

The three pillars of our new initiative are trade, investment, and debt. To expand trade, I propose that we begin the process of creating a hemisphere-wide free-trade zone; to increase investment, that we adopt measures to create a new flow of capital into the region; and to further ease the debt—the burden of debt—a new approach to debt in the region with important benefits to our environment.

I know there is concern that the revolutionary changes we've witnessed this past year in Eastern Europe will shift our attention away from Latin America. But I want to assure you all today, as I've assured many democratic leaders in Central and South America and the Caribbean and Mexico, the United States will not lose sight of the tremendous changes and opportunities right here in our own hemisphere. And indeed, as we talk with the leaders of the G-24 about the emerging democracies in Europe—I've been talking to them also about their supporting democracy and economic freedom in Central America. Our aim is a closer partnership between the Americas and our friends in Europe and in Asia.

Two years from now, our hemisphere will celebrate the 500th anniversary of an epic event, Columbus' discovery of America, our New World. And we trace our origins, our shared history to the time of Columbus' voyage and the courageous quest for the advancement of man. Today the bonds of our common heritage are strengthened by the love of freedom and a common commitment to democracy. Our challenge, the challenge in this new era of the Americas is to secure this shared dream and all its fruits for the people of the Americas—North, Central, and South.

Suggestions for Further Reading

Carothers, Thomas. *In the Name of Democracy*. Berkeley: University of California Press, 1991.

Connell-Smith, Gordon. *The Inter-American System*. New York: Oxford University Press, 1962.

Gil, Federico G. *Latin American-United States Relations*. New York: Harcourt Brace Jovanovich, 1971.

Green, David. *The Containment of Latin America: A History of the Myths and Realities of the Good Neighbor Policy*. Chicago: Quadrangle Books, 1971.

LaFeber, Walter. *The New Empire: An Interpretation of American Expansion, 1860–1898*. Ithaca: Cornell University Press, 1963.

———. *Inevitable Revolutions*. New York: Norton, 1985.

Lowenthal, Abraham F. *Partners in Conflict: The United States and Latin America*. Baltimore: Johns Hopkins University Press, 1990.

———. *Exporting Democracy: The United States and Latin America*. Baltimore: Johns Hopkins University Press, 1992.

Munro, Dana G. *Intervention and Dollar Diplomacy in the Caribbean, 1900–1921*. Princeton: Princeton University Press, 1964.

Pastor, Robert A. *Whirlpool: U.S. Foreign Policy toward Latin America and the Caribbean*. Princeton: Princeton University Press, 1992.

Perkins, Dexter. *A History of the Monroe Doctrine*. Boston: Little, Brown, 1963.

Perloff, Harvey S. *Alliance for Progress: A Social Invention in the Making*. Baltimore: Johns Hopkins University Press, 1969.

Tulchin, Joseph S. *The Aftermath of War: World War I and United States Policy toward Latin America*. New York: New York University Press, 1971.

Wagner, R. Harrison. *United States Policy toward Latin America: A Study in Domestic and International Politics*. Stanford: Stanford University Press, 1970.

Whitaker, Arthur P. *The United States and the Independence of Latin America, 1800–1830*. Baltimore: Johns Hopkins University Press, 1941.

———. *The Western Hemisphere Idea: Its Rise and Decline*. Ithaca: Cornell University Press, 1954.

Wood, Bryce. *The Making of the Good Neighbor Policy*. New York: Columbia University Press, 1961.

Latin American Silhouettes
Studies in History and Culture

William H. Beezley and
Judith Ewell
Editors

Volumes Published

William H. Beezley and Judith Ewell, eds., *The Human Tradition in Latin America: The Twentieth Century* (1987). Cloth ISBN 0-8420-2283-X Paper ISBN 0-8420-2284-8

Judith Ewell and William H. Beezley, eds., *The Human Tradition in Latin America: The Nineteenth Century* (1989). Cloth ISBN 0-8420-2331-3 Paper ISBN 0-8420-2332-1

David G. LaFrance, *The Mexican Revolution in Puebla, 1908–1913: The Maderista Movement and the Failure of Liberal Reform* (1989). ISBN 0-8420-2293-7

Mark A. Burkholder, *Politics of a Colonial Career: José Baquíjano and the Audiencia of Lima*, 2d ed. (1990). Cloth ISBN 0-8420-2353-4 Paper ISBN 0-8420-2352-6

Kenneth M. Coleman and George C. Herring, eds. (with Foreword by Daniel Oduber), *Understanding the Central American Crisis: Sources of Conflict, U.S. Policy, and Options for Peace* (1991). Cloth ISBN 0-8420-2382-8   Paper ISBN 0-8420-2383-6

Carlos B. Gil, ed., *Hope and Frustration: Interviews with Leaders of Mexico's Political Opposition* (1992). Cloth ISBN 0-8420-2395-X Paper ISBN 0-8420-2396-8

Charles Bergquist, Ricardo Peñaranda, and Gonzalo Sánchez, eds., *Violence in Colombia: The Contemporary Crisis in Historical Perspective* (1992). Cloth ISBN 0-8420-2369-0 Paper ISBN 0-8420-2376-3

Heidi Zogbaum, *B. Traven: A Vision of Mexico* (1992). ISBN 0-8420-2392-5

Jaime E. Rodríguez O., ed., *Patterns of Contention in Mexican History* (1992). ISBN 0-8420-2399-2

Louis A. Pérez, Jr., ed., *Slaves, Sugar, and Colonial Society: Travel Accounts of Cuba, 1801–1899* (1992). Cloth ISBN 0-8420-2354-2 Paper ISBN 0-8420-2415-8

Peter Blanchard, *Slavery and Abolition in Early Republican Peru* (1992). Cloth ISBN 0-8420-2400-X Paper ISBN 0-8420-2429-8

Paul J. Vanderwood, *Disorder and Progress: Bandits, Police, and Mexican Development*. Revised and Enlarged Edition (1992). Cloth ISBN 0-8420-2438-7 Paper ISBN 0-8420-2439-5

Sandra McGee Deutsch and Ronald H. Dolkart, eds., *The Argentine Right: Its History and Intellectual Origins, 1910 to the Present* (1993). Cloth ISBN 0-8420-2418-2 Paper ISBN 0-8420-2419-0

Jaime E. Rodríguez O., ed., *The Evolution of the Mexican Political System* (1993). ISBN 0-8420-2448-4

Steve Ellner, *Organized Labor in Venezuela, 1958–1991: Behavior and Concerns in a Democratic Setting* (1993). ISBN 0-8420-2443-3

Paul J. Dosal, *Doing Business with the Dictators: A Political History of United Fruit in Guatemala, 1899–1944* (1993). ISBN 0-8420-2475-1

Marquis James, *Merchant Adventurer: The Story of W. R. Grace* (1993). ISBN 0-8420-2444-1

John Charles Chasteen and Joseph S. Tulchin, eds., *Problems in Modern Latin American History: A Reader* (1994). Cloth ISBN 0-8420-2327-5 Paper ISBN 0-8420-2328-3